Nation Branding and Sports Diplomacy

Yoav Dubinsky

Nation Branding and Sports Diplomacy

Country Image Games in Times of Change

Yoav Dubinsky
Lundquist College of Business
University of Oregon
Eugene, OR, USA

ISBN 978-3-031-32549-6   ISBN 978-3-031-32550-2 (eBook)
https://doi.org/10.1007/978-3-031-32550-2

© The Editor(s) (if applicable) and The Author(s), under exclusive licence to Springer Nature Switzerland AG 2023

This work is subject to copyright. All rights are solely and exclusively licensed by the Publisher, whether the whole or part of the material is concerned, specifically the rights of translation, reprinting, reuse of illustrations, recitation, broadcasting, reproduction on microfilms or in any other physical way, and transmission or information storage and retrieval, electronic adaptation, computer software, or by similar or dissimilar methodology now known or hereafter developed.

The use of general descriptive names, registered names, trademarks, service marks, etc. in this publication does not imply, even in the absence of a specific statement, that such names are exempt from the relevant protective laws and regulations and therefore free for general use.

The publisher, the authors, and the editors are safe to assume that the advice and information in this book are believed to be true and accurate at the date of publication. Neither the publisher nor the authors or the editors give a warranty, expressed or implied, with respect to the material contained herein or for any errors or omissions that may have been made. The publisher remains neutral with regard to jurisdictional claims in published maps and institutional affiliations.

This Palgrave Macmillan imprint is published by the registered company Springer Nature Switzerland AG.
The registered company address is: Gewerbestrasse 11, 6330 Cham, Switzerland

Preface

It started a few weeks after I turned 9, during the first Gulf War in the winter of 1991. My family and I moved from Tel Aviv, spending over a month away from home with our relatives, going to a bomb shelter and wearing a gas mask when sirens sounded the alarm that Saddam Hussein and Iraq were firing rockets with potential chemical heads towards Israel. It was then when I felt enormous pride watching on television between sirens Maccabi Tel Aviv Basketball Club compete in the European Champions Cup and qualify for the Final Four. Despite hosting abroad due to security concerns, a team from my hometown, representing a West-Asian country in a European competition and reinforced by foreign players from America, inspired me through their resilience. Later, I learned the club plays in yellow jerseys as a reminder of the yellow badges Jewish people were forced to wear by the Nazis, and of the six million Jews murdered in the holocaust. I sympathized with the club's winning ethos, and the local pride as summarized by trailblazing team captain Tal Brody who coined the most iconic phrase in Israeli sports after an unlikely victory over Soviet Union giants CSKA Moscow in 1977: "We are on the map and we're staying on the map, not just in sports but in everything." That passion and curiosity for the intersection between sports and geopolitics followed me through my childhood, adolescence, and adulthood. Since 2003, for the next two decades I have studied, researched, covered, or presented about implications of sports nation branding, and public diplomacy in every continent around the world, including through four Olympic Games. I attended hundreds of sports events in over a dozen countries. Through involvement with the International Olympic Academy in Olympia, Greece, as a student, a coordinator, and a lecturer, starting in 2009, I experienced how sports connects people from different countries, ages, nationalities, races, genders, and backgrounds. The book argues that while the use of sports for nation branding and public diplomacy is not new, during the years 2020 and 2022, the world of sports is adjusting to new global challenges. While this book focuses on the period between January 2020 to December 2022, it was shaped by all my past experiences.

Eugene, OR, USA   Yoav Dubinsky

Acknowledgments

The book focuses on the years 2020 to 2022, but it galvanizes professional work of around two decades. I thank my brother Dr. Itamar Dubinsky for his comments through the writing and editing process, and my parents Nitay and Karyn for their ongoing support. In terms of reviewing, editing, proofing, and production, I thank the lovely team at Palgrave Macmillan making this book possible. I acknowledge the help of previous editors and dozens of press officers and media directors who enabled me to attend local, national, and international sports events over the past decades, furthering my research and education on the intersections between sports, nation branding, and public diplomacy. Thank you to Israeli sports journalists, members, and participants in the International Olympic Academy, other Olympic stakeholders, and fellow academics, with whom I spent countless hours debating about sports and geopolitics. I specifically acknowledge Honorary Dean of the International Olympic Academy Professor Kostas Georgiadis, my former PhD supervisor at the University of Tennessee Dr. Lars Dzikus, and the head of the marketing department in the Lundquist College of Business at the University of Oregon Professor T. Bettina Cornwell for making me a better global scholar. Of course, I send my gratitude to the thousands of students I had the pleasure and privilege teaching and learning from. While any mistakes in the book are my own, you are all part of this journey. Thank you all for helping me walk on with hope in my heart.
    YNWA

Contents

1 **Nation Branding and Sports Diplomacy in Times of Change**   1
   Introduction   1
   A Different World   2
   Global Sports and the Pandemic   5
   Beyond the Pandemic   11
   Book Structure   15
   Professional and Academic Contribution   20
   References   21

2 **Theoretical and Conceptual Frameworks of Nation Branding and Sports Diplomacy**   25
   Introduction   25
   Contested Definitions   26
   Public Diplomacy   28
   Nation Branding   30
   National Identity   33
   Soft Power, Cultural Diplomacy, and Sports   34
   Colonization and Globalization   37
   Sports Diplomacy and Ethical Concerns   40
   Conclusion   43
   References   44

3 Country Image, Nation Branding, and the FIFA World Cup (1930–2022) 51
Introduction 51
The FIFA World Cup, Nation Branding, and Country Image 53
   Public Diplomacy 53
   National Identity 56
   Commercialization and Globalization 59
   Nation Branding and Sportswashing 61
   Future Challenges and Opportunities 66
   References 68

4 Nation Branding, Tokyo 2020, and the New Era of the Olympic Movement 75
Introduction 75
Previous Eras of Nation Branding and the Olympic Movement 76
A Survival-Oriented Era 77
A Questionable Legacy Era 78
An American-Influenced but Democracy-Limited Era 80
A Post-Woke of Athletes-to-People Diplomacy Era 83
A Global Geopolitical Era 86
A Digital-Cultural Era 90
An Era of Global Challenges and Backlash 91
Conclusion 94
References 95

5 American Sports Diplomacy Amid the 50 Years Anniversary of Title IX 101
Introduction 101
Nation Branding, Country Image, and Brand America 102
Lesson 1: Title IX Adds to America's Identity as "Land of Opportunity" 104
Lesson 2: Title IX Is America's Sustainable Competitive Advantage 106
Lesson 3: Title IX Is an Ongoing Revolutionary Process 108
Lesson 4: Title IX Is a Tool for US Foreign Policy 111
Lesson 5: Title IX Covers Up American Hypocrisy 113
Lesson Six: Title IX Fosters Globalization 118
Conclusion 120
References 121

6	**The European Super League as a Nation Branding Geopolitical Battlefield**	129
	Introduction	129
	Nation Branding and Club Football	131
	Nation Branding and the European Super League	136
	England	137
	Spain	139
	Italy	141
	Germany and France	142
	Foreign Ownership	144
	Non-State Actors	146
	The Aftermath	148
	References	150
7	**Nation Branding, Public Diplomacy, and the Dirty Business of Sportswashing**	157
	Introduction	157
	What Is Sportswashing?	159
	China	161
	Russia	165
	Gulf Cooperation Council Countries	170
	Other Manifestations	176
	What About Western Democracies?	179
	Conclusion	183
	References	184
8	**From "TrackTown USA" to Oregon22 World Athletics Championships**	193
	Introduction	193
	City Branding and Sports	194
	Place Branding and Oregon	195
	Place Branding and Track and Field in America	197
	Place Branding, TrackTown USA, and the Oregon22 World Athletics Championships	200
	Local	201
	Regional	203

	National	205
	International	208
	Global	211
	Conclusion	214
	References	215
9	**Sport-Tech Diplomacy**	223
	Introduction	223
	What Is Sport-Tech Diplomacy?	224
	An Authentic Narrative of Innovation	228
	A History of Innovation in Sports	231
	A Diverse Sport-Tech Ecosystem	234
	Galvanizing State and Non-State Actors Around Sport-Tech Diplomacy	236
	Conclusion	241
	References	242
10	**Sports, Country Image, and the Global Order in an Ever-Changing World**	251
	Introduction	251
	Sustainability and the Environment	253
	Social Justice	256
	Economic Vulnerabilities	260
	Geopolitics	262
	Technology and Innovation	267
	Conclusion	270
	References	271
Index		275

About the Author

Yoav Dubinsky is an Instructor of Sports Business in the Lundquist College of Business at the University of Oregon. Dr. Dubinsky's research focuses on sports, nation branding, and public diplomacy, especially in the contexts of international sports, the Olympic Movement, the USA, and Israel. Born and raised in Tel Aviv, Israel, Dr. Dubinsky is a sports researcher and sports journalist with two decades of experience covering and researching sports around the world, including the last four summer Olympic Games from Beijing, London, Rio de Janeiro, and Tokyo. Dr. Dubinsky has also been involved for several years with the International Olympic Academy as a lecturer, coordinator, and student, using sports as a tool for inclusion in diverse international environments. Dr. Dubinsky completed his PhD at the University of Tennessee, Knoxville, in 2018, writing his dissertation on Israel's use of sports for nation branding and public diplomacy. He also owns a BA in political science (Tel Aviv University, Israel), and MA in political communication (Tel Aviv University, Israel), an MA in Olympic Studies and Sport Management (University of Peloponnese, Greece), and a professional graduation diploma in media and journalism (Koteret Media and Journalism College, Israel). Dr. Dubinsky published over two dozen peer-reviewed academic manuscripts, articles, and chapters about the intersections of sports, nation branding and public diplomacy, and is often interviewed by international, national, and local media outlets. Dr. Dubinsky is also an avid football fan of his home club Maccabi Tel Aviv, Ajax Amsterdam in the Netherlands, and Liverpool FC in England, and a strong supporter of women's football in the USA and around the world.

LIST OF TABLES

Table 1.1 Mega-sports events cancelled or postponed 8
Table 3.1 Nation branding, country image, and the evolution of the FIFA World Cup 54
Table 5.1 Lessons on Title IX Brand America and US sports diplomacy 104
Table 6.1 Clubs' ownerships and involvement in the European Super League as of its creation and collapse 132

CHAPTER 1

Nation Branding and Sports Diplomacy in Times of Change

INTRODUCTION

The use of sports for nation branding and public diplomacy goes back to antiquity and to the athletic competitions in Ancient Greece, as they did not just provide an opportunity for the different city-states to expose their image but were one of the most important Pan-Hellenic traditions and were even partly used for colonization purposes (Dubinsky, 2019a; Miller, 2004). Through modernization and institutionalization of sports, especially since the second half of the nineteenth century and during the twentieth century and the first two decades of the twenty-first century, sports have been globalized, affecting every country on Earth (Dubinsky, 2019b; Krechmar et al., 2017). With around 10,000 athletes representing over 200 countries and territories and global broadcasting to over 220 countries and territories (Dubinsky, 2022b), states, communities, organizations, and individuals have been using the Olympic Games, for example, to try and achieve a favorable image and leverage their social, political, and economic goals. Yet the globalized nature of sports was also one of the reasons why the outbreak of the COVID-19 pandemic spread so swiftly and harshly, causing in March 2020 a domino effect, leading to pausing, cancelling, postponing, and modifying the way sports are practiced and held (Frawley & Schulenkorf, 2023). The pandemic did not just cause a health crisis but provoked global waves of activism and protest on social

© The Author(s), under exclusive license to Springer Nature Switzerland AG 2023
Y. Dubinsky, *Nation Branding and Sports Diplomacy*,
https://doi.org/10.1007/978-3-031-32550-2_1

issues that were already challenging social order, politics crises around the world, and economic recessions. While the world found ways to live through what became an endemic by the end of 2022, social, economic, and geopolitical factors growing or emerging during these years changed the ways countries use sports for nation branding and public diplomacy.

The book analyzes intersections between sports and the multidisciplinary fields of nation branding, including public diplomacy and country image, through the period of 2020–2022. Disciplines, theories, and lenses used in the book include international relations and public diplomacy theories, soft power, product-country-image, tourism destination image, social identity, agenda-setting and framing, and others (Buhmann & Ingenhoff, 2015; Cull, 2008; Fan, 2010; Nye, 2004). The main argument made through the book is that the use of sports for nation branding and public diplomacy goals is not new, but the changes the world went through during the period of 2020–2022 required nations, places, communities, and individuals to modify and adapt the ways they use sports for country image purposes. The different chapters in the book dive into the nuances of that change, the power struggles behind them, and how countries, cities, people, communities, organizations, and other stakeholders are adapting or leading that change.

A Different World

The world is in a different place than it was in December 2019. SARS-CoV-2—a new version of the coronavirus known as COVID-19—was first detected by the World Health Organization on the last day of 2019 (Frawley & Schulenkorf, 2023). Within months, the virus spread across the world, and the ways countries reacted to the pandemic reflect some of the national values and priorities (Best & Howard, 2022; Kettemann & Lachmayer, 2022). A globalized world means that as people, products, and ideas, cross-national borders, so do viruses—leading to every country going through some sort of trauma during the pandemic. The pandemic exposed how unprepared the USA was for a pandemic and the downsides of private health systems which expose economic gaps and availability of resources. Personal freedom in the USA manifested through backlash over federal and state requirements and led to over a million deaths despite vaccines becoming available to most Americans in early 2021 (World Health Organization, n.d.). The Swedish Model that relied on the developed public health system and had limited state-led restrictions, was scrutinized at first, as other countries forced mandated quarantined and isolations. Asian countries with more collectivist cultures who were well prepared for a pandemic going through the MERS crises, such as Taiwan, Singapore, South Korea, and Hong Kong, were more inclined to follow public regulations, especially if accustomed to mask wearing, and were better prepared for outbreak. Zero-COVID policies such as in Japan proved efficient at first but being late on vaccinations in comparison to Europe and North America kept the country in and out of states of emergency through 2021 and 2022.

Some democratic states such as the USA, Italy, France, Spain, Brazil, and India were among the countries hurt the most by the pandemic (Best & Howard, 2022), as their health systems were not prepared, hospitals lacked enough ventilators, and personal hygiene products such as masks and hand sanitizer were limited, all causing a raising death toll in the early stages of the pandemic. Germany and New Zealand, two democratic countries led by female heads of states during the outbreak, using science-based policies about public health, had less deadly initial responses. European countries sharing borders, but having different COVID-19 policies, had different death tolls, which further highlighted internal divisions within the European Union. Perhaps the biggest manifestation of lack of European cohesiveness was the Brexit, led by populist British former Prime Minister Boris Johnson, who was one of the most outspoken heads of states and divisive voices against the dangers of the pandemic. Science denying played a significant part in populist nationalism (Bobbitt, 2022), as seen by Donald Trump in the USA, Boris Johnson in the UK, and Jair Bolsonaro in Brazil, rejecting or downplaying the danger of the pandemic or the importance of social distancing, mask wearing, or even vaccinations. This was in contrast to Queen Elizabeth II who gave a heartfelt uniting speech about the need for unity amid a collective challenge which became one of the most iconic moments in her over 70-year reign as a monarch. African countries were hit later by the pandemic but also recovered late, as vaccines were first available in wealthier countries. South Africa was even blamed for the outbreak of the Omicron variant. In fact, Africa became a platform for both Chinese and American vaccine diplomacy, as both countries tried to strengthen their soft power in the continent through vaccine donations (Wall Street Journal, 2021). In the Middle East, the branding of Israel as an innovative country manifested through its adaptability to the outbreak of the pandemic with a mobile-based monitory system and an early adopter of the vaccines. The UAE was also among the first countries to vaccinate most of its population. Of course, not all is known about the real impact of the pandemic, as reporting and transparency are not consistent around the world. China, the source of SARS-CoV-2, restricted information from the world about the origins of the virus and limited personal freedom by taking strict measurements against its own population. Russia, which already developed a reputation for spreading misinformation, is assumed to underreport the death toll. The pandemic exposed fragility, lack of preparedness, and lack of domestic and international solidarity, along with the global connection between countries and communities.

The chaos manifested globally well beyond a health crisis. The 2020 presidential elections in the USA ended with an insurrection of Donald Trump's supporters attacking the Capitol denying the legitimacy of the results. The inauguration of President Joe Biden was taken under extreme security measures as the mall in Washington, D.C., resembled a warzone. The USA left Afghanistan, letting the Taliban to take over. Months later, Russia invaded Ukraine, with the USA and Europe imposing economic sanctions that were retaliated by Russian sanctions and gas prices rising across the world. If the Soviet Union was framed by American President Ronald Reagan as "The Evil Empire" during the Cold War, in 2022 the new boogeyman is Vladimir Putin, with President Biden warning of "a nuclear Armageddon" as the West was arming Ukraine. All while North Korea is demonstrating its own ballistic capabilities, launching missiles over Japan. The Western support for Ukraine against Russia and criticism over Chinese and North Korean defiance were also portrayed in the Global South as a hypocritical proxy war between East and West, accusing Western countries of double standards and showing more sympathy to blonde Europeans than to war victims and refugees in Afghanistan, Iraq, or Syria or concerns to ethnic crimes against the Tigray population in Ethiopia. In the Middle East and Africa, the Abraham Accords normalizing relations between Israel, the UAE and Bahrain, Oman, Morocco, and Sudan, brought hope for stability, yet the ongoing Israeli occupation of Palestinians also keeps leading to escalation of the conflict.

Protests are global but also provoke counterreactions. Calls for Black Lives Matter are associated with supporting Free Palestine, and demanding gender equality leads to global support of women in Iran taking off their hijabs in defiance to modesty police oppression. Yet progressive movements also lead to backlash, against liberal and international institutions, manifesting with the Brexit of the UK from the European Union and the rise to power of the extreme right in Italy. The culture war also leads to spread of disinformation and fake news to create chaos and challenge the legitimacy of democratic institutions, denying science amid climate change, global warming, and natural disasters becoming deadlier every year. In addition, Angela Merkel who was the longest reigning head of state in the European Union is no longer the Chancellor of Germany, former Japanese Prime Minister Shinzo Abe who tried to lead the country during the pandemic and resigned for health reasons was assassinated in 2022, and the people in England sang "God Save the King" again after over 70 years. Thus, the world went through significant change between January 2020 and December 2022.

Beyond the health risk causing millions of deaths, the global pandemic of COVID-19 led to financial, social, and political crises worldwide, impacting how countries used sports for nation branding and public diplomacy in every continent. From mental health to supply chain shortages, the pandemic disrupted every sphere of normalcy. Social, economic, and political pressures also reflected in the ways countries approached sports during the pandemic, including using sports for nation branding and public diplomacy purposes, and in ways that reflect functional, normative, aesthetic, and sympathetic dimensions of the countries' images (Buhmann & Ingenhoff, 2015).

Global Sports and the Pandemic

Before COVID-19 evolved into a global pandemic, 2020 was off to a promising start in terms of the connection between sports, nation branding and public diplomacy. Lausanne, a small Swiss city on Lake Geneva, solidified its official branding as the Olympic Capital by hosting the 2020 Winter Youth Olympic Games, not only showing that a small city can host an international event in a sustainable fashion but also using some of the International Olympic Committee's (IOC) Agenda 2020 policies and holding some of the events in the French Alps. The year 2020 was supposed as a celebration for Europe, with the UEFA Euro 2020 Championship spread across the continent celebrating 60 years of the governing body and joint European identity. In the USA, Shakira and Jenifer Lopez celebrated Latino culture through their performance in the Super Bowl Half Time Show, with the latter also protesting President Donald Trump's anti-immigration policies (Dubinsky, 2021, 2022a). Yet most of the optimism was around the Tokyo 2020 Olympic Games, as after the turbulent competitions in Rio de Janeiro 2016, this time all facilities were ready on time, and Japan was ready to put on a show that celebrates its ancient traditions along with new modern innovations (Dubinsky, 2022b). Yet along with the optimism started the rumors and reports about postponed sports events and travel restrictions in East Asia due to a mysterious virus originating in Wuhan, China (Frawley & Schulenkorf, 2023). Due to the global nature of sports that relies on people and products crossing national borders, the virus spread quickly, and by mid-March 2020, professional sports around the world stopped. In an unprecedented situation, not even seen during World Wars or following the September 11 terror attacks, within days, hundreds of local, national, and international sports events worldwide were postponed or cancelled (ESPN News Services, 2020). Following pressure and demand for certainty by sports associations, governments, sponsors, television right holders, and other stakeholders, and with athletes socially isolated at home sharing training videos bouncing toilet paper during government-mandated lockdowns, international sports federations also decided to postpone mega-events, including Euro 2020 and the Tokyo 2020 Olympic Games, causing a domino effect of postponements and cancellations in the following years.

As a result of the cancellations and the domino effect created by the postponement of the Tokyo 2020 Olympic Games, directly or indirectly, every country in the world was affected by the decision. The pandemic required governments, organizations, communities, and people to adapt to an unprecedented new situation, as the virus impacted the entire sports business ecosystem, including leagues, clubs, athletes, broadcasters, sponsors, federations, spectators, the betting industry, the fitness industry, amateur sports clubs, youth sports, sports for development organizations, disability sports, volunteering, community sports, and any other stakeholder (Frawley & Schulenkorf, 2023). Some of the solutions were practical and tactical: hosting sports events in closed bubbles such as the NBA and WNBA in closed facilities in Florida, open bubbles which enabled athletes to travel to and from the venues from designated hotels such as the Tokyo 2020 Olympic Games, a closed loop system such as in the Beijing 2022 Winter Olympic Games where the city was divided between official accredited stakeholders and residences, or sports held with limited or no fans. These solutions mostly depended on the competencies of the hosting countries and the financial incentives and pressures by corporate partners such as sponsors or broadcasting rightsholders to continue to host sports, at times in spite of the recommendations of health officials. In some countries and some sports where media rights are not the main source of revenues, leagues and competitions were cancelled, deepening inequality gaps between privileged and underserved communities. Yet some of the solutions required deeper strategic planning, aligned with public health policies and overall long-term plans for returning to what is commonly described as "the new normal."

The global sports ecosystem is a $2.3 trillion industry (Best & Howard, 2022), and the cancellations cost billions to local economies, and hosting sports events without fans hurt the tourism industries and the abilities of countries, cities, and places to capitalize on the event and brand themselves as attractive tourism destinations (Dubinsky, 2022a). The abilities to use technological advancement to host sports events might be seen as positive reflections of the functional dimension of a country's image, but the country's normative dimension can also be scrutinized for questionable priorities or putting more people at risk. As seen from Table 1.1, international sports events in every continent were postponed or cancelled, and some of the direct and indirect impacts continued to manifest even beyond 2022.

In North America, capitalist pressure drove the US sports organizations to find ways to resume sports leagues, while over 1 million people died from COVID-19, and athletes protested social injustice. The contested ethical culture in American sports also manifested through the pandemic through the collegiate system, first in chaos as different conferences and divisions took different approaches to the outbreak and especially in the fall of 2021 as all Power Five conferences held football seasons despite a vaccine not being ready and the death tolls in America rising. Athletes also took a stand in the 2020 presidential elections, mobilizing underrepresented communities to vote, criticizing the January 6, 2021, attack on the Capitol, and even Atlanta Dream WNBA players supporting a senate campaign against the team owner. The interpretation of personal freedom, along corporate pressure, populist science-denying leaderships, consistent reporting systems, and other factors, led to the USA becoming the only country to officially count over one million deaths from the pandemic (World Health Organization, n.d.). No other Western country has significantly put its people at risk as the USA. The social and economic chaos during the pandemic inflated by President Trump's populist rhetoric, including using the term "Kung Flu," led to a wave of racist manifestations towards Asian-Americans in the USA (Dubinsky, 2021). This is not the first time Trump used sports-related terminology in his controversial

Table 1.1 Mega-sports events cancelled or postponed

Continent	Selected international competitions	Impact of COVID-19
Europe	UEFA EURO 2020	Postponed to 2021, games from Dublin were moved to St. Petersburg and London
	UEFA Champions League Final 2020	The tournament was stopped in March 2020 and resumed in August 2020 in a single-game knockout tournament in Portugal, the final was moved from Istanbul to Lisbon
	Euroleague	Cancelled
	UEFA Women's Euro England 2021	Postponed by a year and rebranded as UEFA Women's Euro England 2022
	The Wimbledon Championships 2020	Cancelled
	UEFA Champions League Final 2022	Final moved from St. Petersburg to Paris following the Russian invasion to Ukraine
North America	World Athletics Championships Oregon21	Postponed by a year and rebranded as World Athletics Championships Oregon22
South America	Copa America 2020	Postponed by a year, moved from Argentina and Colombia to Brazil, and rebranded as Copa America 2021
Africa	Dakar 2022 Youth Olympic Games	Cancelled. Senegal will host the Youth Olympic Games in Dakar in 2026.
	2020 African Nations Championships	Postponed from April 2020 and held in January/February 2021 in Cameroon
	2022 African Nation Championships	Postponed from 2022 to 2023
Asia	Tokyo 2020 Olympic Games	Postponed by a year to 2021, held in an open bubble without local or international fans
	Beijing 2022 Winter Olympic Games	Held in China in closed loop under "dystopian conditions"
	World University Games Chengdu 2021	Postponed to 2022 and again to 2023, replacing the planned Games in Yekaterinburg (Russia)
	Hangzhou 2022 Asian Games	Postponed to 2023
Oceania	2020 Australian Formula 1 Grand Prix	Cancelled
	Solomon Island 2021 Pacific Games	Postponed to 2023

rhetoric, as after being caught on tape saying people with power can grab women, he justified that as locker-room banter (Dubinsky, 2021). American companies were even blamed for pressuring Japan to host the Olympic Games in 2021 despite the objection of Tokyo residences (Dubinsky, 2022b) and not taking a stand against China when hosting the Beijing 2022 Winter Olympic Games. This is aligned with previous accusations of American hypocrisy of sports leagues, commercial partners, and even athletes, who vocally and financially support social justice causes in America but keep silent amid human rights violations in China, fearing to risk commercial growth in the Asian market (State of the Union, 2022). Canada, on the other hand, was one of the first countries to officially withdraw from Tokyo 2020, before they were postponed to 2021. Canada took a much more measured and responsible approach than its southern neighbors, having the NHL resume only in Canadian cities and the Toronto Raptors hosting NBA games in the 2021 season in Florida. On the other hand, operation Warp Speed to reach safe vaccinations was a powerful display of the distribution capabilities of the American industry, which helped the recovery of the American economy and the sports system even faster than countries which took more prudent health measures but were behind on vaccinations.

In Europe, following the domino effect of cancellation of sports events in March 2020, different countries had different policies regarding postponement or cancellation of their domestic leagues, showing that the European market is not a cohesive one. The UEFA Champions League match in Bergamo, Italy, in February 2020, between Italian team Atalanta and Spanish team Valencia, became a super-spreader event of COVID-19 across the continent. Financial pressures in European football had multiple nation branding implications. Euro 2020 was postponed to 2021 and was held in 13 different countries and cities across the continent, despite not all of them having the same vaccination and health policies. The financial turmoil in European football also led top clubs in England, Spain, and Italy to try and break away from the existing system, leading to backlash against foreign ownerships and pressures from Russia, the Arabic Gulf, and the USA. Furthermore, travel restrictions were implemented on international players, limiting abilities to represent their countries in continental competitions in Africa and South America. Yet as vaccines became widely available and sports resume, European countries returned to use mega-events for nation branding and public diplomacy purposes. England hosted the final stages of Euro 2020 in 2021 and the Birmingham 2022 Commonwealth Games and won the UEFA Women's Euro in a packed Wembley Stadium. Germany hosted the Munich 2022 European Championships, 50 years after the Munich Massacre—the terror attack in which 11 Israeli athletes, coaches, and referees were murdered by Palestinian terrorists in the Munich 1972 Olympic Games—and flirted with a potential future Olympic bid marking 100 years after Nazi Germany hosted the Berlin 1936 Olympic Games. Yet perhaps the most significant manifestation of geopolitics in European sports was the exclusion of Russia following the country invading Ukraine.

When it comes to pandemic diplomacy, perhaps the country that received the most international praise was New Zealand. Prime Minister Jacinda Ardern implemented strict monitoring policies, closed the country's boarders, demanded obedience from her cabinet, and led through example, and within months, even before a vaccine was manufactured, New Zealanders were enjoying local rugby games in front of full stadiums. While such policy proved effective and lifesaving in the first year of the pandemic, the closed borders also had negative impact on the country's economy due to its reliance on tourism. Australia implemented lockdown policies and vaccination requirements, positioning itself as another country which took COVID-19 seriously, even at the expense of not allowing tennis superstar and vaccine-denier Novak Djokovic to compete in the 2021 Australian Open. In early 2020 New Zealand and Australia won a joint bid to host the 2023 FIFA Women's World Cup. Since then, both countries emphasized social and environmental justice through the preparations, including sustainability and climate change, gender equality, and the historic and cultural significance of first nations, indigenous, and aboriginal people and communities, thus positioning themselves as normative leaders in the world of sports.

Asia of course had a significant impact on COVID-19, with Japan hosting the Tokyo 2020 Olympic Games in the summer of 2021 under unprecedented conditions without local and international fans and China hosting the Beijing 2022 Winter Olympic Games through dividing the city in what was described as "dystopian conditions" in "an Orwellian surveillance state." In the Middle East, Qatar hosted the 2022 FIFA World Cup under international scrutiny over human rights violations, and Saudi

Arabia also joined the sportswashing initiatives by buying Newcastle United from the Premier League and signing Cristiano Ronaldo. The Israeli-Arab dispute took several turns as the Abraham Accords led to normalization and even sports collaborations with the UAE, yet whenever violence escalated with the Palestinians, international athletes took a stand supporting Palestine and affiliating woke movements such as Black Lives Matter with the Palestinian struggle.

In Africa, Senegal was supposed to become the first African country to host an Olympic event, yet the Dakar 2022 Youth Olympic Games were cancelled during the pandemic. The Games will be held in Senegal in 2026. South Africa, once the face of the continent as host of the 2010 FIFA World Cup, ended 2019 with a feel-good moment of winning the Rugby World Cup, yet following the outbreak of the pandemic, the country was scrutinized for the emergence of the Omicron variant. Sports events in Africa received mixed reactions, as football players felt a need to justify why they should be allowed to compete in the African Cup of Nations during the 2021/2022 season, something European athletes do not. Furthermore, despite Kenya being one of the most successful countries in long runs, Nairobi was not chosen to host the 2025 World Athletics Championships. There was some history made in Africa, as the Basketball Africa League (BAL)—a basketball league organized by the NBA and FIBA—held its first season in Kigali, Rwanda, in 2021, a country that went through an ethnic genocide of hundreds of thousands of members of the Tutsi minority ethnic group in the mid-1990s. Despite the NBA being predominantly black, despite the growing wave of black athletes' activism, and despite players from Africa such as Joel Embiid or African descent such as Giannis Antetokounmpo being among the most dominant ones in the league, as of the end of 2022 the league has not conducted any regular season or preseason games in Africa while playing regularly in Western Europe, across Asia, in Central and South America, and post-pandemic even in the Arabian Gulf.

Beyond the Pandemic

In all fairness, most challenges the world of sports is facing did not start with the coronavirus pandemic. Racism, gender inequality, gentrification, sportswashing, greenwashing, public spending, corruption and lack of transparency, sexual violence, child abuse, mental health, and community resistance were part of the world of sports before COVID-19. Yet the pandemic created urgency, surfacing challenges the world of sports was forced to address. Because of the global nature of sports, these challenges spread across national and continental borders.

Sports sociologist professor Harry Edwards studied and influenced the role of black athletes' activism in America (2017), arguing that the impact on society comes in different waves (Cooper et al., 2019). The first wave started at the beginning of the twentieth century when black athletes suffered from racism in America but managed to achieve international glory. Significant examples include boxer Joe Louis and of course Jesse Owens who won four medals in Berlin 1936 held in Nazi Germany (Edwards, 2017; Cooper et al., 2019). The second wave emerged after World War II and was influenced by democratization and emancipation, manifesting in the USA with desegregation of sports leagues and with Jackie Robinson breaking the color barrier in professional baseball. The third wave occurred in the 1960s and 1970s and was influenced by social movements such as the Civil Rights Movement and spiritual leaders such as Dr. Martin Luther King Jr. and Malcolm X and resulted in some of the most successful athletes in America taking a stand against systematic racism, including Muhammad Ali refusing to be drafted to the Vietnam War, Tommie Smith and John Carlos protesting on the podium during the Mexico City 1968 Olympic Games, Lou Alcindor (who changed his name to Kareem Abdul-Jabbar after converting to Islam) boycotting the Olympics in Mexico, and Bill Russell marching with King and protesting racism in the NBA, among others. Yet with the commercialization of American sports and especially since the 1980s and especially since the end of the Cold War and the Collapse of the Soviet Union, instead of a wave of activism, the USA shifted toward a perception of a post-racial America, focusing on the commercial success of black athletes as a proof the American system works. Perhaps the most known example of this apolitical period is Michael Jordan who refused to take a side in elections in North Carolina and support a black candidate against a racist white one, saying "Republicans buy gym shoes too" (Edwards, 2017). Yet racism in America did not stop during the 1990s. There are some examples of athletes such as Mahmoud Abdul-Rauf taking a stand against immoral ethics in the USA, yet these voices were shut up quickly by the system. In the 2010s a fourth wave of black athletes' activism emerged along with the Black Lives Matter movement following the killings and murders of African Americans and especially against police brutality. The fourth wave was led by athletes with both social and capital power, using social media to spread their messages. LeBron James and Colin Kaepernick were among the leaders of this wave (Edwards, 2017). Yet while LeBron and multiple other NBA and WNBA players were embraced by their leagues, Kaepernick's kneeling protest during the national anthem resulted in backlash from the NFL and became another polarizing topic in the 2016 elections and in Donald Trump's political campaign and agenda. Some white athletes, including female soccer star Megan Rapinoe, joined the caused kneeling until she was told to stop by the American federation (Dubinsky, 2021). Following the murder of George Floyd and the killings of Breonna Taylor and Ahmaud Arbery in the spring of 2022 and Jacob Blake in the summer of that year, athletes in America were in the front line of social protests against systemic racism, including suspending resumed sports events. Edwards, along with other scholars, classifies these events as a fifth wave of athletes' activism (Williams, 2022). The protests crossed genders, political affiliations, and even borders, leading to social change in American sports, including sports organizations such as the NFL and US Soccer apologizing for not restricting athletes' protests, the NFL franchise from Washington finally changing its racist "Redskins" name which is associated with genocide of Native Americans following corporate pressure, and international athletes joining the calls for social justice and race and gender equality (Dubinsky, 2021). The pandemic did not start racial injustice in America, but the health and financial crisis, along with Trump's divisive rhetoric, already led to resistance that was sparked by the murders and killings.

Protests in America against governmental policies in 2020 were ignited by a new wave of athletes' activism supporting Black Lives Matter and revolting police brutality, which led to black football players in England protesting domestic racism, clubs and national teams kneeling before European football games, and athletes around the world demanding policy changes by the IOC who relaxed its anti-protest regulations and allowed structured protests for social justice in the Tokyo 2020 Olympic Games (Dubinsky, 2022b). Yet the capitalist corporate forces that pushed to hold a college football season during the COVID-19 pandemic, despite the athletes not being compensated or vaccinated, also pressured Japan to host the Olympic Games against the will of local communities who were left out of the event and funded and financially supported the Beijing 2022 Winter Olympic Games despite diplomatic boycotts and international criticism over Chinese human rights violations.

Athletes can also serve diplomatic roles, such as role models and United Nations Goodwill Ambassadors, to promote social and humanitarian causes but can also lead to opposite outcomes (Cooper, 2020). American gymnast Simone Biles and Japanese tennis player Naomi Osaka became vocal ambassadors for mental health awareness. Biles, one of the most decorated international gymnasts who also survived sexual abuse in American gymnastics, and Rapinoe, a two-time world champion who took a stand against domestic racism and fought for women's rights, received the Medal of Freedom, the highest civic honor American citizens can receive, from President Biden in 2020. Negative athletes diplomacy manifested through vaccination-rejecting approaches of NBA Star Kyrie Irving who was banned from playing some of the home games of the Brooklyn Nets and Serbian tennis player Novak Djokovic who missed several Grand Slam tournaments due to vaccination policies in Australia and New York. Djokovic is of course not the first controversial athlete to be adored nationally and globally. Celebrity diplomacy in sports could be seen following the deaths of global icons Kobe Bryant and Diego Armando Maradona, as the NBA named the All-Star MVP trophy after the late player, and the government of Argentina declared three national days of mourning to commemorate the late and controversial football player. Bryant's life was celebrated by female athletes across America and became a symbol for supporting women's sports despite facing rape charges. Maradona became a symbol of Argentinian pride by bringing glory to the country by winning the 1986 FIFA World Cup and of defiance against the West from cheating England in the quarter finals of the tournament to having close relations with Cuban socialist dictator Fidel Castro. The year 2022 ended with the death of Pele, the Brazilian football superstar who embodied the Jogo Bonito—the beautiful game—a style of play that is associated not just with the attractive Brazilian national team but with Brazil's culture of samba and carnival.

The financial crisis during the pandemic exposed the faults of the political economy in European football, leading local and foreign owners to try and change the traditional system, and were met with backlash from local communities. Populist leadership that manifested with Trump, Bolsonaro, Johnson, and other leaders downplaying the pandemic manifests worldwide with far-right Giorgia Meloni winning the elections in Italy speaking against progressive movements and American politicians continuing Trump's divisive rhetoric on the expense of transgender athletes as they campaign for their own elections. After decades in which the world of sports stood by as Russia was manipulating the system, finally sports organizations took practical measures following Vladimir Putin's invasion to Ukraine such as excluding Russian athletes, terminating contract with Russian sponsor Gazprom, or going after the wealth of oligarchs who own Western clubs, adding to the sanctions the international community put on the country. Yet these sanctions over Russia also led to counterreactions, such as not selling gas to the West, leading to gas prices rising, further financial pressures on working classes across the world, and further criticism on democratic leaderships. These are just a few examples of how the pandemic played a direct or indirect role in igniting border-crossing challenges that had geopolitical impacts through sports.

Book Structure

The book is constructed from 10 different but complementary chapters. This chapter discusses how the outbreak of the COVID-19 pandemic and the followed health crisis, financial, social, and political turmoil impacted the ways countries used sports for nation branding and public diplomacy. Due to the global nature of sports and its already existing challenges, these crises manifested around the world. This chapter reviews how different countries around the world addressed and adapted to the needed change while keep using sports for nation branding and public diplomacy purposes. The chapter also outlines the structure of the book.

Chapter 2, "Theoretical and Conceptual Frameworks of Nation Branding and Sports Diplomacy," discusses the theoretical and conceptual frameworks used to research and analyze the multidisciplinary fields of country image, nation branding, and public diplomacy. This chapter discusses the theoretical and conceptual connections between sports, soft power, public diplomacy, and nation branding, especially in the context of trying to improve countries' images to achieve foreign policy goals. The term soft power refers to the ability to shape preferences of others and getting them to do what you want through attraction without the use of payments or of military force (Nye, 2004). The three main resources of soft power are culture, political values, and foreign policy. Cultural diplomacy refers to the way culture is used for public diplomacy and soft power purposes. Countries, cities, and communities have been using sports for public diplomacy and branding purposes to achieve social, political, and financial goals and improve the image of the country. The international exposure, the focus on culture, and peaceful values in sports make it a useful tool for countries to use soft power to achieve international goals and improve their public diplomacy. The chapter is based on the article I published in *Place Branding and Public Diplomacy* (Dubinsky, 2019a) and on the literature review from my PhD dissertation "Israel's Use of Sports for Nation Branding and Public Diplomacy" at the University of Tennessee, Knoxville (Dubinsky, 2018). The chapter also leads the readers through major historic intersections between sports, nation branding, and public diplomacy into the 2020s.

Following the theoretical and conceptual introduction, Chap. 3, "Country Image, Nation Branding, and the FIFA World Cup (1930–2022)," explores and analyzes how nation branding and public diplomacy played significant roles through the historic development of one of the largest global events. With the growing popularity of international football, this chapter tries to address the research question of how can the evolution of the FIFA World Cup from 1930 to the 2020s be understood through nation branding, country image, and public diplomacy lenses? This chapter explores and discusses dozens of academic literatures, media articles, documentaries, and other sources related to the intersections between the FIFA World Cup, nation branding, country image, public diplomacy, and international politics. The chapter identifies how, through the historical development of the competitions, hosting and participating countries applied more efforts and significance of trying to achieve a more favorable image and different social, political, and economic goals. In addition to exploring the implications of nation branding and public diplomacy through one of the most popular international mega-events, the following areas are identified as having significant implications on the FIFA World Cup and require further research: (a) public diplomacy in international football, (b) national identity in international football, (c) commercialization and globalization and international football, (d) nation branding and sportswashing in international football, and (e) future challenges and opportunities in international football. The chapter discusses social, political, and economic manifestations by hosting and participating countries, the significance of football as the world's most popular sport, and latest manifestations of nation branding and sports diplomacy in the Qatar 2022 FIFA World Cup.

Chapter 4, "Nation Branding, Tokyo 2020, and the New Era of the Olympic Movement," focuses on arguably the biggest impact of COVID-19 on the world of sports—the postponed Tokyo 2020 Olympic Games that were held in 2021. The Olympic Games are the largest international event humanity holds in terms of participating countries and delegations, countries and territories the event is broadcasted to, and the logistics involved. Postponing the Olympics for a full year and holding them without local or international fans were both unprecedented and controversial. The Tokyo 2020 Olympic Games were the first postponed Olympic Games, held in 2021, during an outbreak of a global pandemic, with strict restrictions and regulations and without international and domestic fans. Despite the challenges and the growing resistance, over 200 countries and delegations still saw value in participating in the most global event humanity holds. The chapter reflects not just on implications on Tokyo and Japan but on the future of the Olympic Movement. This chapter is based on my research in Japan during the summer of 2021 on the Tokyo 2020 Olympic Games and my article published in *Place Branding and Public Diplomacy* (Dubinsky, 2021).

The pandemic did not just lead to a health crisis but also exposed and accelerated social processes. Chapter 5, "American Sports Diplomacy amid the 50 Years Anniversary of Title IX," focuses on the USA especially through gender. The chapter discusses how Title IX, an amendment to the American education law from 1972 that prohibits discrimination based on sex in the education system, did not just change sports domestically over the past 50 years but how gender and social activism impact nation branding and public diplomacy as well. The chapter explores and discusses the role of Title IX in Brand America and US sports diplomacy 50 years after the legislation of the anti-sex discrimination Education Amendment in 1972. The chapter argues that Title IX enhances Brand America through sports, leading to the success of female American athletes and leaders on a global stage, exposing American culture and history to foreign publics, creating networks and relations with international stakeholders, and adding authenticity to values such as opportunities, innovation, competition, rebellion, and freedom association with the image of the USA. Yet the chapter also argues that while US governments used Title IX to promote foreign policy goals, it also covered up exploitative, unethical, and hypocritical practices in the American political economy that most countries reject, questioning the normative dimension of the country's image. Using multidisciplinary theoretical and conceptual frameworks from nation branding, country image, and related fields, along with existing literature on the image of the USA and relevant media coverage, the chapter suggests six lessons scholars and practitioners should consider when analyzing the different impacts of Title IX and shaping and refining Brand America.

The COVID-19 pandemic exposed the vulnerability of the financial structure of global sports, including the unsustainable challenges of the political economy in European football. Chapter 6, "The European Super League as a Nation Branding Geopolitical Battlefield," focuses on Europe and the global and glocal challenges posed by international and local pressure groups. The COVID-19 pandemic exposed the financial crises in European football, and with the winds of the Brexit, when elite football clubs from England, Spain, and Italy tried to break out from the existing system, they were met by backlash and resistance from their own fans and from the football community. On the night of April 18, 2021, 12 European football clubs, 6 from England, 3 from Spain, and 3 from Italy announced they are forming a new private midweek competition—the European Super League (ESL). Within the next 72 hours the football community, including fans, players, coaches, media pundits, and head of states and royalty, revolted against the move, leading to a domino effect of clubs withdrawing and the project officially ceasing. The chapter uses nation branding lenses to discuss the roles of (a) England, (b) Spain, (c) Italy, (d) France, and Germany whose teams declined to join, (e) foreign ownership from Russia, the Arabian Gulf, the USA, and China, and (f) non-state actors. Based on the discussion, the article argues that (a) no one explanation can be sufficient to understand the fiasco and (b) most of the actors who contributed to the creation of the ESL were also responsible for its collapse and vice versa. This chapter analyzes the European Super League fiasco as a nation branding battlefield and power struggles.

The financial and social crises also led to political turmoil and to countries trying to take advantage of the situation through sports. Chapter 7, "Nation Branding, Public Diplomacy, and the Dirty Business of sportswashing," discusses the role of sportswashing in nation branding and public diplomacy. The Beijing 2022 Winter Olympic Games were held during the global COVID-19, under extreme monitory conditions and with ongoing global criticism over Chinese human rights violations, leading to diplomatic boycotts and to the framing of China's use of the Olympics for sportswashing purposes. The term sportswashing refers to countries, predominantly with nondemocratic or authoritarian regimes, using sports to distract international attentions from human rights violations and by that launder the country's images. Among the countries often accused of sportswashing are China, Russia, and countries from the

Arabian Gulf along with other nondemocratic countries or countries facing accusations of human rights violations. This chapter discusses the term sportswashing and how it manifested through the period of 2022, including during the Beijing 2022 Winter Olympic Games, the 2022 FIFA World Cup held in Qatar, Vladimir Putin's use of sports amid the Russian invasion of Ukraine, questionable manifestations of sports and nation branding in the Middle East, and reflections on how Western countries use sports for colonization purposes and if liberalization and globalization of sports essentially require the inclusion of non-liberal countries not just as participants but as equal partners as policymakers. The chapter also compares practices framed as "sportswashing" to ones of liberal democracies who traditionally used sports for soft power purposes to maintain or increase their institutional power and their centrality in the international system.

Chapter 8, "From 'TrackTown USA' to Oregon22 World Athletics Championships," focuses on multilayered approaches to place branding. In July 2022, the USA hosted the World Athletics Championships, arguably the third most significant international sports event after the Olympic Games and the FIFA World Cup. The competition was hosted for the first time on US soil, not in a global city such as Los Angles, New York, or Atlanta, which have history of hosing mega-sports events, but in Eugene, Oregon, a university town in the Pacific Northwest that does not have an international airport or even have money exchange services for non-American tourists. Yet, Eugene has rich history in track and field, including a long legacy of elite athletes developed at the University of Oregon, being the birthplace of Nike, igniting amateur jogging traditions, and hosting annual events. This chapter discusses the 2022 World Athletics Championships and the branding of Eugene as TrackTown USA through place branding lenses on local, regional, national, international, and global levels. The chapter argues that Oregon22 World Athletics Championships was a double-edged sword for the branding of Eugene as the capital of track and field in America resulting in glocal dissonance. On the one hand, the competitions reaffirmed the significance of the city to the sport, but on the other, they also exposed the limitations of hosting an international sports event in a small university town and to stakeholders considering hosting future events in bigger cities to attract larger audiences. The chapter gives insight not just about Eugene, OR, but on the potential and risks of small towns trying to market and differentiate themselves through sports.

Chapter 9, "Sport-Tech Diplomacy," focuses on Israel and the branding attempt of the country as a start-up nation through sports. This chapter explores and discusses the role of the growing sport-tech ecosystem as a soft power tool used for nation branding and public diplomacy purposes. The chapter specifically focuses on the role of the growing sport-tech ecosystem and the branding of Israel as a start-up nation in the country's sports diplomacy. When analyzing Israel's deteriorating image, scholars and practitioners recommended to focus the country's branding and diplomatic efforts on micro-marketing and in creating bypassing messages to the Israeli-Arab dispute. While other countries manage to use sports for such purposes, international politics often limited Israel's possibilities. Being the number one country in the world in start-ups per capita and having a growing sport-tech ecosystem used by some of the biggest international sport-related organizations, Israel embodies new opportunities especially in the context of "sport-tech diplomacy." The chapter explores the intersections of technology, innovation, sports, and diplomacy, using the term "sport-tech diplomacy." The chapter is based on an article I published in *Place Branding and Public Diplomacy* (Dubinsky, 2022b).

Lastly, Chap. 10, "Sports, Country Image, and the Global Order in an Ever-Changing World," tries to analyze the future intersections of sports, nation branding, and public diplomacy. The chapter summarizes key arguments and ideas raised in the previous nine chapters, followed by a discussion on how sports, nation branding, and public diplomacy might intersect in the near future through continents, countries, nongovernmental organizations, communities, and other stakeholders around the world amid the global changes. The chapter also discusses the potential implications of cross-national global challenges and trends and their implications through sports, such as climate change, sustainability, growing social activism, populism, gender classifications, and others. The chapter ends with suggestions for future research on the intersections between sports, nation branding, and public diplomacy in decades to come.

Professional and Academic Contribution

Within two years of the outbreak of the pandemic, international scholars published multiple books discussing implications of COVID-19 on public diplomacy (Aarts et al., 2021; Best & Howard, 2022; Kettemann & Lachmayer, 2022) and on the sports industry and in dozens of different countries (Frawley & Schulenkorf, 2023; Krieger, et al., 2021; Pedersen et al., 2021), adding timely and significant contribution to an ongoing developing challenge. This book focuses predominantly on the use of sports for nation branding and public diplomacy, with the pandemic being mostly an accelerating factor to ongoing changes. Internationally oriented practitioners and academics in the fields of governance, diplomacy and public policy, marketing and branding, and sports management will find this book useful. While the book is not written as a textbook, it does fit to serve courses related to international sports either as the core readings or as supplementary materials scholars can assign in their syllabi when teaching wide variety of courses in political science, communication, and sports management. The book is edited in a way in which each chapter can stand on its own, yet together they portray a mosaic telling a story of nation branding and sports diplomacy in a changing world. The book focuses on three specific years, 2020, 2021, and 2022, as the world went through a turmoil, and countries, organizations, and communities found more and less successful ways to navigate through it, as they adapt to new realities and to a new normal. While I wrote about international sports being on a verge of a new era even before the outbreak of the pandemic (Dubinsky, 2019b), in the last few years that argument received more support from sports governing bodies such as the IOC discussing a new era in the Olympic Movement (IOC News, 2022) and scholars defining a new era in sports management (Gammelsaeter & Anagnostopoulos, 2022). Country image games are ongoing. They do not start or end on a specific date, nor is there an end-game winner. For thousands of years, countries, cities, and communities have been using sports to improve their images and achieve social, political, and economic goals. This is one constant that survives even in unprecedented times of change.

References

Aarts, E., Feuren, H., Sitskoorn, M., & Wilthagen, T. (eds.). (2021). *The New Common*. Cham, Switzerland: Springer.

Best, R., & Howard, D. (2022). *The global sports industry*. Independently Published.

Bobbitt, P. (2022). Future scenarios: "We are all failed states, now". In H. Brands & F. J. Gavin (Eds.), *COVID-19 and world order* (pp. 56–71). John Hopkins University Press.

Buhmann, A., & Ingenhoff, D. (2015). The 4D Model of the country image: An integrative approach from the perspective of communication management. *The International Communication Gazette, 77*, 102–124.

Cooper, A. F. (2020). UN celebrity-driven public diplomacy: Causes, critiques, and trajectories. In N. Show & N. J. Cull (Eds.), *Routledge handbook of public diplomacy* (pp. 187–194). Routledge.

Cooper, J. N., Macaulay, C., & Rodriguez, S. S. (2019). Race and resistance: A typology of African American sport activism. *International Review for the Sociology of Sport, 54*(2), 151–181. https://doi.org/10.1177/1012690217718170

Cull, N. J. (2008). Public diplomacy: Taxonomies and histories. *ANNALS of the American Academy of Political Science, 616*(1), 31–54.

Dubinsky, Y. (2018). *Israel's use of sports for nation branding and public diplomacy*. Unpublished doctorate dissertation, University of Tennessee, Knoxville. https://trace.tennessee.edu/utk_graddiss/4868/

Dubinsky, Y. (2019a). From soft power to sports diplomacy: A theoretical and conceptual discussion. *Place Branding and Public Diplomacy, 15*, 154–164. https://doi.org/10.1057/s41254-019-00116-8

Dubinsky, Y. (2019b). Analyzing the roles of country image, nation branding, and public diplomacy through the evolution of the modern Olympic movement. *Physical Culture and Sport. Studies and Research, 84*(1), 27–40. https://doi.org/10.2478/pcssr-2019-0024

Dubinsky, Y. (2021). Sports, Brand America and U.S. public diplomacy during the presidency of Donald Trump. *Place Branding & Public Diplomacy, 19*, 167. https://doi.org/10.1057/s41254-021-00230-6

Dubinsky, Y. (2022a). Country image, cultural diplomacy, and sports during the COVID19 pandemic: Brand America and Super Bowl LV. *Place Branding & Public Diplomacy.*, 1–17. https://doi.org/10.1057/s41254-021-00257-9

Dubinsky, Y. (2022b). The Olympic Games, nation branding, and public diplomacy in a post-pandemic world: Reflections on Tokyo 2020 and beyond. *Place Branding & Public Diplomacy.*, 1–12. https://doi.org/10.1057/s41254-021-00255-x

Dubinsky, Y. (2022c). Sport-tech diplomacy: Exploring the intersections between the sport-tech ecosystem, innovation, and diplomacy in Israel. *Place Branding & Public Diplomacy, 18*(2), 169–180. https://doi.org/10.1057/s41254-020-00191-2

Edwards, H. (2017). *The Revolt of the Black Athlete (50th Anniversary Edition)*. The University of Illinois.

ESPN News Services. (2020, March 23). List of sporting events canceled because of the coronavirus. *ESPN*. Retrieved from https://www.espn.com/olympics/story/_/id/28824781/list-sporting-events-canceled-coronavirus

Fan, Y. (2010). Branding the nation: Towards a better understanding. *Journal of Place Branding and Public Diplomacy, 6*(2), 97–103.

Frawley, S., & Schulenkorf, N. (Eds.). (2023). *Routledge handbook of sport and COVID-19*. Routledge.

Gammelsaeter, H., & Anagnostopoulos, C. (2022). Sport management: mission and meaning for a new era. *European Sport Management Quarterly, 22*(5), 637–642. https://doi.org/10.1080/16184742.2022.2100918

IOC News. (July 26, 2022). With two years until Paris 2024, IOC President looks ahead to "new era" of Olympic Games. *Olympics*. Retrieved from https://olympics.com/ioc/news/with-two-years-until-paris-2024-ioc-president-looks-ahead-to-new-era-of-olympic-games

Kettemann, M. C., & Lachmayer, K. (eds.). (2022). *Pandemocracy in Europe*. Oxford, UK: Hart Publishing.

Krechmar, R. S., Dyreson, M., Llewellyn, M. P., & Gleaves, J. (2017). *History and philosophy of sport and physical activity*. Human Kinetics.

Krieger, J., Henning, A., Pieper, L., & Dimeo, P. (Eds.). (2021). *Time out: National perspectives on sport and the Covid-19 lockdown*. Common Ground Research Networks. https://doi.org/10.18848/978-1-86335-232-1/CGP

Miller, S. G. (2004). *Ancient Greek athletics*. Yale University Press.

Nye, J. S., Jr. (2004). *Soft power: The means to success in world politics*. PublicAffairs.

Pedersen, P. M., Ruihley, B. J., & Li, B. (Eds.). (2021). *Sport and the pandemic: Perspectives on Covid-19's impact on the sport industry*. Routledge.

State of the Union. (2022, February 6). Jake Tapper calls over China's move during Olympics Opening Ceremony. *CNN*. Retrieved from https://edition.cnn.com/videos/world/2022/02/06/china-olympics-corporations-human-rights-jake-tapper-sotu-vpx.cnn

Wall Street Journal. (2021, December 23). How Omicron Challenges U.S. and China on Vaccine Diplomacy. *YouTube*. Retrieved from https://www.youtube.com/watch?v=W-_YOw94grg

Williams, L. A. (2022). The heritage strikes back: Athlete activism, Black Lives Matter, and the iconic fifth wave of activism in the (W)NBA bubble. *Cultural Studies ↔ Critical Methodologies, 22*(3), 266–275. https://doi.org/10.1177/15327086211049

World Health Organization. (n.d.). *WHO coronavirus (COVID-19) dashboard*. https://covid19.who.int/table

CHAPTER 2

Theoretical and Conceptual Frameworks of Nation Branding and Sports Diplomacy

INTRODUCTION

The connection between sports and politics goes back to the athletic competitions in Ancient Greece and was strengthened again as sports developed through the nineteenth, twentieth, and twenty-first centuries (Dubinsky, 2019; Murray, 2012). With over 200 countries participating in the Summer Olympic Games (IOC, 2018), marching in ceremonies, and displaying their flags and symbols, every kind of political regime has been using sports to achieve social, political, and economic goals (Boykoff, 2016; Dubinsky, 2019). The ever-growing media exposure (IOC, 2018), the uncertainty of the outcome, and the universal language of an athletic competition make sports appealing platforms for countries, cities, and communities to use. While Nelson Mandela, who used sports to unite post-Apartheid South Africa, said, "Sport has the power to change the world" (Murray, 2018, p. 257), George Orwell had a different take, referring to sports as "war minus shooting" (Orwell, 1945). While some countries, communities, and organizations have been using sports as a tool to build bridges, some have used it as a powerful tool for diplomatic purposes targeting other foreign policy goals (Boykoff, 2016; Murray, 2018). This chapter[1] discusses the connection between sports, nation branding, public diplomacy, country image, and their related fields (Fan, 2010; Buhmann & Ingenhoff, 2015), suggesting different lenses and theories from multidisciplinary fields of analysis.

CONTESTED DEFINITIONS

The term public diplomacy was applied during the Cold War (Cull, 2008; Gilboa, 2008) referring to the process of international organizations trying to achieve foreign policy goals by engaging with foreign publics. Gilboa (2008) argued that while classic public diplomacy refers mostly to states, new public diplomacy refers also to non-state actors. The term soft power refers to the ability to shape preferences of others and getting them to do what you want through attraction without the use of payments or of military force (Nye, 2004). Nye (2004) who coined the term argued that the three main resources of soft power are culture, political values, and foreign policy. Cultural diplomacy (Signitzer & Coombs, 1992) refers to the way culture is used for public diplomacy and soft power purposes.

Public diplomacy also played a role in the competitions in the Ancient Games, especially through the peaceful tradition of "Ekecheiria," a declared cease-fire to ensure a secure passage for all the delegation to come from the different city-states to Olympia even if they were at war with each other (Miller, 2004). In more modern times, countries, cities, and communities have been using sports for public diplomacy (Arning, 2013) and branding purposes (Preuss, 2015) to achieve social, political, and financial goals (Chalip, 2006) and improve the image of the country. The international exposure, the focus on culture, and peaceful values in sports make it a useful tool for countries to use soft power (Nye, 2004) to achieve international goals and improve their public diplomacy.

Sports events have become a political tool for countries and governments to promote themselves, leverage political and economic goals, regenerate, expose local products and local businesses as the local culture, promote tourism, and thus improve their international image (Chalip &

---

[1] This chapter is an adapted and updated version of the article I published: Dubinsky, Y. (2019). From soft power to sports diplomacy: A theoretical and conceptual discussion. Place Branding and Public Diplomacy, 15, 154–164. https://doi.org/10.1057/s41254-019-00116-8. For the chapter, the article was edited to discuss more concepts in related fields to nation branding and public diplomacy, using more examples leading 2020.

Leyns, 2002; Heslop et al., 2010; Laroche et al., 2003; Nadeau et al., 2008). The unit of analysis may vary from a country or a nation to a global city, a region, or even a small town (Papadopoulos & Heslop, 2002). Country image may change in time, although the process is rather slow. Preuss (2008) differentiates between different types of sports events according to the number of sports (multi-sports events such as the Olympic Games and single sport like the Super Bowl), the location of the event (different location each time like with the Olympics or in a particular location like branding the Wimbledon Tennis tournament), and the region affected by the event (a city or a region like the Olympics or the whole country like the FIFA World Cup). Some one-time sports events can be associated with not just the place they took place in but an entire region or continent, such as "The Rumble in the Jungle" heavyweight boxing championship match between Muhammad Ali and George Foreman in Kinshasa, Zaire, which was perhaps the most internationally famous sports event that happened in Africa in the twentieth century. The following year Ali boxed against Joe Frazer III in the Philippines, in a championship fight known as "The Thrilla in Manila," making it one of the most famous sports events in Southeast Asia in the last century. Some cities officially associate their image with sports, such as Lausanne, Switzerland, being the Olympic Capital; Eugene, Oregon, branded as "Track-Town USA"; and the small coastal town Torquay, being the surfing capital of Australia (I Am Torquay, 2022). Sports also serve as a tool for small countries like Qatar (Brannagan & Giulianotti, 2015), to reposition themselves and become more significant political actors. Thus, while connecting to culture and history and enjoying international exposure, countries see sports as a useful tool for countries and governments to demonstrate their soft power (Nye, 2004) and become more attractive for domestic and foreign audiences. This article discusses the connection between soft power and sports.

The terms public diplomacy, nation/place branding, and national identity have some overlaps but are inherently different. The term public diplomacy originated during the Cold War and comes from the fields of political science and public relations (Cull, 2008; Nye, 2008). The term nation branding is directly connected to business management and marketing, analyzing images and brands (Anholt, 2010; Fan, 2010), and researching destinations (Kotler et al., 1993). National identity comes from the fields of sociology and psychology or sociopsychology (Buhmann & Ingenhoff, 2015; David & Bar-Tal, 2009) and is rooted in social identity theory (David & Bar-Tal, 2009). One important commonality between public diplomacy, nation branding, and national identity is that they all impact countries' images and reputations (Anholt, 2010; Buhmann & Ingenhoff, 2015). To better understand the relations between sports, nation branding, public diplomacy, and country image, a clearer dichotomy of definition is needed.

Public Diplomacy

Traditional definitions of public diplomacy refer to the communications and interactions by governments, policymakers, organizations, and individuals to influence foreign publics to achieve a more favorable image of the nation and ultimately achieve foreign policy goals (Cull, 2008; Gilboa, 2006; Nye, 2008). Signitzer and Coombs (1992) differentiate between traditional diplomacy that refers to the national governments trying to influence each other through negotiations and public diplomacy that is aimed at foreign publics and refers to how governments, organizations, and individuals shape public opinions and through them their government's foreign policies.

The term public diplomacy is relatively new, applied first in the 1960s to research as an emerging dimension in international relations about "the conduct of foreign policy through engagement with international publics" (Cull, 2010, p. 11). The term was first applied in 1965 by Edmund Gullion, a former US Ambassador and the Dean of the Fletcher School of Diplomacy at Tufts University, in Medford Massachusetts (Cull, 2010). The term referred "to the process by which international actors seek to accomplish the goals of their foreign policy by engaging with foreign publics and has gained international currency only since the end of the Cold War" (Cull, 2008, p. 31). Gilboa (2006) also refers to the Cold War as the origin of public diplomacy arguing that because of the emergence of nuclear weapons, "information and persuasion campaigns would be the principal weapons that the two superpowers, the US and Soviet Union, would utilize in their global ideological and strategic struggle" (Gilboa, 2006, p. 717). According to Gilboa (2006), public diplomacy is used by policymakers to communicate with foreign people and influence them and their governments. In most cases, the goals of public diplomacy are to achieve a better social, political, and economic image of the nation (Gilboa, 2006). Nye (2008) adds that when the term public diplomacy was introduced in the 1960s, it was defined as "interactions not only with foreign governments but primarily with non-governmental individuals and organizations, and often presenting a variety of private views in addition to governmental views" (Nye, 2008, p. 101).

Public diplomacy has been associated with propaganda (Cull, 2010) as they both focus on influence. However, unlike propaganda, where the message goes through a one-way street between the government and the audience, public diplomacy when done right is a two-way street, an ongoing process with a mutual influence. Wang (2006a) suggests that public diplomacy encompasses three main dimensions: (a) "Promoting nation states' goals and policies," (b) "communicating their values," and (c) "developing common understanding and mutual trust among countries and peoples" (p. 43). The focus on message, target, and audiences makes public diplomacy multidisciplinary (Fitzpatrick, 2007). Although the term comes from international relations through the context of analyzing the Cold War, as strategic communications (Nye, 2008) is an essential part of it, public diplomacy has also been very much studied in the fields of communications and public relations (Fitzpatrick, 2007; White, 2015). While more traditional definitions of public diplomacy refer to the engagement of government to government or government to people (Wang, 2006a), more recent definitions also emphasize non-state actors such as people-to-people diplomacy (Handelman, 2012), also referred to as citizen diplomacy (Cull, 2010), and even the private sector (White, 2015), looking at corporate diplomacy. Amiri (2022) also adds the classification of city diplomacy, analyzing not just communications by the state but the different relations a city fosters to enhance its global image.

While the term public diplomacy might be relatively new, the parts that constitute it are much older and were used for foreign policy before the term was coined (Cull, 2008). Nye (2008) goes back to the nineteenth century, and to the French-Prussia War in 1883, and how the French government needed to repair the French image. Similar arguments were made about Italy and Germany after World War I. Cull (2008) divided the practices of public diplomacy into five: listening, advocacy, cultural diplomacy, exchange diplomacy, and international broadcasting. According to Gilboa (2006), some of the techniques used in public diplomacy are "international broadcasting; cultural and scientific exchanges of students, scholars, intellectuals and artists; participation in festivals and exhibitions; building and maintaining cultural centers; teaching a language; establishing local friendship leagues and trade associations" (Gilboa, 2006, p. 717).

According to Murray and Pigman (2014), "international sport is used as an instrument of diplomacy by governments can generate important prescriptive conclusions that can enable governments to use sport for diplomatic purposes more effectively" (p. 1115). The connection between sports and diplomacy goes back over 2700 years ago, to the Ancient Olympia and the "Ekecheiria," the "Olympic Truce" that was respected by the different Greek city-states and became one of the most significant Pan-Hellenic traditions (Murray, 2018). In the twentieth century, sports played a role in both war and peace. Sports played a diplomatic role by promoting truce during "The Christmas Truce" in which during World War I in December 1914 British and German soldiers stopped fighting and had an informal day of football or through "Ping Pong Diplomacy" (Carter & Sugden, 2011), a table tennis game that led to official relations between the USA and Communist People's Republic of China and a meeting between American President Richard Nixon and Chairman Mao Zedong. However, sports also became a platform for political boycotts such as between the Olympic boycotts of the USA and the Soviet Union during the 1980s (Murray, 2012; Murray & Pigman, 2014; Murray, 2018) and political exclusions, like in the case of South Africa, which was excluded from the Olympic movement while it was under the Apartheid Regime (MacLean, 2014). According to Murray (2012), sports diplomacy offers governments an alternative channel to form relationships. Murray (2012) argued that "sports does so in a unique fashion: by demonstrating that people share affinity through a love of sports" (p. 588) but warned about using sports as "a gimmick, or a photo-op" (p. 589). Good public diplomacy needs to be rooted in sound policies (Cull, 2010). The same goes to sports diplomacy.

Nation Branding

The research of nation branding comes especially from business studies perspectives that focus on management, marketing, and sponsorship (Kotler et al., 1993; Olins, 2002). According to Aaker (1991), a brand is the name or symbol that identifies one group and differentiates it from its competitors. According to Keller (1993), brand equity is defined in terms of marketing effects uniquely attributable to the brand and assets and liabilities that are associated with the brand. Fan's (2010) definition of a nation brand is "the total sum of all perceptions of a nation in the minds of international stakeholders, which may contain some of the following elements: people, place, culture/language history, food, fashion, famous faces (celebrities), global brands and so on" (Fan, 2010, p. 98). While branding is the process done by the government or the country itself, the image and the reputation of the country are determined by their target audiences, which in the case of nation branding are foreign people and foreign governments (Fan, 2010). While Fan (2010) uses the term nation branding as a comprehensive one of capturing different fields of study, it is mostly used to suggest business and marketing lenses of analysis (Buhmann & Ingenhoff, 2015). Branding a nation is commonly analyzed through two main approaches: (a) the products associated with the place (Jaffe & Nebenzahl, 1993; Johansson, 1989) and (b) the place as a tourism destination (Kang & Perdue, 1994; Nadeau et al., 2008).

A destination-oriented branding focuses on a country as a tourism destination, trying to have an attractive image for future tourists (Nadeau et al., 2008). This approach to nation branding received several names such as marketing places (Kotler et al., 1993), tourism destination image (Nadeau et al., 2008), or various variations of country brand, city brand, or place branding (Papadopoulos & Heslop, 2002). Some of the categories that are commonly analyzed in tourism-based research are the attractions, the scenery, the culture, the nature, the history, the reputation of the people and the country, the economic and political systems, and others (Nadeau et al., 2008; Papadopoulos & Heslop, 2002). Kavaratzis and Ashworth (2015) identify different tactics of using culture for place branding purposes, such as event hallmarking, personality association, and flagship building and signature district. Beyond targeting foreign publics, festivals and sports events "are held to strengthen local appreciation of the place's cultural past or to showcase the place's potential for cultural creativity and contemporary cultural production" (Kavaratzis & Ashworth, 2015, p. 158).

While tourism-based research focus on the country's attempts to attract future tourists, the product-based approach targets future consumers of products and businesses associated with a country (Nadeau et al., 2008). Product-based branding in nation branding literature receives various names such as product-country image (Nadeau et al., 2008), country-of-origin (Dinnie, 2003), or various variations with the words "made in" (Johansson, 1989; Nebenzahl et al., 1997). The "made in" label (Johansson, 1989) embodies various characteristics and values that may influence the consumer's decision whether to purchase a product associated with the country. Nebenzahl, Jaffe, and Lampert (1997) add that the ways countries are branded and the images they have in the eyes of the consumers are important in every stage of the process: from the home country (HC) where the consumer resides, the origin country (OC) of the consumer, the made-in country (MC) of the product where and the product was made, and the designed-in country (DC) where the product is designed. Some of the factors that impact product-based branding are nationalism, the economic system, the people and country's competencies, culture, nationalism, education, and demographics.

Another factor that might influence a consumer to either travel to a country or buy products from a certain country is animosity (Batra et al., 2000; Klein et al., 1998; Laroche et al., 2003). War is a factor that creates animosity (Klein et al., 1998) between people from the fighting countries. Moreover, an international crisis raises negative feelings towards a country's products (Heslop et al., 2008; Magnusson et al., 2019). Thus, improving an image of a nation that is going through war or a conflict is much more complex.

There are inconsistencies in academic literature about the definitions and goals of nation branding. Fan (2010) points out five different definitions of the purpose and outcomes of nation branding in academic literature: (a) to remold national identities; (b) to enhance a nation's competitiveness; (c) to embrace political, cultural, business, and sports activities; (d) to promote economic and political interests at home and abroad; and (5) to alter, improve, or enhance a nation's image/reputation. Fan (2010) divides nation branding into four fields: political branding as public diplomacy, export branding as country of origin or product-country image, place branding as tourism destination image, and cultural branding as national identity. Country image is one of the outcomes of nation branding (Fan, 2010). Thus, while there is a general agreement that nation branding is an attempt by governments and other non-state actors to achieve a better image of the country, there are various definitions to the term and to what exactly it captures, especially with the relations with public diplomacy and national identity. The terms place branding, nation branding, and country branding are at times used interchangeably, and at times nation branding refers to the entire branding of a country, while place branding refers mostly to the tourism side of branding a specific place or destination (Avraham, 2009; Anholt, 2010; Jun et al., 2009).

Countries, cities, and communities have been using sports events for branding purposes (Chalip & Costa, 2005; Preuss, 2015) to improve the image of the country and through that achieve social, political, and financial goals and leverage future opportunities (Chalip, 2006). Different regimes use sports in different ways (Dubinsky, 2018, 2019). For example, while the Chinese government used the 2008 Olympic Games to showcase a powerful image of China by spending over $40 billion on the games and exposing Chinese technologies, the British tried to use the London 2012 Olympic Games to renovate East London and focused on sustainability (Dubinsky, 2018). Some countries go beyond nation branding and use sports even for nation building purposes. The State of Israel, as a Jewish country, and the Zionist Movement that galvanizes Jewish people around the idea of having a homeland for Jewish people use the Maccabiah Games to connect the Jewish Diaspora to the State of Israel, encourage to make Aliyah, and to immigrate to Israel or to strengthen relations with the country. Qatar, a rich country due to its natural resources, is using its wealth for hard power purposes to ensure its security, and sports competitions became a tool not just to showcase the country to the world but to build infrastructure around them. Thus, again, the multidisciplinary nature of the fields creates overlapping classifications for attempting to use sports to improve a country's image and achieve domestic and international goals.

National Identity

According to social identity theory, the self-concept of an individual is influenced by one's membership in a social group (David & Bar-Tal, 2009). Membership in a social group embodies emotions, values, knowledge, norms, behaviors, and self-categorization. According to David and Bar-Tal (2009), the process of social identity goes through two processes: (a) a cognitive process of categorizing oneself into groups and defining the meanings of these groups and of external groups and (b) a motivation to differentiate between one's groups to external groups. According to social identity theory, social identity has impact on various social effects, including collective feelings or behaviors such as discrimination, collaborations, and the possibility of mobilizing people to act together under a shared social reality (David & Bar-Tal, 2009). Collective identity is the acknowledgment of individuals that they share the same social identity.

National identity is a specific case of collective identity, based on nationalism. According to David and Bar-Tal (2009), national identity embodies a shared history, values, ideology, identity, territory, common myths and memories, public culture, common duties, commonalities, beliefs, and other socially constructed collective characteristics. Social identity theory and the term national identity come from the research fields of sociology and psychology (Buhmann & Ingenhoff, 2015; David & Bar-Tal, 2009). From a sociological perspective, sports play different roles in creating national identities (Gleaves & Llewellyn, 2014) and imaged community (Hobsbawm, 1992), where athletes and teams represent a nation of millions. According to Hobsbawm (1992), between World War I and World War II, sports became "an expression of national struggle, and sportsmen representing their nation or state, primary expression of their imagined communities" (p.143). One of the more famous examples of the use of sports to expose local identities to a global audience is the "Haka dance" that the "All Blacks," the National Rugby Team of New Zealand, conducts before every game. By using the dance, the rugby team sheds light on the indigenous Māori culture while making capital profit through global sponsorships (Jackson & Hokowhitu, 2002).

Soft Power, Cultural Diplomacy, and Sports

Through the lenses of international relations and political science, countries use public diplomacy and soft power to achieve a better image and international goals (Cull, 2008; Gilboa, 2008; Nye, 2004). In his book *Soft Power: The Means to Success in World Politics*, Nye (2004) demonstrated how the USA has been using different sources of power to influence other countries and players. According to Nye (2004), power is the capability to affect others and to create outcomes, and relationships are involved. In international relations, Nye (2004) described hard power as military and economic capabilities, as these are the main tools that can pose threats or incentives. Nye (2004) suggests other forms of power in world politics to attract players and influence agendas, rather than just military force or economic sanctions.

Soft power does not rely on military force or on sanctions, but on the possibility to shape the preferences of others through attractions and seductions. Nye (Nye, 2004, 2008) argued that the sources of soft power are culture, political values, and foreign policy. According to Nye (2008), the sources of credibility of soft power are governments, nongovernmental organizations, intergovernmental organizations, media, and markets, and the receivers of soft power are foreign governments and foreign publics. According to Nye (2004), "when a country's culture includes universal values and its policies promote values and interests that others share, it increases the probability of obtaining its desired outcomes because of the relationship of attraction and duty that it creates" (p. 11).

Thus, culture, either high culture or popular culture (Nye, 2004), plays a role in public diplomacy. According to Signitzer and Coombs (1992), "cultural diplomacy's goal is to convey a favorable image of one's culture with a view forward facilitating diplomatic activities as whole" (p. 142). Signitzer and Coombs (1992) separated cultural diplomacy into two stages: creating cultural agreements and executing them. They argue that cultural diplomacy and cultural cooperation influence cultural communications, which influences a state's public diplomacy. According to Anholt (2010), culture also enriches a nation's brand, rooting the brand in culture and history.

Meaning and values are not universal and vary between cultures (Szondi, 2010). According to Nye (2004), using culture for soft power purposes will be more effective between countries that share similar values. Yet, when the cultures are not similar, using culture for soft power will most likely achieve a lesser outcome. Nye (2004) argued that the use of culture for public diplomacy is contextual, and American films that can showcase an attractive USA in China and South America can have the opposite effect in Saudi Arabia and Pakistan. He argued that "the background attraction (and repulsion) of American popular culture in different regions and among different groups may make it easier or more difficult for Americans to promote their policies" (p. 12). The limitations of America's soft power and cultural diplomacy are especially evident when addressing the Arab and Muslim world that does not have a democratic culture (Nye, 2004; Wang, 2006b).

The declining of the USA's reputation is discussed in the book *Rebuilding Brand America* (Martin, 2007). Martin (2007) argued that products that were "made in America," such as McDonald's, Coca-Cola, and Levi's, not only were respected but gave bits of American experiences to people all over the world and helped associating America with money, freedom, and pursuit of happiness. However, the strength of Brand America also caused a polarizing affect, associating Americans with arrogance, self-absorption, and ignorance. Martin (2007) also raises the importance of public opinion research on Brand America and the connection between public relations and public diplomacy (Wang, 2006a).

When assessing the US cultural engagement with different countries, Nye (2004) argued that when compared with the Soviet Union, popular culture is very different, but both countries are interested in sports and in winning the most medals in the Olympic Games. "In science and technology, classical music, ballet, and athletics, Soviet culture was attractive, but the absence of popular culture exports limited its impact" (Nye, 2004, p. 75). Szondi (2010) makes a connection between the roles of sports and culture in the contexts of nation branding and public diplomacy, arguing that governments lobbying to host "cultural or sports events also come under the auspices of PR where relationships are developed with key decision makers" (Szondi, 2010, p. 340).

In the context of sports, one of the most efficient platforms to use soft power and cultural diplomacy is through the opening ceremonies of the Olympic Games (Arning, 2013). Over 200 National Olympic Committees participate in the Olympic Games that are broadcasted to 220 countries and territories around the world drawing an audience of around 4 billion viewers (Arning, 2013). The Opening Ceremony gives the hosting countries an opportunity to showcase their culture and history and leave a lasting memory. Arning (2013) studied all Opening Ceremonies of the Summer Olympic Games between 1980 and 2012. During that period of time, the countries that hosted the Summer Olympic Games were the Soviet Union (Moscow 1980), the USA (Los Angeles 1984, Atlanta 1996), South Korea (Seoul 1988), Spain (Barcelona 1992), Australia (Sydney 2000), Greece (Athens 2004), China (Beijing 2008), and Great Britain (London 2012). He breaks down his analysis into six categories: (a) mass orchestration, (b) technological prowess, (c) symbolic ingenuity, (d) esthetic enchantment, (e) whimsy and humor, and (f) musical grandeur.

When discussing mass orchestration, Arning (2013) focused mostly on the amount of people participating in the parades during the Opening Ceremonies in Moscow, Beijing, and Seoul. He particularly emphasized the Soviet use of military in the opening ceremony, combined with the cultural capital of the Bolshoi ballet. For technological prowess, some of the examples Arning gives were the Soviet Union showing a message from a cosmonaut in space, of the USA landing a jet in the Olympic Stadium in Los Angeles, and the South Koreans forming the Olympic Rings by a coordinated parachute team. In symbolic ingenuity, Arning (2013) analyzed the symbols that were used. He gives examples of the shapes the different performances create such as English and Korean alphabet in Seoul or creating a human pyramid in Barcelona, which had some symbols that represented the 12 European Union countries but also some that represented Catalan folklore. For esthetic enchantment, Arning (2013) gives examples of the use of colorful performances to reference historic events and local cultures and communities, such as the indigenous flowers in Sydney or imperial designs and cherry blossoms in Beijing. Whimsy was defined as a playful creation, and examples included the mascots that were used during the ceremonies. The last category Arning (2013) analyzed was music, which he describes as one of the most powerful media tools. Some of the examples include the massive dance performances, the different dance routines while using iconic and symbolic signs. According to Arning (2013), "opening ceremonies enable countries to smuggle in and project soft power through the guise of Olympic stewardship" (p. 539).

Colonization and Globalization

Another way of analyzing the evolution of the use of sports for nation branding and public diplomacy since Ancient Greece is through the lenses of colonization and globalization. Athletic competitions were not just used in Greece for public diplomacy by city-states or as a Pan-Hellenic tradition (Murray, 2018), but Alexander the Great used to implement traditional ancient Greek athletic competitions in new conquered colonies as part of the Hellenization process (Miller, 2004). The Roman Empire introduced the Colosseum and the gladiator fights and with those different violent competitions between captured slaves and animals brought from different conquered areas of the Roman Empire. Thus, colonization is bounded in sports since antiquity, and with Ancient Greece and Ancient Rome setting some of the foundations of modern society, this includes sports and colonialism. In more modern times, the institutionalization of sports in Europe and especially in Great Britain led to the spreading of different sports across different colonies, either organically or even structurally through the Commonwealth Games, enhancing the British Empire's cultural richness through sports (Krechmar et al., 2017). In some cases, countries developed their own sports and traditions out of institutionalized British sports. Perhaps the most notable examples are ball kicking games such as football and rugby, which spread across the world and led to the creation of American football in the USA and Australian football in Australia. In South Africa, the Springboks, the national rugby team, became a symbol of the Apartheid Regime and also of its abolishment following the elections of Nelson Mandela and the 1995 Rugby

World Cup. As mentioned, in Oceania, New Zealand and other Pacific Islands, such as Tonga, Samoa, and Fiji, perform Haka dances to honor native tribes. Hundreds of thousands of aboriginals died due to British colonialism of Oceania, and entire cultures were lost. Cricket, another British sport spread through the Empire, was especially adopted in India and Pakistan, making it one of the most popular sports worldwide due to the population sizes in the countries.

The evolution of using sports for public diplomacy in the twentieth century can also be analyzed through predominant international relations theories (Dubinsky, 2017). The institutionalization of modern sports in the late nineteenth and early twentieth century, including the creation of the International Olympic Committee (IOC) in 1984, can be seen as part of utopianism and idealism in international relations (Dubinsky, 2017), reflecting times of peace and creating institutions to foster international collaborations (Carr, 1964). Yet since the cancellations of the Berlin 1916 Olympic Games because of World War I and especially since the Berlin 1936 Olympic Games which was used for Nazi propaganda and through World War II and the Cold War, the realist approach (Dubinsky, 2017; Legro & Moravcsik, 1999) in international relations can better explain states taking pragmatic rational approaches putting national security and foreign policy above any other factor, including sports, leading also to boycotts of international sports events. The liberal and neoliberal approaches that emphasize mutual growth rather than the realists' zero-sum game including the significance of non-state actors (Keohane & Martin, 1995) also fill some of the gaps, especially with pressure groups using the exposure of mega-sports events to send social and political messages either peacefully through the Black Power Salute in the Mexico City 1968 Olympic Games or through terrorism during the Munich 1972 Olympic Games (Dubinsky, 2017). Either way, the ever-growing significance of sports in geopolitics and international relations could not happen without globalization.

Globalization refers to the movements of people, goods, and ideas across national borders. The institutionalization of modern sports is mostly associated with Western Europe and linked to social class and to the education system in the second half of the nineteenth century reflecting some of the values in these countries. In Great Britain sports were used to build character and values in private and public schools, while in Prussia/Germany the turnen was part of a patriotic way to prepare youth to be military fit (Krechmar et al., 2017). In the USA, on the other hand, sports in the education system was a form of entertainment. The philosophy and practice of the IOC as formed by Baron Pierre de Coubertin was shaped by synthesizing the use of sports in different countries, connecting it back to Ancient Greek athletics. In some countries Western institutionalization of sports changed local traditions, such as the formation of judo in Japan from an educational martial arts practice into a competition with winners and losers. Colonization of African countries also led to institutionalization of national talents, and the development of running programs in Kenya and Ethiopia led to the branding of these countries as long-running specialists. Some countries invest in specific sports to differentiate themselves from others using their sociopolitical system, weather, and genetics, such as Jamaica in sprints, Cuba in boxing, ice hockey in Canada, or cross-country skiing in Norway which established itself as the most dominant country in the history of the Winter Olympic Games despite having a population of just over five million.

The impacts of globalization go along with technological developments, especially of broadcasting and media, leading to both the global popularity of sports and resistance against its negative impacts. On the one hand, globalization led to spread sports worldwide and make mega-events such as the FIFA World Cup or the Olympic Games globally popular, having international members and hosting international competitions in non-American and non-European countries. Yet it also led to sports leagues and institutions in Western countries and the global north widening financial gaps through attracting talents from lesser developing economies, through football academies in Africa, for example. With sports becoming globally popular, every country in the world sees some benefit through representation on international stages. The flow of ideas galvanizes pressure groups, such as NOlympics, across the world to unite behind causes such as climate change or social justice and protests against bidding cities or against the Olympic Movement itself.

Globalization theories, which analyze border-crossing patterns, are also linked with other social theories such as the feminist, critical, and conflict (Woods & Butler, 2021). Through feminist lenses of social structures in society shaped by gender power struggles, the women's rights movement led to Title IX, an antidiscrimination law in the American education system from 1972. Title IX led to the growth and specialization of American women in sports, to be successful in international competitions, and became a public diplomacy tool through attracting international talents to improve the system or through international programs to teach about the

American way of life. Through conflict lenses though, which rely on Marxism and analyze power struggles based on social capital, the base of the social structure of the American sports system has been highly scrutinized for exploitation of athletes who generate billions in college athletics but are not allowed to receive a salary or share of the revenues. Critical lenses, which analyze hegemony in society and the systematic evolution of dominant social classes and especially critical-race theories that focus on racial and ethnic historic injustice, have been especially dominant when discussing the civil rights movements and anticolonization movements, empowering resistance and athletes activism and diversifying national teams through immigrations and naturalizations of athletes.

Since the 1980s, and especially after the collapse of the Soviet Union, America and capitalism shape international sports from Californization of the Olympic Movement and adjustments to American-oriented sports and television rights (Dyreson, 2013) to Disneyfication of international sports, trying to make international sports commercially attractive to the largest audience possible. The twenty-first century though introduces new global players adopting such tactics for their own nation branding and public diplomacy benefits. Abu Dhabi, a small emirate from the Arabian Gulf, has created an international network of football franchises under the umbrella of City Football Group, almost as they were just another evolutionary form of an American fast food franchise in Europe, Japan, or Australia. Foreign investments in international sports also provoke resistance from local communities, fearing their history and traditions will be erased or changed to accommodate global needs. More broadly, this could also be seen through the rise of populist leaderships and a revolt against globalization, immigration, and progressive movements, including their manifestations in sports.

Sports Diplomacy and Ethical Concerns

By hosting sports events and participating in sports events, countries receive international exposure not only on the competitions but on the culture and values of the country, making sports a useful tool for countries to demonstrate their soft power (Arning, 2013; Nye, 2004) to achieve international goals and improve their public diplomacy (Cull, 2010). Sports diplomacy is one example of how through nation branding soft power can be used for diplomatic purposes to achieve foreign policy goals (Arning, 2013; Murray & Pigman, 2014). There is not one consistent theory that captures sports diplomacy or one clear definition, beyond the intersections between diplomacy and sports (Postlethwaite et al., 2022). In his book *Sports Diplomacy* (Murray, 2018), author Dr. Stuart Murray divides the field into four subfields: traditional sports diplomacy, sports diplomacy, the specialized diplomacy of non-state sporting actors, and sports anti-diplomacy. According to Rofe (2021), sports diplomacy focuses on three main features: communication, representation, and negotiation. Such intersections can be seen through governmental use of sports for official public diplomacy purposes ranging from a Department of State initiating sports-related programs or even implementing international boycotts that align with foreign policy goals. Sports for development and peace (SDP) are often also referred to as sports diplomacy initiatives especially when their goal is to bridge between communities, varying between sports, governing bodies that could be the government, a federation or association, a nongovernmental organization, or any other private initiative (Rofe, 2021; Woods & Butler, 2021). International institutions such as the United Nations or the IOC also invest in SDP. Athletes play a role in sports diplomacy, whether officially as envoys or even diplomats or unofficially through citizen diplomacy and through the way they behave and engage with foreign publics.

Perhaps one of the most known examples of sports diplomacy is *ping-pong diplomacy* (Carter & Sugden, 2011), when the USA and China formed relations after having a friendly table tennis game between delegates. Using athletes as ambassadors is another cultural channel where sports serve for public diplomacy purposes (Pigman, 2014). While there are ample examples of violence erupting through sports (Boykoff, 2016; Murray, 2018), sports can also play as a tool building bridges between rival communities. Sports for development and peace organizations such as Right to Play, Free to Run, Beyond Sport, the Peres Center for Peace, and other nongovernmental organizations (NGOs) operate all over the world using sports as a tool to create bridges between communities (Murray, 2018). According to Murray (2018), "Not only do they represent universality, they remind the world that sport promotes progress, inclusivity and inter-connectivity over static, regressive and traditional security approaches to foreign policy" (p. 169). The Olympic Movement emphasizes the concept of Ekecheiria (Spaaij, 2012), the declared truce between city-states in Ancient Greece. The movement also emphasizes the philosophy of Olympism (International Olympic Committee, 2015) which aspires to promote educational values through sports and rejects any sort of discrimination.

There are also some subcategories that emerged over the years such as ping-pong diplomacy or cricket diplomacy (Murray, 2018) that are specific to a certain sport and stadium diplomacy that refers, for example, to China building sports facilities across Africa to establish more control across the continent (Dubinsky, 2021). The jersey itself can serve for diplomacy with designs of official outfits reflecting some of a country's or a place's culture and heritage or through sponsorships. For example, Maccabi Tel Aviv Basketball Club plays in yellow jerseys referring to the yellow badges Jews were forced to wear under Nazi Germany and during the holocaust. With the evolution of technology, there are also new diplomatic implications receiving subcategories such as sport-tech diplomacy (Dubinsky, 2022c) that refers to investment in technology and sports as part of nation branding and public diplomacy strategies or esports diplomacy (Murray et al., 2020) referring to the relations between the different stakeholders around electronic sports.

While sports diplomacy can lead to building bridges between communities (Murray, 2018), there are ethical concerns about the use of sports for soft power purposes (Boykoff, 2016; Coakley, 2015). In Ancient Greece athletic competitions were used for political purposes (Coakley, 2015; Miller, 2004). Governments, pressure groups, and individuals have used sports for a variety of soft power purposes. These purposes include leveraging tourism, making political statements, showing different sides of the country, exposing the culture (Arning, 2013), promoting products and technologies, shaping the countries' image (Chalip & Costa, 2005; Preuss, 2015), and for different international relations purposes (Guttmann, 2002).

The idealistic philosophy of Olympism faced a very different reality when during the Munich 1972 Olympic Games Palestinian terrorists kidnapped and murdered 11 Israeli athletes, capitalizing on the international exposure of the games (Galily et al., 2015). Aspirations of governments and of different pressure groups to use sports to improve their images and reach political goals manifested in negative and even catastrophic outcomes (Boykoff, 2016; Coakley, 2015). Some of these outcomes include public spending (Coakley, 2015) and financial debts (Boykoff, 2016), mass boycotts (Boykoff, 2016; Guttmann, 2002), systematic doping systems (Guttmann, 2002), greenwashing and destruction of the environment (Boykoff & Mascarenhas, 2016), and even different manifestations of violence such as terrorism (Galily et al., 2015). Different regimes have used sports for political purposes, including some of the most democratic countries. Examples include the USA and Canada (Boykoff, 2016) and authoritarian regimes such as the Soviet Union and China (Boykoff, 2016; Guttmann, 2002). Since the end of World War II the Soviet Union has been using sports for public diplomacy purposes very bluntly. The bloody water polo match between the USSR and Hungary during the 1956 Melbourne Olympic Game manifested the role of sports in expression of hyper-nationalism as it followed the Soviet invasion to Hungary and the Hungarian Revolution (Boykoff, 2016; Murray, 2018). The boycotts of the 1980 and 1984 Olympic Games also showed how the two main superpowers use sports for foreign policy purposes. In recent years, Vladimir Putin's Russia used mega-sports events for nationalistic purposes hosting the most expensive Olympic Games in Sochi in 2014 costing over US$50 billion, invading the Crimea Peninsula in Ukraine while hosting the 2014 Winter Paralympic Games, developing a systematic government-led doping system, and hosting the FIFA World Cup in 2018 after a corruption clouded bid (Boykoff, 2016; Murray, 2018). The use of sports to promote nationalistic ideologies goes back to the 1930s with Il Duce Benito Mussolini using the Italy 1934 FIFA World Cup to promote fascism and of course Adolf Hitler, who used the 1936 Olympic Games in Berlin to unite Germany behind the leadership of the National Socialist Party and to promote the racist Nazi propaganda (Boykoff, 2016; Guttmann, 2002). The use of sports for country image purposes can lead to terrible outcomes in some cases, and with Russia, China, countries from the Arabian Gulf, or states facing human rights violations in hosting mega-sports events or purchasing Western sports clubs in the first decades of the twenty-first century, the use of sports to launder a country's image has been classified as "sportswashing" (Boykoff, 2022).

Conclusion

City-states, countries, governments, and communities have been using sports as a form of soft power and for public diplomacy purposes for over two and a half millennia. There are ample examples of how sports is the last town hall, building a global community around the Olympic Games which are broadcasted to over 200 countries and territories (IOC, 2018; Murray, 2018). Athletes from rival countries competing peacefully in stadiums and arenas, countries hosting joint sports events (Murray, 2012), or children from conflict-struck areas getting to know each other through sports and physical activities (Murray, 2018), yet the use of sports for soft power and public diplomacy purposes is controversial and has a lot of gray areas. On the one hand, when governments use sports for propaganda purposes, there could be negative implications. Hundreds of athletes who trained rigorously anticipating their moments of glory in the international competitions, including the Olympic Games, have been stripped from the opportunity to compete because of political reasons (Boykoff, 2016; Guttmann, 2002). Corruption (Sugden & Tomlinson, 2017), doping, boycotts, exclusions, mass public spending, and destruction of nature are all negative outcomes of governments attempting to try and better their image through sports (Boykoff, 2016; Coakley, 2015). Adolf Hitler used the 1936 Berlin Olympic Games to show the German people how strong and organized Germany could be under the leadership of the Nazi Party.

On the other hand, countries try to maximize their potential in the international system. Soft power, cultural diplomacy, sports diplomacy, and nation branding through sports give countries other options to shape the country's images and try to reposition themselves in the international system through peaceful means. One might ask whether the world is really going to be a better place if instead of public spending on grand sports events, cheating in athletic competitions, or boycotting a competition, countries will spend these efforts and money on more tanks, more sophisticated bombs, and even deadlier war machines. Despite social and political evolutions and technological developments and the different manifestations, using sports for nation branding and public diplomacy to achieve a better image and domestic and foreign goals goes back almost three millennia. Only the methods change.

REFERENCES

Aaker, D. A. (1991). *Managing brand equity: Capitalizing on the value of a brand name*. The Free Press.
Amiri, S. (2022). City diplomacy: An introduction to the forum. *The Hague Journal of Diplomacy, 17*(1), 91–95.
Anholt, S. (2010). *Places: Identity, image and reputation*. Palgrave Macmillan.
Arning, C. (2013). Soft power, ideology and symbolic manipulation in Summer Olympic Games opening ceremonies: A semiotic analysis. *Social Semiotics, 23*, 523–544.
Avraham, E. (2009). Marketing and managing nation branding during prolonged crisis: The case of Israel. *Journal of Place Branding and Public Diplomacy, 5*, 202–212.

Batra, R., Ramaswamy, V., Alden, D. L., Steenkamp, J.-B. E. M., & Ramachander, S. (2000). Effects of brand local and nonlocal origin on consumer attitudes in developing countries. *Journal of Consumer Psychology, 9*(2), 83–95.

Boykoff, J. (2016). *Power games: A political history of the Olympics*. Verso.

Boykoff, J. (2022). Toward a theory of sportswashing: Mega-events, soft power, and political conflict. *Sociology of Sport Journal, 39*(4), 342–351. https://doi.org/10.1123/ssj.2022-0095

Boykoff, J., & Mascarenhas, G. (2016). The Olympics, sustainability, and greenwashing: The Rio 2016 summer games. *Capitalism Nature Socialism, 27*(2), 1–11. https://doi.org/10.1080/10455752.2016.1179473

Brannagan, P. M., & Giulianotti, R. (2015). Soft power and soft disempowerment: Qatar, global sport and football's 2022 World Cup finals. *Leisure Studies, 34*, 703–710.

Buhmann, A., & Ingenhoff, D. (2015). The 4D model of the country image: An integrative approach from the perspective of communication management. *The International Communication Gazette, 77*, 102–124.

Carr, E. H. (1964). *Twenty years crisis: 1919–1939: An introduction to the study of IR*. Harper Perennial.

Carter, T., & Sugden, J. (2011). The USA and sporting diplomacy: Comparing and contrasting the cases of table tennis with China and baseball with Cuba in the 1970s. *International Relations, 26*(1), 101–121.

Chalip, L. (2006). Towards social leverage of sport events. *Journal of Sport & Tourism, 11*(2), 109–127.

Chalip, L., & Costa, C. (2005). Sport event tourism and the destination brand: Towards a general theory. *Sport and Society, 8*(2), 218–237.

Chalip, L., & Leyns, A. (2002). Local business leveraging of a sport event: Managing an event for economic benefit. *Journal of Sport Management, 16*, 132–158.

Coakley, J. (2015). *Sports in society issues and controversies* (11th ed.). McGraw-Hill.

Cull, N. J. (2008). Public diplomacy: Taxonomies and histories. *ANNALS of the American Academy of Political Science, 616*(1), 31–54.

Cull, N. J. (2010). Public diplomacy: Seven lessons for its future from its past. *Journal of Place Branding and Public Diplomacy, 6*, 11–17.

David, O., & Bar-Tal, D. (2009). A sociopsychological conception of collective identity: The case of national identity as an example. *Personality and Social Psychology Review, 13*, 354–379. https://doi.org/10.1177/1088868309344412

Dinnie, K. (2003). Literature review place branding: Overview of an emerging literature. *Place Branding, 1*, 106–110.

Dubinsky, Y. (2017). The evolution of the Olympic Games through international relations theories. *World History Bulletin, 33*(1), 10–15.

Dubinsky, Y. (2018). The image of Beijing and London in Israeli media coverage of the 2008 and 2012 Olympic Games. *The International Journal of Sport and Society, 9*, 2152–7857.

Dubinsky, Y. (2019). Analyzing the roles of country image, nation branding, and public diplomacy through the evolution of the modern Olympic movement. *Physical Culture and Sport. Studies and Research, 84*(1), 27–40. https://doi.org/10.2478/pcssr-2019-0024

Dubinsky, I. (2021). China's stadium diplomacy in Africa. *Journal of Global Sport Management, 1*, 1–18. https://doi.org/10.1080/24704067.2021.1885101

Dubinsky, Y. (2022). Sport-tech diplomacy: Exploring the intersections between the sport-tech ecosystem, innovation, and diplomacy in Israel. *Place Branding & Public Diplomacy, 18*(2), 169–180. https://doi.org/10.1057/s41254-020-00191-2

Dyreson, M. (2013). The republic of consumption at the Olympic Games: Globalization, Americanization, and Californication. *Journal of Global History, 8*, 256–278. https://doi.org/10.1017/S1740022813000211

Fan, Y. (2010). Branding the nation: Towards a better understanding. *Journal of Place Branding and Public Diplomacy, 6*(2), 97–103.

Fitzpatrick, K. R. (2007). Advancing the new public diplomacy: A public relations perspective. *The Hague Journal of Diplomacy, 2*, 187–211.

Galily, Y., Yarchi, M., & Tamir, I. (2015). From Munich to Boston, and from theater to social media: The evolution landscape of world sporting terror. *Studies in Conflict & Terrorism., 38*, 998. https://doi.org/10.1080/1057610x.2015.1076640

Gilboa, E. (2006). Public diplomacy: The missing component in Israel's foreign policy. *Israel Affairs, 12*, 715–747.

Gilboa, E. (2008). Searching for a theory of public diplomacy. *Annals of the American Academy of Political and Social Science, 616*, 55–77.

Gleaves, J., & Llewellyn, M. (2014). Ethics, nationalism, and the imagined community: The case against inter-national sport. *The Journal of Philosophy of Sport, 41*, 1–20.

Guttmann, A. (2002). *The Olympics: A history of the modern games* (2nd ed.). University of Illinois Press.

Handelman, S. (2012). The minds of peace experiment: A laboratory for people-to-people diplomacy. *Israel Affairs, 18*(1), 1–11. https://doi.org/10.1080/13537121.2012.634278

Heslop, L. A., Lu, I. R. R., & Cray, D. (2008). Modeling country image effects through an international crisis. *International Marketing Review, 25*, 354–378.

Heslop, L. A., Nadeau, J., & O'Reilly, N. (2010). China and the Olympics: Views of insiders and outsiders. *International Marketing Review, 27*, 404–433.

Hobsbawm, E. (1992). *Nations and nationalism since 1780 programme, myth, reality*. Cambridge University Press.

I Am Torquay. (2022). Surfing in Torquay. *Great Ocean Road Regional Tourism*. Retrieved from https://torquaylife.com.au/explore/surfing/

International Olympic Committee. (2015). *Olympic charter*. International Olympic Committee. Retrieved from https://stillmed.olympic.org/Documents/olympic_charter_en.pdf

IOC. (2018). *Olympic marketing fact file 2018th edition*. International Olympic Committee. Retrieved from https://stillmed.olympic.org/media/Document%20Library/OlympicOrg/Documents/IOC-Marketing-and-Broadcasting-General-Files/Olympic-Marketing-Fact-File-2018.pdf

Jackson, S. J., & Hokowhitu, B. (2002). Sport, tribes, and technology: The New Zealand All Black Haka and politics of identity. *Journal of Sport & Social Issues, 26*, 125–139.

Jaffe, E., & Nebenzahl, I. (1993). Global promotion of country image: Do the Olympics count? In N. Papadopoulos & L. Heslop (Eds.), *Product-country images: Impact and role in international marketing* (pp. 433–452). International Business Press.

Johansson, J. K. (1989). Determinants and effects of the use of "made in" labels. *International Marketing Review, 6*, 47–58.

Jun, W. J., Lee, H. S., & Park, J. H. (2009). Roles of media exposure and interpersonal experiences on country brand: The mediated risk perception model. *Journal of Promotion Management, 15*, 321–339.

Kang, Y.-S., & Perdue, R. (1994). Long-term impact of a megaevent on international tourism to the host country: A conceptual model and the case of the 1988 Seoul Olympics. *Journal of International Consumer Marketing, 6*, 205–225.

Kavaratzis, M., & Ashworth, G. (2015). Hijacking culture: The disconnection between place culture and place brands. *The Town Planning Review, 86*(2), 155–176. https://doi.org/10.3828/tpr.2015.10

Keller, K. L. (1993). Conceptualizing, measuring, and managing customer-based brand equity. *Journal of Marketing, 57*, 1–22.

Keohane, R. O., & Martin, L. L. (1995). The promise of institutional theory. *International Security, 20*(1), 39–51.

Klein, J. G., Ettenson, R., & Morris, M. D. (1998). The animosity model of foreign product purchase: An empirical test in the People's Republic of China. *Journal of Marketing, 62*, 89–100.

Kotler, P., Haider, D. H., & Rein, I. (1993). *Marketing places*. The Free Press.

Krechmar, R. S., Dyreson, M., Llewellyn, M. P., & Gleaves, J. (2017). *History and philosophy of sport and physical activity*. Human Kinetics.

Laroche, M., Papadopoulos, N., Heslop, L., & Bergeron, J. (2003). Effects of subcultural differences on country and product evaluations. *Journal of Consumer Behaviour, 2*, 232–247.

Legro, J. W., & Moravcsik, A. (1999). Is anybody still a realist? *International Security, 2*(24), 5–55.

MacLean, M. (2014). Revisiting (and revising?) sports boycotts: From rugby against South Africa to soccer in Israel. *International Journal of the History of Sport, 31,* 1832–1851.

Magnusson, P., Westjohn, S. A., & Sirianni, N. J. (2019). Beyond country image favorability: How brand positioning via country personality stereotypes enhances brand evaluations. *Journal of International Business Studies, 50,* 318–338. https://doi.org/10.1057/s41267-018-0175-3

Martin, D. (2007). *Rebuilding brand America: What we must do to restore our reputation and safeguard the future of American business abroad.* Amacom.

Miller, S. G. (2004). *Ancient Greek athletics.* Yale University Press.

Murray, S. (2012). The two halves of sports-diplomacy. *Diplomacy & Statecraft, 23,* 576–592.

Murray, S. (2018). *Sports diplomacy: Origins, theory and practice.* Routledge.

Murray, S., & Pigman, A. G. (2014). Mapping the relationship between international sport and diplomacy. *Sport in Society, 17*(9), 1098–1118.

Murray, S., Birt, J., & Blakemore, S. (2020). eSports diplomacy: Towards a sustainable 'gold rush'. *Sport in Society, 25,* 1419. https://doi.org/10.1080/17430437.2020.1826437

Nadeau, J., Heslop, L., O'Reilly, N., & Luk, P. (2008). Destination in a country image context. *Annals of Tourism Research, 35,* 84–106.

Nebenzahl, I., Jaffe, E., & Lampert, S. (1997). Towards a theory of country image effect on product evaluation. *Management International Review, 37*(1), 27–49.

Nye, J. S., Jr. (2004). *Soft power: The means to success in world politics.* PublicAffairs.

Nye, J. S., Jr. (2008). Public diplomacy and soft power. *Annals of the American Academy of Political and Social Science, 616*(1), 94–109.

Olins, W. (2002). Branding the nation—The historical context. *Brand Management, 9,* 241–248.

Orwell, G. (1945, December 14). The sporting spirit. *The Tribune.* Retrieved from https://www.orwellfoundation.com/the-orwell-foundation/orwell/essays-and-other-works/the-sporting-spirit/

Papadopoulos, N., & Heslop, L. A. (2002). Country equity and country branding: Problems and prospects. *Journal of Brand Management, 9,* 294–314.

Pigman, G. A. (2014). International sport and diplomacy's public dimension: Governments, sporting federations and the global audience. *Diplomacy & Statecraft, 25,* 94–114.

Postlethwaite, V., Jenkin, C., & Sherry, E. (2022). Sport diplomacy: An integrative review. *Sport Management Review, 26,* 361. https://doi.org/10.1080/14413523.2022.2071054

Preuss, H. (2008). Signaling growth: China's major benefit from staging the 2008 Olympics in Beijing. *Harvard Asia Pacific Review, 9*(1), 45–49.

Preuss, H. (2015). A framework for identifying the legacies of a mega sport event. *Leisure Studies, 34,* 643–664.
Rofe, S. (2021). Sport diplomacy and sport for development SfD: A discourse of challenges and opportunity. *Journal of Global Sport Management,* 1. https://doi.org/10.1080/24704067.2021.2010024
Signitzer, B. H., & Coombs, T. (1992). Public relations and public diplomacy: Conceptual convergences. *Public Relations Review, 18*(2), 137–147.
Spaaij, R. (2012). Olympic rings of peace? The Olympic movement, peacemaking and intercultural understanding. *Sport in Society, 15,* 761–774.
Sugden, J., & Tomlinson, A. (2017). *Football, corruption, and lies.* Routledge.
Szondi, G. (2010). From image management to relationship building: A public relations approach to nation branding. *Place Branding and Public Diplomacy, 6,* 333–343. https://doi.org/10.1057/pb.2010.32
Wang, J. (2006a). Public diplomacy and global business. *Journal of Business Strategy, 27*(3), 41–49.
Wang, J. (2006b). Managing national reputation and international relations in the global era: Public diplomacy revised. *Public Relations Review, 32,* 91–96.
White, C. J. (2015). Exploring the role of private-sector corporations in public diplomacy. *Public Relations Inquiry, 4,* 305–321.
Woods, R., & Butler, N. (2021). *Social issues in sport (4th ed.).* Human Kinetics.

CHAPTER 3

Country Image, Nation Branding, and the FIFA World Cup (1930–2022)

Introduction

The purpose of this chapter is to explore, discuss, and analyze the roles of nation branding, country image, and related fields (Buhmann & Ingenhoff, 2015; Fan, 2010) through the evolution of the FIFA World Cup.[1] Over 3.5 billion people, more than half of the world's population above the age of 4, watched the 2018 FIFA World Cup (2018 FIFA World Cup Russia, 2018). Four years later, beIN Media Group, the Qatari-based official broadcaster of Qatar 2022 FIFA World Cup, reported over five billion accumulated views (beIN Sports, 2022). Football is the most practiced sport in the world (Woods & Butler, 2021), and the organizing body that regulates it is the International Federation of Football Associations (FIFA), with the World Cup being the crown jewel. According to the official global broadcast and audience summary (2018 FIFA World Cup Russia, 2018), over 1.1 billion watched at least part of the final between France and Croatia having 884.37 million in-home TV viewers and 231.82 million out-of-home and (or) digital-only viewers. At least 10 games in the tournament were viewed live by an average of at least a quarter of a billion

---

[1] The article refers to the men's world championship in football as the FIFA World Cup as this is how the competition is referred to in existing scholarship and official reports. The article also uses the word football for the same reasons, despite the sport being called soccer in North America.

© The Author(s), under exclusive license to Springer Nature Switzerland AG 2023
Y. Dubinsky, *Nation Branding and Sports Diplomacy*,
https://doi.org/10.1007/978-3-031-32550-2_3

live audience (2018 FIFA World Cup Russia, 2018), and all of the last three FIFA World Cup Finals had over half a billion viewers (Richter, 2020). Just for comparison, the 2019 Super Bowl, the most viewed annual TV programming in the USA, had a global rating of 160 million viewers, significantly less than some of the group state matches in Russia (2018 FIFA World Cup Russia, 2018; Richter, 2020). The only event comparable to the exposure and popularity of the FIFA World Cup is the Summer Olympic Games (OG), as according to the International Olympic Committee (2016), "half of the world's population" watched the 2016 Olympic Games in Rio de Janeiro, reaching a global audience of 3.2 billion through television, 1.3 unique users through digital platforms of rights-holding broadcasters, and having 4.4 billion video views (International Olympic Committee, 2020). The Sochi 2014 Winter Olympic Games, followed by the 2018 FIFA World Cup, are considered a pivotal point in Vladimir Putin's strategy to brand Russia as a global powerhouse as strategic way to achieve imperialist goals. International media and scholars frame countries, regimes, and governments who use sports to launder their reputation from human rights violations as sportswashing (Boykoff, 2022a; Chadwick, 2018, 2022a). While the term pertains mostly to authoritarian regimes, democratic countries have been accused of sportswashing as well (Boykoff, 2022a). Russia is not the first or last to use the FIFA World Cup for soft power and foreign policy goals (Brannagan & Rookwood, 2016; Wolfe, 2020). Countries, cities, and communities have been using sports to achieve social, political, and economic goals, by improving their countries' images (Dubinsky, 2019a). With football being the most popular sports in the world (Woods & Butler, 2021) and with such a significant international audience, the FIFA World Cup embodies ample opportunities for hosting and participating countries.

This chapter further discusses and analyzes the international impact of the FIFA World Cup, using the different lenses of nation branding, country image, and related fields (Buhmann & Ingenhoff, 2015; Fan, 2010) focusing specifically on the World Cup. In their edited book *The FIFA World Cup 1930–2010: Politics, Commerce, Spectacle*, editors Rinke and Schiller (2014) identify four different periods in the manifestation of politics in the FIFA World Cups; (a) prewar World Cups between 1930 and 1936, (b) World Cups between tradition and modernity between 1950 and 1962, (c) World Cups before the "Gold Rush" between 1966 and 1982, and (d) multiculturalism and commercialization through capturing the next tournaments until 2010. These eras somewhat correspond with the way Dubinsky (2019b) analyzed the evolution of the modern OG through country image, nation branding, and public diplomacy lenses. Dubinsky identified five different and overlapping eras in the history of the Olympic Movement: (a) the revival of the Games between 1896 and World War I, (b) recognizing the Games' potential between the World Wars, (c) the political era between 1948 and 1984, (d) the commercialized era between 1984 and the end of the millennium, and (e) the legacy-oriented era in the early twenty-first century. The following discussion examines how can the evolution of the FIFA World Cup from 1930 to the 2020s be understood through nation branding, country image, and public diplomacy lenses. Based on the analysis of the classified periods by Rinke and Schiller (2014) and Dubinsky (2019b), the geopolitical commentary of Chadwick (2022a) and through analysis of dozens of books, articles, media publications, official reports, and documentaries, this chapter explores the intersections between country image, nation branding, public diplomacy, and football and suggests applicable taxonomy through outlining the different developmental stages of the FIFA World Cup (Dubinsky, 2019a).

The FIFA World Cup, Nation Branding, and Country Image

In the following sections, the chapter explores how nation branding, country image, and their related field manifested through the evolution of the FIFA World Cup. The manifestations are discussed in chronological order but should not be read as separate eras from each other but as a continuum in which the fields overlap with each other and become more significant over time. Table 3.1 exemplifies the roles and manifestations of nation branding and country image through the evolution of the FIFA World Cup.

Public Diplomacy

The role of public diplomacy and political use of the FIFA World Cup to achieve foreign policy goals go back to earliest stages of the FIFA World Cup, a period Rinke and Schiller (2014) defined as the "prewar World Cups" section, between 1930 and 1938. From the early days of the competitions, countries recognized the potential use of the games to achieve

Table 3.1 Nation branding, country image, and the evolution of the FIFA World Cup

Nation branding and country image lenses	FIFA World Cup (winner)	Examples of nation branding and country image manifestations
Public diplomacy(1930–World War II)	Uruguay 1930 (Uruguay), Italy 1934 (Italy), France 1938 (Italy)	Benito Mussolini using the 1934 World Cup to spread fascism
National identity(end of World War II to end of Cold War)	Brazil 1950 (Uruguay), Switzerland 1954 (West Germany), Sweden 1958 (Brazil), Chile 1962 (Brazil), England 1966 (England), Mexico 1970 (Brazil), West Germany 1974 (West Germany), Argentina 1978 (Argentina), Spain 1982 (Italy),Mexico 1986 (Argentina)	"Garra charrua" as description for bravery in Uruguay; "jogo bonito" expressing Brazilian lifestyle; Germans win with efficiency, Italians with pragmatism; "Maracanazo" a Brazilian national trauma; Argentinian dictators hijacking the World Cup for propaganda
Commercialization and globalization(1990–2000)	Italy 1990 (West Germany), USA 1994 (Brazil), France 1998 (France)	World Cup held only in Western countries; Corruption in FIFA; France wins with diversity
Nation branding and sportswashing(2000–2022)	Japan and South Korea 2002 (Brazil), Germany 2006 (Italy), South Africa 2010 (Spain), Brazil 2014 (Germany), Russia 2018 (France), Qatar 2022 (Argentina)	First World Cup in Asia and Africa; rebranding Germany; global and local protests against FIFA, governments and hosting World Cups; "Mineirazo" a national trauma; Russia and Qatar laundering their images, deaths of migrant workers building infrastructure

foreign policy goals. The culture was set by Uruguay, host of the first FIFA World Cup in 1930. As described by Sugden and Tomlinson (2017), "The first world cup was a politically motivate statement by a national government. It was staged by a small country anxious to show its bigger neighbours how well it could perform on a global stage" (p. 22). Uruguay was one of the first global power in football, winning the Olympic tournament in 1924 and 1928, before winning the first World Cup at home. With

Uruguay beating Argentina both in the 1928 OG football finals and the 1930 World Cup Final, the rivalry between the South American sides became one of the first derby matches in international football, known as the "clásico del Rio de la Plata" (Revelez, 2018). While there are not many political boycotts in the history of the World Cup, there are some football-related boycotts. England, seeing itself as the birthplace of football, and the other home nations (Scotland, Wales, and Northern Ireland) did not join the first competitions due to internal disputes with FIFA. Uruguay also had a boycott of its own, not competing in the 1934 and 1938 World Cup partly as a retaliation against the European hosts who did not travel to Montevideo in 1930 (Rinke, 2014).

The use of the tournament for public diplomacy escalated when Benito Mussolini, the fascist dictator of Italy, used the hosting of the second World Cup in 1934 to spread a wave of nationalism through a victorious home team and "to show the world the superiority of the fascist regime" (Lisi, 2015, p. 19). Mussolini is described as "a very active diplomat" (Impiglia, 2014, p. 74) in bringing the World Cup to Italy and was accused of manipulating the competitions. Accusations include meetings with the referee before the semifinal between Italy and Austria, bribing and fixing games, and visiting the referees in the locker rooms before the final against Czechoslovakia (Impiglia, 2014). According to Impiglia (2014), before the final *Il Duce* "spend suspiciously long time with the referee and linesmen," who during the Italian national anthem "proffered the Roman Salute" (p. 81). The Swedish team also performed the salute when facing Italy during the tournament (Radmann & Andersson, 2018). When describing the final, Impiglia writes, "Il Duce was the Nero of the situation, who would be expected to give the thumbs down in a gladiatorial battle whose outcome was already decided" (p. 83). Four years later, the connection between the Italian national team and fascist symbolism manifested in the third World Cup in France when the Italian players wore a black strip in the color of fascism and made the fascist salutes to the fans (Impiglia, 2014). A tournament that Italy eventually won, becoming the first national team to successfully defend its title. Perhaps the most significant impact of the decade was Mussolini using sports for political fascist propaganda, which will be adopted by other dictatorships including in future World Cup (Murray, 2018; Dubinsky, 2019a). Thus, while the term sportswashing (Boykoff, 2022a; Chadwick, 2022a) is relatively new, the authoritarian use of sports is not.

National Identity

Following World War II, national identity became central in the FIFA World Cup, not just by hosting country but by participating ones as well. During World War II and through the entire 1940s, FIFA did not hold world championships (Lisi, 2015) before reinstating the World Cup, going back to South America, this time in Brazil. In the final, Uruguay, the first host and champion of the competition, stunned the host winning 2–1 at the packed Maracanã Stadium with 200,000 Brazilian fans (Watts, 2014). Uruguay cemented itself as world cup legends, and their uncompromising approach to the game, known as "garra charrua," refers to the identity of a small country with a population of just over 3 million people, fighting with bravery against larger opponents. Such passion for the game is part of Uruguayan culture, transferring to other spheres in social life. Late Uruguayan author Eduardo Galeano captured the emotional history of the game of football in his monumental book, *El fútbol a sol y sombra* (2013)—*Football in Sun and Shadow*—which was translated into dozens of languages and sold millions of copies all over the world.

Still in South America, the Brazilian national team, led by Pelé, dominated the next few decades winning the World Cup three times in 1958, 1962, and 1970 in this era and twice more in 1994 and 2002. The free and attractive style of play received the nickname "jogo bonito"—the beautiful game. In the book *The Invention of the Beautiful Game: Football and the Making of Modern Brazil*, author Greg Bocketti (2016) explains:

> Brazilians demand a very particular version of football, which is what makes it an essential part of Brazilian culture. This is *O jogo bonito* – "the beautiful game" of creativity and fantasy and joy – which ostensibly enacts Brazil's authentic identity, one rooted in the country's history of mixing cultures and people, among which the contributions of people of African descent are said to be especially important. (Bocketti, 2016, 11)

Along with being celebrated for capturing the imagination through play, there is also national trauma in Brazil when the talented team loses. The loss in the 1950 World Cup final to Uruguay was traumatic for Brazilian national identity and is remembered as the "Maracanazo" (Lisi, 2015)—the agony of the Maracanã. The commitment to attractive style of play backfired at times, such as in the 1982 World Cup game against Italy, where an attractive Brazilian side needed a draw to qualify from the second group stage but lost 2–3 to Italy, which eventually won the cup after beating West Germany in the final.

The Italian style of play, known as "catenaccio," results from a practical perception of life that is integrated in national and collective identity going back to the renaissance and Machiavelli, of doing what is necessary to win without concerns about beauty or morality (Kalife, 2018). That can explain, to some extent, how while in 1934 and 1938 the Italians were ambassadors of fascist propaganda, and in 1982 and 2006 Italian football was dealing with corruption scandals, "*la Squadra azzura*" still managed to come out victorious.

Another example of a connection between tactical approach and national identity is Germany's style of play in the twentieth century, defined by efficiency, precision, and discipline (Kaelberer, 2017). A style that has not only been associated with German bureaucratic culture but proved successful for winning the World Cup by beating the Hungarian *Golden Team* in 1954 in a final known as "the Miracle of Bern" and defeating the attractive Dutch *Total Football* in the Olympic Stadium in Munich in the 1974 World Cup Final. World War II had long-term implications on the collective memory in Germany and by opponents. According to Kaelberer (2017), the victory over Hungary in 1954 "reflected the emergence of Germany from the trauma of World War II and the Nazi period" (p. 293). While arguing the 1974 World Cup Final focused on football, Simon Kuper describes in his book, *Soccer Against the Enemy* (2010) the game between the Netherlands and Germany in the 1988 European Championship writing "Holland vs Germany, good vs. evil" (p. 10), and "the Dutch players were the Resistance, and the Germans the Wehrmacht" (p. 11). War memories were also associated with West Germany over this period, especially around the 1966 World Cup Final loss to England in London (Ramsden, 2006). The group-stage game against East Germany in the 1974 World Cup produced political tension (Kaelberer, 2017; Lisi, 2015) and when facing Austria in 1982, a game known as the "disgrace of Gijon" after reaching a score that fits the needs of both. International media were critical of Germany, even referring to the game as "Anschluss," the annexation of Austria in 1938 by Nazi Germany (Smyth, 2018).

Collective and national identity manifested regularly through participating teams and players. The Mozambique-born football star, Eusebio, played for Portugal leading the team to the third place in the 1966 World Cup finishing as the top scorer of the competition and one of the first African-born international stars (Darby, 2007). According to Darby

(2007), when analyzing the colonization of Africa, while Eusebio's success "was a source of immense pride for Mozambican's, his career can also be interpreted in a similar vein that it perpetuated a desire for either assimilation into Portuguese citizenship or cultural emulation" (p. 503). Overlaps of international relations, public diplomacy, and collective identity manifested through the 1986 World Cup quarter-final game between Argentina and England, four years after the Falklands War between the countries (Salazar-Sutil, 2008). The political tension became part of the myth of one of the most iconic games in the World Cup, as within a span of five minutes, Diego Armando Maradona scored two iconic goals, one with his hand, which he referred to as "the hand of god," and one by exceptional dribbling skills. Maradona's style of play, controversial lifestyle, and dominant personality made him a national hero and a mythical figure in Argentina (Salazar-Sutil, 2008). After analyzing the collective narrative around Maradona, Salazar-Sutil writes: "Argentinean fans, for one, would agree that the ball and the world never turned the same way again since their God Diego Armando Maradona stepped onto the pitch" (Salazar-Sutil, 2008 p. 442).

The use of the World Cup for soft power (Nye, 2004) purposes by totalitarian regimes continued in 1978 (Murray, 2018). The 1978 World Cup in Argentina became known not for the host nation winning the Cup but for a military dictatorship regime "hijacking" (Murray, 2018, p. 64) a sports event for political, ideological, or national reasons. As Kuper (2010) writes, "The Generals staged the World Cup to impress their own people and the world" (Kuper, 2010, p. 212). In other words, "the Beautiful's Game's ugliest moment'" (Murray, 2018, p. 64). Apart from the 1978 World Cup, political manifestation in the FIFA World Cup were relatively mild. Examples include qualification rounds of Israel competing in different continents after Arab countries refused to play them or even an escalation of a short armed conflict between Honduras and El Salvador after a playoffs meeting (Dubinsky, 2019b; Zimbalist, 2016), yet in that case the connection to football was mostly anecdotal. African countries boycotted the 1966 World Cup, but not because of colonialism or racism but due to a dispute with FIFA about quotas. The realist political approach dominated the parallel years in the Olympic Movement with mass boycotts during the Cold War and even terrorism (Dubinsky, 2019b; Murray, 2018), putting foreign policy ahead of international institutions and collaborations. In the World Cup though, country image manifested mostly through different forms of representation and national identity (Dubinsky, 2019a).

Commercialization and Globalization

The end of the Cold War and the collapse of Communism left America as the sole world superpower and the capitalist system as the predominant economic global approach (Dubinsky, 2019b). A new world order was formed in the 1990s, as new countries received independence, the Berlin Wall fell, and the European Union was formed. The changing of transfer laws, much due to the Bosman Rule in 1995, made it easier for players to migrate between clubs and for ideas to be shared. This period is identified by commercialization and globalization, which impacted how countries approached and used the World Cup. The three World Cups played during the 1990s were held in the Western world: in Italy, the USA, and France. Although the Berlin Wall fell in 1989, it was still West Germany which competed and won.

From agenda setting and framing lenses (Entman, 1993; McCombs & Shaw, 1972) to analyzing what the media finds important and how issues are framed, one of the most interesting narratives of 1990 FIFA World Cup was around the Cameroonian national team. For the first time a competitive African team captured the hearts of the world, including beating the defending champion, Argentina, in the group stage. The image of Roger Milla dancing next to the corner flag became one of the most iconic images in World Cup history, showcasing African talent and joy. According to Porro and Conti (2014), the narrative the media created on Cameroon focused on two aspects: "(i) the involvement of all black African countries in supporting Cameroon, and (ii) the leading role of an eponymous hero like Roger Milla. His four goals and flamboyant goal celebrations made him one of the tournament's biggest stars" (p. 281). Milla continued to make a name for African football in the following World Cup in the USA, becoming the oldest player to score in the tournament at the age of 42. Nigeria followed the steps of Cameroon in the 1998 FIFA World Cup in France. After winning the gold medal in the 1996 OG in Atlanta, the talented Nigerian team, based on players competing in the top clubs in Europe, also showcased an attractive style of play, beating Spain in the group phase and reaching the knockout stage. With the Bosman Law and with the establishment of the European Union, the success of African countries on the world's stage led to globalization of talents from Africa to top football clubs and European clubs investing in academies in Africa but also to European countries further exploiting Africa's natural resources.

As Darby (2005) argues, "the discourse on Africa's place at the World Cup can be read as a reflection of broader First World-Third World power relations" (p. 883).

After decades of playing a marginal role in the world of football, the USA finally hosted the World Cup in 1994, becoming the first country to do so outside of Europe and Latin America. The Americans used American football stadiums, setting average attendance records of almost 69,000 fans per game (Zimbalist, 2016) and creating an estimated financial impact of US$4 billion (Vierhaus, 2019). The US Men's National Team (USMNT) did not leave a significant competitive impact, beyond in one of the most political games of the decade, losing 0–2 to Iran in the group stage of the 1998 World Cup (Delgado, 2003). However, the US Women's National Soccer Team (USWNT) did. FIFA introduced the FIFA Women's World Cup in 1991, and in 1996 the USA hosted and won the first Olympic women's football tournament in Atlanta. Enjoying the benefits of Title IX, an amendment to the American educational law (Woods & Butler, 2021), the USWNT dominated international football in the next decades while also fighting for gender equality. Thus, nationalism, liberalism, and capitalism that are integrated in Brand America also manifested through FIFA as the Cold War ended.

Collective identity and cultural affiliations can manifest differently. In the semi-final of the 1990 FIFA World Cup, the fans in the stadium in Naples were split if to support the Italian national team or Argentina, led by Maradona who played for the local club Napoli. Being a crime-struck southern Italian city, Maradona was locally adored for leading the local team to beat the rich teams of the North. Thus, fans were torn if to show nationalism towards home-country Italy, consisting of many players from Juventus and Milan, or local pride, supporting Maradona who perhaps represented better the hard struggles of the people of Naples. While that was an example of divisions of local identity, an example of football bringing diverse populations together could be seen in the national team of France, who won the 1998 FIFA World Cup on home soil. As a former colonizing empire, the French society consists of various ethnic populations who immigrated from Africa and the Caribbeans. With a team consisting of defenders and midfielders from African descent, such as Marcel Desailly, Patrick Viera, and Lilian Thuram, a truly diverse French team won its first world championship. Perhaps the player who represented that integration the best was team star Zinedine Zidane, whose parents immigrated to France from Algeria. After scoring twice in the 3–0 victory against Brazil in the final, the Arc de Triumph paid respect by lighting the words "Merci Zizou." As Sonntag (2014) writes:

> Out of the blue, the World Cup winners of 1998, from their emblematic coach Aime Jacquet to their extraordinary new star Zinedine Zidane, suddenly offered exactly what French society was longing for. For each and every citizen, there seemed to be a possibility to identify with the team and its success. (p. 318)

After changing various formats during the previous phase, the tournament finally settled on 32 teams in the 1998 FIFA World Cup, setting the structure for the upcoming decades. The 1998 World Cup was also technologically innovative, as after some TV rights disputes were settled, the organizers provided giant screens in public place across France, giving fans a new and unique international experience. The mega screens gave the huge crowds a "stadium-like atmosphere" (Sonntag, 2014, 322) and made the colorful and noisy fans a part of the show as they travel across the country or engage with locals. Perhaps the biggest personal change in the world of football was the retirement of FIFA President João Havelange in 1998, after almost a quarter of a century in office (Sugden & Tomlinson, 2017). During his time at the realm, Havelange managed to grow the game of football globally but also created a culture of "omertà," "by which the real truth is what is most kept within the family" (Sugden & Tomlinson, 2017, p. 44). A culture that will continue through his successor Sepp Blatter.

Nation Branding and Sportswashing

Entering the new millennium, the FIFA World Cup built on successful experiences from earlier competition while making innovative choices about the next future hosts of the World Cup: (a) Japan and South Korea became not only the first joint hosts of the FIFA World Cup in 2002 but the first Asian ones as well, (b) Germany from Western Europe hosted in 2006, (c) South Africa became the first African country to host the World Cup in 2010, and (e) Russia became the first Eastern European country to host the World Cup in 2018. With the FIFA World Cup diversifying into new markets, the use of nation branding and country image becomes more complex, embodying impactions through every lens and discipline of the field. The significance countries see in hosting the FIFA World Cup for nation branding purposes also led to counter-movements arising, protesting FIFA, the governments, and the organizations for corrupting mega-events for political purposes at the expense of the public.

Much public diplomacy needed to occur for Japan and South Korea to host a World Cup together, first and foremost between the countries addressing the atrocities of the past, when Imperial Japan annexed South Korea between 1910 and 1945 (Goldblatt, 2019; Tagsold, 2014). While the two countries found mutual goals in hosting the tournament and did manage to open Asia as an attractive market for FIFA, it "did not produce an image of overall image of the two nations overcoming the past" (Tagsold, 2014, p. 351). According to Tagsold (2014), "the long-term consequences of Japan's imperialist misdoings were much too deeply rooted to be overcome by four weeks of common joy, festivity and football" (p. 351). A country that did manage to disassociate from its past war crimes was Germany through the way the 2006 World Cup was hosted, through the diverse composure of the national team, and through their attractive style of play. The mega screens that were introduced in France and used in Korea and Japan became structured fan zones. After using the 1936 Berlin Olympic Games from Nazi propaganda and having the 1972 Olympic Games being overshadowed by a terror attack, finally Germany managed to project a fun, open, and welcoming image to the world (Dubinsky, 2019b; Kaelberer, 2017). Perhaps the most interesting case of nation branding and sports was South Africa hosting the FIFA World Cup in 2010 as the tournament was a celebration not only of Nelson Mandela and the "Rainbow Nation" but was meant to be a landmark for the renaissance of the continent (Goldblatt, 2019). According to several studies, the success has been limited. From a product-country-image approach, branding South Africa as an emerging economy, such as India, China, or Brazil, needed more than a mega-event (Maguire, 2011). Scholars argue that while there was generally a positive coverage of South Africa during the tournament (Maguire, 2011; Bolsmann, 2014), there was much criticism on unneeded spent of public money. According to the revenue distribution system that was introduced, the host country covers all the opening budget including infrastructure, stadiums, transportation, and communication based on FIFA's approval, while FIFA covers the operating expenses and retains all the revenues (Zimbalist, 2016). FIFA generated US$1.291 billion (FIFA, 2011), leading to criticism that once again Europe, now in the form of FIFA in Zurich, was enjoying the money generated in Africa, much at the expense of the locals who were left with unsustainable stadiums (Maguire, 2011). Brazil had ambitions to become a regional leader and make Rio de Janeiro the most central city in South America through hosting the 2014 FIFA World Cup and the 2016 OG, but due to financial, political, and social crises, the plan backfired (Boykoff, 2016; Dubinsky, 2019a, b). Instead, the country barely managed to host the events, local residents protested corruption and public spending, strikes erupted across all sectors (Zimbalist, 2016), and the country's image was framed negatively through international media resulting in negative attitudes (Schalhorn, 2020). All while FIFA enjoyed another record year, generating over $2 billion in 2014 (FIFA, 2015). That number more than doubled four years later, when FIFA reported a revenue of 4.6 billion USD in 2018 after the World Cup in Russia (FIFA, 2019).

National identity, which defined some of the characteristics of how national teams approach football, has changed. The traditionally organized and efficient German became a symbol for diversity and attacking football (Kaelberer, 2017). That was a result of a structural change in German football, after losing the 2002 World Cup Final to Brazil, resulting in highly attractive and diverse squads that culminated in 2014, winning the World Cup in Brazil. The Brazilians on the other hand went through the exact opposite process, neglecting the traditional jogo bonito to a more tactical approach, which resulted in another national tragedy, a 7–1 loss, to Germany in the semi-final in the 2014 hosted World Cup, a game now known as the "Mineirazo." Continuing on national identity and sports as a uniting tool, the Spanish national team, "La Rocha," consists of players from rival regions, including separatist Catalonia and the Basque region (Ortega, 2016). One of the most politically rooted games in European football was the "el classico" between FC Barcelona representing Catalonia and Real Madrid associated with federal Spain. Much like the French national team in 1998 and 2018 and the German team in 2014, a diverse Spanish team consisting of players from Barcelona, Madrid, Basque origins, and different ethnicities dominated the world of football winning the 2010 World Cup. The Spaniards had their own style of play, known as *tiki-taka*, an evolution of the Dutch Total Football. The Netherlands, on the other hand, neglected their developed style and adopted a more tactical and practical approach to the game, reaching the final in 2010 and the semi-final in 2014 but still coming up short. Thus, traditional approaches to national identity and football have been changed due to different social and political developments.

The 2018 FIFA World Cup in Russia is more than anything associated with the corruption scandal in FIFA that led to the resignation of former FIFA President Sepp Blatter and dozens of other officials across the different federations and associations (Chadwick, 2022a; Sugden & Tomlinson, 2017). With words such as "omertà," "bad fellas," "boss," and "mafia" (Jennings, 2015; Sugden & Tomlinson, 2017), one of the strongest organizations in charge of the world's most popular sports was constantly compared to the Cosa Nostra. Investigative journalist Andrew Jennings writes, "I sniffed around FIFA in the 1990s and from 200 began to focus on Blatter and Havelange. Soon I realized that I was back in the dark ethos of Sicily and criminal culture of Omertà" (Jennings, 2015, p. 12) FIFA's decision in 2010 to award Russia to host the World Cup in 2018 and Qatar in 2022 was received with much criticism and suspicion, leading to research on how the countries are using football for soft power purposes (Brannagan & Rookwood, 2016; Wolfe, 2020) and even framing that as sportswashing (Boykoff, 2022a; Chadwick, 2022a, b). Accusations of reviving the USSR or a new Cold War almost immediately came up after Putin's Russia won the bid (Goldblatt, 2019). The 2018 World Cup did not resemble the 1934 FIFA World Cup in terms of political interference or the 1936 OG in terms of ideological propaganda. Although the 2018 World Cup did not necessarily create a more positive image of Russia (Rocha & Wyse, 2020) and the host team did not win the cup, the tournament was organized relatively smoothly, and even new technology was introduced in the form of the video assistant referee (VAR). Yet as Goldblatt explains:

> President Putin had no expectations that Russia would win on the pitch, but as this, the clearest signal of all that Russia held the international rule of law in contempt, suggested, he was conducting the battle and making gains on other fronts. (Goldblatt, 2019, p. 526)

Dubinsky (2019b) defines the parallel era in the Olympic Movement as the "legacy-oriented era," arguing that host cities are aiming for long-term impacts when holding the Games. Japan and Korea, Germany, South Africa, Brazil, Russia, and Qatar all saw the World Cup as part of a larger plan for the place of the country in the world, at times at the expense of local communities. As a result, counter-movements started to protest the need of mega-events, against international and national sports organizations and against governments and local authorities. When analyzing the

Olympic Movement, Dubinsky (2019b) suggested that perhaps the third decade of the twenty-first century will be starting a new era. The COVID-19 pandemic hitting the world in early 2020 forced countries, communities, and people to change their ways of life and adapt. The pandemic had an immediate impact on the world of football, causing countries to stop, postpone, or even cancel competitions (Drewes et al., 2020). Unlike the 1990s that ended with a solid tournament structure, a growing revenue model, and a new approach for fans engagement, the 2020s start with much uncertainty about how the world of sports is going to look like in the foreseeable future amid a global pandemic. Yet despite the growing criticism about corruption, public spendings, or deaths of thousands of migrant workers, neither the 2018 nor the 2022 FIFA World Cup was stripped from Russia and Qatar (Ludvigsen & Bond, 2022). The 2018 FIFA World Cup should be seen as part of Putin's long-term geopolitical strategies through sports that have often been framed as sportswashing (Zeimers & Constandt, 2022). Only after invading Ukraine in February 2022, international sports authorities, including FIFA and UEFA, took sanctions against Russia, banning the country from the playoffs of the 2022 FIFA World Cup, banned Russian clubs from continental competitions, and stripped Russia from hosting other events such as the 2022 UEFA Champions League Final.

Both FIFA and Qatar received ample criticism since the Middle Eastern country was awarded to host the 2022 World Cup. FIFA was accused of corruption leading to dozens of arrests and resignations in the following years (Zeimers & Constandt, 2022). Qatar was accused of sportswashing, trying to use football to clean its image from human rights violations, exploitations of migrant workers living in subhuman conditions, corruption, and even supporting terrorism (Ludvigsen & Bond, 2022). Among the issues Qatar was accused of were the kafala system and the deaths of thousands of migrant workers, anti-LGBTQ laws, gender discrimination, corruption and lack of transparency, oppression of freedom of speech, and supporting terror organizations (Brannagan & Giulianotti, 2015; Brannagan & Reiche, 2022; Griffin, 2019). Yet the Qataris and their supporters responded by framing the competition as a nation building event, using the World Cup to build necessary infrastructure to modernize the country (Chadwick, 2022b; Reiche, 2022). The initial scrutiny Qatar received turned into a cultural clash between the global north and the global south, with counteraccusations of orientalism and islamophobia and whataboutism (Al Jazeera Staff, 2022; Hussain & Cunningham,

2022). The organization of Qatar 2022 was unique, as while all stadiums were within about an hour drive from the capital Doha and did not require stakeholders to fly from venue to venue and switch hotels between games, the organization was also accused of greenwashing and spending over $200 billion on an unsustainable event (Boykoff, 2022a, b). While Western media scrutinized Qatar 2022 as a prize for corruption and lack of accountability (Liew, 2022; Slot, 2022), the Qataris and FIFA emphasized the change the tournament led to, not just in modernized infrastructure but also in legislation abolishing the kafala system and improving migrant workers' rights (Media Release, 2022; Olley, 2022; Reiche, 2022). The legacy of Qatar 2022 is very much in the eyes of the beholders. While being defiant against the West, the Global North, and liberalism, Qatar 2022 also galvanized Arab support around the Palestinian cause and around Morocco, the first Arab and African team to reach the semi-final of a World Cup. Thus, even the discussion if Qatar 2022 was uniting or polarizing was polarizing.

Future Challenges and Opportunities

With the FIFA World Cup ever-evolving, so do the implications of nation branding, adding new and old challenges and opportunities. The 2026 FIFA World Cup will be hosted by three countries for the first time, Canada, Mexico, and the USA. The Americans see value in hosting mega-events, being scheduled to host the FIFA World Cup Final in 2026 and the OG in 2028. However, with over a million Americans dead from COVID-19, a financial crisis, and a wave of activism that perhaps even originated in American football, there are bound to be domestic challenges. The growing counter-movements, combined with the waves of social protests around the world, are bound to challenge the FIFA World Cup and every hosting country moving forward.

Physical, structural, and technological changes will also shape the future as well. With the exposure and revenue possibilities growing, FIFA expanded the World Cup to 48 teams, giving more countries a chance to capitalize on football through participation in the next tournaments. Moreover, FIFA continues to attract new markets and try innovative approaches for hosting, such as having the 2022 World Cup in the winter and the 2026 World Cup in three different countries. Following Qatar's use of sports and especially football for nation branding purposes, Saudi Arabia, a military regional powerhouse in the Middle East, started to invest billions of dollars in international football for soft power purposes, aiming to host a future World Cup (Chadwick & Widdop, 2022). The recognition of the growth of the women's game after the 2019 FIFA Women's World Cup attracted 1.12 billion viewers (FIFA, 2019) led FIFA to increase the number of participating teams to 32 and engage new markets as well, with Australia and New Zealand elected to host the FIFA Women's World Cup in 2023. While there is critic about the increase of teams based on some one-sided results, football can become another tool for countries to show their values by investing in the women's game. From a product-country-image approach, the new phases of the evolution of the FIFA World Cup will also be defined by the use of technology. New artificial intelligence (AI) and automatic recording technologies might change the way sports are being produced and how crowds experience the games during the coronavirus pandemic. Even regardless of COVID-19, other technological challenges and opportunities emerge. The introduction of the VAR in the 2018 World Cup in Russia met a need for more accurate refereeing but has since met with criticism for ruining the game. The rise of the popularity of esports and the ability to connect people through football regardless of geographic borders were adopted by leagues, teams, and federations including FIFA. Climate change is already making an impact on the world of sports and is expected to continue to do so. Protests against unsustainable hosting started in the previous competitions, including ruining the environment for the sake of hosting mega-events. When Qatar bid for the 2022 World Cup, they planned to host it in the summer in artificially cooled stadiums. Yet after winning the bid, they acknowledged it will not be possible to host such a tournament in the summer heat of the Middle East. In America, every year hurricanes strike the East Coast of the USA or the Gulf of Mexico, and wildfires burn across the West Coast. Yet while sportswashing, foreign governments, and foreign investments have changed the world of football, the backlash against the European Super League, and especially against the Americanization of the European-based game, demonstrates the strengths of local communities in keeping the traditions and shaping the future.

The chapter explored and discussed the evolution of the FIFA World Cup through the lenses of country image, nation branding, and public diplomacy. In each period new influences of country image emerge, which continued to shape the FIFA World Cup in the following periods as well. The outbreak of COVID-19, counter-movements protesting against FIFA and the hosting governments, anti-American backlash following the

European Super League initiative, sportswashing manifestations, technological changes, the growth of women's football, and climate change will shape how countries will be using the World Cup as it continues to evolve. Much is unknown about the future of football, but the growth of the popularity of the game indicates that people will still be kicking a ball around for a few more years, and countries will try to capitalize on that. As long as football remains the most popular sport worldwide, while the geopolitical manifestations might be different, countries using the FIFA World Cup for nation branding and public diplomacy are not likely to change.

References

2018 FIFA World Cup Russia. (2018). Global broadcast and audience summary. *FIFA*. Retrieved from https://resources.fifa.com/image/upload/2018-fifa-world-cup-russia-global-broadcast-and-audience-executive-summary.pdf?cloudid=njqsntrvdvqv8ho1dag5

Al Jazeera Staff. (2022, November 8). 'Racism': Qataris decry French cartoon of national football team. *Al Jazeera*. Retrieved from https://www.aljazeera.com/news/2022/11/8/islamophobia-qataris-decry-french-cartoon-of-football-team

beIN Sports. (2022, December 16). beIN Sports broadcast FIFA World Cup Qatar 2022 Final on free-to-air and YouTube. *beIN Sports*. Retrieved from https://www.beinsports.com/en/fifa-world-cup-qatar-2022/news/bein-sports-to-broadcast-fifa-world-cup-qatar/2006715

Bocketti, G. (2016). *The Invention of the Beautiful Game: Football and the Making of Modern Brazil*. Gainesville, FL: University Press of Florida.

Bolsmann, C. (2014). The 2010 World Cup in South Africa A Continent Spectacle? In S. Rinke & K. Schiller (Eds.), *The FIFA World Cup 1930–2010: Politics, commerce, spectacle, and identities* (pp. 372–388). Wallstein Verlag.

Boykoff, J. (2016). *Power games: A political history of the Olympics*. Verso.

Boykoff, J. (2022a). Toward a theory of sportswashing: Mega-events, soft power, and political conflict. *Sociology of Sport Journal, 39*(4), 342–351. https://doi.org/10.1123/ssj.2022-0095

Boykoff, J. (2022b, November 23). The World Cup in Qatar is a climate catastrophe. *Scientific American*. Retrieved from https://www.scientificamerican.com/article/the-world-cup-in-qatar-is-a-climate-catastrophe/

Brannagan, P. M., & Giulianotti, R. (2015). Soft power and soft disempowerment: Qatar, global sport and football's 2022 World Cup finals. *Leisure Studies, 34*, 703–710.

Brannagan, P. M., & Reiche, D. (2022). *Qatar and the 2022 FIFA World Cup: Politics, controversy, change*. Palgrave Macmillan.

Brannagan, P. M., & Rookwood, J. (2016). Sports mega events, soft power and soft disempowerment: International supporters' perspectives on Qatar's acquisition of the 2022 FIFA World Cup finals. *International Journal of Sport Policy and Politics*, 8(2), 173–188. https://doi.org/10.1080/19406940.2016.1150868

Buhmann, A., & Ingenhoff, D. (2015). The 4D model of the country image: An integrative approach from the perspective of communication management. *The International Communication Gazette*, 77, 102–124.

Chadwick, S. (2018, August 24). Sport-washing, soft power and scrubbing the stains. *Asia & Pacific Policy Forum*. Retrieved from https://www.policyforum.net/sport-washing-soft-power-and-scrubbing-the-stains/

Chadwick, S. (2022a). From utilitarianism and neoclassical sport management to a new geopolitical economy of sport. *European Sport Management Quarterly*, 1-20. https://doi.org/10.1080/16184742.2022.2032251

Chadwick, S. (2022b, November 14). Qatar's hosting of the FIFA Men's World Cup: The issues and challenges ahead. *SKEMA*. Retrieved from https://publika.skema.edu/qatar-hosting-fifa-men-world-cup-issues-and-challenges-ahead/

Chadwick, S. & Widdop, P. (2022, December 19). World Cup 2022: Who won the prize for 'soft power'? *The Conversation*. Retrieved from https://theconversation.com/world-cup-2022-who-won-the-prize-for-soft-power-195867

Darby, P. (2005). Africa and the 'World' Cup: FIFA politics, eurocentrism and resistance. *The International Journal of the History of Sport*, 22(5), 883–905. https://doi.org/10.1080/09523360500143745

Darby, P. (2007). African football labour migration to Portugal: Colonial and neocolonial resource. *Soccer & Society*, 8(4), 495–509. https://doi.org/10.1080/14660970701440774

Delgado, F. (2003). The fusing of sport and politics: Media constructions of US versus Iran at France '98. *Journal of Sport & Social Issues*, 27(3), 293–307. https://doi.org/10.1177/0193732503255760

Drewes, M., Daumann, F., & Follert, F. (2020). Exploring the sports economic impact of COVID-19 on professional soccer. *Soccer & Society*, 17(2), 85–95. https://doi.org/10.1080/14660970.2020.1802256

Dubinsky, Y. (2019a). From soft power to sports diplomacy: A theoretical and conceptual discussion. *Place Branding and Public Diplomacy*, 15, 154–164. https://doi.org/10.1057/s41254-019-00116-8

Dubinsky, Y. (2019b). Analyzing the roles of country image, nation branding, and public diplomacy through the evolution of the Modern Olympic Movement. *Physical Culture and Sport. Studies and Research*, 84(1), 27–40. https://doi.org/10.2478/pcssr-2019-0024

Entman, R. (1993). Framing toward clarification of a fractured paradigm. *Journal of Communication*, 43(4), 51–58. https://doi.org/10.1111/j.1460-2466. 1993.tb01304.x

Fan, Y. (2010). Branding the nation: Towards a better understanding. *Journal of Place Branding and Public Diplomacy*, 6(2), 97–103.

FIFA. (2011, May 31). *FIFA financial report 2010*. Retrieved from https://resources.fifa.com/image/upload/fifa-financial-report-2010-1392046.pdf?cloudid=n4hhe0pvhfdhzxbbbp44

FIFA. (2015, May 28). *Financial report 2014*. Retrieved from https://img.fifa.com/image/upload/e4e5lkxrbqvgscxgjnhx.pdf

FIFA. (2019). *Financial report 2018*. Retrieved from https://resources.fifa.com/image/upload/xzshsoe2ayttyquuxhq0.pdf

Galeano, E. (2013). *Soccer in sun and shadow*. Bold Type Books.

Goldblatt, D. (2019). *The age of football*. Macmillan.

Griffin, T. R. (2019). National identity, social legacy and Qatar 2022: The cultural ramifications of FIFA's first Arab World Cup. *Soccer & Society*, 20(7–8), 1000–1013. https://doi.org/10.1080/14660970.2019.1680499

Hussain, U., & Cunningham, G. B. (2022). The Muslim community and sport scholarship: A scoping review to advance sport management research. *European Sport Management Quarterly*. https://doi.org/10.1080/16184742.2022.2134434

Impiglia, M. (2014). 1934 FIFA World Cup: Did Mussolini rig the game? In S. Rinke & K. Schiller (Eds.), *The FIFA World Cup 1930–2010: Politics, commerce, spectacle, and identities* (pp. 66–84). Wallstein Verlag.

International Olympic Committee. (2016). *Marketing report Rio 2016*. Retrieved from https://stillmed.olympic.org/media/Document%20Library/OlympicOrg/Games/Summer-Games/Games-Rio-2016-Olympic-Games/Media-Guide-for-Rio-2016/IOC-Marketing-Report-Rio-2016.pdf

International Olympic Committee. (2020). *Marketing fact file 2020 edition*. Retrieved from https://stillmed.olympic.org/media/Document%20Library/OlympicOrg/Documents/IOC-Marketing-and-Broadcasting-General-Files/Olympic-Marketing-Fact-File.pdf

Jennings, A. (2015). *The dirty game*. Century.

Kaelberer, M. (2017). From Bern to Rio: Soccer and national identity discourses in Germany. *International Journal of Politics, Culture, and Society*, 30, 275–294. https://doi.org/10.1007/s10767-016-9234-6

Kalife, F. (director). (2018). Becoming Champions, episode 2: Italy: Against All Odds. *Netflix*. Retrieved from https://www.netflix.com/title/80226279

Kuper, S. (2010). *Soccer against the enemy*. Nation Books.

Liew, J. (2022, November 17). Qatar 2022 is actually happening: A horrifying but irresistible prospect. *The Guardian*. Retrieved from https://www.theguardian.com/football/2022/nov/17/qatar-2022-is-actually-happening-a-horrifying-but-irresistible-prospect

Lisi, C. (2015). *A history of the World Cup*. Rowman & Littlefield.
Ludvigsen, J. A. L., & Bond, A. J. (2022). Chapter 13: Managing risk and security at FIFA World Cups. In S. Chadwick, P. Widdop, C. Anagnostopoulos, & D. Parnell (Eds.), *The business of the FIFA World Cup* (pp. 179–189). Routledge.
Maguire, J. (2011). Invictus or evict-us? Media images of South Africa through the lens of the FIFA World Cup. *Social Identities, 17*(5), 681–694. https://doi.org/10.1080/13504630.2011.595208
McCombs, M. E., & Shaw, D. L. (1972). The agenda-setting function of mass media. *The Public Opinion Quarterly, 36*, 176–187.
Media Release. (2022, December 16). FIFA World Cup 2022 praised for its "unique cohesive power". *FIFA*. Retrieved from https://www.fifa.com/about-fifa/organisation/fifa-council/media-releases/fifa-world-cup-2022-tm-praised-for-its-unique-cohesive-power
Murray, S. (2018). *Sports diplomacy: Origins, theory and practice, 2018*. Routledge.
Nye, J. (2004). *Soft power: The means to success in world politics*. PublicAffairs.
Olley, J. (2022, November 19). World Cup: FIFA president Infantino slams Europe's 'hypocrisy' in speech. *ESPN*. Retrieved from https://www.espn.com/soccer/fifa-world-cup/story/4806508/world-cup-fifa-president-infantino-slams-europe-hypocrisy-in-astonishing-speech
Ortega, V. R. (2016). Soccer, nationalism and the media in contemporary Spanish society: La Roja, Real Madrid & FC Barcelona. *Soccer & Society, 17*(4), 628–643. https://doi.org/10.1080/14660970.2015.1067793
Porro, N., & Conti, F. (2014). Italia Novanta: "Magic Nights", globalization and a country at the crossroads. In S. Rinke & K. Schiller (Eds.), *The FIFA World Cup 1930–2010: Politics, commerce, spectacle, and identities* (pp. 279–297). Wallstein Verlag.
Radmann, A., & Andersson, T. (2018). Sweden. In J.-M. De Waele, S. Gibril, E. Gloriozova, & R. Spaaij (Eds.), *The Palgrave international handbook of football and politics* (pp. 139–162). Palgrave Macmillan. https://doi.org/10.1007/978-3-319-78777-0
Ramsden, J. (2006). England versus Germany, soccer and war memory: John Huston's Escape to Victory (1981). *History Journal of Film, Radio and Television, 26*(4), 570–590. https://doi.org/10.1080/01439680600916892
Reiche, D. (2022, December 14). A successful FIFA World Cup 2022. How Qatar proved its critics wrong and can continue to do so. *Georgetown University Qatar*. Retrieved from https://cirs.qatar.georgetown.edu/a-successful-fifa-world-cup-2022-how-qatar-proved-its-critics-wrong-and-can-continue-to-do-so/?fbclid=IwAR0bvfWhX3-fmnC0Sbm8fDiLVmHpZg37Pcnvw7EygSM5QqiuJ54IRGL2590
Revelez, L. B. (2018). Uruguay. In J.-M. De Waele, S. Gibril, E. Gloriozova, & R. Spaaij (Eds.), *The Palgrave international handbook of football and politics* (pp. 557–578). Palgrave Macmillan. https://doi.org/10.1007/978-3-319-78777-0

Richter, F. (2020, January 31). Super Bowl can't hold the candle to the biggest game in soccer. *Statista*. Retrieved from https://www.statista.com/chart/16875/super-bowl-viewership-vs-world-cup-final/

Rinke, S. (2014). Globalizing football in times of crisis: The first World Cup in Uruguay in 1930. In S. Rinke & K. Schiller (Eds.), *The FIFA World Cup 1930–2010: Politics, commerce, spectacle, and identities* (pp. 49–65). Wallstein Verlag.

Rinke, S., & Schiller, K. (2014). *The FIFA World Cup 1930–2010: Politics, commerce, spectacle, and identities* (pp. 66–84). Wallstein Verlag.

Rocha, C., & Wyse, F. (2020). Host country brand image and political consumerism: The case of Russia 2018 FIFA world cup. *Sport Marketing Quarterly*, 29(1), 62–76. https://doi.org/10.32731/SMQ.291.032020.05

Salazar-Sutil, N. (2008). Maradona Inc. Performance politics off the pitch. *International Journal of Cultural Studies*, 11(4), 441–458. https://doi.org/10.1177/1367877908096053

Schalhorn, C. (2020). Samba, sun and social issues: How the 2014 FIFA World Cup and the 2016 Rio Olympics changed perceptions of Germans about Brazil. *International Review for the Sociology of Sport*, 55(5), 603–622. https://doi.org/10.1177/1012690218822994

Slot, O. (2022, December 19). Invisible Qataris showed no accountability. *The Times*. Retrieved from https://www.thetimes.co.uk/article/ba569a2a-7ef3-11ed-bc2d-0c63022989a8?shareToken=fa51614c0b17c76fbec667a5e3944530

Smyth, R. (2018, March 20). World Cup stunning moments: Wes Germany 1–0 Austria in 1982. *The Guardian*. Retrieve from https://www.theguardian.com/football/blog/2014/feb/25/world-cup-25-stunning-moments-no3-germany-austria-1982-rob-smyth

Sonntag, A. (2014). France 98 – A watershed World Cup. In S. Rinke & K. Schiller (Eds.), *The FIFA World Cup 1930–2010: Politics, commerce, spectacle, and identities* (pp. 318–337). Wallstein Verlag.

Sugden, J., & Tomlinson, A. (2017). *Football, corruption, and lies*. Routledge.

Tagsold, C. (2014). Remember – Forget: The 2002 FIFA World Cup Korea/Japan as reconciliation of a dark past? In S. Rinke & K. Schiller (Eds.), *The FIFA World Cup 1930–2010: Politics, commerce, spectacle, and identities* (pp. 318–337). Wallstein Verlag.

Vierhaus, C. (2019). The international tourism effect of hosting the Olympic Games and the FIFA World Cup. *Tourism Economics*, 25(7), 1009–1028. https://doi.org/10.1177/13548166188143

Watts, S. (2014). How Uruguay broke Brazilian hearts in the 1950 World Cup. *BBC*. Retrieved from https://www.bbc.com/news/magazine-27767298

Wolfe, S. D. (2020). 'For the benefit of our nation': Unstable soft power in the 2018 men's World Cup in Russia. *International Journal of Sport Policy and Politics*, *12*(4), 545–561. https://doi.org/10.1080/19406940.2020.1839532

Woods, R., & Butler, N. (2021). *Social issues in sport* (4th ed.). Human Kinetics.

Zeimers, G., & Constandt, B. (2022). Chapter 7: An integrity design of the FIFA World Cups. In S. Chadwick, P. Widdop, C. Anagnostopoulos, & D. Parnell (Eds.), *The business of the FIFA World Cup* (pp. 89–105). Routledge.

Zimbalist, A. (2016). *Circus Maximus*. Brookings Institution Press.

CHAPTER 4

Nation Branding, Tokyo 2020, and the New Era of the Olympic Movement

INTRODUCTION

The Olympic Movement is in a constant state of crossroads, needing to navigate through and adapt to changing global realities. Manifestations of nation branding and public diplomacy can be traced back to the athletic competitions in Ancient Olympia and through the entire history of the Modern Olympic Games (Dubinsky, 2019a, b; Murray, 2018). Dubinsky (2019b) analyzed the evolution of the modern Olympic Games through such lenses, identifying prior to the pandemic that the Movement might be facing a new era, and addressed it as the survival-oriented era (Dubinsky, 2022a), following his research on the postponed Tokyo 2020 Olympic Games. International Olympic Committee (IOC) President Thomas Bach also used the term "new era" when discussing the future of the Olympic Movement but here referred to Paris 2024 as the point of change (IOC News, 2022). Based on Dubinsky's[1] reflections on the postponed Tokyo

---

[1] This chapter is an adapted and updated version of the article I published following my research in Japan during the Tokyo 2020 Olympic Games: Dubinsky, Y. (2022). The Olympic Games, nation branding, and public diplomacy in a post-pandemic world: Reflections on Tokyo 2020 and beyond. *Place Branding & Public Diplomacy*. 1–12. https://doi.org/10.1057/s41254-021-00255-x. For the chapter, the article was edited to discuss the new era of the Olympic Movement, adding further discussion on events happening until the end of 2022, including the Beijing 2022 Winter Olympic Games and the Qatar 2022 FIFA World Cup.

© The Author(s), under exclusive license to Springer Nature
Switzerland AG 2023
Y. Dubinsky, *Nation Branding and Sports Diplomacy*,
https://doi.org/10.1007/978-3-031-32550-2_4

2020 Olympic Games, this chapter conceptualizes and discusses the nature of the new era of the Olympic Movement and its intersections with nation branding, public diplomacy, country image, and related fields.

Previous Eras of Nation Branding and the Olympic Movement

The Tokyo Olympic Games were unprecedented and mark a beginning of a new era, not just because of the pandemic or being the first postponed Games, but because they, and future Games, offer a new evolution of the Olympic Movement. Dubinsky (2019b) divides the modern Olympic Games into five different eras of nation branding and public diplomacy. In the first era, the revival of the Olympic Games lasted between the first Modern Olympic Games in 1896 in Athens and the outbreak of World War I, during which the Berlin 1916 Olympic Games were canceled. In this era, the Games were relatively small and at times hosted as part of another international event such as the Paris 1900 and St. Louis 1904 Olympic Games being part of the World's Fair and the London 1908 Olympic Games part of the British-Franco Exhibition. In the second era that lasted between World War I and World War II, countries started to recognize the potential of the Games, and new traditions were implemented, leading to Nazi Germany hosting the Berlin 1936 Olympic Games with clear nation branding and public diplomacy goals. During World War II, the 1940 and 1944 Olympic Games were canceled. The political era of the Olympic Movement started after World War II and lasted until the end of the Cold War. After World War II, the Olympic Movement became more international, and as the name of the era indicates, the era is characterized by countries, organizations, and individuals trying to achieve political goals through the Games. Examples included the Black Power Salute in Mexico City 1968, the Munich Massacre—the terror attack in which 11 Israeli athletes, coaches, and referees were kidnapped and murdered during the Munich 1972 Olympic Games—the African boycott of the Montreal 1976 Olympic Games, the American-led 60-countries boycott of Moscow 1980 after the Soviet Union invaded Afghanistan, and the retaliation of the Eastern Bloc with the boycott of the Los Angeles 1984 Olympic Games. The commercialized era from the end of the Cold War until the beginning of the twenty-first century is characterized by the end of amateurism, the introduction of private sponsorships, the rise of television rights, and exposure of corruption scandals in the bidding process. In the legacy-oriented era, from the beginning of the twenty-first century until 2020, hosting countries and cities include long-term strategy, while local and international resistance is growing. While there are overlaps between the different eras, according to Dubinsky (2019b), each of these eras is unique as it adds a new dimension to the use of nation branding and public diplomacy through the Olympic Games. Despite identifying the eras before the outbreak of the COVID-19 pandemic, Dubinsky (2019b) already recognizes a shift in the Olympic Movement, arguing that the 2020s "might signal if the Olympic movement is still focusing on legacy or will be starting a new Olympic era where countries will be targeting other opportunities to use the games to improve their images" (p. 37).

A Survival-Oriented Era

While every Olympic Games are different, the Tokyo 2020 is the first in a series of several Olympic Games that were either elected or hosted in an unprecedented way. Tokyo 2020 was held in 2021, being the first Olympic Games to be postponed, without international or local fans being able to attend the Games and with ample restrictions on athletes, media, and other accredited stakeholders (Kuhn, 2021; Tokyo 2020, 2021a, b, c, d, e, f). The Games were held under a state of emergency, and as the coronavirus was not being contained, Japanese people and Tokyo residents repeatedly showed their objection to the Games in a variety of surveys (Kuhn, 2021). The following Games in 2024 in Paris and 2028 in Los Angeles were awarded together for the first time after multiple cities withdrew from the 2024 bid due to lack of local or governmental support (Dubinsky, 2019b; GamesBids, n.d.). Los Angeles was even the second choice of the United States Olympic and Paralympic Committee (USOPC), which originally chose Boston to bid to host in 2024 but had to change its candidate due to the growing opposition in Massachusetts. After awarding Paris and Los Angeles to host the 2024 and 2028 Olympic Games, respectively, the International Olympic Committee (IOC) changed its bidding regulations, and instead of competing bids, a special committee negotiates with candidate cities. Under the new regulations, a few days before the Opening Ceremony of Tokyo 2020, the IOC awarded Brisbane to host the 2032 Olympic Games (Zirin & Boykoff, 2021).

Thus, while the future of the Olympic Games seems somewhat secure with the next three host cities already selected, the Olympic Movement is entering a new survival-oriented era in which it constantly has to change and adapt its policies amid ongoing threats and challenges. The IOC is often criticized for being extravagant and generating billions on the backs of local communities (Boykoff, 2016; Zimbalist, 2016; Zirin & Boykoff, 2021), but a series of events leading to the Tokyo Olympic Games, and the decisions about future competitions, indicate that the Olympic Movement is more fragile than it might be seen. Despite having over 200 countries and delegations participating in the Games (International Olympic Committee, 2021a), when local communities get a chance to speak their minds, they usually vote against hosting the Games (Zirin & Boykoff, 2021). The wave of athletes' activism (Abdul-Jabbar, 2021), along with growing demand for free speech and flexibility on protesting, jeopardize the political neutrality of the Olympics. Of course, the pandemic caused the postponement of the Tokyo Olympic Games and the cancellation of the 2022 Youth Olympic Games (GamesBids, n.d.) and is expected to continue to impact and challenge future Olympic Games. The new era differentiates from previous ones and is characterized by the IOC making practical changes in policies, norms, and traditions, to ensure the survival of the Olympic Movement amid new challenges.

A Questionable Legacy Era

According to the Tokyo 2020 Organizing Committee of the Olympic and Paralympic Games (TOCOG), the total bid stage budget of hosting the Tokyo 2020 Olympic and Paralympic Games in 2021 was US$15.4 billion (McCurry, 2021), $2.8 billion more than if they would have not been postponed, games which locals could not attend and could not generate revenues from international visitors. The Japanese government covered all the costs except $6.7 billion. Thus, the legacy of the short-term and long-term legacies of the Games remains questionable, and the decision to host the Games has been criticized by international media and was protested locally in Japan (Nolympics LA, n.d.; Zirin & Boykoff, 2021). Such a decision can hurt a country's normative dimension (Buhmann & Ingenhoff, 2015). With that said, canceling the Olympics would have cost Japan US$16 billion (McCurry, 2021).

The narrative around Tokyo 2020 changed several times. Japan used the Tokyo 1964 Olympic Games to reposition the country's image from a devasted country after World War II to a technological powerhouse through the reconstruction of the capital, introduction of the bullet train, and use of newly developed technology including satellite broadcasting for the first time in the Olympics (Abel, 2021; International Olympic Committee, 2021a). The original bid for the Games in 2013 focused on the recovery and reconstruction from the 2011 tsunami and the nuclear disaster in Fukushima (Boykoff & Gaffney, 2020; Tokyo, 2021a, b). Yet in March 2020, when the Games were postponed due to the outbreak of the coronavirus, the narrative of the Games changed as well, for the Games to become a victory of humanity over a global pandemic. According to Cull (2010), effective public diplomacy needs to be credible and connected to policy. As the Japanese government was not able to contain the virus, the vaccination rates in Tokyo and Japan were lower than in the USA and Europe, Tokyo went into several states of emergency, and more and more restrictions were published, it became clear that the 2020 Olympic Games would not be a global celebration of a victory over the virus. Thus, the latest narrative focused on the importance of holding the Olympic Games despite the virus and the significance of having the Games for the athletes. There was still a place in the Main Press Center (MPC) dedicated to recovery and reconstruction (Tokyo, 2021a, b), and measurements and restrictions were put to try and prevent further outbreaks of the virus. Movement was restricted, the ceremonies were less celebratory than in previous Olympic Games, and integration with the public was limited and at times prohibited (Tokyo, 2021a, b), all to secure that the Games could go on.

Japan was originally positioned relatively well to fight the virus. It is an island that could have taken measures such as New Zealand to prevent the virus from coming from abroad, the government took the virus seriously and took measurements early, the Japanese public is already accustomed to wearing masks and has a collectivist culture, and the Japanese technology is the most advanced in the world. Thus, falling behind on vaccinations, not being able to contain the virus, and holding the Olympic Games without fans and with ample restrictions projected a problematic image of Japan's functional dimension (Buhmann & Ingenhoff, 2015). TOCOG and the IOC try to market Tokyo 2020 to the world through the slogan "United by Emotion" (Tokyo 2020, 2021a, b, c, d, e, f, g). Yet such a motto also hides the sad reality that organizational failures prevented the world from being united in person and limited Japan from leveraging the Olympic Games to showcase its rich and diverse history and culture and use them for nation branding and public diplomacy, to achieve social, political, and economic goals.

The legacy of Tokyo 2020 was mixed, questionable, and controversial. Following the Games, there was further backlash in Japan against hosting Winter Olympic Games in Sapporo, and former Prime Minister Shinzo Abe, one of the strongest advocates for hosting the Tokyo Olympics, was assassinated. Less than six months after Tokyo 2020, China hosted the Beijing 2022 Winter Olympic Games under unprecedented restricting conditions both to local populations and participating delegates, facing international scrutiny for human rights violations and being held in "an Orwellian surveillance state" (Ingle, 2022). The plannings of Paris 2024, Los Angeles 2028, and Brisbane are all legacy oriented, focusing on social inclusion and sustainability, yet each of the future hosts faces its own unique problems. Thus, with the long-term implications of the COVID-19 pandemic still unknown and with the growing doubt and resistance about the benefits of hosting the Olympic Games, the legacies of the Olympic Games held during the new era are questionable.

An American-Influenced but Democracy-Limited Era

The 1984 Los Angeles Olympic Games changed the Olympic Movement after several Games in which international politics overshadowed the competitions. Being privately funded, Los Angeles 1984 Olympic Games started the commercial era of the Olympic Movement, leading to The Olympic Partners (TOP) sponsorship program in 1985 and to the official abolishment of amateurism in the Seoul 1988 Olympic Games (Dubinsky 2019a, b). That, along with the end of the Cold War, gave the USA significant influence in the Olympic Movement. With broadcasting rights being the most profitable stream of revenues (International Olympic Committee, 2021a) and most television revenues coming from North America and the USA, the American influence of the Olympic Movement and the Olympic Games manifest in a variety of ways. Some of the critics over hosting the 2020 Olympic Games argued that the organizers folded under pressure from TV rights holders and sponsors, with several of these stakeholders being American. Furthermore, Los Angeles was awarded the 2028 Olympic Games 11 years in advance, which potentially blocked any chance of further postponing the Tokyo Games as well.

The influence of American television rights holders also manifested in scheduling events according to American prime time. For example, the swimming finals were held in the morning and not in Japanese prime time. The basketball final was also held in the morning, hours before the bronze medal match. Originally the women's football (soccer) final was scheduled to be held in the morning despite the heat in Tokyo, but after the United States Women's National Team (USWNT) did not qualify, the organizing committee agreed to the requests of Canada and Sweden to hold the final in the evening in Yokohama.

Despite having a questionable ethical Olympic history, the USOPC or American governing bodies are very rarely sanctioned by the IOC. After leading a 60-countries boycott of the Moscow 1980 Olympic Games from political reasons, not only the USA was not suspended from the Olympic Movement, but Los Angeles was allowed to fund the 1984 Games through private sponsors (Dubinsky, 2019b). Just as a point of reference, after North Korea did not send a delegation for the Tokyo 2020 Olympic Games, the IOC suspended the Olympic Committee of North Korea from participating in the Beijing 2022 Winter Olympic Games (Morgan, 2021). Another famous scandal in which the Americans suffered almost no consequences was the corruption around the bid for the Salt Lake City 2002 Winter Olympic Games, where IOC members were bribed by bid-related stakeholders (Boykoff, 2016). Yet, while the IOC did reform some of its policies and suspended a few members, Salt Lake City was not stripped from hosting the Games. Over the years, several American athletes have been caught doping in some of the most notorious doping scandals, such as Marion Jones as part of the BALCO doping scandal (CNN Editorial Research, 2021) and Lance Armstrong and the US Postal Service Pro Cycling Team who as the US Anti-Doping Agency (USADA) defined "ran the most sophisticated, professionalized and successful doping program that sport has ever seen" (USADA, 2021). More recently, the Nike Oregon Project, a project promoting long runs supported by Nike—the official outfitter of Team USA—was closed after USADA banned coach Alberto Salazar for doping violations (Grez, 2019). Yet, while Russian athletes were forced to compete under their Olympic Committee and not under the Russian flag for systematic doping scandal, American sports-governing bodies such as the USOPC or USA Track & Field did not suffer international consequences. The USOPC or USA Gymnastics also did not suffer international sanctions after the sexual abuse scandal in which former Team USA doctor Larry Nassar sexually abused hundreds of gymnasts over decades, including Olympic champions (Kwiatkowski, 2021). According to the 2020 version of the Olympic Charter (International Olympic Committee, 2020), part of the mission of the IOC is "to promote safe sport and the protection of athletes from all forms of harassment and abuse" (p. 17). Yet, despite the systematic sexual abuse scandal in the USOPC and USA Gymnastics, these organizations were not retroactively suspended from future Olympic Games, which eventually enabled the USA to top of the medal table podium (Tokyo 2020, n.d.) much thanks to the two gold medals won in women's gymnastics.

As mentioned, the Tokyo 2020 Olympic Games were the last summer Olympic Games which were awarded in a traditional bid, seven years in advance, after IOC members chose the Japanese capital over Istanbul and Madrid in the 125th IOC Session in 2013 (GamesBids, n.d.). In the same session, the IOC also elected Thomas Bach as the organization's ninth president, succeeding Jacque Rogge. One of Bach's first initiatives as IOC president was to review and revise the Olympic Movement, through what was defined as "Agenda 2020"—a list of 40 recommendations and guidelines of how to improve the Olympic Movement (International Olympic Committee, 2014). As much of the criticism over the IOC was about the costly bidding process and the delivery of the Games, some potential reforms were suggested in the Agenda 2020 Recommendations. Yet, while the IOC was projecting optimism, the following bids during Bach's presidency continued to show resistance and lack of trust from local populations (Zirin & Boykoff, 2021). During the bid for the 2022 Winter Olympic Games, either due to lack of governmental support or due to lack of public support, Stockholm, Krakow, and Oslo withdrew from the bid, leaving only Almaty from Kazakhstan and Beijing from China as the only candidate (GamesBids, n.d.; Zimbalist, 2016). Munich, who bid for the 2018 Winter Olympic Games, did not enter the bid for 2022 after the people of Bavaria voted against hosting the Games in a referendum (Zimbalist, 2016). The result in the Munich referendum might also be seen as a vote of lack of confidence by the German people against the German president of the IOC. The Ukrainian city Lviv dropped its bid following the Russian invasion to the Crema Peninsula. Beijing won the bid by a small margin becoming the first city to host both the Olympic Games and Winter Olympic Games, and China used the event as another power play opportunity to defy the West and showcase its hard power. All show that people and communities have doubts and reservations about the benefit of the Olympic Games and authoritarian countries and taking advantage of that gap.

As the bid for the 2022 Winter Olympic Games started before the implementation of Agenda 2020, there was hope in the IOC that the bid for the 2024 Olympic Games will be different under the new flexible recommendations. Yet, despite a promising start, bids from Budapest, Rome, Boston, and Hamburg all failed to get to the finish line due to lack of public or political support (GamesBids, n.d.; Zirin & Boykoff, 2021). Once again Bach received an international humiliation from the people of Germany, this time in the Hamburg bid referendum. The USOPC chose Boston after a preliminary bid process as the American candidate city for the 2024 Olympic Games, but after a growing opposition in Massachusetts, the bid collapsed. Going back to the lab again, the Americans chose runner-up Los Angeles to bid to host the Games for the third time, and without going IOC constantly changing its rules and regulations, transparency and democracy are becoming a burden (Zirin & Boykoff, 2021). Thus, on one hand with France, the USA, and Australia hosting the Olympic Games through the 2020s and early 2030s in Paris, Los Angeles, and Brisbane, the future of the Olympic Movement seems to be in democratic control and linked with American interest. Yet, when diving deeper into the bids and how the Games were awarded, democracy and transparency are a growing limitation of the Olympic Movement.

A Post-Woke of Athletes-to-People Diplomacy Era

From a people-to-people diplomacy perspective (Handelman, 2012), athletes could be a resource for sports diplomacy (Abdi et al., 2019) through their competitions, behaviors, and athletic success, protecting their country's image to diverse international audiences and effecting the sympathetic dimension of a country (Buhmann & Ingenhoff, 2015). In the context of the Olympic Movement, examples include Jesse Owens defying the racist ideology of Nazi Germany, Abebe Bikila winning the Marathon in Rome barefoot and starting the glorious legacy of long running in Africa, Nadia Comaneci exposing Romanian gymnastics and breaking barriers through the Cold War, Cathy Freeman celebrating with the Aboriginal flag a gold medal in the Sydney 2000 Olympic Games paying tribute to the history of indigenous people in Australia, or Usain Bolt and Jamaican sprinters in the twenty-first century (Dubinsky, 2019a; Murray, 2018). Perhaps contrary to the decline of the power of the people, Tokyo 2020 also signifies a rise in the power of the athletes. Tokyo 2020 was the first Olympic Games held after the COVID-19 pandemic, which did not only cause a health challenge around the world but was followed by a wave of social activism, especially after the murder of African American George Floyd by a police officer in Minnesota (Abdul-Jabbar, 2021).

Yet, to fully understand the events, one needs to go back to shortly after the 2016 Olympic Games in Rio de Janeiro, when American football player Colin Kaepernick started kneeling in preseason football games as a protest against racism and police brutality in the USA (Cooper et al., 2019). Kaepernick's actions were followed by numerous protests not just in American sports but in international competitions as well including former Olympic champion Megan Rapinoe kneeling during the American national anthem in a friendly international competition before she was instructed to stop and Olympic athletes protesting on the podium during the 2019 Pan-American Games, which resulted with the USOPC reprimanding them (Dance, 2020; Zaccardi, 2020). Professor Harry Edwards, one of the leading voices on athlete's activism and a mentor to Tommie Smith and John Carlos who protested racial injustice in America during the Mexico City 1968 Olympic Games, classified the series of protests as the fourth wave of athletes' activism (Cooper et al., 2019). Unlike in previous waves, this wave was characterized by athletes with social, political, and economic power, who used social media to bypass traditional white establishments and directly correspond with their followers. Following the murder of George Floyd in 2020, the wave of activism spread to more sports, more athletes, more minority groups, and beyond the boundaries of the USA. As a result of the growth of activism, several American sports organizations that originally objected to the protests changed their policies and even apologized to their athletes (Zaccari, 2020).

Leading up to the Tokyo 2020 Olympic Games, Thomas Bach and the IOC repeatedly emphasized the importance of Rule 50 in the Olympic Charter. According to the rule: "No kind of demonstration or political, religious or racial propaganda is permitted in any Olympic sites, venues or other areas" (IOC, 2020, p. 90). When Smith and Carlos protested in 1968, Avery Brundage, the American president of the IOC, instructed the USOC to send the athletes back. Smith and Carlos were scrutinized and suffered from racism and financial difficulties after their return (Cooper et al., 2019; Zimbalist, 2016). It took decades before they were accepted as national heroes, and in 2019 they were finally introduced into the USOPC Hall of Fame. The shift in the approach towards athletes' activism in the USA also manifested through the Tokyo 2020 Olympic Games as the IOC relaxed some of the restrictions (International Olympic Committee, 2021d). While the IOC continued to emphasize the need for political neutral Games, athletes were allowed to kneel before competitions, which happened in several soccer games and other sports (Abdul-Jabbar, 2021). While the fear that relaxing the regulations about protesting will result in a variety of political causes raised by athletes, there were only a handful of athletes who tested the water and were not sanctioned for it. Perhaps the most visible protest was done by gay African American silver medalist Raven Saunders, who used the time on the podium to create an X with her hands symbolizing "the intersection of where all people who are oppressed meet" (Bates & Locker, 2021). American fencer Race Imboden and American hammer thrower Gwen Berry who protested during the 2019 Pan-American Games made modest protests during the Tokyo Olympic Games as well (Abdul-Jabbar, 2021). Neither the IOC nor the USOPC sanctioned the athletes for the gestures, which is a significant difference from the response both organizations had to the protest of Smith and Carlos in 1968.

While the Black Lives Matter movement was significant for activism against racism, the #MeToo movement also influenced reforms and more vocal and opinionated athletes. The growing importance of inclusion and gender in sports also manifested with a transgender athlete from New Zealand and a trans-nonbinary athlete in Canada competing in the Tokyo Olympic Games (Abdul-Jabbar, 2021), changing not only perceptions on gender fluidity but branding their countries as progressive and democratic. Perhaps the two most significant female athletes in the Games in terms of social change were American gymnast Simone Biles and Japanese tennis player Naomi Osaka using sports to raise awareness for mental health (Abdul-Jabbar, 2021).

One of the most horrific scandals in sports history was revealed just after the 2016 Olympic Games, as hundreds of American gymnasts testified against Dr. Larry Nassar for sexual assaults during his roles at the USOC, USA Gymnastics, and Michigan State University (Kwiatkowski, 2021). Simone Biles, who was assaulted by Nassar, continued to compete and represented Team USA in Tokyo as well. During the Olympics Biles withdrew in the middle of the team competition and from four of the five individual finals she qualified for because of mental health reasons. While several athletes have been talking in the past about mental health, the Tokyo 2020 Olympic Games are unique as Biles decided to prioritize her mental health over competing. Biles' decision came a few months after Naomi Osaka started withdrawing from Grand Slam tennis tournaments, speaking on mental health reasons as well. The acceptance of athletes prioritizing their health over taking part in the competitions also shows a culture shift because of a variety of civil rights movements. From a nation branding, public diplomacy, and people-to-people diplomacy perspectives, it is also evident that these shifts of culture were ignited or led by American athletes and American culture.

Lastly, when discussing cultural shifts, the new generation of athletes and fans also manifests through newly introduced sports, which pertain to urban cultures, such as skateboarding and climbing, as the IOC is trying to attract younger audiences. In skateboarding, some of the medalists were young teenagers at the age of 13, who are already social media influencers. While some celebrate the change, there is also a growing criticism against the pressure put on children to become elite athletes at such a young age by their environment, including the sports federations and even governments. With the growing awareness of mental health and burnout, and with the constant use of social media, these issues will continue to challenge the Olympic Movement.

Progressive and woke movements are shaping and changing international sports, but there are also setbacks and challenges. The Beijing 2022 Winter Olympic Games showed that not all countries are falling in line with progressive movements. The international scrutiny China received prior to the Games did not result in athletes' activism during the competitions, and child safety was very much scrutinized, especially around Russia and the figure skating competitions. Although not in an Olympic event, the Qatar 2022 FIFA World Cup, oppressed athletes' activism and their support of the LGBTQ community, with FIFA calling international stakeholders to focus on football. With the growing financial influence of countries from the Arabian Gulf and resistance from populist leaderships, the new era of the Olympic Movement is characterized by a rise of athletes' activism and their role as influencers through people-to-people diplomacy but also by counterreactions.

A Global Geopolitical Era

The athletic field has always been a stage for nation branding and public diplomacy battlefield through participation and performance (Dubinsky, 2019a, b). Overall, 206 delegations competed in the Tokyo Olympic Games, including a refugee delegation and the National Olympic Committee of Russia (Tokyo, 2020a, b, c, d, e, f, g, 2021d). The only country that did not send athletes to compete in Tokyo was North Korea

(Morgan, 2021). For the third straight Summer Olympic Games, the USA finished first in the medal table, winning the most gold medals and overall medals (Tokyo 2020, 2021a, b, c, d, e, f, n.d.). Much like in 2016, once again American women won most of these medals, demonstrating the significance of Title IX in the American system and in American sports diplomacy. Some of the athletes who starred in Tokyo participated in diplomatic initiatives as envoys of the US Department of State, including two of the stars of the Olympic Games: Allyson Felix, who won a gold and a bronze medal in Tokyo, became the track and field athlete with most Olympic medals in the history, and Swimmer Katie Ledecky, who won three gold medals and two bronze ones (Norlander, 2021), making further history as one of the most decorated female Olympians (Bureau of Educational and Cultural Affairs, n.d.). Yet the American dominance was much less significant than in previous Games as only on the day of the closing ceremony did the USA pass China in the gold medal ranking (Tokyo 2020, Tokyo 2020, 2021a, b, c, d, e, f, g, n.d.). Through most of the Games, the Chinese anthem was the most played anthem on the podiums, especially in dominated events such as table tennis, weightlifting, and diving.

Aligning national goals with athletic success led to different attempts to improve the country's rankings, varying from specializing in specific disciplines, through naturalizing athletes who were born in other countries, to different forms of cheating including systematic doping going back to East Germany and the Soviet Union during the Cold War (Pigman, 2014; Zimbalist, 2016). In Tokyo 2020, the Russians due to a government-led doping scandal, and when athletes won gold medals, instead of the Russian national anthem, Tchaikovsky's "Piano Concerto No. 1" was played, demonstrating at least part of Russia's cultural depth. Much like many other hosting countries, Japan also enjoyed athletic success finishing third in the gold medal ranking, dominating some of the country's popular sports such as judo where Japanese athletes won 9 gold medals and 12 overall medals from 15 possibilities in the historic venue the Nippon Budokan (Tokyo 2020, 2021a, b, c, d, e, f, n.d.). Japan also won gold medals in some of the new or returning disciplines such as baseball and softball, three gold medals in skateboard, and one in karate.

Some countries specialize in specific disciplines or specific sports (Dubinsky, 2019a). In Tokyo 2020, Jamaican women and Caribbean athletes excelled in the sprints, while athletes from Kenya, Uganda, and Ethiopia excel in the long runs (Tokyo 2020, 2021a, b, c, d, e, f, n.d.). Perhaps one of the most extraordinary performances in the Tokyo Olympic

Games was by Ethiopian-born Dutch athlete Sifan Hassan, winning gold medals in 10,000 m and 5000 m, and a bronze medal in 1500 m. Australian women dominated the pool winning eight gold medals, led by Emma McKeon who won four gold medals and three bronze ones.

The Tokyo Olympic Games had two records of 88 different countries winning at least one medal, and 63 countries winning gold. Turkmenistan, San Marino, and Burkina Faso won their first Olympic medals, having their flags risen during the medal ceremony for the first time. The Philippines, Bermuda, and Qatar won their first gold medals, having their anthem played on the podium for the first time (Fowler, 2021). While Qatar's investment in sports has often been criticized for naturalization, sportswashing, or corruption (Zimbalist, 2016), a very different image of the country was projected when Qatari high jumper Mutaz Essa Barshim and Gianmarco Tamberi from Italy were tied at the end of the event, yet instead of having a jump-off, they both decided to share the top of the podium with each getting a gold medal (Abdul-Jabbar, 2021; Fowler, 2021), giving the Games an emotional feel-good moment.

While the IOC did give more flexibility to athletes to protests, the IOC still prohibits political boycotts through athletic competitions. The political manifestations and boycotts in the twenty-first century have been more subtle or even silent compared to the mass boycotts of the 1976, 1980, and 1984 Olympic Games (Dubinsky, 2019a). Yet there are still political manifestations in the Olympic Games, such as athletes from certain Arab and Muslim countries forced by their governments to withdraw from competing against Israelis under the guise of an injury (Dubinsky & Dzikus, 2019). Before the Tokyo 2020 Olympic Games, the Iranian Judo Federation was suspended for continuing with such policies (Palmer, 2021). Perhaps the most astonishing case was of judoka Saeid Mollaei, a former Iranian world champion who publicly criticized Iran's policies after being forced to lose a match to avoid facing an Israeli. As a result, Mollaei said he was afraid to return to Iran and fled to Europe, before officially becoming a citizen of Mongolia. He won a silver medal in Tokyo (Trouillard, 2021). There were two suspected silent boycotts in judo, with athletes from Algeria and Sudan. The Algerian athlete and his coach were suspended for 10 years by the International Judo Federation because of the incident (Reuters Staff, 2021). On the other hand, for the first time, an athlete from Saudi Arabia competed against Israeli Raz Hershko (Palmer, 2021). This should also be looked at through the lenses of the growing criticism of Israeli policies against the Palestinians and the growing support of international athletes and of Black Lives Matter with the Palestinian cause. Another issue related to the Israeli–Palestinian conflict that pertains to public diplomacy and the Olympic Games is the demand to officially commemorate the 11 Israeli athletes, coaches, and referees that were murdered in Munich during the 1972 Olympic Games (Dubinsky & Dzikus, 2019). For decades the families of the victims have been demanding that the 11 Munich victims will be commemorated in the opening ceremony, and in Tokyo 2020 for the first time they were mentioned as part of a moment of silence.

Much like in the 2016 Rio de Janeiro Olympic Games, Tokyo 2020 also included a delegation of refugees. The IOC Refugee Olympic Team included 29 athletes from 11 host countries, competing in 12 sports (International Olympic Committee, 2021b, c). Emphasizing the significance of the team, the delegation marched second in the opening ceremony, following Greece who always marches first. During the Games Belarusian athlete Krystsina Tsimanouskaya sought help from the IOC through social media after being taken to the airport for criticizing her government but refused to board the flight (Dunbar, 2021). Eventually, the athlete was granted a Polish visa after seeking refuge from Belarusian authorities. Such an example demonstrates the political significance countries see in participating in the Olympic Games, the challenge of containing freedom of speech and criticism in different cultures and regimes, some of the diplomatic roles the IOC is taking as a nongovernmental international organization, and the potential impact on the normative and sympathetic dimension of a country's image (Buhmann & Ingenhoff, 2015) through the framing of a country by international media.

Since World War II, every era in the Olympic Movement had some level of geopolitics impacting the Olympic Games (Dubinsky, 2019b). Issues such as the Israeli-Arab dispute or refugees are likely to continue to manifest through next Olympics, especially as they are tied to the growing waves of social justice. Furthermore, Russia broke the Olympic Truce during the Beijing 2022 Winter Olympic and Paralympic Games by invading Ukraine, which led to international suspensions of Russian and Belarusian athletes from several international sports competitions. The USA and several other Western countries announced a diplomatic boycott of Beijing 2022 due to Chinese ongoing human rights violations. Thus, the global nature geopolitics will manifest as well through the new era of the Olympic Movement.

A Digital-Cultural Era

The Olympic Games have been a platform for countries to improve the aesthetic dimensions (Buhmann & Ingenhoff, 2015) of their images through the exposure of their culture, heritage, and tourist attractions. Yet, without international fans arriving, much of these opportunities either are lost or depend on other gatekeepers such as the media. However, in the Tokyo (2020a, b, c, d, e, f, g) Olympic Games, even accredited journalists who were able to attend and cover the Games were under strict movement restrictions due to the pandemic. During the first months of 2021, the IOC and TOCOG published three versions of the *Playbook*—a book of guidelines for different stakeholders, with each version having more restrictions (Tokyo 2020, 2021a, b, c, d, e, f). As explained in the thirrd version of the *Playbook* for media, international media were under quarantine for their first 14 days in Japan, during which they were followed through mobile applications and were only allowed to go to Olympic venues and use Olympic-sanctioned transportation (Tokyo 2020, 2021a, b, c, d, e, f). This meant that even the media covering the Olympic Games were not allowed to visit tourist attractions or interact with locals during most of the Games. The windows of possibilities to capitalize on cultural diplomacy and/or on destination branding (Fan, 2010) and enrich the aesthetic and sympathetic dimensions (Buhmann & Ingenhoff, 2015) of Japan's image through in-person activities during the Olympic Games were extremely limited.

Traditionally, hosting and participating countries try to capitalize on Olympic Games through hosting cultural events. Some participating countries have an "Olympic House" in which they host different stakeholders and expose some of their food, music, and culture when hosting events, celebrations, or watch parties open to international fans traveling to the Olympic Games (Gordon, 2016). As no international fans were traveling to Tokyo, Olympic Houses were not used for nation branding and public diplomacy purposes as used in previous Games. Hosting countries and cities usually have a Cultural Olympiad during the Olympic Games, which includes education collaborations with schools and different exhibitions and programs. TOCOG, the Japanese government, and the city of Tokyo did hold several activities or events, including the Nippon Festival and the Olympic Agora (Tokyo 2020, 2021a, b, c, d, e, f). While some of the content was also available online, the main issue remained through most of the Games because of the restrictions that the only people who could attend were local Japanese; thus the impact on foreign publics was very limited.

Perhaps the events where the intersection between sports, culture, and diplomacy is the strongest are the opening and closing ceremonies. These ceremonies allow the hosting country to showcase its soft power by exposing its history and culture (Arning, 2013). In the closing ceremony for Rio de Janeiro 2016, during the section dedicated to the next hosting city Tokyo, Shinzo Abe, then the Prime Minister of Japan, appeared dressed as Super Mario (Rich, 2016). While the ceremonies in Tokyo did expose some Japanese traditions and even used popular video games music as athletes marched into the stadium (Dubinsky, 2022b), the comic and light-headed references from Rio de Janeiro 2016 rarely appeared. The opening ceremony was described in words such as "somber," "minimalist" (Akbar, 2021), "subdued" (Fadel, 2021), and even "depressing as hell" (Fallon, 2021). The closing ceremony traditionally has a celebratory theme, yet again was described as "somber" but also with "grace" (Ronay, 2021). With no fans, a minimal number of athletes in the stadium, and with increasing COVID-19 cases, the use of the ceremonies as a soft power tool to improve the aesthetic dimension and sympathetic dimension (Buhmann & Ingenhoff, 2015) of Japan was limited.

In 2021 the IOC (2021e) replaced its Agenda 2020 strategic plan with Agenda 2020+5, which included 15 recommendations on 5 new topics, with digitalization being one of them, along with sustainable development, credibility, and economic and financial resilience. The IOC especially recognizes the popularity and economic growth of esports with Gen Z and in new markets, but due to governance issues, violence in the games, and especially the question of physical activity, electronic games have yet to become an Olympic medal event. Dubinsky (2022b) uses the term sport-tech diplomacy to discuss the intersection between technology, sports, and diplomacy, which includes video games and esports, along with other technological innovations. Sport-tech diplomacy and the digitalization of cultural diplomacy are bound to share the future of the Olympic Movement.

An Era of Global Challenges and Backlash

The IOC draws its moral justification through a philosophy defined in The Olympic Charter (International Olympic Committee, 2020) as Olympism. The Olympic Charter outlines seven principles of Olympism, focusing on what it defines as "fundamental ethical principles" (International Olympic Committee, 2020, p. 11), using big words such as "harmonious development of humankind," "promoting a peaceful society," "preservation of human dignity," "friendship, solidarity, and fair play," and "political neutrality." Through the history of the Olympic Movement, political and commercial forces have challenged these ideals, with countries and other stakeholders using the Olympics to achieve their own social, economic, and political goals, resulting also in discrimination, wars, boycotts, cheating, and even terrorism (Dubinsky, 2019a; Murray, 2018). In recent years, the backlash against the IOC focused on the pragmatic manifestations of the Olympic Games, leading also to public spendings, social and financial negative legacies, and accusations of greenwashing (Boykoff, 2016; Boykoff & Gaffney, 2020). Examples vary from the financial debt of the Montreal 1976 Olympic Games, unused facilities and neglected facilities in previous Olympic Games, and environmental damage the organizations caused (Boykoff, 2016; Dubinsky, 2019b). In Agenda 2020+5 (IOC 2021e), the strategy the IOC published in 2021, the organization interlinks Olympism with its recommendations to strengthen the role of sport as an important enabler for the United Nations Sustainable Development Goals. Thus, having a sustainable legacy is linked with the philosophy of the movement and is challenged by capitalist and political forces.

For the Tokyo Olympic Games to go ahead, almost every stakeholder needed to compromise. From athletes needing to adjust their preparations to media needing to accept restrictions of freedom of the press to the Japanese people who were not allowed to attend the Games, all stakeholders had to adjust to a new reality for the Games to happen, and willingly or not, they did (Tokyo 2020, 2021a, b, c, d, e, f). Thus, from a macroperspective, over 200 countries and delegations saw more value in participating in the Tokyo 2020 Olympic Games and accepting restricting rules, than withdrawing. The IOC and TOCOG used slogans such as "United by Emotion," or even adjusted the Olympic Moto to "Faster, Higher, Stronger – Together" (Tokyo 2020, 2021a, b, c, d, e, f), reinforcing that message. Whether the cost was worth it or not, all stakeholders saw enough value in having the Games happening to collaborate.

An even larger global challenge than the pandemic that pertains to every country and person on this planet is the environment and global warming. Each hosting city tries to emphasize in its bidding process how hosting the Olympic Games will improve the quality of life or how sustainable the organization will be. In 2021 the IOC introduced Olympic

Agenda 2020 + 5, adding 15 recommendations to the original 40, including further emphasizing sustainability and the environment (International Olympic Committee, 2021e). Yet the practical challenges often overshadow such plans, and the IOC is often accused of greenwashing (Boykoff, 2016; Boykoff & Gaffney, 2020). As mentioned earlier, the Tokyo 2020 was originally framed as recovery and reconstruction games from a natural disaster, and the organization tried to demonstrate having sustainable policies that protect the environment. Examples include using electric and even automatic cars, temporary venues, and even awarding recycled medals. Global warming and climate change create a challenge in every continent, regardless of the economic status of the countries. Organizing committees and the IOC publish their sustainable activities of policies, but much of the growing criticism against the IOC is hosting Olympic Games in non-sustainable ways, damaging the environment (Boykoff, 2016; Zimbalist, 2016), and greenwashing (Boykoff & Gaffney, 2020). Perhaps if the Olympic Games would be in jeopardy of cancellation because of the environment, that would lead to a more united front against one of the world's greatest challenges.

There was no shortage of criticism against the Japanese government, the organizing committee, and the IOC about the Tokyo 2020 Olympic Games (Boykoff & Gaffney, 2020). The majority of the people of Tokyo did not support hosting the Games in the summer of 2021, sponsors and partners moderated their presence, there was a corruption scandal around the Games, numerous high-level officials resigned for various reasons, and protests against the Olympics followed the torch relay and occurred during the Games including outside the opening ceremony (Boykoff & Gaffney, 2020; Rosenberg, 2021). Much of the criticism focused on lack of transparency, misinformation, or misuse of data. The IOC and the organizing committee took pride in holding over 675,000 tests and having a 0.02% positivity rate (Burke, 2021), but still, there were over 500 positive COVID-19 cases related to the Olympic Games, including the lambda variant (The Japan Times, 2021). On July 23, the day of the opening ceremony, the Tokyo Media Center reported 1359 new daily cases in Tokyo (TMC, 2021). Within a few days after the Olympic Games, the daily cases have risen to over 5000 (Staff Report, 2021).

The local backlash against hosting the Tokyo 2020 Olympic Games also impacted Japan's corporate diplomacy. With the country being associated as a technological powerhouse, there were several Japanese TOP sponsors (Abel, 2021; International Olympic Committee, 2021a). Toyota, for example, provided a self-driving bus in the Olympic Village and hybrid electric cars for different stakeholders as part of a sustainability effort. Panasonic also provided tech services in the MPC and other Olympic venues. Yet, despite investing

hundreds of millions in the sponsorship agreements, after TOCOG announced that the Olympic Games will be held without fans, Toyota scaled back its advertising efforts in Japan, and Panasonic announced that the CEO of the company will not attend the opening ceremony (Kuhn, 2021).

The backlash against the Olympic Games has been gaining momentum over the years (Zimbalist, 2016). NOlympics groups emerge in almost every candidate, bidding, or hosting cities, protesting hosting the Games, demanding transparency, and emphasizing how the Games will hurt local communities (Nolympics LA, n.d.). Scholars have also been criticizing the Olympic Movement, questioning if the Olympic Games in their current form should even go ahead (Boykoff, 2016; Zimbalist, 2016). While the IOC does not necessarily depend on the support of local communities, the mayors and governments in the hosting cities and countries do need the people's support in upcoming elections. Thus, in countries such as France, the USA, and Australia, and next hosting cities such as Paris, Los Angeles, and Brisbane, ignoring the voices of the public can have a personal price. Whether through the unknown long-term implications of the pandemic, global warming, the environment, or social justice, border-crossing challenges are bound to galvanize resistance and impact the new era of the Olympic Movement.

Conclusion

This chapter emphasizes the ongoing importance of the Olympic Games for nation branding and public diplomacy, as, despite all the challenges, over 200 countries and delegations still see the importance of taking part in the most global event humanity holds (Tokyo 2020, 2021a, b, c, d, e, f). Tokyo 2020 showed that despite the pandemic and the related health risks, almost every country on Earth sees some value in taking part in the Olympic Games. Yet the Olympic Movement is also under extreme scrutiny, and the resistance is likely to keep growing. The Olympic Movement is changing, facing unprecedented backlash from local communities and different pressure groups, leading it to try and bypass dependency on the public's opinion.

The chapter identifies and discusses a variety of stakeholders that play significant roles in shaping the new era of the Olympic Movement through nation branding and public diplomacy lenses, including countries, NGOs, athletes, sponsors, broadcasters, and local and international communities. The chapter identifies different repeating characteristics that will shape the new era of the Olympic Movement, framing it as survival-oriented, mixed-legacy, post-woke, American-led but democracy-limiting, geopolitical, culturally digital, globally challenging, and backlash-facing era. The Olympic Movement also identified the dawn of a new era through its Agenda 2020+5 policies published in 2021 (International Olympic Committee, 2021e), where the IOC made 15 new recommendations related to solidarity, digitalization, sustainable development, credibility, and economic and financial resilience. They, of course, address at least some of the challenges identified in this chapter. This chapter and Dubinsky (2022a, b) argue that the new era starts with Tokyo 2020, while President Bach targets Paris 2024 (IOC News, 2022). The starting point of the era might only be determined retrospectively, and a more precise classification will be given in time. Either way, the Olympic Movement is in the process of change.

References

Abdi, K., Talebpour, M., Fullerton, J., Ranjkesh, M. J., & Nooghabi, H. J. (2019). Identifying sports diplomacy resources as soft power tools. *Place Branding & Public Diplomacy, 15*(3), 147–155. https://doi.org/10.1057/s41254-019-00115-9

Abdul-Jabbar, K. (2021, August 8). Kareem Abdul-Jabbar: What I learned watching the Tokyo Games. *The Hollywood Reporter*. Retrieved from https://www.hollywoodreporter.com/tv/tv-news/kareem-abdul-jabbar-olympics-lessons-1234994649/

Abel, J. R. (2021). Technologies of Cold War diplomacy: Transforming postwar Japan. *Technology and Culture, 62*(1), 128–155. https://doi.org/10.1353/tech.2021.0005

Akbar, A. (2021, July 23). Tokyo Olympic opening ceremony: Toil and mourning bloom into sparkling extravaganza. *The Guardian*. Retrieved from https://www.theguardian.com/sport/2021/jul/23/tokyo-olympic-opening-ceremony

Arning, C. (2013). Soft power, ideology and symbolic manipulation in Summer Olympic Games opening ceremonies: A semiotic analysis. *Social Semiotics, 23*, 523–544.

Bates, J., & Locker, M. (August 3, 2021). Despite IOC Restrictions, Team USA athletes are protesting at the Tokyo Olympics. TIME. Retrieved from https://time.com/6086632/us-olympic-protest-tokyo-rules/

Boykoff, J. (2016). *Power games: A political history of the Olympics*. Verso.

Boykoff, J., & Gaffney, C. (2020). The Tokyo 2020 games and the end of Olympic history. *Capitalism Nature Socialism, 31*(2), 1–19. https://doi.org/10.108 0/10455752.2020.1738053

Buhmann, A., & Ingenhoff, D. (2015). The 4D Model of the country image: An integrative approach from the perspective of communication management. *The International Communication Gazette, 77*, 102–124.

Bureau of Educational and Cultural Affairs. (n.d.). *Sports Envoy*. United States Department of State. Retrieved from https://eca.state.gov/sports-diplomacy/sports-envoy

Burke, P. (2021, August 11). Tokyo 2020-related COVID-19 cases top 500 as Japanese capital again reports more than 4,000 new infections. *Inside the Games*. Retrieved from https://www.insidethegames.biz/articles/1111525/tokyo-2020-covid-cases-top-500

CNN Editorial Research. (2021, April 15). BALCO Fast Facts. *CNN*. Retrieved from https://www.cnn.com/2013/10/31/us/balco-fast-facts/index.html

Cooper, J. N., Macaulay, C., & Rodriguez, S. S. (2019). Race and resistance: A typology of African American sport activism. *International Review for the Sociology of Sport, 54*(2), 151–181. https://doi.org/10.1177/1012690217718170

Cull, N. J. (2010). Public diplomacy: Severn lessons for its future from its past. *Place Branding and Public Diplomacy, 6*, 11–17. https://doi.org/10.1057/pb.2010.4

Dance, B. (2020, January 13). 'We shouldn't be silenced': IOC's protest ban cops backlash from athletes. *FOX Sports*. Retrieved from https://www.foxsports.com.au/olympics/we-shouldnt-be-silenced-iocs-protest-ban-cops-backlash-from-athletes/news-story/ca1e0cb83ef78088d00d129b3f02743c

Dubinsky, Y. (2019a). From soft power to sports diplomacy: A theoretical and conceptual discussion. *Place Branding and Public Diplomacy, 15*, 154–164. https://doi.org/10.1057/s41254-019-00116-8

Dubinsky, Y. (2019b). Analyzing the roles of country image, nation branding, and public diplomacy through the evolution of the modern Olympic movement. *Physical Culture and Sport Studies and Research, 84*(1), 27–40. https://doi.org/10.2478/pcssr-2019-0024

Dubinsky, Y. (2022a). The Olympic Games, nation branding, and public diplomacy in a post-pandemic world: Reflections on Tokyo 2020 and beyond. *Place Branding & Public Diplomacy*, 1–12. https://doi.org/10.1057/s41254-021-00255-x

Dubinsky, Y. (2022b). Sport-Tech Diplomacy at the Tokyo 2020 Olympic Games. *CPD Perspectives on Public Diplomacy*. USC Center for Public Diplomacy and

Figueroa Press. Retrieved from https://uscpublicdiplomacy.org/sites/default/files/Sport-Tech%20Diplomacy_11.21.22.pdf

Dubinsky, Y., & Dzikus, L. (2019). Israel's country image in the 2016 Olympic Games. *Place Branding and Public Diplomacy, 15*, 173–184. https://doi.org/10.1057/s41254-018-0105-y

Dunbar, G. (2021, August 2). Poland grants visa to Belarus Olympian who fears for safety. *AP*. Retrieved from https://apnews.com/article/2020-tokyo-olympics-krystsina-tsimanouskaya-belarus-asylum-8467db47e3dc84a0719e76a0eb0481a2

Fadel, L. (2021, July 23). With a subdued Opening Ceremony, the Tokyo Summer Olympics have officially kicked off. *npr*. Retrieved from https://www.npr.org/2021/07/23/1019892681/with-a-subdued-opening-ceremony-the-tokyo-summer-olympics-have-officially-kicked

Fallon, K. (2021, July 23). The Tokyo Olympics Opening Ceremony was depressing as hell. *Daily Beast*. Retrieved from https://www.thedailybeast.com/the-tokyo-olympics-opening-ceremony-was-depressing-as-hell

Fan, Y. (2010). Branding the nation: Towards a better understanding. *Journal of Place Branding and Public Diplomacy, 6*(2), 97–103.

Fowler, W. (2021, August 6). Which nations have claimed their first-ever medals in Tokyo? *NBC Olympics*. Retrieved from https://www.nbcolympics.com/news/which-nations-have-claimed-their-first-ever-medals-tokyo

GamesBids. (n.d.). Past Olympic host election results. *GamesBids*. Retrieved from https://gamesbids.com/eng/past-bid-results/

Gordon, A. (2016, August 8). Olympic hospitality houses are a place to cry and party during the Games. *Vice*. Retrieved from https://www.vice.com/en/article/jp7g5x/olympic-hospitality-houses-are-a-place-to-cry-and-party-during-the-games

Grez, M. (2019). Nike Oregon Project to shut down following Alberto Salazar ban. *CNN*. Retrieved from https://www.cnn.com/2019/10/11/sport/nike-oregon-project-shut-down-alberto-salazar-spt-intl/index.html

Handelman, S. (2012). The Minds of Peace Experiment: A laboratory for people-to-people diplomacy. *Israel Affairs, 18*(1), 1–11. https://doi.org/10.1080/13537121.2012.634278

Ingle, S. (2022, January 18). Athletes warned about speaking out against China at Winter Olympics. *The Guardian*. Retrieved from https://www.theguardian.com/sport/2022/jan/18/athletes-warned-speaking-out-china-winter-olympics

International Olympic Committee. (2014). *Olympic Agenda 2020 −20+20 Recommendations*. International Olympic Committee. Retrieved from https://stillmed.olympics.com/media/Document%20Library/OlympicOrg/Documents/Olympic-Agenda-2020/Olympic-Agenda-2020-20-20-Recommendations.pdf

International Olympic Committee. (2020). *The Olympic Charter.* International Olympic Committee. Retrieved from https://stillmed.olympic.org/media/Document%20Library/OlympicOrg/General/EN-Olympic-Charter.pdf

International Olympic Committee. (2021a, March). *Olympic Marketing Fact File 2021 Edition.* International Olympic Committee. Retrieved from https://stillmed.olympics.com/media/Documents/International-Olympic-Committee/IOC-Marketing-And-Broadcasting/IOC-Marketing-Fact-File-2021.pdf

International Olympic Committee. (2021b, August 8). Olympic Solidarity inspires record number of NOCs to medal. *Olympics.* Retrieved from https://olympics.com/ioc/news/olympic-solidarity-inspires-record-number-of-nocs-to-medal?fbclid=IwAR0wqyAooc66B9l06eBBcRMsIWjHdKgpPuscCbFH0JUSri5xorXNFAyVVZg

International Olympic Committee. (2021c). IOC Refugee Olympic Team Tokyo 2020. *Olympics.* Retrieved from https://olympics.com/ioc/refugee-olympic-team-tokyo-2020

International Olympic Committee. (2021d). *IOC extends opportunities for athlete expression during the Olympic Games Tokyo 2020.* International Olympic Committee. Retrieved from https://olympics.com/ioc/news/ioc-extends-opportunities-for-athlete-expression-during-the-olympic-games-tokyo-2020

International Olympic Committee. (2021e). *Olympic Agenda 2020+5– 15 Recommendations.* International Olympic Committee. Retrieved from https://stillmedab.olympic.org/media/Document%20Library/OlympicOrg/IOC/What-We-Do/Olympic-agenda/Olympic-Agenda-2020-5-15-recommendations.pdf

IOC News. (2022, July 26). With two years until Paris 2024, IOC President looks ahead to "new era" of Olympic Games. *Olympics.* Retrieved from https://olympics.com/ioc/news/with-two-years-until-paris-2024-ioc-president-looks-ahead-to-new-era-of-olympic-games

Kuhn, A. (2021, July 20). Toyota and other big Olympics sponsors are downplaying their ties to the Games. *npr.* Retrieved from https://www.npr.org/sections/tokyo-olympics-live-updates/2021/07/20/1018390493/toyota-and-other-big-olympics-sponsors-are-downplaying-their-ties-to-the-games

Kwiatkowski, M. (2021, July 27). Larry Nassar's abuse of gymnasts, including Simone Biles went back decades. Why it still matters in Tokyo. *USA Today.* Retrieved from https://www.usatoday.com/story/sports/olympics/2021/07/27/usa-gymnastics-larry-nasser-abuse-scandal-looms-over-tokyo-olympics/5375279001/

McCurry, J. (2021, June 10). 'Claims could run into billions': The interests at stake if Olympics in Japan were cancelled. *The Guardian.* Retrieved from https://www.theguardian.com/sport/2021/jun/10/claims-could-run-into-billions-the-interests-at-stake-if-olympics-in-japan-were-cancelled

Morgan, L. (2021, September 8). North Korea banned from Beijing 2022 after IOC suspends NOC. *Inside the Games*. Retrieved from https://www.insidethegames.biz/articles/1112768/ioc-suspends-north-korea-noc-beijing2022

Murray, S. (2018). *Sports diplomacy: Origins, theory and practice*. Routledge.

Nolympics LA. (n.d.). Retrieved from https://nolympicsla.com/

Norlander, M. (2021, August 8). Katie Ledecky makes history with 6th individual gold, cements Olympic icon status, and she'll be back in 2024. *CBS Olympics*. Retrieved from https://www.cbssports.com/olympics/news/katie-ledecky-makes-history-with-6th-individual-gold-cements-olympic-icon-status-and-shell-be-back-in-2024/

Palmer, D. (2021, July 30). IJF praises Saudi Arabian for facing Israeli opponent at Tokyo 2020. *Inside the Games*. Retrieved from https://www.insidethegames.biz/articles/1110991/judo-israel-saudi-arabia-bout

Pigman, G. A. (2014). International sport and diplomacy's public dimension: Governments, sporting federations and the global audience. *Diplomacy & Statecraft*, 25(94), 94–114. https://doi.org/10.1080/09592296.2014.873613

Reuters Staff. (2021, September 13). Judo-Algerian Nourine gets 10-year ban for withdrawing from Olympics to avoid Israel. *Reuters*. Retrieved from https://www.reuters.com/article/judo-algeria-sanctions-idAFL4N2QG1A0

Rich, M. (2016, August 22). A morning surprise for Japan: Shinzo Abe as Super Mario. *The New York Times*. Retrieved from https://www.nytimes.com/2016/08/23/world/asia/shinzo-abe-super-mario-tokyo-rio-olympics.html

Ronay, B. (2021, August 8). Tokyo says goodbye to the Games with grace and sense of relief. *The Guardian*. Retrieved from https://www.theguardian.com/sport/2021/aug/08/tokyo-says-goodbye-to-the-games-with-grace-and-sense-of-relief

Rosenberg, M. (2021, July 23). Pandemic, protests loom over lackluster Opening Ceremony at Tokyo Olympics. *Sports Illustrated*. Retrieved from https://www.si.com/olympics/2021/07/23/opening-ceremony-tokyo-olympics-pandemic-protestors-empty-stadium

Staff Report. (2021, August 14). COVID-19 tracker: Tokyo logs over 5,000 new cases as number of severely ill patients continues to rise. *The Japan Times*. Retrieved from https://www.japantimes.co.jp/news/2021/08/14/national/japan-cases-wrap-august-14/

The Japan Times. (2021, August 13). First Japan case involving lambda COVID-19 variant linked to Olympics. *The Japan Times*. Retrieved from https://www.japantimes.co.jp/news/2021/08/14/national/japan-cases-wrap-august-14/

TMC. (2021, July 23). COVID-19 Updates from the TMC – July 23, 2021. Tokyo Media Center. *TMC Newsletter*.

Tokyo 2020. (2021a). The playbooks. *Olympics*. Retrieved from https://olympics.com/tokyo-2020/en/games/tokyo-2020-playbooks/
Tokyo 2020. (2021b, May). Media handbook. The Tokyo Organising Committee of the Olympic and Paralympic Games.
Tokyo 2020. (2021c, July). *Tokyo 2020 Olympic Games opening ceremony media guide*. Tokyo 2020.
Tokyo 2020. (2021d, August). *Tokyo 2020 Olympic Games opening ceremony media guide*. Tokyo 2020.
Tokyo 2020. (2021e, June 30). First Olympic Agora cultural hub opens in Tokyo. *Olympics*. Retrieved from https://olympics.com/tokyo-2020/en/news/first-olympic-agora-cultural-hub-opens-in-tokyo
Tokyo 2020. (2021f). Explore Japan. *Olympics*. Retrieved from https://olympics.com/tokyo-2020/en/events/
Tokyo 2020. (n.d.). Olympic medal table. *Olympics*. Retrieved from https://olympics.com/tokyo-2020/olympic-games/en/results/all-sports/medal-standings.htm
Trouillard, S. (2021, July 28). Freedom-flavoured silver medal for Iranian-born judoka competing for Mongolia. *France 24*. Retrieved from https://www.france24.com/en/sport/20210728-tokyo-games-freedom-flavoured-silver-medal-for-iranian-born-judoka-competing-for-mongolia
USADA. (2021, October 10). Statement from USADA CEO Travis T. Tygart regarding The U.S. Postal Service Pro Cycling Team doping conspiracy. *USADA*. Retrieved from https://www.usada.org/statement/statement-from-usada-ceo-travis-t-tygart-regarding-the-u-s-postal-service-pro-cycling-team-doping-conspiracy/
Zaccardi, N. (2020, June 4). Gwendolyn Berry gets apology from USOPC CEO after reprimand for podium gesture. *NBC Sports*. Retrieved from https://olympics.nbcsports.com/2020/06/04/gwen-berry-protest/
Zimbalist, A. (2016). *Circus Maximus*. Brookings Institution Press.
Zirin, D., & Boykoff, J. (2021, June 16). The IOC says the 2032 Olympics are coming to Brisbane. *The Nation*. Retrieved from https://www.thenation.com/article/society/ioc-brisbane-olympics-2032/

CHAPTER 5

American Sports Diplomacy Amid the 50 Years Anniversary of Title IX

Introduction

The purpose of this chapter is to explore and discuss the role of Title IX on nation branding and country image 50 years after the legislation came into effect. Title IX of the Education Amendments of 1972 is an amendment to the US Education Act signed by President Richard Nixon on June 23, 1972, stating: "No person in the United States shall, on the basis of sex, be excluded from participation in, be denied the benefits of, or be subjected to discrimination under any education program or activity receiving Federal financial assistance" (U.S. Department of Education, 2021; NCAA, 2022). Title IX prohibits discrimination based on sex in any education system that receives financial support, pertaining predominantly to the following areas: "recruitment, admissions, and counseling; financial assistance; athletics; sex-based harassment, which encompasses sexual assault and other forms of sexual violence; treatment of pregnant and parenting students; treatment of LGBTQI+ students; discipline; single-sex education; and employment" (U.S. Department of Education, 2021). There is ample scholarship discussing the impacts of Title IX, power struggles based on gender and race, growth of women's sports, limitation of Title IX on compensation of student-athletes, inclusion and exclusion of transgender athletes, and other social, financial, and economic, psychological, and health issues affecting American society (Cooky et al., 2015; Staurowsky, 2012; Woods & Butler, 2021). Yet most of the scholarships focus domestically on American society.

© The Author(s), under exclusive license to Springer Nature Switzerland AG 2023
Y. Dubinsky, *Nation Branding and Sports Diplomacy*,
https://doi.org/10.1007/978-3-031-32550-2_5

The chapter discusses the roles of Title IX as it relates to foreign publics and the place of the USA within the international system. Due to its popularity and international exposure, countries, cities, and communities have been using sports to try and achieve social, political, and economic goals by projecting an attractive positive image (Dubinsky, 2019; Murray, 2018). Nation branding and one of its outcomes—country image—are multidisciplinary fields, analyzed through theories and lenses drawn from political science, marketing, sociology, and communication (Buhmann & Ingenhoff, 2015; Fan, 2010). The chapter follows the structure of previous work by Cull (2010) when suggesting seven lessons on public diplomacy and by Dubinsky's reflections on nation branding and public diplomacy implications of the Tokyo 2020 Olympic Games (Dubinsky, 2022a) and on sports, Brand America, and US sports diplomacy during the presidency of Donald Trump (Dubinsky, 2021a). Much like the mentioned studies (Cull, 2010; Dubinsky, 2021a, 2022a), this chapter synthesizes dozens of relevant academic scholarships with contemporary conceptual sources, providing lessons scholars and practitioners can use when analyzing the role of Title IX in Brand America and US sports diplomacy and why the world adopts some American values but rejects the practices behind them.

Nation Branding, Country Image, and Brand America

Due to the multidisciplinary nature of nation branding (Fan, 2010), a country's image is complex, dynamic, and multileveled (Buhmann & Ingenhoff, 2015), including the image of the USA, which is also referred to as Brand America (Martin, 2007; Dubinsky, 2021a, 2022b). One of the key theoretical lenses when analyzing political branding and public diplomacy is soft power (Nye, 2004), which refers to attempts to achieve foreign policy goals through attractions, rather than through military force and or economic sanctions. The USA used smart power (Nye, 2008), a combination of soft power and hard power, during the Cold War, which helped the Americans to prevail over the Soviet Union that collapsed. The use of soft power to expose American culture and American lifestyle, along with the USA becoming the sole superpower and the capitalist system becoming the predominant economic system worldwide, helped shape the image of the USA as the Land of Opportunity (Martin, 2007) with some of the values attributed to Brand America being freedom, personal opportunity, capitalism, competition, individualism, rebelliousness, and respect for others, along with arrogance, ignorance insensitivity, and self-absorption. Yet relying on hard power in recent decades exemplified by the invasion of Iraq in 2003 deteriorated the country's image and increased anti-American sentiments (Martin, 2007; Nye, 2004, 2008). According to the Nation Brands Index, "disapproval of American invasion of Iraq affected the world's view of the American population American products, American culture, and even the American landscape itself" (Anholt, 2010a, p. 68). All led to criticism of American foreign policy as hypocrisy and to rejection of the American way of life (Glaser, 2006; Martin, 2007). The USA is also being internationally scrutinized for its negative impact on the planet and climate (The Good Country Index, n.d.) and questionable policies and practices regarding gun control, healthcare, and racism (Dubinsky, 2022a, b).

There are many examples of how the USA has used sports over the years for nation branding and public diplomacy, such as boycotting the Olympic Games in Moscow during the Cold War (Murray, 2018; Pigman, 2014), exposing American culture in the Opening Ceremonies (Arning, 2013), shaping international sports through American commercialism (Dubinsky, 2022b), diplomatic initiatives by the US Department of States through athletes (Cooper, 2019), or even "ping-pong diplomacy" between American and Chinese delegates that led to official meetings between the heads of states (Dubinsky, 2019; Murray, 2018). In recent years, Dubinsky has been researching the intersection of sports, nation branding, and country image in America, through the United States Women's National Team (USWNT) in soccer (Dubinsky, 2021b), during the presidency of Donald Trump (Dubinsky, 2021a), through the projected images in the long-running animated political satire South Park (Dubinsky, 2021c) and international coverage of the 2021 Super Bowl Game (Dubinsky, 2022b). Through the analyses, Dubinsky (2021a, b, c, 2022a, b) argues that (a) sports does not just play a nation building role in the USA but is also a significant component associated with American culture that helps construct the aesthetic dimension of the country's image, (b) gender plays a role in Brand America's image through sports, and (c) the constructed image of the USA also relies on questionable values on social, economic, and racial exploitations. This chapter explores and discusses how Title IX complements, contradicts, and manifests through Brand America and US sports diplomacy, suggesting six lessons for scholars and practitioners. The lessons and their manifestations are summarized in Table 5.1.

Lesson 1: Title IX Adds to America's Identity as "Land of Opportunity"

One of the core images of branding is being labeled as the "Land of opportunity" (Martin, 2007, p. 57). According to Fan (2010), nation branding reflects also domestic branding through national identity, which he refers to as cultural branding. Social identity theory argues that individuals' self-identity is influenced by the social groups they associate with (David and Bar-Tal, 2009). According to David and Bar-Tal (2009), national identity is a specific example of collective identity, based on shared history, culture, traditions, myths, memories, and other social

Table 5.1 Lessons on Title IX Brand America and US sports diplomacy

Lesson on Title IX and the USA	Nation branding and public diplomacy manifestations
1. Title IX adds to America's identity as "Land of Opportunity"	More girls and women participate in high school and collegiate sports Growing sports business ecosystem targeting women International female students come to study in the USA
2. Title IX is America's sustainable competitive advantage	High-level facilities and conditions in American collegiate sports system Advantage in depth and breadth in international competitions
3. Title IX is an ongoing revolutionary process	Results from the women's liberation movement Every generation uses the achievements of previous generations to continue the fight for equality A culture of struggles and protests Protests in America have international implications
4. Title IX is a tool for US foreign policy	Official foreign programs by the US Department of State regardless of partisan leadership Aligned with foreign policy following the terror attacks of September 11, 2001 Athletes sent abroad as ambassadors International leaders come to America to learn about the American way of life
5. Title IX covers up American hypocrisy	A culture of sexual violence in American sports American institution systematically covered up sexual violence against hundreds of female gymnasts Political economy of collegiate sports relies on racial exploitation
6. Title IX fosters globalization	Movement of athletes, ideas, and coaches between borders Globalization improved women's sports in the USA and abroad Opportunities for corporate diplomacy and sport-tech diplomacy through a growing sports business ecosystem

characteristics. President Joe Biden repeated that message during his presidential acceptance speech, saying "I've always believed we can define America in one word: 'Possibilities'. That in America everybody should be given an opportunity to go as far as their dreams and God-given abilities will take them" (The Associated Press, 2020). Thus, the words "opportunity" and "possibilities" are used not only to Brand America's image to foreign publics but also as part of shaping US national identity.

With a perspective of half a century, Title IX embodies the authenticity of that message as over 10 times more girls participate in organized high school sports and over seven times more in college sports since the law passed in 1972, making female student-athletes over 40% of collegiate athletes in the USA (NCAA, 2022; Woods & Butler, 2021). According to the National Collegiate Athletics Association's (NCAA) Title IX 50th Anniversary Report (NCAA, 2022), 47% of Division I student-athletes are female. Title IX revolutionized American sports by providing more opportunities for girls and women to engage and compete for longer periods on high levels. It also organically developed an industry for women's sports equipment, clothes, and merchandise, creating more job opportunities in sports for women and expanding the entire sports business ecosystem (Dees et al., 2022; Woods & Butler, 2021). Nike, one of America's most recognized brands (Martin, 2007), was one of the first companies to recognize the social change through its commercials, using female athletes in advertising in the 1980s (Nike News, 2015) and leading to campaigns in the 1990s directed towards girls and women such as "If you let me play" in which they emphasize the benefits on women's development and health (Lucas, 2000). Export branding (Fan, 2010) perspectives of nation branding through the lenses of product-country image and country of origin, also analyzing the brand equity of the "made in" label (Johansson, 1989; Nebenzahl et al., 1997). According to Martin (2007) who analyzed Brand America, "The Nike Swoosh is a badge that identifies the wearer as someone who's energetic and a bit of the rebel, whether roller-blading or lying in a hammock" (p. 99). As a market leader, Nike continued to headline female athletes such as Serena Williams, USWNT players, and other top American and international athletes, while innovating women's sportswear by designing a hijab allowing Muslim female athletes to compete and practice sports without violating their religious beliefs and traditions (Dubinsky, 2021b; Martin, 2007). Following multiple campaigns featuring the USWNT and other top athletes to domestic American audiences, Nike also used the soccer team as part of the international campaign "Dream Further," along with female soccer stars from around the world, before the 2019 FIFA Women's World Cup (Dubinsky, 2021b). Such exposure also leads to commercial success, with the jersey of the USWNT becoming the most sold jersey on Nike.com (Dubinsky, 2021b). Thus, Title IX created more opportunities for more girls and women to engage in sports in the USA, and, as a result, developed the American sports business ecosystem and opened further opportunities abroad for American stakeholders to engage with the international publics.

Lesson 2: Title IX Is America's Sustainable Competitive Advantage

According to Martin (2007), one of the values associated with Brand America is competition, along with innovation and entrepreneurship. As seen in the discussion on opportunities, by increasing the number of participating girls and women, the market responds with innovative solutions to the growing demand. That demand also reflects on and off the field competition. As college football is the most revenue-generating sports in collegiate athletics and Division 1, the highest level of competitions, universities allocated between 60 and 85 full-time scholarships to a men's sport. This means that the universities will need to create women's sports teams and provide the same number of scholarships and conditions to women (Woods & Butler, 2021). While American football in the big Division I conferences generates billions of dollars, according to the NCAA financial reports, on average every collegiate women's sports are losing money (NCAA, 2021a; Woods & Butler, 2021). With college tuition being a financial burden on American families, athletics for women became a competitive option for households. This led to a constant state of ongoing competition for scholarships, competition within the team and against other colleges, and an increasing level of talents and technical bars to reach the next level. Furthermore, with equaled level conditions, training, medical support, and facilities, the elite of the American collegiate system is world-class level.

American female athletes are the USA's sustainable competitive advantage in international sports. In the last summer Olympic Games, London 2012, Rio de Janeiro 2016, and Tokyo 2020, female athletes were over 50% of Team USA, winning most of the American medals and leading the USA to the top of the medal rankings (Dubinsky, 2021a, 2022b). In soccer, the USWNT has won a medal in each FIFA Women's World Cup or Olympic Games except for Rio 2016. In basketball, the US Women's National Team won a gold medal in each Olympic Games since the domestic hosted competitions in Atlanta 1996 (Olympics, n.d.). These Games were also the first ones where the USA won its first all-around women's gymnastics team gold medal, achievements repeated in London 2012 and Rio 2016 under the leadership of Aly Raisman. Simone Biles is the most decorated gymnast when combining world champions and Olympic Games. While many Olympic-level gymnasts who train intensively from a young age, including Raisman and Biles, did not develop through the collegiate sports system, they still exemplify how Title IX encourages girls across America to participate in sports, leading to elite-level performances. Allyson Felix is the most decorated track and field Olympian, and Katie Ledecky is the most decorated female Olympic swimmer—both studied at universities in California. According to the NCAA (2021b), over 75% of Team USA athletes competed in college. Title IX is responsible for the development of these athletes, as they develop through high intense competitions, in high-level facilities, and with expert coaching, medical, and technological support, regardless of the revenue generation of their collegiate program. This is unique to the USA, as in other countries professional sports do not develop through the educational system but through clubs (Ridpath, 2018), which are not protected from open-market competitions and needs by legislation such as Title IX. A legislation that equals conditions regardless of market demand, benefitting from billions-of-dollars revenue-generating American football (Dubinsky, 2021a, 2022b; NCAA, 2021a). Countries see nation branding opportunities in winning, showing the superiority of their system, rising their national flags on the podium while having their anthem played, and generating interest in the background stories of their athletes and where they grew up (Dubinsky, 2019; Murray, 2018). Some countries specialize in specific sports or disciplines such as Jamaica in sprints or Norway in winter sports, and some develop holistic training programs, some naturalize athletes born in other countries to increase competitiveness, and some result in corruption, cheating, and even doping systems (Dubinsky, 2019). Thus, the sustainable competitive advantage the USA has on the playing field thanks to American women topping Olympic podiums can potentially translate to soft power as well.

The appeal of the American collegiate system also attracts international talents, which also have nation branding and public diplomacy implications. Over 1000 athletes representing over 100 countries in Tokyo 2020 also competed in the NCAA, winning 282 medals in Japan for over 20 countries (Johnson, 2021). International talents who compete in collegiate sports increase the level of training and competition, bring foreign knowledge to the American system, and push the level even further. The investments in collegiate sports also make American colleges and universities appealing to international students (Zhou et al., 2021), who in 2019 contributed $38.7 billion to the US economy. Thus, through competition in collegiate athletics as manifested with and through Title IX, the USA not only manages to separate itself on the medal rankings (Olympics, n.d.) and generate more interest and exposure but also reaches out to foster relations with international stakeholders.

Lesson 3: Title IX Is an Ongoing Revolutionary Process

Revolution and constant strive for growth, change, and freedom are embodied in American history and the American image, especially as it pertains to fights for freedom and capital (Martin, 2007). The American Revolution was influenced by the French Revolution and the Industrial Revolution, leading to the Boston Tea Party of 1773—protests against British colonial tax (Martin, 2007). From its Founding Fathers who wrote the Declaration of Independence and US Constitution, through community leaders such as Martin Luther King Junior Jr., to twenty-first-century presidents such as Barack Obama, American leaders framed the narrative of American democracy as a revolutionary experiment, an ongoing process of nonlinear growth of making a more perfect union and dreaming on a brighter unknown future (King Jr., 1965; npr, 2018). Through these lenses, of history and culture of revolution embodied in the American DNA, and with revolution tied to financial gains, Title IX is another manifestation of this ongoing process. Title IX was born out of the Women's Liberation Movement in the 1960s and 1970s, and every step of progress required a fight for change (Woods & Butler, 2021). One of the champions of Title IX was Billie Jean King, former world number one tennis player, who fought nationally and internationally to improve women's rights in sports. Although known for the symbolic Battle of the Sexes victory over retired world number one male tennis player Bobby Riggs, her lasting legacies were fighting for and creating a future for women's sports, through a professional tennis tour and through Title IX (Ware, 2011). After the passage of the legislation, female leaders and athletes needed to continue to fight for schools to follow it.

Title IX created a culture of generational protests, as every improvement was not given but earned through resistance, and every generation of women used the achievements of previous generations to take the fight for equality forward. One of the most famous protests was in Yale in 1976, where female rowers stripped naked in front of the director of women's athletics, having the words "Title IX" written on their chests and backs protesting the team's conditions (Sharrow, 2017). Billie Jean King helped form Title IX under which Pat Summitt fought for growing women's college basketball in Tennessee since the 1970s (Parker et al., 2022), which led to the development of talents across America. Talents such as Cheryl Miller from the University of Southern California (USC) in the 1980s helped grow women's basketball through domestic collegiate rivalries and made it more popular by leading the USA to win its first Olympic gold medal in a women's basketball in the Los Angeles 1984 Olympic Games, under the coaching of Summitt at the national team (Zaccardi, 2016). Despite professional women's basketball leagues struggling to sustain themselves, that growth of talent through Title IX inspired more African Americans to excel in basketball, including Sheryl Swoopes and Lisa Leslie, who not only led the USA to win gold in the Atlanta 1996 Olympic Games but were also among the first stars of the Women's National Basketball Association (WNBA) which started the following year (Parker et al., 2022) and celebrated its 25th season in 2021. With a professional league on the horizon, a new generation of athletes such as Candace Parker developed under Pat Summitt in Tennessee, and Sue Bird, Diana Taurasi, Maya Moore, and countless other top athletes developed in the emerging collegiate powerhouse Connecticut, along with dozens of talents across America who followed their footsteps (Parker et al., 2022). And when their generation reached the WNBA, they took social fights forward, about women's rights, gender equality, and social justice, with some of them being in the front end of Black Lives Matter (Williams, 2022). And the next generations continue such struggles, as seen by University of Oregon student Sedona Prince exposing gender inequality in the NCAA National Championship Tournaments leading to the organization improving the women's training conditions and marketing both tournaments under the March Madness brand (Murphy, 2022), female basketball players capitalizing on the newly introduced laws and regulations that enable student-athletes to get compensation on their name, image, and likeness (NIL) (NIL Summit, 2022), and the basketball community on all levels calling the White House to bring former WNBA, NCAA, and Olympic champion Brittney Griner back to the USA from Russia after being arrested and sentenced to 25 years in prison (Jackson, 2022a; Greenwalt, 2022). After spending 10 months in Russian prison, Griner was returned to the USA as part of a prisoner exchange deal, for notorious arms dealer Viktor Bout (Greenwalt, 2022), which signifies the diplomatic significance of top female American athletes in American foreign policy.

Title IX provides depth and breadth of talents, along with education, so when athletes take the next step, they have social awareness. The USWNT is an example of that generational fight, in which every group of athletes needed to fight for further development of a women's sport that was introduced to the Olympic Movement only in 1996 (Dubinsky, 2021b; Olympics, n.d.). The USWNT did not just need to win the FIFA Women's World Cup in 1992 and the Olympic Medal in 1996 but had to physically advertise the 1999 FIFA Women's World Cup in schools, so fans will attend a US-hosted tournament, leading up to fill the Rose Bowl Stadium in the final (Foudy & Leyden, 2013). The success of Mia Hamm, Brandi Chastain, and their group inspired future generational athletes such as Abby Wambach who also fought for LGBTQ rights and Hope Solo, Carli Lloyd, Alex Morgan, and Megan Rapinoe, who showed the commercial potential of the team when receiving unprecedented ratings for soccer in America when winning the 2015 FIFA Women's World Cup, leading to a growing dispute with U.S. Soccer about equal pay (Dubinsky, 2021b). Rapinoe was in the front of challenging the status quo of on-field protests for social justice in 2016 being one of the first white athletes to join Colin Kaepernick in kneeling. Rapinoe's act was labeled as unpatriotic, she was not allowed to protest that way by U.S. Soccer, and she was criticized by former President Donald Trump before the 2019 FIFA Women's World Cup (Dubinsky, 2021a, b; Fredrick et al., 2020; Schmidt et al., 2018). All these actions manifested with structural changes, as U.S. Soccer appointed 1999 world champion Cindy Parlow Cone as its president apologized to Rapinoe and reached an equal pay for equal work agreement with the players, equaling the prize money received from FIFA, despite the men's bonuses being significantly higher (Dubinsky, 2021a, b; U.S. Soccer, 2022). These ongoing fights for change could not be successful without the on-field success that generates interest from the American public who want to celebrate the national team's success which increases exposure and revenues. Title IX provides the depth and breadth of talent that creates that generational continuity. Yet, with the understanding that the American public is the target audience for the players to achieve their social and financial goals, USWNT players have been accused of manifestation negative American stereotypes such as being self-centered and arrogant in international competitions (Dubinsky, 2021b; Martin, 2007).

Parlow Cone (2022) is just one of many top-level administrators who benefited from Title IX as a student-athlete, leading to a career in a leadership position where they can make policies and create change. Becky Hammon broke gender barriers by becoming the first full-time female assistant coach of an NBA team (Dubinsky, 2021a), Dawn Staley received a multimillion-dollar salary for coaching the University of South Carolina's basketball team (Coleman, 2021), and every year more and more former female athletes get into the front office or coaching positions in the National Football League (NFL), Major League Baseball (MLB), and other professional sports. The success of American athletes also led to inspiring athletes around the world to take a stand. Billie Jean King inspired Serena and Venus Williams (AP, 2018), who kept fighting for social justice and gender equality, inspiring Japanese tennis player Naomi Osaka to support Black Lives Matter and raise awareness of social challenges she was facing in the form of mental health. Following social protests in the USA, including by leading American female athletes such as Gwen Berry who protested on the podium in the Pan-American Games against racial inequality in the USA, the International Olympic Committee relaxed its anti-protest policies in Tokyo 2020 Olympic Games (Dubinsky, 2021a, 2022a). Following the USWNT resolving their dispute with U.S. Soccer and the federation announcing the equal allocation of revenues from FIFA, other football associations also took equaling steps to improve their nation teams (Dixon, 2022; U.S. Soccer, 2022). Progress and change are not linear, including—and maybe especially—in the USA. There are ample obstacles and challenges, yet revolution is in the American DNA, and Title IX provides human capital to manifest, foster, and grow that demand for change through amateurish, professional, domestic, and international platforms.

Lesson 4: Title IX Is a Tool for US Foreign Policy

Nation branding and country image potential of Title IX are not lost on the US government, regardless of its partisan leadership (Bureau of Educational and Cultural Affairs, n.d.-a). Buhmann and Ingenhoff (2015) analyze a country's image through four dimensions: functional, normative, aesthetic, and sympathetic. The functional dimension pertains to the capabilities of a country, its infrastructure, telecommunication, and overall functionality. Through the impact of Title IX, the USA manages to demonstrate a system where women have growth opportunities, dominating international sports, leading to the market demand for new innovative solutions, and establishing themselves in leadership positions of governance. The normative dimension pertains to the ethics of countries, such as laws and forms of government. Title IX demonstrates an investment in women and that even the most capitalist country on Earth has socialist laws that benefit society. The aesthetic dimension of a country pertains to its nature, scenery, culture, and history. Title IX embodies the rich history of the USA, the athletes reaching international success expose the diversity of the country, and with their success, international federations see the USA as a favorable venue to host events, which bring further opportunities to promote the country as an attractive tourism destination. The fourth dimension is the sympathetic, constructed by the first three dimensions and captures attitudes and feelings towards a country. To capitalize on that, the US government takes active steps and measures.

After the terror attacks of September 11, 2001, the US Department of State revisited its public diplomacy, trying to identify the growing anti-American sentiments worldwide. One of the operational actions the Department of State took was to create a sports diplomacy branch under the Bureau of Educational and Cultural Affairs, later to be named the US Department of State's Sports Diplomacy Division (Bureau of Educational and Cultural Affairs, n.d.-a). Nye (2008) argues that after becoming the only global superpower after the Cold War, the USA overemphasized its military strength, neglecting some of its useful soft power strategies. With the invasion of Iraq further damaging America's international image (Martin, 2007), Nye (2008) recommended the USA rediscover its smart power. Culture is one of the key components of soft power (Nye, 2004) as a form of attraction, and sports can be seen and used as a subset of cultural diplomacy (Dubinsky, 2019). The US Department of State's Sports Diplomacy Division (Bureau of Educational and Cultural Affairs, n.d.-a) emphasizes the significance of women's sports and Title IX through international initiatives. Such initiatives include sending athletes abroad to play diplomatic roles and inviting delegations to the USA to teach about the American way of life, using traditional public diplomacy aligned which is designed by the state and aligned with foreign policy goals and people-to-people diplomacy through individual citizens (Handelman, 2012) and corporate diplomacy in which private companies are involved (Ordeix-Rigo & Durate, 2009; White, 2015). Title IX and women empowerment are at the center of some of these programs. For example, the Global Sports Mentorship Program is a joint effort by the US Department of State and espnW in which international leaders visit the USA and meet with executives in the sports sector receiving mentorship for promoting inclusion and gender equality (Bureau of Educational and Cultural Affairs, n.d.-a, b; Office of the Spokesperson, 2022). The Sports Visitor Program brings youth elite athletes to the USA and includes sessions discussing the "impact on sports in America such as the Civil Rights Movement, Title IX, and the Americans with Disabilities Act" (Evaluation Division, December 2020, p. 1). The Sports Envoy Program recruits professional American athletes to travel on behalf of the US government to improve bilateral relations (Bureau of Educational and Cultural Affairs, n.d.-b). Over 300 sports envoys from 24 sports participated in such programs, including some of the most decorated American female athletes such as former WNBA MVP and four times Olympic gold medalist Tamika Catchings, dozens of USWNT players including two-time world champion Alex Morgan, swimming royalty Katie Ledecky, track and field star Allyson Felix, two-time Olympic gold medalist snowboarder American Korean Chloe Kim, and many more decorated athletes. Kim continues a legacy of successful Asian-American athletes who excelled in the Winter Olympic Games, including five-time world champion and two-time Olympic medalist former figure skater Chinese American Michelle Kwan who became an official public diplomacy envoy, serving during the Republican administration of George W. Bush and the Democratic administrations of Barack Obama and Joe Biden. Thus, the use of Title IX and gender for official public diplomacy purposes to create an attractive image of America is bipartisan and state-orchestrated.

Lesson 5: Title IX Covers Up American Hypocrisy

Over a third of the countries in the world had a female head of state at least once, 63 of them after 1960, but as of 2022, not the USA (Geiger & Kent, 2015; Statista, 2022). Yet, despite that, American governments are trying to frame the USA as a champion and revolutionary for gender equality. As established in the previous lesson, Title IX is used by the US government for foreign policy purposes, predominantly to enhance the normative image of the USA with international audiences (Dubinsky, 2021a, b). Yet much of the critique against US foreign policy is being hypocritical (Glaser, 2006) and pretending to act in a virtuous way while having weak morals and other motives. According to Glaser (2006), the USA does not practice what it preaches, and the state, as an actor, does not act consistently in a moral way. Successful public diplomacy and nation branding result from credible messages and moral policies (Cull, 2010). Thus, being consistently framed as hypocritical contradicts the credibility of a country, limiting nation branding and diplomatic efficiency, and questions the authenticity of the moral dimensions of a country's image. Title IX has some limitations. To name a few, Title IX applies only to the education system and has a limited direct impact on the open market where most women's sports struggle to compete financially (Woods & Butler, 2021). Part of the critics about the incarceration of Brittney Griner in Russia was around the need for professional female American basketball players to play abroad during the offseason of the WNBA, as the league's salaries are significantly lower not just in comparison to men's professional sports but to other countries (Owens, 2022). Other limitations of Title IX in open-market economies are that women's sports receive very little coverage on ESPN SportsCenter and national news (Cooky et al., 2015). Furthermore, as only men's football and men's basketball generate profits, schools need to consider a double financial loss whenever they offer more men's sports as they will need to offer a similar women's team that will also lose money, and it has not provided a viable solution for trans-female athletes who went through puberty as males before making the transition to compete in women's sports (Dubinsky, 2022a; Sharrow, 2017; Woods & Butler, 2021). Yet these limitations do not classify Title IX as morally wrong or question America's integrity when celebrating it. The issues that do emphasize systematic American hypocrisy though are (a) the unauthenticity of anti-sex discrimination practices in the USA including systematic cover-ups of Title IX violations and (b) the racially exploitative system that enables Title IX to have a significant impact.

Title IX is an anti-sex discrimination amendment to the Education Act, used by the US government to preach to other countries about gender equality and its role in the American way of life (Bureau of Educational and Cultural Affairs, n.d.-a). Yet the USA has systematically covered up the abuse of girls and women in sports, including in the education system. For decades, gymnastics doctor Larry Nassar sexually abused hundreds of women and children under the guise of medical treatment under his official roles in the most prestigious athletic institutions in the USA, including Division I NCAA powerhouse Michigan State University (MSU), the National Olympic Committee of the USA—now called the US Olympic and Paralympic Committee (USOPC)—and the sports' governing body USA Gymnastics (USG) (Alesia et al., 2016; Lansing State Journal and IndyStar, n.d.). Following the complaints, a network of systematic failures emerged, of misreporting, underreporting, and dismissing complaints, about the abuse, enabling Nassar to continue to molest. Heads of these organizations resigned after the exposure, and the organizations paid hundreds of millions of dollars to the survivors through settlement agreements, avoiding public trials. After the US Department of Justice decided not to prosecute FBI agents who have been accused of mishandling the complaints after being offered positions in sports organizations, over 90 gymnasts demanded over $1 billion in compensation from the FBI for mishandling the complaints (Durkee, 2022). The sexual abuse in American gymnastics was exposed in 2016, during the presidential election campaign in which Donald Trump was tapped bragging that men in power can force themselves on women and dismissed it as locker room talk (Alesia et al., 2016; Dubinsky, 2022a). Despite that, the American people elected him as president instead of a more government-experienced woman.

During his presidency, Trump appointed conservative Supreme Court judges, which on June 24, 2022, the day following the 50th anniversary of Title IX, overturned Roe v. Wade, eliminating the constitutional right for abortion. While male and female American athletes and private sports organizations and leagues expressed their outrage (Taylor & Limón Romero, 2022), many sports federations, including the NCAA and conferences, stayed relatively silent despite the damaging impact the ruling is expected to have on girls and women's opportunities to engage in competitive sports (Mangan, 2022). Thus, while US governments, regardless of partisan leadership, have been using Title IX for foreign policy purposes to preach about women's rights and gender equality as part of the American lifestyle, the Supreme Court, the Department of Justice, allegedly the FBI, the Olympic Committee, the governing body, Division I university, and public sports institutions have systematically contributed to a culture in which hundreds of women and children were sexually abused in sports for decades or stayed silent amid systematic discrimination or sexual violence against women. The blame for such a culture does not fall only on American institutions but also on the American people who elected to the White House a president who bragged about grabbing women by the pussy (Dubinsky, 2021a, b, c). The sexual assaults of gymnasts at MSU add to almost incomprehensible estimations in studies from 2000, 2007, and 2015 that between 20% and 25% of female students experienced attempted rape or rape during their college years (McCray & Taylor, 2021), portraying a culture that violates Title IX. All leading to systematic hypocritical use of Title IX to promote a narrative about a normative dimension of the image of the USA, while the state as an actor, its institutions, and people clearly do not follow what they preach.

The other aspect of the hypocritical use of Title IX to promote American values is the exploitative system that enables women's sports to grow through Division I colleges that generate revenues through men's football (Jackson, 2021). As women's DI college sports lose money, their funding depends also on revenues generated by American football, a sport in which African American athletes are overrepresented (Woods & Butler, 2021), and can cause short-term and long-term brain damage. Student-athletes are considered amateurs in the USA and as of the 50th anniversary of Title IX are not allowed to receive a salary for their labor. With African Americans being in the lowest income demographic in the USA due to a history of slavery, segregation, and racial discrimination, athletic scholarships are often the only path to social mobility. Or in other words, to get a college education, increase cognitive abilities, and have a better chance to find a job, they need to engage in a sport in which they risk brain damage that can reduce their cognitive abilities and hurt their chances of holding a job. The money generated by the athletes funds not just the salaries of the football coaches and staff but the entire athletic departments, including women's sports. While African Americans are overrepresented in NCAA Division I football and men's basketball, the only two sports that generate revenues, that is not the case with the overall demographic distribution of Division I female student-athletes. While the NCAA (2022) shows growth in the representation of minority female student-athletes, African American women are not overrepresented in Division I women's sports (Woods & Butler, 2021). Meaning that to comply with Title IX and to equal the scholarships African American males receive, the same proportions of scholarships do not go to African American female student-athletes, and white families who already enjoy a higher average income further benefit from the system. The political economy of the American collegiate system that classifies student-athletes as amateurs has been long scrutinized, including comparisons to "modern-day slavery" (Kalman-Lamb et al.,

2021) as a "new plantation" (Hawkins, 2010) in which old white men in a leadership position such as coaches and athletic directors enjoy the financial benefits of the system while having authority on African American athletes who have limited choices.

In recent years there has been some change in terms of increasing the amounts student-athletes get for the cost of attendance and allowing student-athletes to receive compensation based on NIL. Yet, as of 2022, pay-for-play is still forbidden, and college players are not allowed to unionize (Silva et al., 2020). Several studies tried to monetize the equity of Division I student-athletes should they be allowed to unionize and reach revenue-sharing agreements such as professional athletes reached with the NFL and the NBA, showing that in the revenue-generating sports, football players and men's basketball players will receive hundreds of thousands of dollars per year on average (Beer, 2020; Witty, 2021). This means becoming millionaires by the time they earn their degrees, taking their families out of poverty, or generally having a different life trajectory. With less than 2% of college athletes going professional and with African Americans being in the lowest income demographic (Woods & Butler, 2021), this is the only chance for most student-athletes in revenue-generating sports to capitalize on their market value.

According to Jackson (2022a) and Staurowsky (2012), some of the justifications not to change the system despite ongoing criticism were about the impact on Title IX on women's sports and gender equality. Some of the arguments against allowing pay-for-play in collegiate sports suggested that it will widen gender inequalities and have an overall negative impact on women's sports (Jackson, 2022a; Staurowsky, 2012), which de facto made Title IX a shield for an exploitative system. Despite these arguments, in recent years there have been several suggestions on how educational institutions can comply with Title IX and create a bypassing system in which students can receive compensation through revenue-sharing models (Jackson, 2022b). Such ideas suggest a new model in which after reducing the costs of scholarships which will be distributed according to Title IX regulations, the revenues will be distributed by the conferences per sport, 50% to the universities and 50% to the athletes according to the revenue generation of the sport (Booker, 2020; Jackson, 2022a). That way athletes will be receiving compensation based on their market value, and schools will still be complying with Title IX. Of course, if half of the revenues will be distributed to the student-athletes and not to the athletic departments, each university sport will be impacted and need to adjust and potentially downsize or cut programs, including women's sports and any other non-revenue-generating sports. Yet, as of 2022, that is not the case, and women's collegiate sports in America, which gives the USA competitive sustainable advantage in international sports, financially rely on racial exploitation. This issue is unique to America, as in most countries the path to professional sports goes through clubs and does not rely on development through a very expensive education system (Ridpath, 2018). Whether for unethical reasons or impractical reasons, most countries do not adopt the American collegiate sports system and the political economy behind it. The American collegiate system has been highly scrutinized, compared domestically to "the new plantation" (Hawkins, 2010), and described internationally as "amateur hypocrisy" (Day, 2014, p. 90). With Title IX benefiting from the money generated by the American collegiate system and with American governments using Title IX as a foreign policy tool, these domestic and international critics all add to the framing of the USA as hypocritical, questioning the ethics behind the system that allows Title IX to flourish and the credibility of the moral dimension of the country.

Lesson Six: Title IX Fosters Globalization

Just because there is hypocrisy in American foreign policy, including through the use of Title IX, does not mean that the legislation cannot or does not contribute to the overall good. Nation branding analyst Simon Anholt (2010b) classified good countries based on the overall benefit they contribute to humanity and the planet. Despite the image of Americans as self-centered, arrogant, and ignorant of other cultures (Martin, 2007), part of Brand America's values about capitalism and freedom also means spreading globalization. The term globalization refers to "the processes by which goods, services, capital, people, information, and ideas flow across national borders" (Grewal & Levi, 2019, p. 178). As nation branding and country image impact foreign publics, globalization manifests through public diplomacy, place branding or tourism destination image, export branding or country of origin, and national identities. And from these perspectives, some of the challenges countries are facing are global as well, including climate change, mass migration, pandemics, and inequality (Anholt, 2010b).

As seen through the first five lessons, Title IX does not impact only the USA. Over 1000 athletes from 100 different countries who competed in the Tokyo 2020 Olympic Games also competed in American colleges (Johnson, 2021). This means that people cross borders to study in the

USA and compete in the collegiate sports system and with that spread knowledge and ideas from their countries into the American system and bring to their home countries knowledge and new training methods from the USA. By training and competing in the USA, international student-athletes improve their performance, increase the level of training of the entire collegiate program, and when going back to train and compete in their home countries improve their national teams. In terms of ideas, as seen, Title IX results from and encourages revolution and strives for change and improvement, which follows athletes into their professional careers when demanding equal play and social justice. And these ideas that manifest in the American context also spread internationally with more soccer federations equaling conditions for men and women and the International Olympic Committee (IOC) relaxing protest policies (Dubinsky, 2022a). The IOC itself is influenced by Title IX as it strives to improve gender equality in the Olympic Games and the Olympic Movement (International Olympic Committee, 2018).

In terms of products, corporate diplomacy, and export branding, Title IX led to a growing sports business ecosystem that transcends America's borders, as exemplified through the Nike commercials targeting international female audiences (Dubinsky, 2021b). Dubinsky (2021c) coined the term sport-tech diplomacy, referring to the intersections between public diplomacy and sports-related technologies. With the ever-growing technological development of sports in American education, schools and colleges are using foreign technologies to provide better services to their student-athletes whether through monitoring, coaching, and performance improvement or for production and media purposes.

These impacts of globalization organically go both ways, improving the American collegiate system, while fostering collaborations with international stakeholders. US foreign policy uses Title IX to preach to foreign publics about American lifestyle, which as seen through lesson five can also be seen as hypocritical. Perhaps to add authenticity and credibility, the USA should emphasize the benefit the American system is getting from other countries, institutions, and people who further improve their relations with the USA and through globalization grow Title IX and gender equality for the greater good.

Conclusion

Title IX had a revolutionary impact on American sports, playing a role not just in gender equality in the USA and increasing sports participation by women and girls but in establishing the USA as an international superpower in international sports, as the country became the sole international superpower in the global system. Since the early twenty-first century, Democratic and Republican administrations have been officially using Title IX as part of American soft power to try to achieve foreign policy goals and create an attractive image of the country and what values Brand America stands for. The chapter used theoretical and conceptual frameworks from nation branding (Fan, 2010) and country image (Buhmann & Ingenhoff, 2015) to discuss the intersections between Title IX, Brand America, and US sports diplomacy amid the 50th anniversary of the amendment offering six lessons: (a) Title IX adds to America's identity as "Land of Opportunity," (b) Title IX is America's sustainable competitive advantage, (c) Title IX is an ongoing revolutionary process, (d) Title IX is a tool for US foreign policy, (e) Title IX covers up American hypocrisy, and (f) Title IX fosters globalization.

The chapter celebrates the achievements of Title IX enhancing Brand America through the growth of women's sports in the USA and the success of female American athletes on a global stage that results in exposing American culture and history to foreign publics and fostering relations with international stakeholders, which are beneficial to the country's image. Yet the chapter also argues that these achievements are hiding a reality in which the American system covers up the abuse of women and girls through sports and a political economy that is racially exploitative and not adopted by other countries, all adding to already existing criticism about the USA not practicing what it preaches and having weak morals which deteriorate the normative dimension of the country's image. Despite these limitations, when looking at the global system, Title IX embodies collaboration opportunities between nations, international institutions, and foreign publics that can lead to mutual growth. With the ever-changing global sports ecosystem, the recent legislation enabling student-athletes to capitalize on their NIL, and the overall growth of women's sports, Title IX is bound to continue to play a significant role in American public life domestically and internationally. With the growing demands for a pay-for-play revenue-sharing module in revenue-generating sports, the inclusion demands of trans-female athletes in women's sports, along with conservative backlash and the overturning of Roe v. Wade, Title IX and its implications on gender equality are likely to be further challenged. Since the celebration of the 50 years to Title IX anniversary, Rapinoe and Biles received the Medal of Freedom from President Joe Biden, and Serena Williams, Sue Bird, and Allyson Felix retired from professional sports after unprecedented careers. Much like Williams, Rapinoe, or Bird who were empowered by Billie Jean King, the 1999 USWNT, and other female athletes who paved the way for them to have long professional careers, now a new generation of female athletes will take over and continue fighting for gender equality and equity and further social change.

REFERENCES

Alesia, M., Kwiatkowski, M., & Evans, T. (2016, September 20). Timeline: Former USA Gymnastics doctor Larry Nassar. *IndyStar*. Retrieved from https://www.indystar.com/story/news/2016/09/20/larry-nassar-timeline/90733320/
Anholt, S. (2010a). *Places: Identity, image and reputation*. Palgrave Macmillan.
Anholt, S. (2010b). *The good country equation: How we can repair the world in one generation*. Berrett-Koehler Publishers.
AP. (2018, April 10). Venus, Serena Williams join Billie Jean King equal pay push. *USA Today*. Retrieved from https://www.usatoday.com/story/sports/tennis/2018/04/10/venus-serena-williams-join-billie-jean-king-equal-pay-push/33696109/
Arning, C. (2013). Soft power, ideology and symbolic manipulation in Summer Olympic Games opening ceremonies: A semiotic analysis. *Social Semiotics*, 23, 523–544.
Beer, T. (2020, September 1). NCAA athletes could make $2 million a year if paid equitably, study suggests. *Forbes*. Retrieved from https://www.forbes.com/sites/tommybeer/2020/09/01/ncaa-athletes-could-make-2-million-a-year-if-paid-equitably-study-suggests/?sh=5c7da3dd5499
Booker, C. (2020, December 17). Senator Booker and Blumenthal introduce College Athletes Bill of Rights. *Cory Booker*. Retrieved from https://www.booker.senate.gov/news/press/senators-booker-and-blumenthal-introduce-college-athletes-bill-of-rights
Buhmann, A., & Ingenhoff, D. (2015). The 4D Model of the country image: An integrative approach from the perspective of communication management. *The International Communication Gazette*, 77, 102–124.
Bureau of Educational and Cultural Affairs. (n.d.-a). *Sports diplomacy. United States of America Department of State*. Retrieved from https://eca.state.gov/sports-diplomacy

Bureau of Educational and Cultural Affairs. (n.d.-b). *Sports Envoy*. United States of America Department of State. Retrieved from https://eca.state.gov/sports-diplomacy/sports-envoy

Coleman, M. (2021, October 15). Dawn Staley receives historic contract extension: 'Huge statement for women'. *SI*. Retrieved from https://www.si.com/college/2021/10/15/dawn-staley-receives-historic-seven-year-contract-extension

Cooky, C., Messner, M. A., & Musto, M. (2015). "It's Dude Time!": A quarter century of excluding women's sports in televised news. *Communication & Sport, 3*(3), 261–287.

Cooper, A. F. (2019). U.S. public diplomacy and sports stars: Mobilizing African-American athletes as goodwill ambassadors from the cold war to an uncertain future. *Place Branding & Public Diplomacy, 15*, 165–172. https://doi.org/10.1057/s41254-018-00114-2

Cull, N. J. (2010). Public diplomacy: Seven lessons for its future from its past. *Journal of Place Branding and Public Diplomacy, 6*, 11–17.

David, O., & Bar-Tal, D. (2009). A sociopsychological conception of collective identity: The case of national identity as an example. *Personality and Social Psychology Review, 13*, 354–379. https://doi.org/10.1177/1088868309344412

Day, D. (2014). America's 'Mysterious "Training Tables"': British Reactions and Amateur Hypocrisy. *Sport in History, 34*(1), 90–112. https://doi.org/10.1080/17460263.2013.844198

Dees, W., Walsh, P., McEvoy, C., & McKelvey, S. (2022). *Sport marketing* (5th ed.). Human Kinetics.

Dixon, E. (2022, June 15). Spain women's and men's soccer teams to receive equal bonuses. *SP*. Retrieved from https://www.sportspromedia.com/news/rfef-spain-womens-national-team-equal-pay-bonuses/

Dubinsky, Y. (2019). From soft power to sports diplomacy: A theoretical and conceptual discussion. *Place Branding and Public Diplomacy, 15*, 154–164. https://doi.org/10.1057/s41254-019-00116-8

Dubinsky, Y. (2021a). Sports, Brand America and U.S. public diplomacy during the presidency of Donald Trump. *Place Branding & Public Diplomacy*. https://doi.org/10.1057/s41254-021-00230-6

Dubinsky, Y. (2021b). Revolutionary or arrogant? The role of the USWNT in Brand America through the 2019 FIFA Women's World Cup. *International Journal of Sport and Society, 12*(1), 147–164. https://doi.org/10.18848/2152-7857/CGP/v12i01/147-164

Dubinsky, Y. (2021c). Country image and political satire in sport management: Analyzing America through sports in South Park. *Sport in Society*, 1–23. https://doi.org/10.1080/17430437.2021.1980781

Dubinsky, Y. (2022a). The Olympic Games, nation branding, and public diplomacy in a post-pandemic world: Reflections on Tokyo 2020 and beyond.

Place Branding & Public Diplomacy, 1–12. https://doi.org/10.1057/s41254-021-00255-x

Dubinsky, Y. (2022b). Country image, cultural diplomacy, and sports during the COVID19 pandemic: Brand America and Super Bowl LV. Place Branding & Public Diplomacy, 1–17. https://doi.org/10.1057/s41254-021-00257-9

Durkee, A. (2022, June 8). Gymnasts – Including Simone Biles – Seek $1 billion from FBI over Larry Nassar case. Forbes. Retrieved from https://www.forbes.com/sites/alisondurkee/2022/06/08/gymnasts-including-simone-biles-demand-1-billion-from-fbi-over-larry-nassar-case/?sh=c7c475f9c6f8

Evaluation Division. (2020, December). Evaluation report. Bureau of Educational and Cultural Affairs. Retrieved from https://eca.state.gov/files/bureau/sports_visitor_program_evaluation_report_final_december_2020.pdf

Fan, Y. (2010). Branding the nation: Towards a better understanding. Journal of Place Branding and Public Diplomacy, 6(2), 97–103.

Foudy, J. (producer), & Leyden, E. (director). (2013). The '99ers. ESPN.

Fredrick, E. L., Pegoraro, A., & Schmidt, A. (2020). "I'm not going to the f***ing White House": Twitter users react to Donald Trump and Megan Rapinoe. Communication & Sport, 1–19. https://doi.org/10.1177/2167479520950778

Geiger, A. W., & Kent, L. (2015). Number of women leaders around the world has grown, but they're still a small group. Pew Research Center. Retrieved from https://www.pewresearch.org/fact-tank/2017/03/08/women-leaders-around-the-world/

Glaser, D. (2006). Does hypocrisy matter? The case of US foreign policy. Review of International Studies, 32(2), 251–268. http://www.jstor.org/stable/40072137

Greenwalt, T. (2022, December 8). Brittney Griner released from Russia prison 10 months after arrest. Yahoo! Sport. https://sports.yahoo.com/brittney-griner-released-from-russian-prison-10-months-after-arrest-132117554.html

Grewal, D., & Levi, M. (2019). M: Marketing (7th ed.). McGraw-Hill.

Handelman, S. (2012). The Minds of Peace Experiment: A laboratory for people-to-people diplomacy. Israel Affairs, 18(1), 1–11. https://doi.org/10.1080/13537121.2012.634278

Hawkins, B. (2010). The new plantation. Palgrave Macmillan.

International Olympic Committee. (2018, April 19). IOC is leading the way in gender equality. Olympics. Retrieved from https://olympics.com/ioc/news/ioc-is-leading-the-way-in-gender-equality

Jackson, V. (2021, March 26). Hey, disruptors! Women's basketball needs you. Global Sport Matters. Retrieved from https://globalsportmatters.com/business/2021/03/26/hey-disruptors-womens-basketball-needs-you/

Jackson, V. (2022a). Want college sports reform? Start with paying Power 5 football players. Arnold Ventures. Retrieved from https://craftmediabucket.s3.

amazonaws.com/uploads/AVCollegeSportWhitePaper_NoPay_VIctoriaJackson-v2B-1.pdf
Jackson, W. (2022b, May 18). Dawn Staley shows support for Brittney Griner in Tweets. *SI*. Retrieved from https://www.si.com/extra-mustard/2022/05/18/dawn-staley-shows-support-for-brittney-griner-in-tweet
Johansson, J. K. (1989). Determinants and effects of the use of "made-in" labels. *International Marketing Review, 6*, 47–58.
Johnson, G. (2021, August 11). Former, current NCAA student-athletes earn 282 Olympic medals. *NCAA*. Retrieved from https://www.ncaa.org/news/2021/8/11/features-former-current-ncaa-student-athletes-earn-282-olympic-medals.aspx
Kalman-Lamb, N., Silva, D., & Mellis, J. (2021, March 17). 'I signed my life to rich white guys': Athletes on the racial dynamics of college sports. *The Guardian*. Retrieved from https://www.theguardian.com/sport/2021/mar/17/college-sports-racial-dynamics?fbclid=IwAR0ixdoThUqGmvgx6-HsYe43RdarE4Kmj2YPboBrjHcmmuz6KrpLyXSwXmY
King, Jr., M. (1965, March 25). *Our God is Marching On!* The Martin Luther King, Jr. Research and Education Institute. Stanford University. Retrieved from https://kinginstitute.stanford.edu/our-god-marching
Lansing State Journal and IndyStar. (n.d.). Who is Larry Nassar? *IndyStar*. Retrieved from https://www.indystar.com/pages/interactives/larry-nassar-timeline/
Lucas, S. (2000). Niek's commercial solution girls, sneakers, and salvation. *International Review for the Sociology of Sport, 35*(2), 149–164.
Mangan, K. (2022, June 24). Supreme Court ruling will upend reproductive rights for college students and compliance medical training. *The Chronicle of Higher Education*. Retrieved from https://www.chronicle.com/article/supreme-court-ruling-will-upend-reproductive-rights-for-college-students-and-complicate-medical-training?utm_source=Iterable&utm_medium=email&utm_campaign=campaign_4544156_nl_Academe-Today_date_20220627&cid=at&source=&sourceid=
Martin, D. (2007). *Rebuilding brand America: What we must do to restore our reputation and safeguard the future of American business abroad*. Amacom.
McCray, K., & Taylor, E. (2021). "I learned that sports teaches rape culture": Assessing Sexual Violence Prevention Education for Intercollegiate Athletes. *Journal of Intercollegiate Sport, 14*(1), 46–65. https://doi.org/10.17161/jis.v14i1.13428
Murphy, D. (2022, March 15). Sedona Prince, March Madness and the ongoing quest for gender equity at NCAA basketball tournaments. *ESPN*. Retrieved from https://www.espn.com/womens-college-basketball/story/_/id/33482596/sedona-prince-march-madness-ongoing-quest-gender-equity-ncaa-basketball-tournaments
Murray, S. (2018). *Sports diplomacy: Origins, theory and practice*. Routledge.

NCAA. (2021a). Finances of intercollegiate athletics database. *NCAA*. Retrieved from https://www.ncaa.org/sports/2019/11/12/finances-of-intercollegiate-athletics-database.aspx

NCAA. (2021b, July 2). NCAA student-athletes at the 2020 summer Olympics. *NCAA*. Retrieved from https://www.ncaa.com/news/ncaa/article/2021-07-21/ncaa-student-athletes-2020-summer-olympics

NCAA. (2022). Title IX 50 years anniversary: The state of women in college sports. *NCAA*. Retrieved from https://s3.amazonaws.com/ncaaorg/inclusion/titleix/2022_State_of_Women_in_College_Sports_Report.pdf

Nebenzahl, I., Jaffe, E., & Lampert, S. (1997). Towards a theory of country image effect on product evaluation. *Management International Review, 37*(1), 27–49.

Nike News. (2015, April 15). Nike puts women front and center for 40 years and counting. *Nike*. Retrieved from https://news.nike.com/news/nike-women-advertising-a-40-year-journey

NIL Summit. (2022). *NIL Awards. NIL Summit*. Retrieved from https://nilsummit.com/nil-awards/

npr. (2018, March 18). Transcript: Barack Obama's speech on race. *npr*. Retrieved from https://www.npr.org/templates/story/story.php?storyId=88478467

Nye, J. S., Jr. (2004). *Soft power: The means to success in world politics*. PublicAffairs.

Nye, J. S., Jr. (2008). Public diplomacy and soft power. *Annals of the American Academy of Political and Social Science, 616*(1), 94–109.

Office of the Spokesperson. (2022, June 22). *Celebrating Global Sports Mentoring Program's 10th Anniversary*. U.S. Department of State. Retrieved from https://www.state.gov/celebrating-the-global-sports-mentoring-programs-10th-anniversary/

Olympics. (n.d.). Olympic results. *Olympics*. Retrieved from https://olympics.com/en/olympic-games/olympic-results

Ordeix-Rigo, E., & Durate, J. (2009). From public diplomacy to corporate diplomacy: Increasing corporations' legitimacy and influence. *American Behavioral Scientist, 53*(4), 549–564. https://doi.org/10.1177/0002764209347630

Owens, J. (2022, September 20). WNBA stars shun Russia, 7 figure salaries amid Brittney Griner's detention, Ukraine invasion. *Yahoo! Sport*. Retrieved from https://sports.yahoo.com/wnba-stars-shun-russia-millions-amid-brittney-griners-detention-ukraine-invasion-215630226.html

Parker, C. (Producer), Porter, D., & Newnham, N. (directors). (2022, April 2). *Title IX: 37 words that changed America*. ESPN.

Parlow Cone, C. (2022, June 24). Title IX helped forge A U.S. Soccer legacy that continues today. *Sportico*. Retrieved from https://www.sportico.com/personalities/executives/2022/title-ix-cindy-parlow-cone-1234678185/

Pigman, G. A. (2014). International sport and diplomacy's public dimension: Governments, sporting federations and the global audience. *Diplomacy & Statecraft, 25*(94), 94–114. https://doi.org/10.1080/09592296.2014.873613

Ridpath, D. B. (2018). *Alternative models of sport development in America: Solutions to a crisis in education and public health*. Ohio University Press.

Schmidt, S. H., Frederick, E. L., Pegoraro, A., & Spencer, T. C. (2018). An analysis of Colin Kaepernick, Megan Rapinoe, and the National Anthem Protests. *Communication & Sport*, 7(5), 653–677. https://doi.org/10.1177/2167479518793625

Sharrow, E. A. (2017). "Female athlete" politic: Title IX and the naturalization of sex difference in public policy. *Politics, Groups, and Identities*, 5(1), 46–66. https://doi.org/10.1080/21565503.2016.1268178

Silva, D., Kalman-Lamb, N., & Mellis, J. (2020, August 12). Cancelling the college football season is about union busting, not health. *The Guardian*. Retrieved from https://www.theguardian.com/sport/2020/aug/12/cancelling-the-college-football-season-is-about-union-busting-not-health

Statista. (2022). Number of countries where de facto highest position of executive power was held by woman from 1960 to 2022. *Statista*. Retrieved from https://www.statista.com/statistics/1058345/countries-with-women-highest-position-executive-power-since-1960/

Staurowsky, E. J. (2012). "A Radical Proposal": Title IX has no place in college sport pay-for-play discussions. *Marquette Sports Law Review*, 22(2), 575–595.

Taylor, M., & Limón Romero, I. (2022, June 24). 'Gutted 💔': WNBA players, sports legends react to Supreme Court's abortion decision. *Los Angeles Times*. Retrieved from https://www.latimes.com/sports/story/2022-06-24/athletes-billie-jean-king-sports-athletes-reaction-abortion-decision

The Associated Press. (2020, November 7). Transcript of President-elect Joe Biden's victory speech. *AP*. Retrieved from https://apnews.com/article/election-2020-joe-biden-religion-technology-race-and-ethnicity-2b961c70bc72c2516046bffd378e95de

The Good Country Index. (n.d.). 1.4. *The Good Country*. Retrieved from https://index.goodcountry.org/?fbclid=IwAR0MeIICz8DZ_c_ce_4wuDiWX9ErDuoWhCKTVS2M8-36SPiksDrIWLqqHCs

U.S. Department of Education. (2021). *Title IX and sex discrimination*. U.S. Department of Education. Retrieved from https://www2.ed.gov/about/offices/list/ocr/docs/tix_dis.html

U.S. Soccer. (2022, May 18). U.S. Soccer Federation, women's and men's national team unions agree to historic collective bargaining agreements. *U.S. Soccer*. Retrieved from https://www.ussoccer.com/stories/2022/05/ussf-womens-and-mens-national-team-unions-agree-to-historic-collective-bargaining-agreements

Ware, S. (2011). *Game, Set, Match: Billie Jean King and the revolution in women's sports*. University of North Carolina Press.

White, C. J. (2015). Exploring the role of private-sector corporations in public diplomacy. *Public Relations Inquiry*, 4, 305–321.

Williams, L. (2022). The heritage strikes back: Athlete activism, Black Lives Matter, and the iconic fifth wave of activism in the (W)NBA bubble. *Cultural Studies ↔ Critical Methodologies, 22*(3), 266–275. https://doi.org/10.1177/15327086211049718

Witty, A. (2021). College athletics spending and the movement towards revenue sharing. *ADU.* Retrieved from https://athleticdirectoru.com/articles/student-athlete-revenue-sharing/

Woods, R., & Butler, N. (2021). *Social issues in sport* (4th ed.). Human Kinetics.

Zaccardi, N. (2016, June 29). Cheryl Miller's cartwheel in front of Pat Summitt put 1984 Olympic hopes in peril. *NBC Sports.* Retrieved from https://olympics.nbcsports.com/2016/06/29/cheryl-miller-pat-summitt-basketball-olympics/

Zhou, X., Pizzo, A., & Funk, D. C. (2021). Outsiders within: College sport as an avenue to integrate East Asian international students. *Journal of Intercollegiate Sport, 14*(2), 42–65. https://doi.org/10.17161/jis.v14i2.14835

CHAPTER 6

The European Super League as a Nation Branding Geopolitical Battlefield

INTRODUCTION

On Sunday, April 18, 2021, around 11:00 PM GMT, 12 European football[1] clubs from England, Spain, and Italy coordinatingly announced a creation of a new mid-week private continental competition—The Super League (European Super League Company, 2021a, b), also referred to as the European Super League (ESL) (BBC, 2021; Wagner et al., 2021). The 12 founding clubs were Liverpool FC, FC Chelsea, FC Arsenal, Tottenham Hotspurs, Manchester City FC and Manchester United from England, FC Barcelona, Real Madrid, and Atletico Madrid from Spain, AC Milan, FC Internazionale Milano (Inter Milan), and Juventus FC from Italy, with three more clubs to be added before the first season (European Super League Company, 2021b). According to the format of the competition, each year 20 clubs – the 15 founding clubs along with 5 more clubs that will go through a qualification system, will compete in a tournament consisting of two groups of 10, leading to a playoff through which a champion will be crowned (European Super League Company, 2021b). The ESL, financially backed by global companies such as American bank JP Morgan, and other investors, was supposed to pay 3.5 billion Euros to the founding teams and generate revenues of around 750 million

---

[1] Known as soccer in North America (Woods & Butler, 2021).

© The Author(s), under exclusive license to Springer Nature Switzerland AG 2023
Y. Dubinsky, *Nation Branding and Sports Diplomacy*,
https://doi.org/10.1007/978-3-031-32550-2_6

for each team, which would have provided financial stability as the majority of clubs were in debts and recorded a loss of 1.5 billion Euros during the pandemic and the 2019/20 season (Daskal, 2021; Gretz et al., 2021).

The creation of the ESL meant breaking away from competitions organized by the Union of European Football Association (UEFA), including the UEFA Champions League (UCL), and creating a closed league at least for the 15 founding clubs, which follow the North American sports system (Wagner et al., 2021). A closed league system, along with shared revenues reduces the financial risks and provides stability (Jakar & Gerretsen, 2021; Wagner et al., 2021). While the ESL did not mean to break away from the domestic league, the guaranteed place in a closed midweek elite competition contradicted the traditional domestic leagues' systems of earning a place in European competitions based on performance, which would have led to unmatched financial advantage over domestic rivals and reduce the need to earn a spot in continental competitions through athletic achievements. Speculations about top European football clubs uniting and creating their closed private league have been growing since the 1990s (Solberg & Gratton, 2004), as UEFA's elite competition, the UEFA Champions League (UCL), has not been maximizing the financial potential of the most popular clubs (Daskal, 2021) in the most popular sport in the world (Woods & Butler, 2021), and UEFA's Financial Fair Play[2] (FFP) Regulations have not created a sustainable financial ecosystem in European club football.

Reports about the creation of the ESL started in the morning of April 18, 2021, followed by criticism by the football community, including the Premier League, and even British Prime Minister Boris Johnson (BBC, 2021). Since the official announcement, football stakeholders, ranging from local fans to heads of states and royalty, caused a wave of backlash that led to a domino effect of teams withdrawing from the project (BBC, 2021; Tharoor, 2021). By the end of Tuesday, April 20, all six English teams had withdrawn from the ESL, and by April 21, Atletico Madrid, Inter Milan, and AC Milan, also jumped ship, leaving Juventus, Real Madrid, and Barcelona as the last members of the project. Within less than 72 hours of its creation, the ESL had officially collapsed (BBC, 2021; Newman, 2021).

---

[2] UEFA's Financial Fair Play (FFP) Regulations is a budgetary framework implemented in 2009 aimed to increase financial transparency and encourage clubs to operate on the basis of their own revenues (UEFA, n.d.).

The ESL was an ambitious project impacting not just football in three Western European countries but had global implications. As seen in Table 6.1, the 12 founding teams of the ESL may compete in three different leagues, but their ownership is much more global. The purpose of this chapter is to explore how different countries and actors led to the rise and fall of the ESL. To discuss the question, the chapter uses nation branding lenses (Fan, 2010), focusing on England, Spain, and Italy—as the countries of the 12 founding teams, France and Germany whose teams declined an invitation to join, foreign ownerships including Russia, the Arabian Gulf, the United States, and China, and non-state actors such as international federations and global movements. Through the discussion, the chapter argues (a) that no one explanation can be sufficient to understand the ESL fiasco and (b) that most actors who contributed to the creation of the ESL were also responsible for its collapse, and vice versa.

NATION BRANDING AND CLUB FOOTBALL

To discuss how different countries and actors led to the rise and fall of the ESL, the chapter uses Fan's (2010) nation branding framework. Football is the most popular sport worldwide and its pinnacle competition the FIFA World Cup is watched by billions (Woods & Butler, 2021; Zimbalist, 2016). As a popular competition between national teams, there are ample manifestations of nation branding, including associated representations with national characters from the fighting spirit of Uruguay—"*Garra Charrua*," the Brazilian *Jogo Bonito*—the beautiful game, associated with a lifestyle of dancing and Carnival, Diego Maradona's *Hand of God* as an Argentinian act of defiance against England's occupation of the Falkland Islands, the traditional German game is based on structure and efficiency (Kaelberer, 2017), to French national team reflecting the country's ethnic diversity of immigrants from former colonies (Oonk, 2021). This section explains the theoretical framework used in this this chapter, by explaining the different lenses of nation branding and how they intersect with club football.

According to Fan (2010), nation branding can be defined as the "sum of all perceptions of a nation in the minds of international stakeholders, which may contain some of the following elements: people, place, culture/language history, food, fashion, famous faces (celebrities), global brands and so on" (p. 98). With football being the most popular sport worldwide (Woods & Butler, 2021), countries, cities, communities, and

Table 6.1 Clubs' ownerships and involvement in the European Super League as of its creation and collapse[a]

Club	Country (League)	ESL status	Owner(s)/controlling shareholder(s) (country)	Estimated value[b] (millions)	Estimated net debt (millions)[c]
AC Milan	Italy (Seria A)	Withdrew April 21	Elliot Management Corporation (United States)	€407	€103.9
Juventus	Italy (Seria A)	Did not withdraw	Agnelli family (Italy)	€1480	€390
Inter Milan	Italy (Seria A)	Withdrew April 21	Zhang Jindong (China)	€877.5	€322.7
Atletico Madrid	Spain (La Liga)	Withdrew April 21	Miguel Gil and Enrico Cerezo (Spain)	€1133	€111.1
Real Madrid	Spain (La Liga)	Did not withdraw	Club members (Spain)	€2908.5	€170
FC Barcelona	Spain (La Liga)	Did not withdraw	Club members (Spain/Catalonia)	€2869	€317.6
Arsenal	England (Premier League)	Withdrew April 20	Kroenke Sports & Entertainment (United States)	€1445	€76.8
Chelsea FC	England (Premier League)	Withdrew April 20	Roman Abramovich (Russia/Israel)	€1874.5	-€19.3
Liverpool FC	England (Premier League)	Withdrew April 20	Fenway Sports Group/John Henry (United States)	€2284	€283.3
Manchester City	England (Premier League)	Withdrew April 20	Sheikh Mansour bin Zayed Al Nahyan/City Football Group (Abu Dhabi)	€2170	€51.9
Manchester United	England (Premier League)	Withdrew April 20	Glazer family (United States)	€2661.5	€524.4
Tottenham Hotspur	England (Premier League)	Withdrew April 20	Joseph Lewis and Daniel Levy/English National Investment Company (England)	€1707.5	€685.5

[a]The table includes information as of April 30, 2021, unless specified otherwise (BBC, 2021; Gretz et al., 2021; KPMG, 2021; Hellier & Nair, 2021; Newman, 2021; Powell, 2021)
[b]Estimated average between higher and lower range as of January 2021 (KPMG, 2021)
[c]As of the end of the 2019/20 season. 11 teams published their debt by June 2020 (Hellier & Nair, 2021), except Liverpool FC who published in April 2021 (Powell, 2021)

other stakeholders are trying to use football to achieve social, political, and economic goals (Chadwick, 2018; Chadwick et al., 2020). Nation branding and its outcome, country image, are multidisciplinary fields, analyzed through lenses of marketing, political science, communications, and sociopsychology (Buhmann & Ingenhoff, 2015; Fan, 2010). According to Fan (2010) nation branding consists of export branding, place branding, political branding, and cultural branding.

Export branding (Fan, 2010), also referred to in the literature as country-of-origin (COO) and product-country-image (PCI) (Jaffe & Nebenzahl, 1993; Papadopoulos et al., 2017), along with place branding (Anholt, 2010), which is also referred to as destination branding or tourism-destination-image (TDI) (Nadeau et al., 2008), are two marketing approaches to nation branding research. While they differ from each other, there is also much overlap as some of the same units of analysis and some of the outcomes are similar. The PCI or COO approach of export branding focuses on the images of products based on the country with which they are associated (Papadopoulos et al., 2017). In the context of club football, the half-century-long relationships and partnerships between leading German sportswear Adidas and German club FC Bayern Munich, illustrate the use of images associated with German industry for commercial gain of sports products (Media, 2011). As a global brand, Bayern Munich has multiple partners and sponsors, but only four are also shareholders—Adidas, Audi, T-Mobile, and Allianz—all German brands (FC Bayern München, n.d.). Place branding, or TDI, analyzes the image of a country as a tourism destination. Dubinsky (2021a) offers a model of branding a city as a sports town, through developing different strategies for local, regional, national, international, and global stakeholders. In the context of club football, TDI approaches can manifest through the impact a team has on the image of a city or country, or through marketing destinations through sponsorships and partnerships, for example, countries sponsoring European football clubs to promote the images of their national airlines. Arsenal, Chelsea, AC Milan, Real Madrid, and PSG are just a few examples of football clubs whose been sponsored by the United Arab Emirates through Fly Emirates (Emirates, n.d.; Koch, 2020). Often such sponsorships and partnerships also involve visiting the countries for exhibition games or training camps as well, thus adding more exposure to the countries as tourism destinations. Azerbaijan took an even more direct approach with the Tourism Office sponsoring Atletico Madrid, having "Azerbaijan Land of Fire" on their jerseys (Chadwick et al., 2020).

Another approach to TDI is countries buying the rights to host prestigious games involving international football clubs, to receive international exposure through the event. Clubs such as Juventus, AC Milan, and Inter Milan have traveled to China to the Supercoppa Italiana; the French Supercup was also held in North America and Africa. Hautbois (2015) analyzed sports and city branding using the football clubs of Manchester United, FC Barcelona, and St. Etienne, exampling how the city of Manchester used to associate itself internationally with the club, including through a giant poster at the airport which sent the "implied message 'you are arriving at the city of Manchester United'" (p. 61).

From international relation perspectives, nation branding analyzes geopolitics though political branding using lenses such as public diplomacy and soft power. Political scientist Joseph Nye (2008) coined the term soft power, referring to the ability to achieve desired outcomes through attractions and without the use of military force or economic sanctions. The main components of soft power are foreign policy, political values, and culture. Public diplomacy is a subset of soft power, referring to communication with foreign publics to achieve foreign policy goals (Cull, 2008). In the early twenty-first century, perhaps the most evident use of club football for soft power and public diplomacy can be seen from countries from the Arabian Gulf purchasing or sponsoring clubs and hosting important international competitions (Chadwick et al., 2020). Qatar Investment Authority purchasing Paris Saint Germain (PSG), sponsoring FC Barcelona, and winning the controversial bid to host the 2022 FIFA World Cup, has been framed not just as an attempt to improve tourism or for corporate goals of generating revenues for their national airlines, but as a soft power play to improve its international image and role on the world's stage (Brannagan & Giulianotti, 2018). Yet, such an initiative also got the name "sport washing," of using sport to launder the country's image from human rights violations (Chadwick, 2018). Abu Dhabi, another Emirate from the Arabian Gulf, has developed a franchise of international sports teams, starting with Manchester City, and expanding across the globe. More contemporary definitions of public diplomacy don't necessarily associate directly to foreign policy, but also individuals through people-to-people diplomacy and companies through corporate diplomacy. FC Liverpool, Manchester United, and Arsenal, all have American owners who also own sports teams in the United States among other businesses. American owners of Premier League clubs often received criticism for applying an American corporate culture without considering the needs and traditions of local fans. The most extreme example of resistance comes from Manchester United fans protesting regularly against the Glazer family (Nauright & Ramfjord, 2010) despite years in which the club had professional success. Since the early 2000s Russian Oligarchs have started buying European football teams as a means to normalize their image in the Western world (Riordan, 2007), including Roman Abramovich buying FC Chelsea in 2003, leading the club to unprecedented national and international glory through unsustainable spending. Whether backed by oil money or other natural resources, foreign countries and people with different agendas have acquired top European football clubs, and despite ongoing success, their motives have been criticized and questioned (Chadwick, 2018; Riordan, 2007).

While public diplomacy refers mostly to targeting foreign audiences, national identity, which Fan (2010) refers to as cultural branding, also applies to domestic audiences. The Spanish "El Classico" has roots in national struggles, with Real Madrid historically representing Castilian and Spanish identity, while Barcelona championing Catalonian ideologies and aspirations and wearing the colors of the Catalan flag (Mwinwelle et al., 2020; Ortega, 2016). Nation identity is a specific case of collective identity, analyzed through social identity theory (David & Bar-Tal, 2009). According to the theory, a social identity is constructed through categorizing oneself into groups, defining the meanings of these groups and external groups, and the motives behind the differences between these groups. According to David and Bar-Tal (2009), a collective identity is a social acknowledgment of individuals sharing the same social identity and national identity is a specific case of these collective sentiments based on history, myths, memories, values, and other socially constructed characteristics. There is no shortage of examples of how football clubs represent the collective identities of their communities. From a social class perspective, FC Liverpool represents the pride of a city with a historic reputation of socialism, unemployment, and popular music, which can also be seen in the collective effort and unity behind the decades-long fight for justice for the 96 fans who died in the Hillsborough disaster (Cronin, 2017) and the emotional anthem "You'll never walk alone" (Evans & Norcliffe, 2016). From a cultural-religious perspective, both Tottenham Hotspurs from England and AFC Ajax Amsterdam from the Netherlands adopted Jewish symbols and traditions, with fans of the English club chanting "Being a

Yid" and those of the Dutch "Super Joden" (Winner, 2019). Other forms of collective identity are political and economic affiliations, such as in Italy, Livorno FC is associated with left-wing communism, and fans of SS Lazio adopted right-wing fascist symbols (Archambault, 2018). Media mogul and former owner of AC Milan Silvio Berlusconi leveraged the national and international success of the "Rossoneri" under his ownership through correlating between the popular chant "Forza Milan!" and his political party "Forza Italia," leading to a turbulent political career as the Italian prime minister in three different terms over three different decades (Friedman, 2015). There are more manifestations of export branding, place branding, political branding, and cultural branding, but these examples demonstrate multidisciplinary lenses of nation branding, and how they intersect with geopolitics and European club football.

Nation Branding and the European Super League

As seen in the previous section, all 12 founding clubs of the ESL have been involved directly or indirectly with nation-branding-related initiatives even before April 2021. From place branding lenses (Fan, 2010) and tourism destination image (Nadeau et al., 2008), there was some shared interest between the cities of the ESL teams. According to Dubinsky (2021a), cities who want to brand themselves as global sports cities have local teams competing on an international stage and have a history of hosting mega sports events. The 12 founding ESL teams come from 7 cities in 3 Western European countries; Chelsea, Arsenal, and Tottenham from London, Manchester City and Manchester United from Manchester, Liverpool FC from Liverpool, AC Milan and Inter Milan from Milan, Juventus from Turin, Real Madrid and Atletico Madrid from Madrid, and FC Barcelona from Barcelona. London and Barcelona hosted the Summer Olympic Games, Turin hosted the Winter Olympic Games, Milan won the bid to host the Winter Olympic Games, Manchester hosted the Commonwealth Games, and Madrid hosted the FIFA World Cup Final. Liverpool hosted more modest international sports events. Meaning that from a destination branding perspective, at least six of the cities are already international sports cities (Dubinsky, 2021a, b), and that all cities had a shared interest of having ESL teams that can improve their global reputation. Yet, beyond some shared place branding goals, when analyzing the ESL through nation branding lenses, the power struggles over geopolitical and socioeconomic differences between the different actors eventually led to the ESL's collapse. The discussion in this section focuses on the following countries and actors: (a) England, (b) Spain, (c) Italy, (d) Germany and France, and (e) foreign ownership, and (f) non-state actors.

England

As the birthplace of association football (Taylor, 2018; Woods & Butler, 2021), the sport is part of the English and British national identity. This could be seen by the national football association called The FA, rather without even mentioning the name of the country like others do (e.g., the French Football Federation), of the famous fans' song "Football's coming home," referring to hosting, winning, or taking ownership on the game. There are ample manifestations of nationalism in English football, ranging from framing the 1966 World Cup Final win against Germany around World War II, to English fans being associated with hooliganism, or internal disputes with the Scottish Football Associations and the nationalities of the players who can represent Great Britain in the Olympic Games (Taylor, 2018). Globalism was a double-edged sword for England and the ESL due to the centrality of football in England's culture and history, celebrated local traditions, and the global popularity of English football and the Premier League, which attracted players, coaches, fans, and owners with different agendas.

Without England, the ESL would likely not have been formed as half of the founding teams came from the Premier League. The global success of the English Premier League led foreign investors to purchase top clubs for social, political, and economic reasons. During the 2010s, all the championships were won by teams with foreign owners or majority shareholders from Abu Dhabi, the United States, Thailand, and Russia. With foreign money also came in foreign corporate culture and foreign interests. On one hand, revenue-sharing models brought from the American sports system, led to the English Premier League being the most revenue-generating football league worldwide as every club received an equal share of television revenues, distributing more talent across to the league and making games more competitive and attractive. In the 2018/19 season, each Premier League team received 34.3 million pounds as equal share and 43.1 million for television rights, so even the team that finished in the last 20th place in the Premier League made 96.6 million pounds which is almost 115 million Euros (Premier League, 2019), equivalent to the club that finished in the 7th place in the Spanish La Liga (Statista, 2021). On the other hand, it is no coincidence that five of the six teams that joined the EFL (FC Liverpool, Chelsea, Arsenal, Manchester United, and Manchester City) are owned by foreigners, who have their agendas on why to invest in English football. The only English-owned team is Tottenham, by the British ENIC Group, but the team has been much less successful than the other English clubs who joined the ESL. Foreign investments, along with problematic salary and transfer fees regulations, politically driven agendas that are not necessarily revenue-oriented along revenue-driven agendas that do not consider local traditions, were all driving forces for English teams to join the ESL.

However, it was also England that brought to the collapse of the ESL. From a collective identity perspective (David & Bar-Tal, 2009), Garry Neville, a media commentator, and a former Manchester United player were among the first to bluntly criticize the ESL, making a clear separation between two different social groups: the English football community who cares about the traditions of the game, and the foreign owners who try to capitalize on it during a global pandemic (Sky Sports Football, 2021a, b). Neville said:

> They're imposters, the owners of these clubs, the owners of Liverpool, the owners of Manchester City, the owners of Chelsea, they have nothing to do with football in this country. There are 100-odd years of football in this country with fans that have lived and loved these clubs and they need protecting, the fans need protecting. (Sky Sports Football, 2021a)

Following backlash from the English football community, including fans turning against their own clubs, on the afternoon of April 20, Chelsea announced it was preparing to withdraw, and Manchester City officially withdrew, which led to the domino effect of all English teams officially breaking away from the ESL within a few hours (Christenson, 2021). As mentioned, the domino started after backlash from the entire football community, including fans of the clubs, fans of rivals, players and coaches of the clubs, ex-players in commentating positions, Prime Minister Boris Johnson called sports authorities to act against the clubs, and the Premier League itself condemned the ESL and announced they are "considering all actions available to prevent it from progressing" (BBC, 2021). Even Buckingham Palace took a stand with the people, with Prince William, who is also the President of The FA tweeting:

> Now, more than ever, we must protect the entire football community – from the top level to the grassroots – and the values of competition and fairness at its core. I share the concerns of fans about the proposed Super League and the damage it risks causing to the game we love. W. (Hellier & Nair, 2021)

There is no one reason why the football community in England took such a strong stand against the ESL. That demonstrates how deep football is integrated in English collective identity. The Premier League and The FA issued a joint statement in which the six clubs will each pay a fine of 25 million British Pounds, a set of sanctions will ensure a breakaway from the current system will not happen again, and that the clubs acknowledged they made a mistake and are committed "to the Premier League and the future of the English game" (Premier League, 2021).

Spain

Nation branding and geopolitics are embedded in Spanish football, through political branding and public diplomacy and cultural branding, and collective identity (Mwinwelle et al., 2020; Ortega, 2016). While Real Madrid embraced its Spanish character and symbols, Catalan nationalism and Basque nationalism are often expressed through the clubs of FC Barcelona and Athletic Bilbao, respectively (Ortega, 2016). It was Generalissimo Franco's dictatorship regime that forbids Catalan political parties and official use of the Catalan language but fostered football rivalries trying to contain non-Spanish national manifestations to the playing field (Ortega, 2016). According to Ortega,

> The ubiquitous status of the Spanish flag during Real Madrid's trophy celebrations and *la Estalada* at Barcelona's rallies signals the role of soccer as a cultural, social and political practice in articulating two competing and non-compatible views of Spain. (Ortega, 2016, p. 9)

By the twenty-first century both clubs became international powerhouses, buying some of the best and most expensive players in the world almost every year. Yet, there are still global and glocal differences, with Real Madrid branded as "Galacticos" and FC Barcelona relying also on players developed through its academy "La Masia"—The Farmhouse—using the "total football" philosophy as embodied and developed by

Dutch legend Johan Cruyff and creating its local version known as "Tiki Taka." Argentinian Lionel Messi, who joined FC Barcelona's academy as a young boy and developed to be one of the game's best players, demonstrates the glocal approach of the club. Issues about Spanish nationality and unity in Spanish football manifest through Spain not having an official national stadium and the national team "La Roja" hosting in different stadiums and the final of the Spanish Cup—Copa del Rey—also rotating between stadiums around the country. With that said, Spain is one of the most dominant forces in international football, with La Roja winning the 2010 FIFA World Cup, the 2008 and 2012 European Championships, and Real Madrid winning the UEFA Champions League in its current or former forms 13 times, FC Barcelona winning 5 times, and the two winnings 7 of the 10 competitions between 2008 and 2018. Two of the UEFA Champions League finals were derby games between Real Madrid and Atletico Madrid. All three teams have been involved with a variety of foreign nation branding initiatives. Real Madrid, FC Barcelona, and Atletico Madrid previously were sponsored by UAE, Qatar, and Azerbaijan (Chadwick et al., 2020), and participated in the Spanish Super Cup in Saudi Arabia in January 2020. Such ongoing duality between localism, globalism, a contested collective identity, amid a financial crisis, led to Spain's contribution to the rise and fall of the ESL.

Real Madrid and FC Barcelona were among the driving forces of the ESL. The two clubs have been dominating the domestic league, yet have not been able to maximize their global popularity through television rights, leading to accumulated debts of almost 3 billion Euros each (Gretz et al., 2021). Unlike the English Premier League, only in recent years, the Spanish LaLiga started to adopt a more equitable revenue-sharing model (McMahon, 2019), which meant that Real Madrid, FC Barcelona, and to a lesser degree Atletico Madrid, enjoy a financial advantage over their rivals (Statista, 2021). The revenue-distribution system in the UCL also did not benefit the Spanish giants, and along with irresponsible financial behavior, a history of banks erasing debts, and a global pandemic leading to a global recession, Real Madrid, FC Barcelona, and to a certain extent Atletico Madrid, desperately needed a structural change. Real Madrid has been pushing towards an elite European league for a while, and Florentino Perez, the club's president, was also the first chairman of the ESL (European Super League, 2021a). Real Madrid and FC Barcelona are owned by club members (Gretz et al., 2021), who periodically elect the club's president. That can help explain why there was not such a significant backlash from local fans against their clubs. In fact, as of the end of April 2021, when the ESL officially collapsed, both Real Madrid and FC Barcelona had not officially withdrawn.

While Real Madrid and Barcelona were among the architects of the ESL, there were also forces in Spain that led to the league's collapse. There was some backlash by fans and in the Spanish media against the ESL (Lowe, 2021), but not in the same magnitude as in England. Arguably, the most significant backlash was the decision by Atletico Madrid to withdraw from the ESL the day after the English domino effect (Newman, 2021), demonstrating again that even among its elite clubs, there is not one united Spanish front.

Italy

Nation branding and football in Italy go back to hosting the second FIFA World Cup in 1934, where "Il Duce" Benito Mussolini ensured a home victory through corruption and intimidation (Sugden & Tomlinson, 2017; Zimbalist, 2016) and promoting the fascist ideology through a grand spectacle for the masses. Corruption, politics, and international glory continued to surround Italian football when the "*Squadra Azzurra*" won the 1982 and 2006 FIFA World Cups, the Camorra—the Neapolitan mafia—surrounded FC Napoli and Diego Maradona in their heydays, Silvio Berlusconi leveraging the success of AC Milan to a political career becoming a corrupted prime mister, and Juventus stripped from championships and relegated for bribery and match-fixing (Archambault, 2018; Buraimo et al., 2016). The Italian TV rights structure applies a 50% revenue-sharing model and 50% distributed based on performance, history, and ratings (Crystal, 2021). That, along with revenues from the UCL, and political and economic turmoil in rival clubs, led to dominant champions, such as Inter Milan winning 5 championships between 2005 and 2010, and Juventus winning 9 between 2011 and 2020.

There are several reasons why Juventus, AC Milan, and Inter Milan—are all former multiple-times European champions from the North of Italy—pushed for the creation of the ESL. First and foremost, it was the debts of the clubs, and especially of Juventus (Gretz et al., 2021). Without a sustainable financial model, with a history of corruption, and with different international regulations, to compete with the best teams in England, Germany, and Spain, Juventus needed to purchase players beyond their revenue capabilities, including Cristiano Ronaldo from Real Madrid. Andrea Agnelli, the chairman of Juventus, was one of the dominant figures behind the ESL and was appointed as the vice-chairman of the new competition. This leads to another significant reason, as the unsustainable financial model of Italian football brought ownership changes in the two clubs from Milano. After decades under the ownership of Silvio Berlusconi and his family, in 2017 Chinese businessman Li Yonghong took over the club, but due to the ongoing debt, in 2018 American financial company Elliot Management Corporation became the sole shareholder. Inter Milan also went through ownership drama, as again, due to financial debts the Moretti family sold the club to Indonesian businessman Erik Tohr who sold it in 2018 to Chinese billionaire Steven Zhang. Thus, despite the two teams having deep roots in Italian ownerships, the ongoing debts, and the frequent change of hands, led both teams owned and controlled by foreigners without ties to Italian football and traditions.

The political and economic climate in Italian football, the different agendas, and foreign influences also led to the collapse of the ESL. There was some domestic clash, as Juventus fans protested the ESL, and Agnelli himself was criticized in Italian media for leading a failed coup and by other Seria A presidents for "betrayal" (Doyle, 2021). From a collective identity perspective (David & Bar Tal, 2009), while all three teams have their cultural traditions, they are also from the North of Italy, Milan, and Turin—representing the richer and more global part of Italy, of rich fashion and high culture, rather than the blue color south, such as FC Napoli (Archambault, 2018). The rivalry between northern and southern Italian football clubs goes back to the 1920s (Archambault, 2018) and the ESL can be seen as the northern teams trying to break away from the rest of the country, which could have also added to domestic backlash. While Agnelli remained a loyal advocate for the league amid the growing pressure and even after the English teams withdrew, the teams from Milano did not. With each club having its interest and agenda, AC Milan and Inter Milan withdrew from the ESL, and Juventus stayed in, showing that Italy as well does not have a united front.

Germany and France

Originally Germany and France were also part of the discussion over the creation of the ESL (ESPN, 2021), being the two economic powerhouses in the European Union (EU) and two of the five strongest European football leagues (Statista, 2022). Bayern Munich and PSG were the last two clubs to play in the last UCL final before the ESL announcement, and the national teams of Germany and France were the last to win the FIFA World Cups in 2014 and 2018, respectively. The way Mussolini used the 1934 FIFA World Cup for fascist propaganda influenced Adolf Hitler in using the Berlin 1936 Olympic Games to showcase to German people how functional, modern, and efficient the country can be under the regime of Nazi Germany (Sugden & Tomlinson, 2017; Zimbalist, 2016). During the second half of the twentieth century German football was mostly associated with traditional German stereotypes such as structural and efficient, yet 70 years after the Berlin Olympics, Germany used the 2006 FIFA World Cup to showcase a diverse, multicultural open, flag-waving country (Kaelberer, 2017). The Bundesliga is third in Europe in terms of revenue generation (Statista, 2022) and is dominated by Bayern Munich who won eight straight national championships before the creation of the ESL. What is also unique about football in Germany is its structural connection to the community, as 50%+1 shares of all Bundesliga teams are owned by club members (Wagner et al., 2021). That situation prevents any majority owner or foreign owners to act according to their agendas or according to a national agenda of foreign countries. That can help explain why both Bayern Munich and Borussia Dortmund declined the invitation to join the ESL.

Having an activist social society, power struggles in France manifest as well through football, whether it is through a representation of ethnic minorities especially from former French colonies through the national teams "Les Bleus" that won the 1998 and 2018 FIFA World Cups (Oonk, 2021). In the French Ligue 1, social struggles can be seen through the rivalry between blue-collar Olympique de Marseille which represents a port city in the South of France influenced by immigration from North Africa, with rich PSG (Ranc & Hourcade, 2018). In 2011, Qatar Sports Investments bought PSG, as part of an overall soft power move, using international sports for nation branding, which included Qatari-owned network *Al Jazeera* buying the TV rights of Ligue 1 (Brannagan & Giulianotti, 2018; Chadwick, 2018). Since the acquisition of PSG, the Qatari bought some of the most glamourous names in world football to play in the French capital, including David Beckham, Zlatan Ibrahimovich, and others winning seven championships between 2012 and 2020. Although not having a history of being a European powerhouse, through its acquisitions PSG often challenged UEFA's FFP regulations, eliminating potential domestic resistance, which made the ESL an attractive possibility. Yet, with Qatar constantly being scrutinized for sportswashing, corruption, and human rights violations after winning the bid to host the 2022 FIFA World Cup (Chadwick, 2018), having PSG break away from existing competitions and join the ESL would challenge UEFA and FIFA and jeopardize its soft power strategies. So, PSG declined the invitation. With clubs from the two powerhouses of the EU not joining the ESL, the project has shown cracks before even starting.

Foreign Ownership

Beyond the countries of the participating clubs, multiple other foreign forces influenced the ESL, especially through ownership. Since the early 2000s Russian oligarch started to purchase Western sports clubs to earn international legitimacy (Riordan, 2007). By investing unsustainable amounts of money, clubs like Chelsea and Portsmouth FC won prestigious trophies, but the financial ecosystem of football was challenged. UEFA's FFP rules have constantly been violated, and as seen through the collapse of Portsmouth who was relegated several leagues, the entire future of the club depended on the owner's commitment. Under the ownership of Roman Abramovich, FC Chelsea became one of the top clubs in Europe, which, beyond the men's team, built a productive academy and an elite women's team led by some of the best athletes and coaches worldwide. Abramovich's agendas have often been questioned, especially about money laundering and Russian influence (Garside, 2018; Martinez, 2018). Being Jewish, Abramovich received Israeli citizenship, yet he does not have a British visa. Abramovich was also constantly linked with Vladimir Putin's agenda (Riordan, 2007), who in the 2010s used mega sports events, including the 2018 FIFA World Cup, for nation branding and soft power purposes. The 2018 and 2022 FIFA World Cups in Russia and Qatar have often been referred to as sportswashing attempts (Chadwick, 2018). Thus, while Russian Oligarchs also fractured the economic ecosystem of football which created a need for the ESL, Russian leadership needed FIFA and UEFA to achieve public diplomacy goals. This can also explain why FC Chelsea was the first team to express its wishes to back off.

As discussed earlier, the countries from the Arabian Gulf have been using European football to promote themselves through ownership, sponsorships, and hosting (Brannagan & Giulianotti, 2018; Chadwick et al., 2020). Yet while some of the tactics of Qatar and the UAE seem similar, their political agendas are significantly different and should be understood through the complex geopolitics of the Middle East. While Qatar is much closer to Iran, the UAE is aligned with Saudi Arabia. Such differences led to an ongoing diplomatic crisis in the region that applied to boycotts of sports events as well. Yet, much like with the Russian oligarchs, countries from the Arabian Gulf are also constantly accused of sportswashing and contributing to the financial instability of football by violating FFP regulations. One of the most unique approaches of the Arabian Gulf was through the Emirate Abu Dhabi, who did not just purchase Manchester City FC and led it to unprecedented success but created an entire franchise around it as part of the City Football Group with teams in Europe, Asia, Oceania, and North America (City Football Group, n.d.; Sky Sports Football, 2021a, b). Thus, while being part of an elite group of clubs such as the ESL was important for Abu Dhabi, the global outreach also means working with football governing bodies. This can also explain why Manchester City was the first club to officially announce its withdrawal from the ESL.

The involvement from American ownership should be analyzed through the lenses of export branding and corporate diplomacy, as the projected image relates generating revenues. While the Russian oligarchs and Arabian Sheikhs were criticized for using European football for political gains, there was rarely backlash by their fans for investing in the teams and making them more competitive (Riordan, 2007; Sky Sports Football, 2021a). However, the involvement of American ownership was often associated with trying to bring American corporate culture and change local traditions for revenue purposes and at times was received by local protests of "Yanks out" (Nalton, 2021). The closed American leagues that give long-term financial security but do not depend on relegations and promotions (Jakar & Gerretsen, 2021; Nauright & Ramfjord, 2010; Wagner et al., 2021), along with the idea that for financial purposes a sports club could relocate to more profitable markets, such as from Seattle to Oklahoma City or from St. Louis to Los Angeles, do not resonate with the European sports system (Szymanski, 2021; Sky Sports Football, 2021a). Thus, much of the backlash from the football community was against John Henry, Stan Kroenke, and the Glazer brothers Joel and Avram—the American owners of FC Liverpool, Arsenal, and Manchester United, respectively. In the case of the Glazers, the backlash goes back to their early days in Manchester United. Much of the criticism in the media was against Liverpool, Manchester United, and Arsenal as English clubs with long traditions and owners who betrayed loyal fans and the game for greed during a global pandemic (Sky Sports Football, 2021a, b). The foreign nationality of the owners was often mentioned, at times to emphasize disconnect from English traditions (Sky Sports Football, 2021a), and at times to emphasize American capitalist values and the American sports system (Szymanski, 2021). Following the protests, American owners issued apologies for letting down the fans (Nalton, 2021). The ESL was led by Real Madrid, Barcelona, and Juventus, with the American owners being on board but not at the realm. Yet, especially in England the backlash was predominantly against the American owners, and the normative image of Americans and the United States was heavily scrutinized.

The role of China in the rise and fall of the ESL needs to be analyzed through smart power lenses (Dubinsky, 2021a, b), and the long-term goal of President Xi Jinping to make China the largest sports economy in the world and a dominant football nation, including targeting hosting a future FIFA World Cup (Chadwick et al., 2020). China has been using sports for smart power purposes, combining both soft and hard power goals (Chadwick et al., 2020; Dubinsky, 2021b)—for example, using the Olympic Movement for nation branding with Beijing becoming the first city to host both the Summer and Winter Olympic Games and investing in football stadiums in Africa as part of smart power goals in the continent (Dubinsky, 2021b). China's investment in football included improving the local league by purchasing famous players, having Chinese companies sponsoring international competitions, buying the rights to host some European competitions such as the Italian Supercup, and wealthy billionaires buying sports clubs, including Li Yonghong previously owning AC Milan, and Zhang Jindong and his company Sunning Holding Group becoming the majority owners of Inter Milan (Chadwick et al., 2020; Gretz, et al., 2021). Much like the City Football Group, as the interest was more on being part of the elite of Europe rather than making a financial profit and with the government's aim of acting along with international sports federations and not against them, once the ESL started to collapse, Inter Milan also withdrew.

Non-State Actors

While the realist approach in international relations analyzes states as unitary actors seeking survival, the liberal approach also emphasizes international organizations and other pressure groups. In the context of the ESL, there have been several non-state actors who played a key role in the conditions that led to the rise and fall of the project. First and foremost, the two relevant sports governing bodies, FIFA and UEFA, failed to create a financially sustainable system and have been constantly criticized for corruption (Sugden & Tomlinson, 2017). FIFA's and UEFA's strategies to accommodate interests of smaller countries, expanding the UCL and other international competitions, adding games and competitions, and even considering holding the FIFA World Cup every two years—all these decisions meant less power and money for the elite clubs, a calendar that jeopardizes the health of football players, and a need to have bigger squads and more expenses. Even the harsher critics of the ESL agreed that football in its current form became financially unsustainable and needed significant reforms (Daskal, 2021).

UEFA reformed the UCL structure to what was described as the "Swiss model" which does not follow the traditional group stages system with home-and-away games against each team in the group. That system was supposed to guarantee more direct games between the top clubs. Yet, for the founding clubs of the ESL, such a solution was not enough and still relied on earning a place in the league through domestic competitions. Trying to block the ESL, FIFA and UEFA threatened the clubs and their players with domestic and international sanctions. While the legality of such actions has not been proven in court, it signaled players, leagues, and fans that the ESL founding clubs are going to be under constant scrutiny. Furthermore, while PSG, Manchester City, and to a lesser extent Tottenham are among the richest teams in football, their history as top competitions in European competitions is much less impressive than clubs and countries that were left out of the ESL including four-time European champions Ajax Amsterdam, and Benfica Lisbon and Porto from Portugal who each won the cup twice. Clubs from small markets often added to the financial complexities of the UCL, leading to the need for a new revenue-generating structure. Yet, by not being among the ESL founding teams, much of Europe was already left out, including clubs with long traditions of success. Ajax condemned the ESL and supported the new format of the UCL which was branded as the "Swiss model" (AFC Ajax, 2021). This example demonstrates that despite the needed reforms in football, clubs from smaller markets preferred to support existing institutions, rather than join the ESL.

The European Union was also a factor, as several heads of state and leaders vowed to fight the ESL (Johnson et al., 2021) through sanctions and legislation. The EU's approach against the ESL and in support of the existing football institutions should be analyzed in the context of a centralized international institution fearing of losing power amid the "Brexit" and the rise of right-wing separatist leaders and parties. Recognizing defeat, Agnelli shifted the blame from Juventus to foreign political and economic forces, blaming the Brexit for the collapse of the ESL, saying to Reuters: "I have had speculation to that extent that if six teams would have broken away and would have threatened the EPL (Premier League), politics would have seen that as an attack to Brexit and their political scheme" (Heffer, 2021).

Lastly, it is also important to acknowledge global movements, such as Black Lives Matter, #MeToo, and others that encouraged global waves of athletes' activism and citizenship, leading to the football community taking a stand against the ESL. The rise and fall of the ESL were often framed by international media along with the narratives of a revolution of fans against greedy owners who wanted to take away their game and a victory of fan power (Rogers, 2021). As phrased in the Spanish *As* "There is a romantic edge to this victory of the people over the multibillionaires who want to subvert football" (Relaño, 2021).

THE AFTERMATH

In December 2022 the Court of Justice of the European Union (CJEU) rejected a lawsuit by the ESL that UEFA is an illegal monology, allowing UEFA and FIFA to expel clubs who break away from their competition (Kirkland & Faez, 2022), which might be a final blow to the Super League. Yet, the embarrassing collapse of the ESL did not follow with a clear sustainable solution to the financial challenges football clubs are facing, nor did it solve geopolitical pressures. In fact, by the end of 2022, further instability was added. Perhaps the most direct geopolitical impact was the invasion of Ukraine by Russia, which led to suspension of Russian clubs from European competitions, dropping Russian sponsors, and Western countries imposing sanctions against Russian oligarchs (Douglas, 2022; Ogden, 2022). As a result, Roman Abramovich sold FC Chelsea, and American billionaire Todd Boehly took over (Douglas, 2022). Yet, to argue that Americans are taking over the Premier League would also not be completely accurate, as the owners of both Manchester United and Liverpool also looked at selling opportunities (Reid, 2022). Geopolitical influences from the Gulf continued to shape European football, with Leo Messi moving in the summer of 2021 from FC Barcelona to Qatari-owned Paris Saint Germain, joining former teammate Neymar and French superstar Kylian Mbappé. The Qatar 2022 World Cup Final between Messi's Argentina and Mbappé's France was a dream conclusion for the host country who invested hundreds of billions in the competition for nation building purposes (Robinson & Clegg, 2022). Furthermore, Messi serves as an ambassador for Saudi Arabia (Zidane, 2022), the new player that entered the geopolitical European football arena since the ESL collapsed. Saudi Arabia's Public Investment Fund bought Newcastle United in late 2021, and in the last days of 2022 Saudi club Al-Nassr signed Cristiano Ronaldo with an unprecedented salary of $200 million per year, all as part of a long-term soft power strategy of the country (Tong & Odeh, 2022). Furthermore, UEFA is facing challenges from multiple directions. Despite the CJEU's decision (Kirkland & Faez, 2022), Real Madrid, who won the UCL in 2022, never officially withdrew from the ESL, along with FC Barcelona and Juventus, so there is still fear the current structure will be challenged in other ways. There are also other threats, as FIFA announced during the Qatar 2022 FIFA World Cup reforms in club competitions, a club world cup of 32 teams from across the globe (BBC, 2022), which will add load on players and cause further challenges to domestic leagues and continental federations.

The unsustainable financial pyramid of European club football, foreign owners with different agendas, a history of corruption in governing bodies, along with losses accumulated due to a global pandemic all accelerated the need to find innovative solutions to the ongoing crises in the world's most popular sport. The ESL was created under these circumstances and should be discussed in this context. Yet, the ESL was also an underdeveloped, half-baked idea that provoked backlash from people, organizations, and countries. Whether it was Qatar using its soft power to prevent PSG from leaving international institutions that chose the Arab country to host the 2022 FIFA World Cup, or if it was English fans and royalty worrying about foreigners taking over the "English game," or if the Americans were blamed for capitalizing on the pandemic, the ESL was a battlefield between nations, people, communities, and non-state actors. The key arguments supported in the chapter are that there are multiple explanations why the ESL ceased after less than 72 hours, and that most of the countries and actors who led to the creation of the league also led to its collapse and vice versa. Yet, despite what can be seen as a temporary victory for traditionalists opposing a closed-league system, the ESL exposed a unsustainable political economy, and for football to accommodate global and local interests, the existing system must adapt and change.

References

AFC Ajax. (2021, April 19). Ajax's reaction to Super League and new Champions League format. *Ajax*. Retrieved from https://english.ajax.nl/articles/ajax-s-reaction-to-super-league-and-new-champions-league-format/

Anholt, S. (2010). *Places: Identity, image and reputation*. Palgrave Macmillan.

Archambault, F. (2018). Italy. In J.-M. De Waele, S. Gibril, E. Gloriozova, & R. Spaaij (Eds.), *The Palgrave international handbook of football and politics* (pp. 105–124). Palgrave Macmillan. https://doi.org/10.1007/978-3-319-78777-0

BBC. (2021, April 21). European Super League timeline: Game changer – Football's volatile 72 hours. *BBC*. Retrieved from https://www.bbc.com/sport/football/56825570

BBC. (2022, December 16). Club World Cup: Fifa to stage 32-team tournament from June 2025- president Gianni Infantino. *BBC*. Retrieved from https://www.bbc.com/sport/football/64001866

Brannagan, P. M., & Giulianotti, R. (2018). The soft power – Soft disempowerment nexus: The case of Qatar. *International Affairs, 94*(5), 1139–1157. https://doi.org/10.1093/ia/iiy125

Buhmann, A., & Ingenhoff, D. (2015). The 4D Model of the country image: An integrative approach from the perspective of communication management. *The International Communication Gazette, 77*, 102–124.

Buraimo, B., Migalli, G., & Simmons, R. (2016). An analysis of consumer response to corruption: Italy's *Calciopoli* scandal. *Oxford Bulletin of Economics and Statistics, 78*(1), 22–41. https://doi.org/10.1111/obes.12094

Chadwick, S. (2018, August 24). Sport-washing, soft power and scrubbing the stains. *Asia & Pacific Policy Forum*. Retrieved from https://www.policyforum.net/sport-washing-soft-power-and-scrubbing-the-stains/

Chadwick, S., Widdop, P., & Burton, N. (2020). Soft power sports sponsorship – A social network analysis of new sponsorship form. *Journal of Political Marketing*, 1–22. https://doi.org/10.1080/15377857.2020.1723781

Christenson, M. (2021, April 20). Timeline: European Super League's rise and fall – In two and a half days. *The Guardian*. Retrieved from https://www.theguardian.com/football/2021/apr/20/timeline-the-rise-and-fall-of-the-european-super-league-in-two-days

City Football Group. (n.d.). *Our Clubs*. City Football Group. Retrieved from https://www.cityfootballgroup.com/our-clubs/

Cronin, M. (2017). Loss, protest, and heritage: Liverpool FC and Hillsborough. *The International Journal of the History of Sport, 34*(3–4), 251–265. https://doi.org/10.1080/09523367.2017.1369965

Crystal. (2021). TV rights revenues Seria A 2020 2021, how much the clubs will collect. *Italy 24 News*. Retrieved from https://www.italy24news.com/sports/football/31857.html

Cull, N. J. (2008). Public diplomacy: Taxonomies and histories. *Annals of the American Academy of Political Science, 616*(1), 31–54.
Daskal, O. (2021, April 20). The big money of football: For members only. *Calcalist*. Retrieved from https://www.calcalist.co.il/sport_news/article/SkWIkHi8d. [Hebrew].
David, O., & Bar-Tal, D. (2009). A sociopsychological conception of collective identity: The case of national identity as an example. *Personality and Social Psychology Review, 13,* 354–379. https://doi.org/10.1177/1088868309344412
Douglas, S. (2022, May 30). Abramovich completes $3.2 billion sale of EPL team Chelsea. *AP*. Retrieved from https://apnews.com/article/russia-ukraine-putin-roman-abramovich-mlb-4b065cf6c13d9761069e0224472c3dfb
Doyle, M. (2021, April 23). Agnelli's failed coup: 'Judas-like Juventus president has lost powerful allies over Super League 'betrayal'. *Goal*. Retrieved from https://www.goal.com/en/news/agnellis-failed-coup-judas-like-juventus-president-has-lost/1ifwmqkn35iqr1l5mhz282d9i3
Dubinsky, Y. (2021a). Branding a city as a sports town: A conceptual model based on 'TrackTown USA'. *Journal of Global Sport Management,* 1–17. https://doi.org/10.1080/24704067.2021.2001354
Dubinsky, I. (2021b). China's stadium diplomacy in Africa. *Journal of Global Sport Management,* 1–18. https://doi.org/10.1080/24704067.2021.1885101
Emirates. (n.d.). Sponsorship football. *Emirates*. Retrieved from https://www.emirates.com/english/about-us/our-communities/sponsorship/football/
ESPN. (2021, April 20). Bayern, PSG reject Super League in favour of Champions League. *ESPN*. Retrieved from https://www.espn.com/soccer/uefa-champions-league/story/4365203/bayernpsg-reject-super-league-in-favour-of-champions-league.
European Super League Company. (2021a). Leading European clubs announce new Super League competition. *The Super League*. Retrieved from https://thesuperleague.com/press.html
European Super League Company. (2021b). The best clubs. The best players. Every week. *The Super League*. Retrieved from https://thesuperleague.com/#who_we_are
Evans, D., & Norcliffe, G. (2016). Local identities in a global game: The social production of football space in Liverpool. *Journal of Sport & Tourism, 20*(3–4), 217–232. https://doi.org/10.1080/14775085.2016.1231621
Fan, Y. (2010). Branding the nation: Towards a better understanding. *Journal of Place Branding and Public Diplomacy, 6*(2), 97–103.
FC Bayern München. (n.d.). Partner. *FC Bayern München*. Retrieved from https://fcbayern.com/en/club/partner
Friedman, A. (2015). *Berlusconi*. Hachette Books.
Garside, J. (2018, September 25). Roman Abramovich posed threat to public security, Swiss police said. *The Guardian*. Retrieved from https://www.the-

guardian.com/world/2018/sep/25/roman-abramovich-posed-threat-to-public-security-swiss-police-said

Gretz, N. et al. (2021). As it happened: European Super League threatens to shake up 'beautiful game'. *CNN*. Retrieved from https://www.cnn.com/world/live-news/european-super-league-updates-live-cmd-spt/index.html

Hautbois, C. (2015). Chapter 5: Sport and city branding. In S. Chadwick, N. Chanavat, & M. Desdordes (Eds.), *Routledge handbook of sports marketing* (pp. 51–67). Routledge.

Heffer, G. (2021, April 21). Number 10 rejects Juventus chair's claim Boris Johnson saw European Super League as 'attack to Brexit'. *SkyNews*. Retrieved from https://news.sky.com/story/number-10-rejects-juventus-chairs-claim-boris-johnson-saw-european-super-league-as-attack-to-brexit-12282644

Hellier, D., & Nair, D. (2021, April 19). European soccer embraced big money. Now it faces all-out war. *Bloomberg*. Retrieved from https://www.bloomberg.com/news/articles/2021-04-20/european-super-league-pits-uefa-against-madrid-liverpool-and-manchester

Jaffe, E., & Nebenzahl, I. (1993). Glob6al promotion of country image: Do the Olympics count? In N. Papadopoulos & L. Heslop (Eds.), *Product-country images: Impact and role in international marketing* (pp. 433–452). International Business Press.

Jakar, G., & Gerretsen, S. (2021). Ownership in European soccer, Financial Fair Play, and performance in UEFA's 2006–2018 Champions League tournaments. *Journal of Sport Management, 35*(1), 511–521. https://doi.org/10.1123/jsm.2020-0217

Johnson, M., Pickard, J., & Abboud, L. (2021, April 20). European political leaders vow to block Super League football plan. *Financial Times*. Retrieved from https://www.ft.com/content/4f7291cf-1225-4127-8972-6e46cc3f1ce1

Kaelberer, M. (2017). From Bern to Rio: Soccer and national identity discourses in Germany. *International Journal of Politics, Culture, and Society, 30*, 275–294. https://doi.org/10.1007/s10767-016-9234-6

Kirkland, A. & Faez, R. (2022, December 15). EU court rejects European Super League claim of illegal UEFA monopoly. *ESPN*. Retrieved from https://www.espn.com/soccer/uefa-champions-league/story/4832443/eu-court-rejects-super-league-claim-of-illegal-uefa-monopoly

Koch, N. (2020). The geopolitics of Gulf sport sponsorship. *Sport, Ethics and Philosophy, 14*(3), 355–376. https://doi.org/10.1080/17511321.2019.1669693

KPMG (2021, May). The European Elite 2021. *KPMG Sports Advisory Practice*. Retrieved from https://www.footballbenchmark.com/documents/files/KPMG%20The%20European%20Elite%202021.pdf

Lowe, S. (2021, April 21). La Liga's Super League fight: How Spain reacted to Barcelona, Real Madrid, Atletico split. *ESPN*. Retrieved from https://www.

espn.com/soccer/spanish-primera-division/story/4367397/la-ligas-super-league-fight-how-spain-reacted-to-barcelonareal-madridatletico-split

Martinez, A. (2018, June 22). World Cup won't give Putin global power. *CNN*. Retrieved from https://www.cnn.com/2018/06/22/opinions/putin-world-cup-plan-wont-work-martinez-opinion/index.html

McMahon, B. (2019, December 15). La Liga distributes €1.4 in TV money; Barcelona and 17 other teams receive record payouts. *Forbes*. Retrieved from https://www.forbes.com/sites/bobbymcmahon/2019/12/15/la-liga-distributes-14b-in-tv-money-barcelona-and-17-other-teams-receive-record-payouts/

Media. (2011, April 19). Adidas and Bayern Munich extend successful partnership until 2020, present New Jersey. *Adidas*. Retrieved from https://www.adidas-group.com/en/media/news-archive/press-releases/2011/adidas-and-fc-bayern-munich-extend-successful-partnership-until-/

Mwinwelle, P., Agbemehia, K. G., & Mwinwelle, R. (2020). A stylo-thematic analysis of rivalry in the anthems of Real Madrid and FC Barcelona. *Advances in Language and Literature Studies, 11*(2), 8–15. https://doi.org/10.7575/aiac.alls.v.11n.2-p.8

Nadeau, J., Heslop, L., O'Reilly, N., & Luk, P. (2008). Destination in a country image context. *Annals of Tourism Research, 35*(1), 84–106. https://doi.org/10.1016/j.annals.2007.06.012

Nalton, J. (2021, April 28). Can Liverpool owners FSG rebuild relationship with fans? *Forbs*. Retrieved from https://www.forbes.com/sites/jamesnalton/2021/04/28/can-liverpool-owners-fsg-rebuild-relationship-with-fans/

Nauright, J., & Ramfjord, J. (2010). Who owns England's game? American professional sporting influences and foreign ownership in the Premier League. *Soccer & Society, 11*(4), 428–441. https://doi.org/10.1080/14660971003780321

Newman, R. (2021, April 21). Inter Milan, AC Milan, Atletico Madrid pull out of European Super League, Juventus accept defeat. *Eurosport*. Retrieved from https://www.eurosport.com/football/champions-league/2020-2021/inter-milan-and-atletico-madrid-join-english-clubs-in-withdrawing-from-the-european-super-league_sto8283147/story.shtml

Nye, J. S., Jr. (2008). Public diplomacy and soft power. *ANNALS of the American Academy of Political and Social Science, 616*(1), 94–109.

Ogden, M. (2022, February 28). FIFA suspends Russia from World Cup, UEFA throws teams out of European competition. *ESPN*. Retrieved from https://www.espn.com/soccer/fifa-world-cup/story/4605670/uefa-removes-russian-teams-from-all-competitions-following-ukraine-invasion

Oonk, G. (2021). Who may represent the country? Football, citizenship, migration, and national identity at the FIFA World Cup. *The International Journal of the History of Sport, 37*(11), 1046–1065. https://doi.org/10.1080/09523367.2020.1844188

Ortega, V. R. (2016). Soccer, nationalism and the media in contemporary Spanish society: La Roja, Real Madrid & FC Barcelona. *Soccer & Society, 17*(4), 628–643. https://doi.org/10.1080/14660970.2015.1067793

Papadopoulos, N., Banna, A. E., & Murphy, S. A. (2017). Old country passions: An international examination of country image, animosity, and affinity among ethnic consumers. *Journal of International Marketing, 25*(3), 61–82. https://doi.org/10.1509/jim.16.0077

Powell, D. (2021, April 28). SG and the truth about Liverpool's £238m debt. *Echo.* Retrieved from https://www.liverpoolecho.co.uk/sport/football/football-news/fsg-truth-liverpools-238m-debt-20485647

Premier League. (2019, May 23). Premier League value of central payments to clubs 2018/9. *Premier League.* Retrieved from https://www.premierleague.com/news/1225126

Premier League. (2021, June 9). Premier League and The FA join statement. *Premier League.* Retrieved from https://www.premierleague.com/news/2167982?sf246616763=1

Ranc, D., & Hourcade, N. (2018). France. In J.-M. De Waele, S. Gibril, E. Gloriozova, & R. Spaaij (Eds.), *The Palgrave international handbook of football and politics* (pp. 31–60). Palgrave Macmillan. https://doi.org/10.1007/978-3-319-78777-0

Reid, J. (2022, December 24). Why Liverpool and Manchester United, two giants of soccer, are up for sale at the same time. *CNBC.* Retrieved from https://www.cnbc.com/2022/12/24/why-two-iconic-soccer-clubs-are-up-for-sale-at-the-same-time.html

Relaño, A. (2021, April 22). England sports the egotistical European Super League. *AS.* Retrieved from https://en.as.com/en/2021/04/22/opinion/1619050333_403067.html

Riordan, J. (2007). Football: Nation, city and the dream: Playing the game for Russia, money, and power. *Soccer & Society, 8*(4), 545–560. https://doi.org/10.1080/14660970701440840

Robinson, J. & Clegg, J. (2022, December 16). Who wins a World Cup Final between France and Argentina? Qatar. *The Wall Street Journal.* https://www.wsj.com/articles/lionel-messi-kylian-mbappe-world-cup-final-qatar-france-argentina-11671134408

Rogers, M. (2021, April 21). The triumph of fan power over the European Super League. *FOX Sports.* Retrieved from https://www.foxsports.com/stories/soccer/fan-power-european-super-league-martin-rogers

Sky Sports Football. (2021a, April 18). I'm absolutely DISGUSTED!|Gary Neville's verdict on the European Super League proposals. *YouTube.* Retrieved from https://www.youtube.com/watch?v=GP05EDm9EB8

Sky Sports Football. (2021b, April 20). Gary Neville slams 'spineless' owners of breakaway clubs! *YouTube.* Retrieved from https://www.youtube.com/watch?v=e9umu7Y2f6c

Solberg, H. A., & Gratton, C. (2004). Would European soccer clubs benefit from playing in a Super League? *Soccer and Society, 5*(1), 61–81. https://doi.org/10.1080/14660970512331391004

Statista. (2021). Net revenue of the football teams in Spain's LaLiga in the seasons 2018/2019 and 2019/2020. *Statista.* Retrieved from https://www.statista.com/statistics/1231398/net-revenue-of-the-football-teams-in-spain-s-laliga/

Statista. (2022). Revenue of the biggest (Big Five) European soccer leagues from 1996/7 to 2021/22. *Statista.* Retrieved from https://www.statista.com/statistics/261218/big-five-european-soccer-leagues-revenue/

Sugden, J., & Tomlinson, A. (2017). *Football, corruption, and lies.* Routledge.

Szymanski, S. (2021, April 27). American sports logic created soccer's failed Super League. *Foreign Policy.* Retrieved from https://foreignpolicy.com/2021/04/27/europeam-super-league-american-sports-model/

Taylor, M. (2018). United Kingdom. In J.-M. De Waele, S. Gibril, E. Gloriozova, & R. Spaaij (Eds.), *The Palgrave international handbook of football and politics* (pp. 181–201). Palgrave Macmillan. https://doi.org/10.1007/978-3-319-78777-0

Tharoor, I. (2021, April 19). The Americanization of the global game reaches a tipping point. *The Washington Post.* Retrieved from https://www.washingtonpost.com/world/2021/04/19/americanization-europes-beloved-game-reaches-tipping-point/

Tong, S., & Odeh, L. (2022, December 30). Ronaldo signs with Saudi Arabia's Al Nassr Football Club. *Bloomberg.* https://www.bloomberg.com/news/articles/2022-12-30/ronaldo-has-signed-to-play-for-saudi-arabia-s-al-nassr-club

UEFA. (n.d.). Financial Fair Play. *UEFA.* Retrieved from https://www.uefa.com/insideuefa/protecting-the-game/financial-fair-play/

Wagner, U., Storm, R. K., & Cortsen, K. (2021). Commercialization, governance problems, and the future of European football – Or why the European Super League is not a solution to the challenges facing football. *International Journal of Sport Communication, 14*(3), 321–333. https://doi.org/10.1123/ijsc.2021-0049

Winner, D. S. (2019, May 10). Don't blame soccer's 'Jewish' teams for Anti-Semitism. *Foreign Policy.* Retrieved from https://foreignpolicy.com/2019/05/10/dont-blame-for-anti-semitism-in-soccer-tottenham-hotspur-spurs-ajax-amsterdam/

Woods, R., & Butler, N. (2021). *Social issues in sport* (4th ed.). Human Kinetics.

Zidane, K. (2022, May 12). Lionel Messi earned $122m last year. He still felt the need to take Saudi money. *The Guardian.* Retrieved from https://www.theguardian.com/football/2022/may/12/lionel-messi-saudi-arabia-deal-tourism

Zimbalist, A. (2016). *Circus Maximus.* Brookings Institution Press.

CHAPTER 7

Nation Branding, Public Diplomacy, and the Dirty Business of Sportswashing

INTRODUCTION

The use of sports for nation branding and public diplomacy goes back to antiquity, not only to the city-states and the athletic competitions in Olympia, in Ancient Greece, but also through the conquests of Alexander the Great. Implementing athletic competitions in newly conquered colonies was a useful Hellenizing tool (Miller, 2004). As modern sports were mostly institutionalized in Western Europe and North America in the second half of the nineteenth century, Great Britain, France, and the United States were among those who shaped the future of international sports (Krechmar et al., 2017). Some implications were the aristocratic nature of the Olympic Movement which relied on amateurism, and having the Olympic Games held only in Europe and the United States until the end of World War II (Boykoff, 2016; Dubinsky, 2019a). After the War, with more countries receiving independence, and the world becoming bipolar, the Olympic Movement became more international, and the Games were spread into more territories and continents. The change was not only semantic, but also meant that non-Western countries had more influence in decision-making positions and the traditional powerhouses started to lose power. Much of the international struggles in sports during the 1950s, 1960s, 1970s, and 1980s was caused by direct or by-proxy backlash between the Eastern Bloc led by the Soviet Union and the Western World led by the USA (Dubinsky, 2019a, b; Murray, 2018; Rofe &

© The Author(s), under exclusive license to Springer Nature Switzerland AG 2023
Y. Dubinsky, *Nation Branding and Sports Diplomacy*,
https://doi.org/10.1007/978-3-031-32550-2_7

Scott-Smith, 2018). The clashes of cultures, nationalism, and economic systems, led to an arms race in international sports, including to state-led and private doping systems, political boycotts, and different ways of bypassing amateurism—ultimately leading the Olympic Games to become fully professional (Dubinsky, 2019a).

With the end of the Cold War and the collapse of the Soviet Union, the USA, the capitalist system, and Western European democracies shaped the future of international sports during the 1990s. Political scientist Samuel Huntington (1996) used the term "clash of civilizations" when discussing the post–Cold War world order, arguing that future conflicts will be between communities with different values and cultures, especially between Western and non-Western civilizations. Huntington (1996) associates values such as universalism, modernity, and democracy with the West, along with superior military capabilities and economic capacities, while also identifying potential challenges, especially in what he classifies as Sinic (which includes China), Islamic, Orthodox (which among others includes Russia and former members of the Soviet Union) civilizations (Huntington, 1996). While there is much critic about the "clash of civilizations" as a theoretical framework (Bottici & Challand, 2010) especially regarding depiction of Muslims (Abozaid, 2018), as of the end of 2022 China, Russia, and dozens of Islamic countries have not fully embraced liberalism and democracy, leading to cultural and social clashes with the West.

Within that context of a unipolar world with only one superpower and with liberalism shaping international sports, new actors identified how the system can work for their own benefit, regardless of their political regime. Predominantly China, Russia, and autocratic countries from the Arabian Gulf recognized liberal paradoxes and loopholes, and identified ways of using international sports for their own geopolitical gain (Chadwick, 2022a; Dubinsky, 2019b; Grix et al., 2019). With the Western world once again losing its hegemony, such attempts are often negatively framed as "sports-washing"—attempts by nondemocratic or totalitarian regimes who use sports to launder their international image that has been tarnished due to human rights violations (Chadwick, 2022a; Fruh et al., 2022; Lenskyj, 2022). This chapter discusses the concept of sportswashing as a nation branding and public diplomacy tool, and questions if it is really a tool used by nondemocratic countries or a negative framing by former empires fearing losing power, and how it manifests especially through multiple international sports events held in 2022.

What Is Sportswashing?

The term "sportswashing" or "sports-washing" was created out of terms such as whitewashing, and descendants such as greenwashing and pinkwashing (Boykoff & Mascarenhas, 2016; Fruh et al., 2022; Kiel, 2020). The idea behind these terms is to present a washed image, meaning to take a negative and dubious feature and present an image in a favorable light. The term whitewashing is used in various contexts, but especially in the context of a history of racism (Fruh et al., 2022). Greenwashing pertains mostly to attempts to wash unsustainable and unecological practices that damage the environment by "claiming credit for providing solutions while doing the bare minimum, if anything at all" (Boykoff & Mascarenhas, 2016). Yet, at times the washing attempts might be to distract the conversation and focus on other negative features and practices, such as human rights violations. Pinkwashing, for example, refers to "the use of LGBTQ rights as a propaganda tool that distracts from rights violations in other areas" (Kiel, 2020, p. 8). According to Fruh, Archer, and Wojtowicz (2022), "In the case of sportswashing, the way attention is routed away from the moral violation is through sport" (p. 3). Amnesty International often uses the term to describe countries using sports to distract from human rights abuses (Zidan, 2022). Yet, there is also much contention to a clear definition of sportswashing, including about sports events that are not state-orchestrated, or how Western democracies been using sports to promote their foreign policy goals, despite their own unethical practices (Dubinsky, 2021a; PtG, 2022).

As mentioned previously, the use of sports to change a place's image goes back to antiquity and is reshaped as modern sports keeps being structured (Dubinsky, 2019b; Murray, 2018). With over 200 states and delegations represented in the Olympic Games, and with the competitions being broadcasted globally, almost every country on Earth sees value in using sports for nation branding and public diplomacy purposes regardless of its size or type of political regime (Dubinsky, 2022a). Thus, sportswashing is a by-product of soft power—an attempt to create a positive image through attraction without the use of military force or economic sanctions (Nye, 2008), and if combined with hard power strategies, sportswashing can be used as part of smart power as well. The use of sports to distract domestic and foreign publics from negative practices of the government to achieve geopolitical goals is not new. Fascist dictator Benito Mussolini used the 1934 FIFA World Cup in Italy to unite the country behind the national team, including through intimidation of referees (Brun & Gomez, 2022). Two years later, Adolf Hitler and his propaganda minister Joseph Goebbels used the Berlin 1936 Olympic Games for their own political goals to show how structured and efficient the country can be under the governance of the Nazi Party, leading to a wave of national pride, including of Nazi propaganda and the "Heil Hitler" salutes. Despite international criticism over terror and crime in Germany by the National Socialist Party and the racist antisemitic "Nuremberg Laws" to protect "German blood," only a handful of countries boycotted the Games (Krüger & Murray, 2003). Due to mixed opinions in the USA, Avery Brundage—who will later become a controversial International Olympic Committee (IOC) President—visited Berlin, met with the organizers, and persuaded the Americans not to boycott, despite the outrage of the Jewish community in the USA (Boykoff, 2016). According to Zirin and Boykoff (2020), "Brundage is infamous for his racism, sexism, and anti-Semitism." Berlin 1936 was a significant moment in the cultivation of Germany behind the Nazi regime, despite its racist propaganda and practices, fostering Hitler's hawkish ambitions and leading to the worst systematic genocide in modern times (Dubinsky, 2019a).

Following World War II, and during the Cold War, there were ample nondemocratic regimes hosting sports events, including Spain hosting the 1964 UEFA European Nations Cup (later to be known as the European Championship) under the dictatorship of Generalissimo Francisco Franco (Simón & Rieck, 2022), and of course in 1978 in Argentina, General Junta used the domestic FIFA World Cup as a nationalistic propaganda tool (Brun & Gomez, 2022), trying to portray a different image of Argentina following the coup d'état of a murderous military regimes. Despite being excluded from the Olympic Movement since the 1960s due to the racial discriminatory laws of the Apartheid Regime, South Africa continued to host boxing and rugby competitions (Dubinsky, 2022b). As a protest of New Zealand being invited to compete in the Montreal 1976 Olympic Games despite its rugby team touring Apartheid South Africa, over 20 African countries withdrew from the Olympics in protest (Boykoff, 2016). Romanian dictator Nicolae Ceaușescu and the Romanian Communist Party used gymnastics superstar Nadia Comaneci and Romanian gymnastics as propaganda tools (Boykoff, 2016; Gilbert, 2015). Thus, despite the term sportswashing being relatively new, the image laundering practices are not.

What has changed is that since the shift from amateurism to capitalization of the Olympic Movement and international sports, and the technological evolution of broadcasting and the internet, sports became a global tool, reaching billions of households across every territory on Earth. To capitalize on the power of sports as a geopolitical tool, sportswashing predominantly manifests through the practices of hosting mega-sports events to bring international attention to the country, buying or sponsoring global sports organizations thus exposing the country's names and products, having administrators in influential positions in international sports governing bodies, and naturalizing athletes to improve the competitiveness and representation of local athletes on an international level (Brannagan & Giulianotti, 2015; Chadwick, 2022a; Fruh et al., 2022). These strategies, along with regular hosting of smaller sports events and training camps, using athletes as ambassadors, and creating different sports for development and peace organizations, are all intended to normalize the image of the country. Sportswashing has been proven as a useful strategy "with the global appeal of competitive sport overshadowing calls for social justice" (Lenskyj, 2022, p. 52).

Boykoff (2022) tried to theorize and conceptualize sportswashing, suggesting that not just authoritarian and autocratic countries practice sportswashing but it can emerge in democratic countries as well, sportswashing can target both domestic and international audiences, it can be tied with military intervention, and that it is evolving and new forms emerge through authoritarian regimes funding teams and events in democratic states. While governments have been using some of these practices, the three countries that have shaped sportswashing as a strategic tool are China, Russia, and Qatar (Boykoff, 2022; Chadwick, 2018, 2022a, b; Fruh et al., 2022). In the next sections the chapter discusses the sportswashing strategies of China, Russia, and Qatar, practices used in other countries facing criticism on human rights violations, and critically discusses about democracies with a history of colonization.

CHINA

Despite being the most populated country in the world, and the second largest global economy (Nye, 2020), for decades China has not capitalized on its potential through sports (Chadwick, 2015; Murray, 2018). Sports in China go back thousands of years, including athletics, martial arts practices such as kung fu, and others (Krechmar et al., 2017). Yet, as modern sports were mostly institutionalized in Europe and North America, China has often been left behind, isolated behind its walls, not participating in the Olympics prior to World War II, and only once prior to the 1980s (Murray, 2018). Yet, even then, during the Cold War and during the Chinese Communist period, sports played a role in Chinese foreign policy through "ping pong diplomacy" (Rofe, 2016)—friendly table tennis games between Chinese and American delegates led to formalizing relations between the People's Republic of China and the USA and to a first official visit of an American President to Beijing in 1971 and a meeting between US President Ronald Reagan and Chinese Chairman Mao Zedong (Murray, 2018).

It took China almost a quarter of a century after the end of the Cold War to challenge Western dominance in sports. The Beijing 2008 Olympic Games are very much considered a coming out of the walls party for China, demonstrating its high-level technologies while hosting the most expensive summer Olympic Games with an estimated cost of over $40 billion (Beech, 2008). For example, Chinese company Lenovo became a Worldwide Olympic Partner, bought part of IBM, designed the torch for the torch relay, and provided tech-services through the Games (Dubinsky & O'Reilly, 2012). While the Beijing 2008 Olympic Games were operationally successful and showcased the world a highly developed powerhouse, they also opened China to criticism about its authoritarian regime, including human rights violations especially against minorities in Tibet and military threat over Taiwan, lack of personal freedom, deportation, public spendings, and lack of sustainability (Boykoff, 2014; Preuss, 2015). In 2014, President Xi Jinping and the Chinese government set an ambitious goal of becoming the largest domestic sports economy in the world by 2025 (Chadwick, 2015). Since Beijing 2008, China's use of sports for nation branding and public diplomacy accelerated through (a) hosting some of the largest sports events, including the Universiade Games and world championships in track and field, swimming, basketball and others; (b) stadium diplomacy in Africa; (c) owning football clubs in European leagues; (d) manufacturing and supplying sports good in North America; and of course (e) becoming a dominant powerhouse in Asian sports (Chadwick, 2015, 2022a, b; Dubinsky, 2021b) China's outreach through sports became global.

Since the collapse of the Soviet Union, political scientists have been singling out China as a growing force in international relations especially through its growing economy, but not necessarily on challenging the USA as the hegemon or change the world's order to a more beneficial one (Nye, 2020). Despite COVID-19 originating in China, and despite its impact on global sports, while the country did cancel or postpone international sports events, it did not back down from hosting the Beijing 2022 Winter Olympic Games. The Winter Olympic Games (WOG) are significantly smaller in terms of participation, with less than 3000 competing athletes representing less than 100 countries, yet they are still broadcasted globally, reaching every county and territory worldwide (Olympics, n.d.-a). In February 2022 Beijing became the first city to host both the summer and winter Olympic Games, and China became the first country to host the OG, the WOG, and the Youth Olympic Games (YOG) (Dubinsky, 2022c). The bid for the 2022 Winter Olympic Games was turbulent, with a series of cities withdrawing due to lack of community or governmental support, leaving Beijing from China and Almaty from Kazakhstan as the only two options International Olympic Committee (IOC) members had to choose from. The Chinese capital was elected in a small majority of 44 to 40 (Olympics, 2015). The Beijing 2022 Winter Olympic Games were held during the global COVID-19, under extreme monitory conditions, and with ongoing global criticism over Chinese human rights violations, even leading to diplomatic boycotts (Boykoff, 2022). Yet, despite the turbulent bid and the ongoing international pressure, around 3900 athletes from 91 countries participated in the 2022 Winter Olympic Games (Olympics, n.d.-a), which were concluded successfully, despite all the challenges.

If Beijing 2008 was a coming out party, Beijing 2022 was an act of defiance (Dubinsky, 2022c). Hosting Winter Olympic Games in dystopian conditions (Crouse, 2022; Wang, 2022a), in what Western media described as "under Orwellian surveillance state" (Ingle, 2022a) while dividing Beijing and separating populations. Athletes and accredited stakeholders went through daily COVID-19 tests, isolations, and extreme monitoring and were warned not to criticize the Winter Olympics while in China (Ingle, 2022a; Wang, 2022a). Other concerns focused on the well-being of Tennis player Peng Shuai who accused a high-level governmental official of sexual assault (Zidan, 2022). Yet, most of the critic was about human rights abuse in Tibet and Hong Kong, and the ongoing military intimidation of Taiwan, especially against the Uighur Muslim minority (Boykoff, 2022; Dubinsky, 2022c). As a result, multiple Western countries including the USA announced diplomatic boycotts of Beijing 2022, sending athletes to compete in the Games but no diplomatic ambassadors of the states (Zidan, 2022).

The manifestation of sportswashing in Beijing 2022 can be seen through the Chinese approach to act as a disruptor, positioning itself as a global powerhouse that can host Winter Olympic Games during a pandemic despite human rights violation accusations. Not only China did not back down from the international criticism and from politicians from the West announcing diplomatic boycotts, but even acted in defiance towards liberal backlash. The Chinese had a Uyghur athlete lighting the torch in the Opening Ceremony and President Xi Jinping invited Russian president Vladimir Putin as a guest of honor. To ensure athletic success, China also naturalized Asian-American freestyle skier and model Eileen Gu, who won two gold medals and one silver medal, becoming one of the most successful athletes in the Games, a national hero, and a normalizing face of China (Olympics, n.d.-b; Wang, 2022b). Western media repeatedly used the term sportswashing to describe the authoritarian Chinese regime and the way it used sports and the 2022 Winter Olympic Games, to launder China's image. And indeed, despite the criticism, political boycotts, and the challenging circumstances (Boykoff, 2022; Wang, 2022a), the show went on, Norwegian athletes dominated the medal table enhancing the Scandinavian reputation as a winter-sport powerhouse (Olympics, n.d.-b), Jamaican bobsled athletes had the feel-good stories of the beloved "Cool Runnings" Disney movie, and China hosted the 2022 Winter Olympic Games in an unapologetic manner (Dubinsky, 2022c; Olympics, n.d.-a). Although China managed to host the Winter Olympics, due to limited success of containing the pandemic, the Asian Games and the Universiade Games were postponed beyond 2022. Despite repeated genocide accusations of the Uighur minorities, exploitations of human rights, criticism on the lack of transparency regarding COVID-19 or even comparisons to the way Nazi Germany used the Berlin 1936 Olympic Games (Ingle, 2022b; State of the Union, 2022), China established itself as Olympic royalty with Beijing being the first city to host both the Olympic Games and the Winter Olympic Games, and the country to be the first to host both types of Olympics along with the Youth Olympic Games (Dubinsky, 2022c). Internally, the Winter Olympics were a success (CNN Beijing, 2022), and the IOC did not report further outbreak of the pandemic (International Olympic Committee, 2022a).

The protests against China did not result with cancelling the Games, but Western companies were also highly criticized for financially supporting the Games as sponsors or television rights holders, and athletes who were vocal on social issues in America were criticized for being hypocritical not taking a stand against China fearing to lose potential revenues (State of the Union, 2022). The NBA, for example, has been highly scrutinized for encouraging athletes' activism in America to take a stand about domestic racial injustice, but staying silent amid social injustice in China allegedly to protect it revenues from a growing market (State of the Union, 2022). In the USA, NBC broadcasted the 2022 Winter Games through television and streaming platforms, branding February 13, 2022, as "Super Gold Sunday" (Johnson, 2022) as for the first time the Winter Olympic Games were held on the same day of the Super Bowl, thus not only normalizing the Olympic Games in Beijing but also co-branding the celebratory broadcasting day with a sports game that is often considered a nationalistic American holiday. Having China's nation branding and sports diplomacy tactics framed as sportswashing by the West or even the comparisons to Berlin 1936 (Ingle, 2022b) did not result in meaningful sanctions. China did not apologize for the spread of the COVID-19 pandemic or for any of the international criticism on human rights abuse, but unapologetically and apparently successfully used 2022 Winter Olympic Games as part of a smart power strategy to position itself as a global powerhouse and a disrupter to the West.

Russia

Much like China, Russia also joined the Olympic Movement relatively late, not competing before World War II (Murray, 2018). Yet, unlike the East-Asian country, the Soviet Union was a major powerhouse in world sports during the Cold War, seeing sports as another clashing platform to display their strength, not just in comparison to the West and the Americans, but also to other Communist countries. Some internal revolutions within the Eastern Bloc manifested through the Olympics, namely, the "Blood in the Pool" water polo final between the USSR and Hungary in Melbourne 1956 after the Soviet Union invaded Hungary, and protests by Czechoslovakian gymnast Vera Caslavska in Mexico City 1968 following the Soviet invasion to her country (Boykoff, 2016). Whether it was dominance in chess, or through dominating the Olympics, the Soviet Union saw sport as another way of highlighting the superiority of their system. Bypassing amateur regulations by employing athletes in governmental positions so they could practice their sport, abusing training of children and athletes, or conducting a state-led doping system, were all fair game behind The Iron Curtain in the Soviet Union and the Eastern

Bloc. Two of the most memorable direct clashes between the USSR and the USA were the basketball final in the Munich 1972 Olympic Games in which the Soviets won in a controversial fashion, and the semifinal of the ice hockey tournament in the Lake Placid 1980 Olympic Games in which the college-players-led Americans surprisingly won—a game known as the "Miracle on Ice." The climax of the clashes manifested in political boycotts, with the Americans leading a 60-country boycott of the Moscow 1980 Olympic Games following the Soviet Union invading Afghanistan, and the Eastern Bloc retaliating 4 years later boycotting the Los Angeles 1984 Olympic Games. With the end of the Cold War, the collapse of the Soviet Union and communism, the democratization of new independent countries, and with capitalism becoming the predominant economic system, the international influence of Russia and its allies has been on the decline, including through international sports.

Despite the collapse of the Soviet Union and Communism as viable economic systems, Russia was still the largest country in the world, and since former KGB agent Vladimir Putin became the head of the state (prime minister 1999–2000, 2008–2012, and president 2000–2008, and since 2012), the country was once again aiming to become a dominant international force, and once again sports became a tool for global empowerment. The collapse of Communism and the privatization of Russian infrastructure and public services enabled businesspeople close to the government to take advantage of the situation and secure contract to own or distribute goods and services in regions of the country, making them extraordinarily rich fast. The Oligarchs, who made their fortunes during the 1990s following the collapse of the Soviet Union (Boykoff, 2016), gradually turned to the West to receive global recognition. Part of the tactic was purchasing sports clubs in Western cities, enjoying the popularity of the masses as their clubs were winning trophies and gain more power and influence. Since Roman Abramovich bought FC Chelsea in 2003, the London club that has not won a championship since the 1950s, won around 20 trophies, including five Premier League championships, and twice in the UEFA Champions League. Such methods changed the political economy of international football, as the money spent by the Oligarchs could not be matched by local owners; led to opening ownerships to more foreign investors; increased transfer fees; and widened the gaps between big clubs and small clubs and big leagues and the rest of Europe. Along with the Oligarchs, Russian power and money bought influence in international sports. By 2010, Vladimir Putin was recognized as an honorary president of the International Judo Federation (AFP, 2022), and international sports events back to the country, including the Champions League Final, Grand Prix Moscow, and others. The Russian influence increased in the 2010s, hosting the world's largest mega-events, including the Sochi 2014 Winter Olympic Games and the 2018 FIFA World Cup, along with Kazan 2013 Universiade Games and the Krasnoyarsk 2019 Winter Universiade Games, the Moscow 2013 IAAF World Athletics Championships, and the FINA 2015 World Aquatics Championships. Russian financial influence on international sports also increased, as Gazprom became one of UEFA's largest sponsors. Despite corruption in the bid for the 2018 FIFA World Cup (Zeimers & Cnstandt, 2022), ongoing doping scandals with Russian athletes, and international criticism over human rights violations, under the leadership of Vladimir Putin, Russia was once again a global force.

Such mega-events enabled Russia to further pursue its branding goals as a global powerhouse and Putin's imperialistic ambitions. The Sochi Winter Olympic Games were surrounded by protests about human rights abuse and discriminative anti-LGBTQ legislation. Furthermore, with an unofficial estimate of over 50 billion dollars (Boykoff, 2016), these were the most expensive Olympic Games held. Despite Russia being a winter country, the Games were held in an area with mild weather that was mostly known as a vacation resort for oligarchs (Boykoff, 2016). Yet, despite the domestic and international critic, not only Russia managed to host the Games, Russian athletes dominated the podium, and the Russian national anthem was played consistently. After years of humiliation, Russian athletes were once again at the top of the world, winning gold medals and reaching the podiums in international events, not only in the Winter Olympics, but in world championships in athletics, swimming, and almost every sport. The year 2014 was also the first time in which Russia demonstrated its smart power, combining soft power and hard power, as while hosting the Sochi Paralympic Games, the Russian army invaded The Crimea Peninsula in Ukraine (Boykoff, 2016). That was not the first time Russian hard power manifests through the Olympic Games, as days prior to the opening ceremony of Beijing 2008, Russia invaded Georgia in a limited armed conflict that continued through the first days of the Olympics (Murray, 2018).

While no international sanctions were held over Russian military aggression, a German television network exposed a state-led systematic doping system in Russia, leading to further investigations by the World

Anti-Doping Agency (WADA) (Wallace & Giambalvo, 2022). Following the exposure and the exclusions demands, Russian athletes were not automatically suspended, but had to compete under the delegation of the Olympic Athletes from Russia in the PyeongChang 2018 Winter Olympic Games. The overwhelming evidence of state-orchestrated doping, through investigations, documents, evidence, and testimonies by whistle-blowers such as in the Academy Awards winning documentary Icarus, WADA issued a 4-year ban over Russia, in 2019, but the following year the Court of Arbitration reduced the sentence to only 2 years (Panja, 2020).

With President Putin using Sochi 2014 and Russia 2018 for geopolitical purposes, and Russian stakeholders being in power positions in international sports, the 2010s were a successful decade for Russia's sportswashing attempts, and the 2020s looked promising as well. Despite the disciplinary sanctions, Russian athletes competed in the postponed Tokyo 2020 under the flag of the Olympic Committee of Russia, and whenever they won a gold medal, a Tchaikovsky's Piano Concerto was played, not only glorifying Russian athletes but also adding to the country's cultural diplomacy and aesthetic image (Dubinsky, 2022a, b, c). Russia continued to play a role in hosting international events, including a group stage and the quarter final of the UEFA Euro 2020 that was postponed to 2021 due to the pandemic, and was scheduled to host other significant competitions. International criticism from the West did not seem to deter Putin's ambitions, and while the USA and other liberal democracies announced toothless diplomatic boycotts of the Beijing 2022 Winter Olympic Games, the Russian president was President's Xi guest of honor in the Opening Ceremony. Since the 1970s the Soviet Union and later Russia usually excelled in the figure skating Olympic competitions. Figure skating competitions are among the highlights of the Winter Olympic Games, embodying nation branding opportunities not just through winning competitions, but also through the music and costumes. Russian superiority was well demonstrated on the ice in Beijing, especially through the depth and quality of its female skaters who seem to effortlessly land quads—four rotations in the air—a routine very few other female athletes have been able to do. When 15-year-old Kamila Valieva's pre-competition doping test came back positive, once again the Russians faced international criticism for manipulating the international doping system and for child abuse (Ryan, 2022; Wallace & Giambalvo, 2022). Yet, once again CAS helped Russian athletes get through legal loopholes. Following Valieva's doping scandal in Beijing 2022, Canadian IOC member Richard Pound suggested Russia might need "a country timeout" (Keating, 2022). Putin awarded the young athlete a special state award as she turned 16 (Associated Press and Reuters, 2022). This could be seen as another one-sided nationalistic act of defiance.

It was only when Russia invaded Ukraine in the days following the closing ceremony of the Beijing 2022 Olympic Games and just before the opening of the Beijing 2022 Winter Paralympic Games, once again violating the Olympic Truce (International Olympic Committee, 2022b, c), that international sprots federation took practical disciplinary action. The comparisons between Beijing 2022 and Berlin 1936 were not lost on the international sports community, including governments and institutions who went along with the Games and are unforgivingly judged by history. While the sanctions against China and Beijing 2022 were mostly symbolic, perhaps due to the financial dependency on the Chinese market and supply chain, the world of sports took practical actions against the Russians. By the end of 2022, teams and clubs representing Russia and Belarus were banned from international football and basketball competitions, Russian and Belarusian athletes were banned from some prestigious individual competitions such as the Oregon22 World Athletics Championships and the Wimbledon Grand Slam in tennis, Russian athletes who were allowed to compete were forced to do so without any type of national identification or symbol, sports events such as the UEFA Champions League Final was moved from Russia or cancelled, UEFA and some other sports organizations cancelled their sponsorship from Gazprom, Western governments started to target the assets of Russian Oligarchs, Roman Abramovich sold FC Chelsea, and Vladimir Putin was stripped from his title as the Honorary President of the International Judo Federation. Defiant to Western sanctions, some Russian athletes who were allowed to compete as individuals used the letter "Z" to show support for the Russian army, and Russia detained American basketball star Brittney Griner on bogus drug possession and smuggling, sentencing the former Olympic champion to 9 years in prison (Quinn, 2022). Unlike with China where the international community, including sport's governing bodies, have not sanctioned the country due to human rights violations, Western countries, the NATO Alliance, the European Union, and many international organizations including sports federations, did take measures against Russia, socially, politically, and economically, isolating the country from the international community.

From the Beijing 2022 Winter Paralympic Games, through Oregon22 World Athletics Championships, to the European Championships Munich 2022, the resistance of Ukraine and the endurance of the country's leadership, army, and people made Ukrainian athletes fan-favorites in every international competition they participated in around the world, celebrated for their fighting spirit and grit. After decades-long silence, 2022 was the year that international sports finally stood up against Russian sportswashing, yet it did not stop Vladimir Putin to continue manipulating the system for foreign policy purposes. It is not unprecedented for sports organizations to ban countries due to military aggression. After World War I and World War II, the IOC excluded Germany from next Olympic Games. Thus, the Russian bans and exclusion from international sports could be seen as a direct result of the military aggression, or as "a lifetime achievement award" for continuously violating and challenging international sports. Symbolically or not, in 2022, Mikhail Gorbachev, the last leader of the Soviet Union who officially dissolved one of the greatest biggest powerhouses of the twentieth century realizing the failures of Marxism, Leninism, and Communism, died, along with much of the hope for a free social-democratic Russia.

GULF COOPERATION COUNCIL COUNTRIES

Huntington's (1996) "clash of civilizations" theories or arguments on the classification of the Islamic World was met with mixed opinions. Those who support Huntington's analysis, would focus on the 9/11 terror attacks as a justification that fundamentalism and jihadism inherently challenge Western values of liberalism, democracy, freedom, and capitalism. Following the 9/11 terror attacks, the Major League Baseball stopped, and several politicians made connections between global terrorism and the 1972 Munich Massacre in which Palestinian terrorists kidnapped and murdered 11 Israelis during the Olympic Games in West Germany. For decades, the IOC refused to commemorate the victims in the Olympic Village or hold a moment of silence during the Opening Ceremony of the Olympic Games, as dozens of Arab and Muslim countries threatened to leave the ceremony should such a commemoration happen. It took almost 50 years for that to happen (Dubinsky, 2019a, b, 2022a, b, c). The two largest jihadist terror attacks in Europe also had sports connections, with the terror attacks in London in July 2005 happening the day after the city was awarded to host the 2012 Olympic Games (which included a commemoration for the victims), and the terror attacks in Paris in 2015 started outside the Stade de France where France and Germany played a friendly football game. In fact, football stadiums have been used in different Muslim countries such as Libya and Afghanistan for public executions, including by the Taliban (Amnesty International, 2019).

Yet, critics of Huntington, argue that the Islamic World could not be classified as one cohesive unite (Abozaid, 2018), and that the demonizing American approach of framing Islam and Arabs as the new bogeymen of the twenty-first century is "inhumane, arrogant, and racist" (p. 155). One of the biggest critics of Huntington's Clash of Civilizations was Palestinian scholar Edward Said who used the word "orientalism" (Said, 1994, 2003) to criticize how Western gatekeepers portray Muslims as inhumane ways as barbaric, blaming the West for colonial imperialism and historic injustices in the Arab world and the Global South. Hussain and Cunningham (2022) argue that in the field of sports management, there is orientalist and Eurocentric bias in Western scholarship when analyzing sports and Islam. Furthermore, despite the antiliberal manifestations discussed above, Muslim leaders and Muslim athletes have significantly contributed to cultural evolutions in the West (Edwards, 2017; Krechmar et al., 2017). Muhammad Ali, who refused to join the Vietnam War for conscientious reasons, and Kareem Abdoul-Jabbar (then named Lou Alcindor) boycotting the Mexico City 1968 Olympic Games due to racial injustice in America, played an important role in the Civil Rights Movement in America and were among the leaders of what sociologist Professor Harry Edwards (2017) defines as the third wave of black athletes' activism. Framing Islam as one cohesive unite of Islamic countries, disregards differences between Sunni and Shia traditions and countries, ignores internal conflicts and wars within the religion, or that people can identify with several "civilizations." The Arabic Gulf consists of Sunni and Shia countries, including Iran, Iraq, Saudi Arabia, Qatar, Bahrain, the United Arab Emirates (UAE), Oman, Kuwait. A region that is very wealthy with oil and natural resources, but also knew multiple wars and conflict in the past decades, including the Iran-Iraq War in the 1980s, Iraq invading Kuwait and the first Gulf War in 1991, the second Gulf War in 2003, the revolutions of the Arab Spring, and of course the rise of The Islamic State. Qatar, the UAE, and Bahrain, are all small and rich countries with military capabilities, who were occupied by the Great Britain following World War I and received independence in the early 1970s. As such, their military power in a very hawkish region is extremely limited, so money, payments, and forming collaborations became essential hard power tools for survival.

In 1981 Bahrain, Kuwait, Oman, Qatar, Saudi Arabia, and the UAE formed the regional union of the Gulf Cooperation Council (GCC), signing political and economic collaborations. It is within this context, of a globalized world along with a raise in post-9/11 Islamophobia and the threat of Iran becoming a nuclear country, that Muslim countries from the nondemocratic Arabic Gulf started to identify ways to position themselves as attractive to the West and better position themselves in the international system. Since the 1990s Qatar gradually identified soft power as a tool to reposition its international significance, beyond its size and military capabilities. Forming the international broadcasting network Al-Jazeera, Qatar managed to communicate to the rest of the Arab World in Arabic, bypassing state-owned television networks that were governed by local authoritarian regimes, and through that criticizing different governments, and playing a role in the Arab Spring, reporting about antigovernmental revolutions in the Arab world.

Since the early 1990s GCC countries targeted sports as a soft power tool, gradually establishing themselves as globally recognized sports hubs (Reiche & Brannagan, 2022). What started with expensive contract to aging football players to end their careers playing in the Gulf gradually expanded to sponsoring some of the biggest football clubs in the world—often from major European cities—either through the state or through their national airways. Among the dozens of sports clubs that were sponsored either by Qatar or the UAE were Real Madrid FC, FC Barcelona, FC Chelsea, Arsenal, AS Roma, AC Milan, Paris Saint Germain (PSG), Olympic Lyonnais, Olympiacos FC, Boca Juniors, and others. Furthermore, members of the royal families also bought European football clubs, changing the political economy of European football. Since the Qataris purchased PSG, the team won the French league almost every season. Since 2008, Abu Dhabi took the football ownership a step further, not just leading Manchester City FC to multiple championships in England but starting a franchise with football clubs in the USA, Australia, Italy, France, Belgium, China, India, Japan, and Uruguay, winning over 40 men's and women's titles under the City Football Group. Through product-country-image and tourism destination image perspectives, the sponsorships branded Qatar Airways, Fly Emirates, and Etihad as reliable airlines, and Doha, Dubai, and Abu Dhabi as luxurious destinations and central connection hubs. Having a sequel movie of *Sex and the City* filmed in Abu Dhabi, Dubai hosting the World's Fair, and the UAE investing in green energy all played a role in sending a softer image of the region. With every sponsorship or ownership, more events were held in the Gulf, more training camps, and more influence the small countries gained in international governing bodies. Through hosting international sports events, the countries also enforced social and political agendas, making Real Madrid removing Christian symbols in one of their tours, forcing Israelis to compete under the flags of the international federations or hiding Israeli symbols, etc. The UAE and Bahrain also owned cycling teams competing in Grand Tours such as the Tour de France, further promoting the name of their countries. To further improve competitiveness, Qatar systematic naturalizes athletes from other countries, giving some of them Arabic names. Such was the case with the handball team that reached the final of the 2015 World Handball Championships in Doha (Dorsey, 2018). In football, Qatar used the Aspire Academy to naturalize international talents. The use of soft power was not limited only to sport. Despite the authoritarian regimes, anti-LGBTQ legislation, and a history of human rights violations, the world of sports has embraced the financial influence of the Arabic Gulf.

Since Qatar won the bid to host the 2022 FIFA World Cup in 2010, the country was held under international scrutiny over bribery, corruption, and human rights violations and being a questionable sports destination (Brannagan & Reiche, 2022; Zeimers & Cnstandt, 2022). Much of the criticism focused on the kafala sponsoring system of migrant workers, who comprise 90% of the population in Qatar. According to human rights organizations, over 6500 migrant workers died in Qatar since the country won the bid to host the World Cup (Pattison et al., 2021). Amnesty International framed the competition as the "World Cup of shame" (Amnesty International, 2016), referring to the workers' conditions as forced labor and raising concerns about abuse and human trafficking. Despite investigations and whistleblowers pointing wrongdoings, mass arrests and resignations in FIFA and different football governing bodies, and players criticizing and protesting around the world (Lahm, 2022), the 2022 FIFA World Cup was not moved from Qatar. Qatar 2022 demonstrated limitations of sportswashing, as international media, especially from the west, highlighted negative issues about the country (The Guardian, 2022).

On the other hand, the Qatari used highly sophisticated public relations and propaganda strategies to counter-criticize international media for Western bias, orientalism, and Islamophobia, and frame the competition as a nation building event that unified the Arab world and the global south (Brannagan & Reiche, 2022; Chadwick, 2022b; Hussain &

Cunningham, 2022; Reiche, 2022). Even Swiss FIFA President Gianni Infantino used such tactics, answering criticism by counter-criticism, saying in the opening press conference of Qatar 2022, "I'm European. I think for what we Europeans have been doing for 3,000 years around the world, we should be apologizing for the next 3,000 years before starting to give moral lessons to people" (Olley, 2022). Unlike China and Russia who took defiant approaches towards the West, the Qataris tried to speak to the West in its own language. Heads of the organizing committee who engage international media are members of the Royal Family who studied in prestigious Western universities and speak flawless English. Qatar owns, sponsors, and funds football clubs and players who normalize Qatar's image through periodic visits and training camps. Qatari international broadcasting network Al Jazeera reports feelgood stories. The country promised to improve workers conditions and cancelled the kafala system, implemented different sports for development and peace initiatives, employed Western marketing firms and scholars who consistently argued about the benefits of the WC, and mostly continued to financially support the football system, ensuring that one of the most morally and financially corrupted events will take place in the country.

The GCC is not always a cohesive unit, as there are internal geopolitical conflicts, especially with Qatar being blamed for inciting the Arab Spring against ruling regimes and having strong affiliations with the Muslim Brotherhood and jihadi terror organizations (BBC, 2017). Such geopolitical complexities led to diplomatic crises including threats of boycotting sports events in the Gulf and television rights disputes (Dorsey, 2018), and prevented an opportunity of having a world cup spread across the region. Yet, Qatar 2022 also created galvanizing moments in the Arab World. Using whataboutism and blaming the west of Islamophobia and orientalism was a useful tool to frame Western criticism on anti-LGBTQ laws and alcohol restrictions as Western bias against Muslims and Muslim traditions. Restricting protests over human rights violations, while promoting issues that the Qatari support, such as the Palestinian cause, united the Arab world and was praised by Western scholars who support social activism. Morocco becoming the first African and Arab country to reach the semifinals of the competition galvanized Arab supporters and immigrant communities around the world. Thus, despite the divisions within the Arab World, Western scrutiny, and constant accusations of sportswashing, Qatar 2022 was also very much framed as a nation branding win for the hosting country (Chadwick & Widdop, 2022; Reiche, 2022; Ronay, 2022).

In comparison to other GCC countries, Saudi Arabia was relatively late to embrace sports as a soft power tool. On one hand, Saudi Arabia is the only GCC country with military capabilities to resist Iran, yet it is also the birthplace of Osama Bin-Laden, and a country facing multiple accusations of human rights violations, criticism over lack of women's rights, and faced international scrutiny following the murder of journalist Jamal Khashoggi in 2018. In relations to sports, only in 2012 the Saudis had a women represent the country in the Olympic Games, there were occasions of athletes withdrawing from competitions to avoid facing Israelis, and there were ongoing frictions between Saudi Arabia and Qatar on TV rights within the region. That said, seeing the successful sportswashing attempts in other GCC countries, the Saudis as well started to invest in international sports, including hosting a Formula 1 Grand Prix and an annual World Wrestling Entertainment event. Since 2020 the investment in sports increased, with hosting prestigious European football games such as the Spanish Supercup tournament, through the Public Investment Fund (PIF)—the wealth fund of Saudi Arabia—purchasing Premier League club Newcastle United in 2021 and starting a new professional golf tour named LIV Golf in 2022. The Saudis ambitions were demonstrated at the end of 2022, when local club Al-Nassr signed international superstar Cristiano Ronaldo for an unprecedented salary of over $200 billion per year, and the royal family using Qatar 2022 FIFA to strengthen the connections with FIFA, promoting a future Saudi bid. Despite the accusations of sportswashing in European, American, and international media, athletes and sports' governing bodies have eventually accepted the Saudi initiatives, leading the country to target ambitious future goals of hosting the Olympic Games and the FIFA World Cup.

Unlike China and Russia, the GCC countries do not aim to be disruptors, but use the financial needs of the international system, to play a more significant role and normalize their place in the global order. While critics of such methods criticize both the sportswashing GCC countries and sports organizations who enable image laundering, some see these initiatives as attempts to take steps towards the west and global collaborations, including having female wrestlers perform in Saudi Arabia, taking steps towards normalizing relations with Israel following the Abraham Accords, or revising workers' conditions in Qatar. Yet perhaps the big picture question here, is will the world be a better place if instead of spending money on soft power initiatives such as sponsoring sports teams or hosting sports events, these rich countries will invest in hard power, adding more military tools to an already conflict-struck region?

OTHER MANIFESTATIONS

China, Russia, and GCC countries are not the only ones engaged in sportswashing activities or who have been accused as such. Former Soviet Union member Azerbaijan has been active on multiple levels using sports to normalize the country's image through hosting the Baku 2015 European Games and being a sponsor of Spanish football powerhouse Atletico Madrid, advertising "Azerbaijan Land of Fire" on the clubs' jerseys. Baku became one of Europe's football capitals, hosting the Europa League Final in 2019, and group stage games and the quarter final of Euro 2020. Kazakhstan, another former Soviet Union Muslim country with questionable human rights practices, owns the Astana Qazaqstan Team that competes in the International Cycling Union World Tour. Under its previous name Astana Pro Team, its riders from the team won all Grand Tours: The Tour de France, Giro d'Italia, and the Vuelta a Espana. In 2021, after ending relations with new Canadian sponsor Premier Tech, the team changed its name to Astana Qazaqstan Team.

While in China, Russia, and the Gulf, the sportswashing initiatives are state-orchestrated, systematic, global, and part of soft power or smart power foreign policy strategy, in other countries such practices are more limited, or might not even be classified as sportswashing. In Africa, Rwanda, a poverty-struck country who went through a genocide of an estimated over half a million Tutsi minority in the 1990s, partnered in 2018 with Arsenal from the Premier League, sponsoring the north London club with "Visit Rwanda" on the sleeves of the club's jerseys (D'Urso & McNicholas, 2022). Per the tourism partnership agreements, players and coaches from Arsenal men's and women's teams visit Rwanda, and club coaches will support development of children in a freedom-oppressing dictatorship through hosting coaching camps (Visit Rwanda, n.d.). As part of a collaboration with the NBA, in 2022 Rwanda hosted the first Basketball African League (BAL) (Official Release, 2022). In terms of ownership, much like Chinese, Russian, and Sheikhs from the Gulf, also wealthy businessmen from other East Asian countries with questionable practices took advantage of European football. When Leicester City FC unlikely won the Premier League in 2016, that was considered one of the biggest upsets in sports history. The team was owned by Thai billionaire Vichai Srivaddhanaprabha, founder of the betting company and club sponsor King Power. After Srivaddhanaprabha tragically died in a helicopter accident in 2018, his son Aiyawatt Srivaddhanaprabha, CEO of the betting company, became the club's owner, under which Leicester FC won the FA Cup in 2021. Indonesian billionaire Erick Thohir owned football clubs, including European powerhouse Inter Milan from Italy, and D.C. United from the MLS, and in 2019 became a member of the IOC.

The State of Israel has been officially using sports for public diplomacy purposes through the Maccabiah Games—a quadrennial multi-sports event for Jewish people with a stated goal of connecting the Jewish diaspora to the state of Israel (Dubinsky & Dzikus, 2019). In the 2022 Maccabiah Games for the first time an "Olim" delegation consisting of Jewish athletes who made Aliayah and immigrated to Israel participated in the Games (Lidman, 2022). The Maccabiah Games are rooted in Muscular Judaism and the change of the Zionist Movement—the national movement of Jewish people seeking a permanent homeland (Dubinsky & Dzikus, 2019). The significance of the Games has changed over the years, but they still have diplomatic Zionistic purposes, especially as the idea of Zionist is internationally contested. Since the 1967 Six-Day War and the occupation of the Gaza Strip (Israel disengaged from Gaza Strip in 2005) and the West Bank, Israel's image is deteriorating as a permanent peace agreement with the Palestinians is not in the horizon, Pro-Palestinian pressure groups call for boycotting Israel, and more antisemitic incidents erupt the world under the guise of anti-Israeli protests. Furthermore, there are ample direct connections between the Israeli government and sports due to the national trauma of the 1972 Munich Massacre. In September 2022 Germany held memorial services marking 50 years to the massacre, taking responsibility for the country's failures, and reaching a compensation agreement with the families.

In recent years, sportswashing practices in the Gulf were also adopted in Israel, a country internationally scrutinized for Palestinian occupation being compared to an Apartheid regime. Most of the sportswashing accusations from the Pro-Palestinian support group Boycotts, Divestments, Sanctions, from Amnesty International, and through Western media were about Israel's cycling diplomacy (Dubinsky, 2019a, b), and particularly hosting 3 days of the 2018 Giro d'Italia (Liew, 2022). Since Canadian Israeli billionaire Sylvain Adams cofounded the Israel Cycling Academy, Adams has been investing in Israeli sports for diplomatic purposes, especially through the sport of cycling. The elite team, Israel Premier-Tech and in its former name Israel Start-Up Nation, competed in all Grand Tours, Adams funded a new Velodrome in Tel Aviv, and donated to bring the Giro d'Italia to Israel, which was also funded by the state. Adams also helped fund a friendly exhibition game between Argentina and Uruguay in Tel Aviv. Furthermore, since 2021, Israel, who plays regularly in European competitions, hosted the Trophee des Champions—the French Super Cup game in Tel Aviv and the I-Tech cup game between Tottenham Hotspur and AS Rome (Eccleshare, 2022). While such practices might resemble the ones seemed in the Gulf, there is a significant different about their sources, as in Israel they are mostly philanthropic, private, or corporate initiatives, rather than state-led ones. This raises the question if sportswashing must be state-orchestrated or if any diplomatic use of sport has aspects of sportswashing?

Another country with borderline arguments of sportswashing is Turkey, sitting geographically and politically between Europe and Iran. When making attempts to take steps towards the West, Arab and Muslim countries are often criticized for not meeting liberal standards. Since the early 2000s, Turkey hosts significant sports events, including the 2005 Champions League Final in Istanbul, the 2010 FIBA Basketball World Cup, the Izmir 2005 Universiade Games and the Erzurum 2011 Winter Universiade Games, and multiple other international sports competitions (Polo, 2015). Furthermore, Turkish Airlines is the main sponsor of the Euroleague—the best professional basketball club competition outside the NBA. Yet, despite the ongoing successful hosting initiatives, Turkey has consistently failed to win a bid to host the Olympic Games, with Istanbul finishing second after Tokyo in the bid to host in 2020. Turkey also lost to France the bid for UEFA Euro 2016 and did not host a game in the UEFA Euro 2020, despite the tournament being split across 11 European cities and countries. These international initiatives could be seen as part of a process Turkey went through to normalize its image to be accepted as a full member state in the European Union (EU). Yet, despite decades-long attempts and negotiations between Turkey and the EU, the ongoing accusations and evidence of human rights violations have slowed and eventually stuck the process. One of the biggest critics of Turkey and President Recep Tayyip Erdogan is Turkish-American NBA player Enes Kanter Freedom, referring to corruption and human rights abuse and being prosecuted by the country. Like with the GCC, Turkey's international ambition is not necessarily to challenge liberalism, but to play a more significant role in global affairs, bridging between Eastern and Western cultures, or playing a more significant role in Europe. By constantly rejecting Turkey for not meeting liberal standards and putting a glass ceiling to the sports events the country hosts, is the West protecting the integrity of sports or pushing a regional powerhouse towards the arms of nondemocratic regimes and fundamentalistic cultures.

What About Western Democracies?

Sportswashing occurs also in Western democracies (Boykoff, 2022). The term and the practice of sportswashing, also raise the issue of whataboutism—questioning unethical practices by countries labelled as liberal democracies, which have not been scrutinized as sportswashing. In fact, critical scholars argue that by framing practices as sportswashing, the Western European and the Anglo-Saxon world, who see themselves as the ones institutionalizing modern sports (Boykoff, 2022; Krechmar et al., 2017), try to protect their power by delegitimizing non-Western countries. In fact, part of the corrupted culture in modern sports was created by or enabled through white, Western men in power positions from France, Switzerland, and the USA (Boykoff, 2016; Jennings, 2015; Sugden & Tomlinson, 2017). There is no shortage of unethical, immoral, or controversial practices in the West.

Almost no country has politicized the Olympic Movement more than the USA, including leading a 60-country boycott as part of domestic foreign policy. Not only were the Americans not sanctioned, but Los Angeles also hosted the Olympic Games in 1984 without any opponent bidding. American doping goes back to the Cold War, but there have also been multiple doping scandals since the collapse of the Soviet Union, including (a) the BALCO lab in American baseball and track and field leading even to 5-time Olympic champion Marion Jones to serve time in jail after lying to federal agents, (b) 7-time Tour de France winner and Olympic medalist cyclist Lance Armstrong running a "mafia-type" doping system, and (c) Nike Oregon long runs program shutting down after coach Alberto Salazar was found guilty doping athletes (Dubinsky, 2022a). The main difference between American and Russian doping is that in the USA the federal government is less central, so it is the private market that provides the opportunities for unethical practices. Yet, there is also much systematic abuse in American sports, including the United States Olympic and Paralympic Committee, USA Gymnastics, and Michigan State University covering up abuse of hundreds of American gymnasts by team doctor Larry Nassar (Dubinsky, 2022a), with the FBI turning a blind eye and the US Department of Justice not prosecuting the agents. While the athletes and their families were financially compensated, American sports institutions were not excluded from future participation in international sports, and in 2017 once again Los Angeles received the rights to host the 2028 Olympic Games without a competing bid, as part of a deal that granted Paris to host the Olympics in 2024. In the bid for the Salt Lake City 2002, American middlemen bribed IOC members with luxury gifts (Boykoff, 2016) to secure the vote. In fact, the morality of the entire American sports system is highly scrutinized, especially as much of the political-economy is based on unpaid college football players, further capitalizing on economic gaps widened through a history of slavery, segregation, and systematic racism (Kalman-Lamb et al., 2021). Despite criticism by scholars and demand by student-athletes to receive a share of the revenues for playing during the pandemic, all five top conferences held college football seasons despite hundreds of thousands of deaths, ensuring that broadcasters and sponsors and their schools will enjoy the financial benefits. Nationalism is also integrated in American sports (Krechmar et al., 2017), not just through playing the national anthem in every domestic league, but through nationalistic and patriotic gestures the armed forces use to improve recruitment. All happening in the country where gun control is limited by the constitution, and mass shootings occur almost on a weekly basis.

Western Europe is not less hypocritical. The roots of amateurism in institutionalized modern sport go back to England and France in the second half of the nineteenth century (Krechmar et al., 2017), including exclusive policies by European aristocracies forming restrictions on participation in the Olympic Movement based on social class (Boykoff, 2016). Despite the shift to professionalism, aristocracy still manifests systematically as Prince William, Prince of Wales and heir to the throne since his father King Charles III succeeded late Queen Elizabeth II in 2022, is also the President of The Football Association (FA). Thus, whether if for formality or governance purposes, while heads of sports associations in other countries are also related to the royal family, Arab countries are the ones framed as sportswashers. Both England and France also systematically used sports as a colonizing tool. Since the first half of the twentieth century, the Commonwealth Games, earlier known as the British Empire Games, and the British Empire and Commonwealth Games, were used as a colonizing tool, to culturally connect between different occupied members of the Empire (Bull, 2022; Krechmar et al., 2017). Despite growing criticism of the ethics behind the quadrennial international multi-sport competition, and even their framing as "sportswashing" (Boykoff, 2022; Bull, 2022), the Commonwealth Games continue to take place every 4 years, including in Birmingham 2022. While mostly former British colonies participate in the Commonwealth Games, their popularity has drawn other countries to join as well. A member of the Royal Family officially opened most Games. Thus, The Crown has systematically used sports as a soft power tool to galvanize Commonwealth Countries behind British culture and wash the crimes of the Empire. Although starting only in the late 1980s and held in a smaller magnitude, the Francophone Games play a similar cultural role for France and its former colonies. Such multi-sports competitions are not framed as sportswashing, despite the violent history and crimes of England and France in their former colonies.

Regarding public opinion and washing the past, German people repeatedly voted against hosting future Olympic Games in referendums in Munich and Bavaria for the 2022 Winter Olympic Games and in Hamburg for the 2024 Olympic Games (Lauermann & Vogelpohl, 2017). Despite that, following the Munich 2022 European Championships, Germany was once again exploring hosting the Olympic Games, this time in 2036, marking 100 years to the Nazi Games of Berlin 1936. Yet in Germany, the Berlin 1936 Olympic Games was supposed to display a highly functional Germany to the world and resulted in a wave of nationalism, establishing the leader as the head of the state for the near future and the country as a European powerhouse, and introduced innovative ways of hosting (Boykoff, 2016). Some similar arguments could be made about the 2006 FIFA World Cup, an inclusive mega-event that normalized flag waving (Sark, 2012): Chancellor Angela Merkel kept her position as head of state for over a decade and a half until 2021, Germany became the most significant economic powerhouse in the European Union, and the tournament integrated new innovations of fan-zones that were adopted in future competitions. Yet, while the 1936 Olympic Games were awarded to Germany before the Nazis came into power as an attempt to show reconciliation following World War II, Germany won the bid to host the 2006 FIFA World Cup through alleged corruption (Sugden & Tomlinson, 2017), delaying the prestigious tournament from being hosted in Africa for the first time.

There is also the question of the responsibilities of countries, leagues, and international organizations who give the rights to use their brands and teams for financial purposes. The football leagues in France, Spain, and Italy financially capitalize on outsourcing their super-cup games to be held in China, Gabon, Saudi Arabia, Israel, or the USA and Canada. Are all these countries sportswashing?

Local communities, pressure groups, and critical scholars repeatedly criticized hosting countries of greenwashing through sports: destroying the environment and hosting the events in unsustainable ways while trying to spin a green image of the organization (Boykoff, 2016; Zimbalist, 2017). The Brazil 2014 FIFA World Cup, followed by the Rio de Janeiro 2016 Olympic Games resulted in mass public spending, unused stadiums, social and political turmoil, and false promises of cleaning pollution (Zimbalist, 2017). In Japan, activists protest Tokyo 2020 before and during the Games (Dubinsky, 2022a). Yet, despite public resistance, the IOC changed its bidding process, and awarded the Olympic Games to Brisbane in 2032 in a nontransparent manner without a competing bid. To try and manage negative image, countries and international organizations often invest in sports for development and peace initiatives to bridge between communities, or in grassroots sports. While such initiatives have merit, they have also been used for public relations photo opportunities to normalize the image of a country or an organization. The IOC embraced United Nations initiatives (Rofe, 2021), created a Refugee delegation that competed in Rio 2016 and Tokyo 2020, emphasized sustainable practices, and in 2022 also developed a strategic framework on human rights (International Olympic Committee, 2022d). Yet, it continuously faces criticism of demanding unsustainable requirements from hosting cities, lack of transparency, supporting or ignoring sportswashing initiatives, and making unethical decisions following corporate pressure. Furthermore, messages on equality and human rights create cognitive loopholes and raise comparative questions if children in the global south, or in China, Russia, or the GCC, have less rights to experience international sports than children in Western developed countries just because the form of the regimes. The argument about whataboutism, comparing the use of sports for soft power purposes in authoritarian countries or countries scrutinized for human rights abuses to unethical and immoral practices in liberal democracies and international institutions frames the use of the term as hypocritical at best, or even as another form of a Western attempt to keep its institutional power.

Conclusion

As mentioned through the chapter, using sports for soft power in an unethical or immoral manner is not a new practice, yet the term "sportswashing" became popular in recent years especially in relations to nondemocratic countries and countries accused of human rights violations. China and Qatar hosting the Winter Olympic Games and the FIFA World Cup and Russia invading Ukraine just before the Winter Paralympic Games and violating Olympic Truce are just a few examples from 2022. Yet, as seen in the chapter, while China, Russia, and Qatar are nondemocratic countries with ongoing human rights violations, their use of sports for soft power purposes plays a different role. While China uses sportswashing to try and position itself as a global powerhouse within the existing system, Russia's goals are to change the system and challenge the west, and GCC countries—including Qatar—to try to normalize their images by getting closer to the west and becoming more meaningful players. Through the success of their attempts, other countries also adopt some of their strategies.

Critics of the term sportswashing will also look at democracies and how they use sports to normalize their image, whether it is England normalizing a colonial history through the Birmingham 2022 Commonwealth Games (Bull, 2022), Germany using the momentum of the Munich 2022 European Championship to explore the potential of Olympic Games in Berlin 100 years after the Nazi used the Games to promote racist propaganda and terror, or the USA commercializing on the Winter Olympics and the Super Bowl together. From critical perspectives, "sportswashing" might be seen as a term dividing the world into good and bad countries by gatekeepers attempting not to lose their acclaimed power. Perhaps the bigger question "sportswashing" poses to the liberal world is whether international sports can be truly inclusive if it excludes countries that do not conform to liberal ideologies and practices. The year 2022 was also the year in which sports organizations stood up against Russia and Putin's aggression, acknowledging the challenge of authoritarian regimes using liberal loopholes to promote their hawkish ambitions. The year 2022 might have not answered all the questions about the nuances of soft power and sportswashing, but a red line has been drawn as sports organizations realize that amid eruption of violence their reaction must change.

References

Abozaid, A. M. (2018). "Clash of Civilizations" at twenty-five. Reappraising Huntington's legacy: View from the Arab world. *Contemporary Arab Affairs*, *11*(4), 135–158. https://doi.org/10.1525/caa.2018.114007

AFP. (2022, February 27). International Judo Federation suspends Putin as honorary President. *France 24*. Retrieved from https://www.france24.com/en/live-news/20220227-international-judo-federation-suspends-putin-as-honorary-president

Amnesty International. (2016). Qatar World Cup of Shame. *Amnesty*. Retrieved from https://www.amnesty.org/en/latest/campaigns/2016/03/qatar-world-cup-of-shame/

Amnesty International. (2019). Reality check: Migrant workers rights with four years to Qatar 2022 World Cup. *Amnesty*. Retrieved from https://www.amnesty.org/en/latest/campaigns/2019/02/reality-check-migrant-workers-rights-with-four-years-to-qatar-2022-world-cup/

Associated Press and Reuters. (2022, April 26). Vladimir Putin defends Kamila Valieva and hots out at bans on Russian athletes. *The Guardian*. Retrieved from https://www.theguardian.com/sport/2022/apr/26/vladimir-putin-kamila-valieva-egveny-rylov-russian-athletes

BBC. (2017, July 19). Qatar crisis: What you need to know. *BBC News*. Retrieved from https://www.bbc.com/news/world-middle-east-40173757

Beech, H. (2008, August 4). The lessons of the Beijing Olympics. *TIME*. Retrieved from http://content.time.com/time/world/article/0,8599,1835582,00.html

Bottici, C., & Challand, B. (2010). *The myth of the clash of civilizations*. Routledge.

Boykoff, J. (2014). *Activism and the Olympics: Dissent at the games in Vancouver and London*. Rutgers University Press.

Boykoff, J. (2016). *Power games: A political history of the Olympics*. Verso.

Boykoff, J. (2022, January 13). The Beijing Olympics are tearing down the IOC's oldest myth: That sports are apolitical. *The Guardian*. Retrieved from https://www.theguardian.com/sport/2022/jan/13/beijing-winter-olympics-human-rights-politics

Boykoff, J., & Mascarenhas, G. (2016). The Olympics, sustainability, and greenwashing: The Rio 2016 summer Games. *Capitalism Nature Socialism*, *27*(2), 1–11. https://doi.org/10.1080/10455752.2016.1179473

Brannagan, P. M., & Giulianotti, R. (2015). Soft power and soft disempowerment: Qatar, global sport and football's 2022 World Cup finals. *Leisure Studies*, *34*(6), 703–719. https://doi.org/10.1080/02614367.2014.964291

Brannagan, P. M., & Reiche, D. (2022). *Qatar and the 2022 FIFA World Cup: Politics, controversy, change*. Palgrave Macmillan.

Brun, F. E., & Gomez, C. (2022). Chapter 4: Politics and geopolitics in staging the FIFA World Cup: What is at stake for the hosting nations? In S. Chadwick, P. Widdop, C. Anagnostopoulos, & D. Parnell (Eds.), *The business of the FIFA World Cup* (pp. 47–60). Routledge.

Bull, A. (2022, July 27). Commonwealth Games must confront the truth about its sportswashing past. *The Guardian*. https://www.theguardian.com/sport/blog/2022/jul/27/commonwealth-games-must-confront-the-truth-about-its-sportswashing-past

Chadwick, S. (2015). Football's 'bamboo revolution'. *Policy Forum*. Retrieved from https://www.policyforum.net/footballs-bamboo-revolution/

Chadwick, S. (2018). Sport-washing, soft power and scrubbing the stains. *Policy Forum*. Retrieved from https://www.policyforum.net/sport-washing-soft-power-and-scrubbing-the-stains/

Chadwick, S. (2022a). From utilitarianism and neoclassical sport management to a new geopolitical economy of sport. *European Sport Management Quarterly, 22*(5), 685–704. https://doi.org/10.1080/16184742.2022.2032251

Chadwick, S. (2022b, November 14). Qatar's hosting of the FIFA Men's World Cup: The issues and challenges ahead. *SKEMA*. Retrieved from https://publika.skema.edu/qatar-hosting-fifa-men-world-cup-issues-and-challenges-ahead/

Chadwick, S. & Widdop, P. (2022, December 19). World Cup 2022: who won the prize for 'soft power'? *The Conversation*. Retrieved from https://theconversation.com/world-cup-2022-who-won-the-prize-for-soft-power-195867

CNN Beijing. (2022, February 21). The Olympics was a success inside China. And that's the audience Beijing cares about. *CNN*. Retrieved from CNN conclusion https://www.cnn.com/2022/02/20/china/china-winter-olympics-domestic-success-intl-hnk/index.html

Crouse, L. (2022, February 13). Why the Beijing Olympics are so hard to watch. *The New York Times*. Retrieved from https://www.nytimes.com/2022/02/13/opinion/culture/beijing-olympics-inspiring-moments.html?partner=naver

D'urso, J., & McNicholas, K. (2022, June 26). Arsenal's Visit Rwanda sponsorship: The impact, criticism and what fans thing. *The Athletic*. Retrieved from https://theathletic.com/3382273/2022/06/27/arsenal-visit-rwanda-sponsorship/

Dorsey, J. M. (2018). Trouble in sport paradise: Can Qatar overcome the diplomatic crisis? *Revista Crítica de Ciências Sociais, 116*, 179–196. https://doi.org/10.4000/rccs.7479

Dubinsky, Y. (2019a). Analyzing the roles of country image, nation branding, and public diplomacy through the evolution of the modern Olympic movement. *Physical Culture and Sport. Studies and Research, 84*(1), 27–40. https://doi.org/10.2478/pcssr-2019-0024

Dubinsky, Y. (2019b). From soft power to sports diplomacy: A theoretical and conceptual discussion. *Place Branding and Public Diplomacy*, 15, 154–164. https://doi.org/10.1057/s41254-019-00116-8

Dubinsky, Y. (2021a). People-to-people sports diplomacy: "Israel Start-Up Nation" in the 2020 Tour de France. *Journal of Global Sport Management.*, 1–21. https://doi.org/10.1080/24704067.2021.1931403

Dubinsky, I. (2021b). China's stadium diplomacy in Africa. *Journal of Global Sport Management*, 1–18. https://doi.org/10.1080/24704067.2021.1885101

Dubinsky, Y. (2022a). The Olympic Games, nation branding, and public diplomacy in a post-pandemic world: Reflections on Tokyo 2020 and beyond. *Place Branding & Public Diplomacy.*, 1–12. https://doi.org/10.1057/s41254-021-00255-x

Dubinsky, I. (2022b). Playing with the Boycott: Israel-South Africa Sports Ties in the Apartheid Era*. *The International Journal of the History of Sport*, 1–22. https://doi.org/10.1080/09523367.2022.2104252

Dubinsky, Y. (2022c). *Nation branding, public diplomacy and the dystopian Beijing 2022 Winter Olympic Games*. USC Center for Public Diplomacy. Retrieved from https://uscpublicdiplomacy.org/blog/nation-branding-public-diplomacy-and-dystopian-beijing-2022-winter-olympic-games

Dubinsky, Y., & Dzikus, L. (2019). Israel's strategic and tactical use of the 2017 Maccabiah Games for nation branding and public diplomacy. *Journal of Applied Sport Management*, 11, 1–13. https://doi.org/10.18666/JASM-2019-V11-I1-9170

Dubinsky, Y., & O'Reilly, N. (2012). The communication strategies of the 2008 Beijing Olympic Games. *The International Journal of Sport and Society*, 3(1), 43–54.

Eccleshare, C. (2022, July 28). Spurs in Israel: Why a pre-season trip to Haifa to face Roma has proven so controversial. *The Athletic*. Retrieved from https://theathletic.com/3456616/2022/07/29/tottenham-roma-friendly-israel/

Edwards, E. (2017). *The revolt of the Black athlete*. University of Illinois Press.

Fruh, K., Archer, A., & Wojtowicz, J. (2022). Sportswashing: Complicity and corruption. *Sport, Ethics and Philosophy, 1-18*. https://doi.org/10.1080/17511321.2022.2107697

Gilbert, M. (2015). *Cold War Europe: The politics of a contested continent*. Rowman & Littlefield.

Grix, J., Brannagan, P. M., & Lee, D. (2019). *Entering the global arena: Emerging states, soft power strategies and sports mega-events*. Palgrave Pivot.

Huntington, S. P. (1996). *Clash of civilizations and the remaking of world order*. Simon & Schuster.

Hussain, U., & Cunningham, G. B. (2022). The Muslim community and sport scholarship: A scoping review to advance sport management research. *European*

Sport Management Quarterly. https://doi.org/10.1080/1618474 2.2022.2134434

Ingle, S. (2022a, January 18). Athletes warned about speaking out against China at Winter Olympics. *The Guardian.* Retrieved from https://www.theguardian.com/sport/2022/jan/18/athletes-warned-speaking-out-china-winter-olympics?CMP=Share_iOSApp_Other

Ingle, S. (2022b, February 1). Spectre of 1936 and 1980 haunts Beijing 2022 as fear and repression breed silence. *The Guardian.* Retrieve from https://www.theguardian.com/sport/2022/feb/01/spectre-of-1936-and-1980-haunts-beijing-2022-as-fear-and-repression-breed-silence-winter-olympics

International Olympic Committee. (2022a, February 21). Beijing 2022 countermeasures ensure safe Games. *Olympics.* Retrieved from https://olympics.com/ioc/news/beijing-2022-countermeasures-ensure-safe-games

International Olympic Committee. (2022b, February 24). IOC strongly condemns the breach of the Olympic Truce. *Olympics.* Retrieved from https://olympics.com/ioc/news/ioc-strongly-condemns-the-breach-of-the-olympic-truce?fbclid=IwAR2YFeIWHAO7Lf5WDU6-ZiHIIUVZAyuU9Ug2Be_0_dHWe55bOftq_IBjUMY

International Olympic Committee. (2022c, February 28). IOC EB recommends no participation of Russian and Belarusian athletes and officials. *Olympics.* Retrieved from https://olympics.com/ioc/news/ioc-eb-recommends-no-participation-of-russian-and-belarusian-athletes-and-officials

International Olympic Committee. (2022d, September). IOC strategic framework on human rights. *Olympics.* Retrieved from https://olympics.com/ioc/news/amp/ioc-approves-strategic-framework-on-human-rights

Johnson, D. (@TheRock). (2022, February 13). Today we celebrate something that hasn't happened in 4.5 Billion years on earth Super Gold Sunday 1st Time EVER- Super Bowl & Olympics take place on the same day. THIS IS #SuperGoldSunday. We earned this one! Enjoy & LFG!!! *Twitter.* Retrieved from https://twitter.com/TheRock/status/1492970751716036611

Kalman-Lamb, N., Silva, D., & Mellis, J. (2021, March 17). 'I signed my life to rich white guys': Athletes on the racial dynamics of college sports. *The Guardian.* Retrieved from https://www.theguardian.com/sport/2021/mar/17/college-sports-racial-dynamics?fbclid=IwAR0ixdoThUqGmvgx6-HsYe43RdarE4Kmj2YPboBrjHcmmuz6KrpLyXSwXmY

Keating, S. (2022, February 11). Russia may need Games "timeout" over doping, says IOC's Pund. *Reuters.* Retrieved from https://www.reuters.com/lifestyle/sports/russia-may-need-games-timeout-over-doping-says-iocs-pound-2022-02-12/

Kiel, C. (2020). Chicken dance (off): Competing cultural diplomacy in the 2019 Eurovision Song Contest. *International Journal of Cultural Policy, 26*(7), 973–987. https://doi.org/10.1080/10286632.2020.1776269

Krechmar, R. S., Dyreson, M., Llewellyn, M. P., & Gleaves, J. (2017). *History and philosophy of sport and physical activity*. Human Kinetics.

Krüger, A., & Murray, W. (2003). *The Nazi Olympics: Sport, politics, and appeasement in the 1930*. University of Illinois Press.

Lahm, P. (2022, January 2). Sports starts can no longer plead ignorance. They have political power and must use it. *The Guardian*. Retrieved from https://www.theguardian.com/sport/blog/2022/jan/02/sports-stars-can-no-longer-plead-ignorance-they-have-political-power-and-must-use-it

Lauermann, J., & Vogelpohl, A. (2017). Fragile growth coalitions or powerful contestations? Cancelled Olympic bids in Boston and Hamburg. *Environment and Planning A*, *49*(8), 1887–1904. https://doi.org/10.1177/0308518X17711447

Lenskyj, H. J. (2022). *The Olympic Games: A critical approach*. Emerald Publishing Limited.

Lidman, M. (2022, July 14). As 21st 'Jewish Olympics' kick off in Israel, organizers set sights on wooing sabras. *The Times of Israel*. Retrieved from https://www.timesofisrael.com/as-21st-jewish-olympics-kick-off-in-israel-organizers-set-sights-on-wooing-sabras/

Liew, J. (2022, January 24). Sportswashing is associated with certain countries – Why not Israel? *The Guardian*. Retrieved from https://www.theguardian.com/sport/blog/2022/jan/24/sportswashing-is-associated-with-certain-countries-why-not-israel

Miller, S. G. (2004). *Arete: Greek sports from ancient sources*. University of California Press.

Murray, S. (2018). *Sports diplomacy: Origins, theory and practice*. Routledge.

Nye, J. S. (2008). Smart power and the "War on Terror". *Asia-Pacific Review*, *15*(1), 1–8. https://doi.org/10.1080/13439000802134092

Nye, J. S., Jr. (2020). Power and interdependence with China. *The Washington Quarterly*, *43*(1), 7–21. https://doi.org/10.1080/0163660X.2020.1734303

Official Release. (2022, May 5). 2022 Basketball African League Season: By the Numbers. *NBA Communications*. Retrieved from https://pr.nba.com/2022-basketball-africa-league-season-by-the-numbers/

Olley, J. (2022, November 19). World Cup: FIFA president Infantino slams Europe's 'hypocrisy' in speech. *ESPN*. Retrieved from https://www.espn.com/soccer/fifa-world-cup/story/4806508/world-cup-fifa-president-infantino-slams-europe-hypocrisy-in-astonishing-speech

Olympics. (2015). *2022 Host City selection*. https://olympics.com/ioc/2022-host-city-election

Olympics. (n.d.-a). *Beijing 2022 facts and figures*. Olympics. Retrieved from https://olympics.com/ioc/beijing-2022-facts-and-figures

Olympics. (n.d.-b). *Beijing 2022 Medal Table*. https://olympics.com/beijing-2022/olympic-games/en/results/all-sports/medal-standings.htm

Panja, T. (2020, December 17). Russia's doping ban is cut to a largely symbolic two years. *The New York Times*. Retrieved from https://www.nytimes.com/2020/12/17/sports/olympics/russia-doping-wada.html

Pattison, P., McIntyre, N., Mukhtar, I., Eapen, N., Uddin Bhuyan, O, Bahattarai, U., & Piyari, A. (2021, February 23). Revealed: 6,500 migrant workers have died in Qatar since World Cup awarded. *The Guardian*. Retrieved from https://www.theguardian.com/global-development/2021/feb/23/revealed-migrant-worker-deaths-qatar-fifa-world-cup-2022

Polo, J.-F. (2015). Turkish sports diplomacy in the service of renewed power? The use and limits of Turkey's "sport power". *European Journal of Turkish Studies, 21*, 1–28. https://doi.org/10.4000/ejts.5241

Preuss, H. (2015). A framework for identifying the legacies of a mega sport event. *Leisure Studies, 34*(6), 643–664. https://doi.org/10.1080/02614367.2014.994552

PtG. (2022, July 27). From sportswashing in autocracies to soft power in democracies. *Play the Game*. Retrieved from https://www.playthegame.org/news/from-sports-washing-in-autocracies-to-soft-power-in-democracies/

Quinn, T. (2022, August 4). Brittney Griner sentenced to nine years in Russian prison. *ESPN*. Retrieved from https://www.espn.com/wnba/story/_/id/34346379/brittney-griner-found-guilty-drug-possession-smuggling

Reiche, D. (2022, December 14). A successful FIFA World Cup 2022. How Qatar proved its critics wrong and can continue to do so. *Georgetown University Qatar*. Retrieved from https://cirs.qatar.georgetown.edu/a-successful-fifa-world-cup-2022-how-qatar-proved-its-critics-wrong-and-can-continue-to-do-so/?fbclid=IwAR0bvfWhX3-fmnC0Sbm8fDiLVmHpZg37Pcnvw7EygSM5QqiuJ54IRGL2590

Reiche, D., & Brannagan, P. M. (Eds.). (2022). *Routledge handbook of sport in the Middle East*. Routledge.

Rofe, S. J. (2016). Sport and diplomacy: A global diplomacy framework. *Diplomacy & Statecraft, 27*(2), 212–230. https://doi.org/10.1080/09592296.2016.1169785

Rofe, S. J. (2021). Sport diplomacy and sport for development SfD: A discourse of challenges and opportunity. *Journal of Global Sport Management*. https://doi.org/10.1080/24704067.2021.2010024

Rofe, S. J., & Scott-Smith, G. (2018). *Sport and diplomacy: Games within Games*. Manchester University Press.

Ronay, B. (2022, December 19). The winner is … Qatar: Curtain comes down on Project Hard Football Power. *The Guardian*. Retrieved from https://www.theguardian.com/football/2022/dec/19/the-winner-is-qatar-project-hard-football-power-world-cup-2022?CMP=Share_iOSApp_Other

Ryan, J. (2022, February 20). Russian Olympic abuses keep happening. When will child athletes be protected? *The Washington Post*. Retrieved from https://www.washingtonpost.com/opinions/2022/02/20/russia-figure-skating-abuse-child-athletes-reforms-needed/

Said, E. W. (1994). *Culture and imperialism*. Vintage Books.

Said, E. W. (2003). *Orientalism*. Penguin Classics

Sark, K. (2012). Fashioning a new brand of "Germanness": The 2006 World Cup and beyond. *Seminar*, *48*(2), 254–266. https://doi.org/10.1353/smr.2012.0013

Simón, J. R., & Rieck, J. (2022). Football, propaganda and international relations under Francoism: The 1960 and 1964 European Nations Cup and their impact on the International Press. *The International Journal of the History of Sport*, *39*(5), 469–488. https://doi.org/10.1080/09523367.2022.2082412

State of the Union. (2022, February 6). Jake Tapper calls over China's move during Olympics Opening Ceremony. *CNN*. Retrieved from https://edition.cnn.com/videos/world/2022/02/06/china-olympics-corporations-human-rights-jake-tapper-sotu-vpx.cnn

Sugden, J., & Tomlinson, A. (2017). *Football, corruption, and lies*. Routledge.

The Guardian. (2022, November 13). The Guardian view on Qatar's World Cup: Sportswashing stains football's image. *The Guardian*. Retrieved from https://www.theguardian.com/commentisfree/2022/nov/13/the-guardian-view-on-qatars-world-cup-sportswashing-stains-footballs-image

Visit Rwanda. (n.d). *About the partnership*. https://www.visitrwanda.com/arsenal/

Wallace, A., & Giambalvo, E. (2022, February 14). A timeline of Russia's state-sponsored Olympic doping scandal. *The Washington Post*. Retrieved from https://www.washingtonpost.com/sports/olympics/2022/02/11/russia-olympics-doping-scandal/

Wang, S. (@SelinaWangtv). (2022a, February 1). Inside v. outside the #WinterOlympics bubble. My colleague @David_Culver & I haven't seen each other in ages. But the closest we could get was meters apart. Inside the closed loop, we're literally fenced in. It's disconnected Beijing residents from the Games @cnn @OutFrontCNN. *Twitter*. Retrieved from https://twitter.com/selinawangtv/status/1488709488249081857?ref_src=twsrc%5Etfw&fbclid=IwAR3fMqTK8NlMe1hDHQhSzSsKDv2XwBCP7hZTapZFaxPD-PIMzm65Vy087ay0

Wang, S. (@SelinaWangtv). (2022b, February 8). Eileen Gu's message is she's proud of her dual heritage. But she's walking a tightrope. Some have accused her of prioritizing profit, while staying silent on human rights issues in China. Eileen's more than just the poster child of Beijing's Olympics... @cnn @ErinBurnett. *Twitter*. Retrieved from https://twitter.com/selinawangtv/status/1491277140729294848

Zeimers, G., & Cnstandt, B. (2022). Chapter 7: An integrity design of the FIFA World Cups. In S. Chadwick, P. Widdop, C. Anagnostopoulos, & D. Parnell (Eds.), *The business of the FIFA World Cup* (pp. 89–105). Routledge.

Zidan, K. (2022, January 5). Could 2022 be sportswashing's biggest year? *The Guardian*. Retrieved from https://www.theguardian.com/sport/2022/jan/05/sportswashing-winter-olympics-world-cup

Zimbalist, A. (Ed.). (2017). *Rio 2016 Olympic myths hard realities*. Brookings Institution Press.

Zirin, D., & Boykoff, J. (2020, June 5). Racist IOC President Avery Brundage loses his place of honor. *The Nation*. Retrieved from https://www.thenation.com/article/society/avery-brundage/

CHAPTER 8

From "TrackTown USA" to Oregon22 World Athletics Championships

INTRODUCTION

The chapter explores and discusses place branding and sports, through the case of Eugene, OR, officially known as "TrackTown USA" and host of the 2022 World Athletics Championships (World Athletics, n.d.). Despite American athletes winning the most medals in the history of the competition, this was the first time the track and field outdoors world championships were held on US soil (World Athletics, n.d.). The World Athletics Championships are considered among the largest and most prestigious international sports events after the Olympic Games and the Men's FIFA World Cup and are usually held in global cities such as London, Berlin, Beijing, Moscow, and other major cities, in large stadiums with a capacity of tens of thousands of seats (World Athletics, n.d.). Yet, in the USA, instead of picking a global city such as Los Angeles that hosted the Olympic Games twice and will host again in 2028, the 2022 World Athletics Championships were held on a university campus of a small town in the remote Pacific Northwest, which does not have an international airport or even money exchange services (WCH Oregon22, 2022). In fact, while all previous World Athletics Championships were named after the host city (i.e., Doha 2019, London 2017, Beijing 2015, etc.), the event was not branded as Eugene 2022, but as the Oregon22 World Athletics Championships—emphasizing the name of the state instead of the city. Branded as "TrackTown USA," Eugene has a rich history in track and

© The Author(s), under exclusive license to Springer Nature Switzerland AG 2023
Y. Dubinsky, *Nation Branding and Sports Diplomacy*,
https://doi.org/10.1007/978-3-031-32550-2_8

field in America, especially through three individuals involved with the University of Oregon (UO): Innovative late track coach Bill Bowerman and entrepreneur and former track athlete Phil Knight who founded Nike together, and late athlete Steve Prefontaine (Pre) who started a running and jogging craze in the 1970s (Dubinsky, 2021a). Their legacy, along with ongoing growth of track and field in Oregon, myths behind the excitement in over-century-old Hayward Field (it was renovated between 2018 and 2021), and passionate track and field fans creating the "Hayward Magic" atmosphere, led Eugene to position itself as the track and field capital of the USA, regularly hosting national championships, Olympic Trials, collegiate champions, and the annual Diamond League meet "Pre Classic" (Dubinsky, 2021a; Hayward Field, n.d.; Howard-Grenville et al., 2013). Hosting the 2022 World Athletics Championships, with around 1700 athletes, representing 179 countries (not including a refugee's delegation, and watched by an estimation of one billion people worldwide (Around the O, 2022; Press Release, 2022), was the crown jewel.

City Branding and Sports

Perhaps the most well-known place for its athletic significance is Olympia, Greece, (Dubinsky, 2019; Murray, 2018)—going back to the competitions in 776 BC. Thus, the connection of sports and places goes back thousands of years. Yet it is only since the early 2000s that scholars have acknowledged the significance of sports in place branding research (Dinnie, 2004). There are ample intersections between sports and place branding, ranging from hosting annual or mega events (Chalip, 2006; Preuss, 2015), local and national identities associated with sports teams (Berendt & Uhrich, 2016), participation and representation (Dinnie, 2004), governmental use for political purposes (Dubinsky, 2019; Murray, 2018), or even officially associating a city as a sports capital, as in the case of Lausanne Capitale Olympique (Lausanne Olympic Capital, 2020), where the headquarters of the International Olympic Committee sits. Another example, of an even smaller town branding itself through sports is the coastal city Torquay in VIC, Australia (I am Torquay, n.d.). Despite having a population of about 20,000 residents, Torquay is branded as the Surfing Capital of Australia for hosting prestigious annual competitions in nearby beaches, being a founding place of international surfing brands Rip Curl and Quiksilver, and home of the Australian National Surfing Museum (Australian Bureau of Statistics, 2021; I am Torquay, n.d.; Gillen, 2022).

While globalization refers to the movement of people, goods, and ideas across national borders, making local adaptation to global standards is referred to as glocalization (Grewal & Levy, 2021). Due to its local affiliation and impact on the identity of local communities, and its global attraction, sports is by nature glocal. This could be seen, for example, through the NBA, marketing both to global markets through international games and camps, but also issuing specific city-edition uniforms aligned with local uniqueness of each team (NBC.com Staff, 2022). City diplomacy is a form of subnational diplomacy that "centres on fostering good relations with international actors through collaboration, co-operation, cultural ties, civic exchanges and shows of goodwill while promoting trade, policies and the city's global image" (Amiri, 2022, p. 92). Using sports events for place branding purposes can strengthen the appreciation of a place's culture (Kavaratzis & Ashworth, 2015). Dubinsky (2021a) analyzed the branding of Eugene, OR, as TrackTown USA, and suggested a multilevel conceptual model for cities to brand themselves as sports-towns. According to the model (Dubinsky, 2021a), there are five levels which a city needs to go through: (a) local—in which the emphasis is on participation sports, local clubs, and community engagement; (b) regional—in which rivalries are created with teams in close proximity, the place starts to host competition, and a fan-base must be built; (c) national—in which the place hosts reoccurring and national competitions, the local teams need to be competitive, and the sportive venue starts to create a halo; (d) international—in which the place bids to host international competitions and reoccurring competitions, sports becomes internationally competitive, but with the exposure and investment also comes backlash; and (e) global—in which the place hosts mega events, bids regularly to host prestigious competitions, and its sports competes on the highest levels. While the local and regional level pertain mostly to create a collective identity, the national level adds external recognition, and the international and global level also create tangible and intangible legacies.

PLACE BRANDING AND OREGON

Brand America (Martin, 2007) is often portrayed as the "Land of Opportunity" with values such as freedom, opportunity, individualism, rebelliousness, competition, and capitalism creating a narrative about a nation of immigrants. Yet, the image of the USA is also associated with patriotism and the military and American people have developed a reputation associated with respect for others, along with arrogance and self-absorption (Martin, 2007). While some of these values can describe Oregon, the branding of the state is unique. Oregon is in the Pacific Northwest on the West Coast of the USA, between California and the State of Washington (Curtis, 2001)—a remote region filled with raw natural scenery ranging from Crater Lake, the wild coastline, forests and parks, waterfalls, hot springs, a wine county, sand dunes, rivers, to snowy peaks of Mount Hood and the Three Sisters. The natural beauty of Oregon is aligned with the enviro-branding of Cascadia—which includes states along the Pacific Ocean such as Oregon and Washington in the USA and British Columbia in Canada, not just ecologically but also ideologically (Smith, 2008). Starting in the 1980s (Curtis, 2001), the branding of Oregon is trying to capitalize on its natural resources, leading to contemporary focus on the mystic of its wilderness and remoteness, including its beauty and "pride of innovation and pioneering spirit" (Carlson, 1998). Branded by Travel Oregon (2022) "Extraordinary is Ordinary," the state's tourism office tries to promote Oregon as naturally and socially diverse, writing on its website "Take in the beauty of it all – wild rivers, scenic bikeways, mountain vistas, abundant farmlands – and show your love for the people who make this place so special." Thus, active lifestyle and recreation culture is also emphasized in the branding. Vineyards in the wine counties, urban breweries, and progressive state legalization of marijuana, are also part of the state's social environment (Eugene, Cascades & Coast, n.d.-a.; Travel Oregon, 2022; Travel Portland, 2022).

The largest city and the only one with professional sports teams in American leagues is Portland, home of the Trailblazers playing in the National Basketball Association (NBA), the Timbers from the Major League Soccer (MLS) and the Thorns playing in the National Women's Soccer League (NWSL). The remoteness, along with the independent culture and artistic scenes all led to the branding of "Keep Portland Weird" (Noorda & Berens, 2020) and the city being known as "quirky" (Travel Portland, 2022). According to Noorda and Berens, "The commercial origin and TV media amplification of Portland's anodyne weirdness obfuscates its truly strange mix of progressive social politics and libertarian skepticism of government regulation and taxation" (p. 6). While the reputation of Portland weirdness also goes back to the 1980s, in more recent years the city has developed a "reputation as a foodie—and green lifestyle—destination" (Noorda & Berens, 2020, p. 5) and sustainable building (Parkman, 2010).

Yet, despite several teams competing in national American professional leagues and being the largest and most cosmopolitan city in Oregon, it is not Portland, nor is it even state-capital Salem, which is branded through sports. Eugene, a city with approximately 170,000 residents, is officially branded as "TrackTown USA" (Eugene, Cascades & Coast, n.d.-a). Travel Lane County's tourism office, Eugene, Cascades & Coast (n.d.-a), promotes the region through its diverse outdoors, including wild beaches, mountains, the Willamette Valley, and the McKenzie River, along with Eugene being known for its track and field affiliation. Much of that connection was created through the significance of the UO, which is central to both Eugene and its neighbor city Springfield. Both cities have significance in American popular culture, as the movie *Animal House* was filmed at the UO in Eugene and is considered a pioneer comedy on American College lifestyle, and Springfield, OR, served as the inspiration for the imaginary town in the decades-long iconic animated show *The Simpsons*. It is with this mindset of wilderness, innovation, imagination, and history that the branding of Eugene, as TrackTown USA should be approached.

PLACE BRANDING AND TRACK AND FIELD IN AMERICA

Sports plays a significant role in the USA, from fostering collective identity around the Super Bowl through nationalistic military exhibitions (Hopsicker, 2017), through public diplomacy of leading a mass boycott of the 1980 Moscow Olympic Games during the Cold War and creating relations with China through Ping Pong Diplomacy (Dubinsky, 2019; Murray,

2018). Almost every social struggle in American life manifested through sports, including the Civil Rights Movement and the Women's Rights Movement (Dubinsky, 2019; Woods & Butler, 2021). While track and field does not enjoy the same ratings and revenues, as American football, or other professional sports league the sport has much significance in American society and the country's image. Track and field are one of the most participated in high school in America, it is the most successful sport for American athletes in the Olympic Games, and the USA won more medals in track and field than any other country in the Olympics or the World Championships. Furthermore, track and field athletes shaped the social structure in America, including Native-American Jim Thorpe who won gold medals in the Stockholm 1912 Olympic Games and later became the first president of what will become the National Football League (NFL), African American sprinters Tommie Smith and John Carlos who protested racism in America during the national anthem in the Mexico City 1968 Olympic Games, and a variety of female athletes developed after the passing of Title IX—an amendment to the education law prohibiting sex discrimination in the education system, such as Allyson Felix, who became the most decorated track and field Olympian in history and pushed for gender equality through her career. The branding of Oregon as weird also manifested with high jumper Dick Fosbury, who won the gold medal in Mexico City 1968 jumping backwards and changing the sport.

Yet, what led to the branding of Eugene as "TrackTown USA" is associated more with a change in culture than with international glory, and more precisely with late UO track coach Bill Bowerman and his business partner and former athlete Phil Knight, who founded Nike together, and UO track star and Oregon-born Steve Prefontaine (Pre), who held every American record between 2000 m and 10,000 m and started a professional and recreational jogging craze across America (Dubinsky, 2021a; Howard-Grenville et al., 2013). The significance of track and field to Eugene goes back to the early twentieth century, with the old Hayward Field named after late coach Bill Hayward, who coached UO for over four decades, and before was a successful athlete who represented UO. Yet, the affiliation of the city with the sport accelerated in the 1970s, when Eugene hosted the 1972 Olympic Trials (Howard-Grenville et al., 2013), with Pre leading the charge. Despite not winning any Olympic medals in his career, his role in spreading a running culture was so significant, that the place marking where he died in a fatal car accident—Pre's Rock—became a pilgrimage destination for track and field enthusiasts. Eugene and Oregon adopted that identity, with the city regularly hosting local, national, and international events—including Diamond League (2020) meet "Prefontaine Classic," and the city, county, and state offering multiple trail paths for running, jogging, and walking, including "Pre's Trail."

The affiliation between Eugene and track and field is both authentic and constructed (Howard-Grenville et al., 2013). The branding of Eugene as the track and field capital of the USA is also very much associated with Nike. According to Martin (2007), Nike is one of America's most known brands, with the Swoosh also representing a rebellious side of the USA. The company's headquarters, Nike Campus—designed as university campus— is in Beaverton, OR, a suburb of Portland, with its buildings and squares dedicated to some of the most known athletes the company sponsored such as Michael Jordan, Serena Williams, Tiger Woods, and of course Steve Prefontaine. These are just a few examples of the deep and authentic affiliation between Nike, UO, Oregon, track and field, and American sports. Phil Knight, his family, and Nike are very much an integral part of that branding, supporting the nonprofit company TrackTown USA (2022a) in its efforts to grow the sport through "TrackTown Tuesday" meetings between athletes and the community and bringing high-profile competitions to Hayward Field, collaborating with "Hayward Magic" to market the sport, etc. Hayward Field, who was renovated thanks to a $270 donation from Phil Knight, is in the center of UO, within half a mile radius of the Knight Library, the Phil and Penny Knight Campus for Accelerating Scientific Impact to which the family donated half a billion US dollars, and the Matthew Knight Arena, named after Knight's late son. Since the renovations were completed and COVID-19 restrictions have been lifted, Hayward Field hosted the 2021 Olympic Trials, two Prefontaine Diamond League meets, PAC-12, NCAA, and national championships, along with local and regional competitions (Diamond League, 2020; Dubinsky, 2021a; TrackTown USA, 2022b). The Oregon22 World Athletics Championships were supposed to be the crown jewel, cementing "the greatest track & field year in the history of Oregon" (TrackTown USA, 2022b).

In fact, when Eugene, OR, was awarded to host the 2021 World Athletics Championships without opening the bid to other opponents, there was some criticism about it including questioning the role of Nike in the decision, especially as the President of World Athletics, Lord Sebastian

Coe, was previously sponsored by the company (Krieger, 2021). Nike has faced much backlash and criticism, including about labor conditions, treatment of women, the Nike Oregon Project in which athletes were doped, and using its financial donations to gain influence at the UO (Hunt, 2018; Ingle, 2019). Despite being a small city, Eugene hosts regularly America's most prestigious annual and quadrennial track and field events, including NCAA championships, national championships, and the Olympic Trials, along with local competitions and of course the international meet "Pre-Classic" (Dubinsky, 2021a). USA Track and Field originally bid to host the world championships in 2019, but World Athletics—then called the International Amateur Athletic Federation (IAAF)—awarded the competitions to Doha, Qatar. A year later, without formally opening the bid to other candidates, Eugene, Oregon, was awarded to become the first American city to host the World Athletics Championships in 2021 in a renovated and extended Hayward Field (IAAF, 2015; Krieger, 2021). Unlike in previous competitions that were named after the hosting city, the 2021 track and field world championships were named after the hosting state—Oregon21. Following the outbreak of the COVID-19 pandemic, the competitions were postponed by a year, leading organizers to change the branding to Oregon22 World Athletics Championships.

Place Branding, TrackTown USA, and the Oregon22 World Athletics Championships

The Oregon22 World Athletics Championships were marketed through several narratives: (a) the first World Athletics Championships on US soil, (b) World Athletics Championships held on a college campus in a city that has historic heritage to the sport and is officially branded as "TrackTown USA," and (c) state-wide efforts of Oregon (WCH Oregon22, 2022; World Athletics Championships Oregon22, 2020). While all these narratives have some validity, they can also self-contradict, and require much planning to maintain authenticity. The organizational tensions between local and glocal goals and objectives, and the gaps of expectations between different stakeholders led to glocal dissonance about the branding of Eugene and Oregon. The following section discusses the branding of Oregon22 World Athletics Championships through Dubinsky's (2021a) model of city branding through sports, on local, regional, national, international, and global levels.

Local

The local level of place branding pertains to the branding of the city of Eugene, OR, and its neighbor city Springfield. The idea of choosing Eugene, OR, as the host of World Athletics Championships was rooted in the history and heritage of the place, and with the idea of demonstrating sustainable hosting of a competition using the facilities of a university campus. World Athletics President Lord Sebastian (Seb) Coe referred to the championship as "scaled down," "sustainable," and "intimate" (World Athletics, 2022). Both local and international media justified the choice of the small and remote city, by briefly mentioning the history and heritage of the place, including the contributions of Bill Bowerman, Phil Knight, and Steve Prefontaine (Bishop, 2022; Futterman, 2022; Ingle, 2022). The branding of Eugene as "TrackTown USA," including the special atmosphere in the stadium, referred to as "Hayward Magic," was also expressed by athletes through mix-zones and press conferences (My CIS, 2022). There were several initiatives to connect the competitions to the community, including "Making Tracks," a youth engagement program focusing on enhancing diversity through sports, and the Oregon Heritage Trail that celebrated athletes from Eugene and the state of Oregon who made a significant impact on the sport (WCH Oregon22, 2022; World Athletics, 2022).

By using the UO's campus, students from different departments enjoyed working, internship, and volunteering opportunities they would not get otherwise (Front Runners, 2022). The use of a university campus as an athletes' village also resulted with no travel time for athletes between their accommodations and the venues, and with athletes spending time in the stadium walking along fans in days they were not competing—enhancing the intimate feeling of the event (Manning, 2022a). So, in that sense, the competition added authenticity of the branding of a city in which track and field is part of its DNA. As for the use of a university campus as an athletes' village and university facilities as competition venues, it is a practice used in the Los Angeles 1984 Olympic Games and will be done again in 2028, but the idea to have an entire international competition in such a model had enough merit to be considered in other cities (Woods, 2022), or at least to justify the attempt in Oregon (Dennehy, 2022).

With that said, there was also local backlash. Beyond the stadium and a few businesses around campus such as "Wild Duck Café" and "TrackTown Pizza" (Caballero, 2022; Manning, 2022a), international stakeholders were rarely exposed to other areas of the city (Kahl, 2022). There were little direct intersections between international stakeholders such as media and athletes and the Riverfront Festival and the Lane County Fair that were happening during the competitions. The organizing committee did not organize media tours of the city, and even iconic places such as Pre's Rock and the Simpsons Mural in Springfield were rarely visited by journalists (Bishop, 2022; Dennehy, 2022). As several journalists mentioned, it was not easy to get around. So, while prior to competitions local authorities prepared residents of a 170,000 city for 200,000 out-of-town visitors (Manning, 2022b), reality was that some businesses not surrounding the stadium lost money on overstocking and overstaffing, many residents left town or were reluctant to go out to avoid the projected masses, and there was local criticism about the championships being overhyped, displacement of homeless people, and overall against the event (Hale, 2022; Kahl, 2022; Smith, 2022; Theen, 2022). Local news outlets, who tried to promote some of the activities in the city such as the Riverfront Festival, also pointed fingers on the multiple mistakes made, including overhyping the championships or holding too many track and field events over a condensed period. Yet, the critic was not just against the local organizers, but also against World Athletics and its president Sebastian Coe. As Dan Kahle from The Register-Guard wrote: "We allowed a technocrat from London to decide how to showcase Eugene." Furthermore, while the branding of Eugene as TrackTown USA is very much associated with the birthplace and evolution of Nike, the sponsor of World Athletics was ASICS (WCH Oregon22, 2022). As a result, competing companies did not receive much visibility in the stadium or through the organizing committee. As most international stakeholders were mostly exposed to events around campus or depended on the organization's transportation system, initiatives by Nike and TrackTown USA (Nike by Eugene Events, 2022; TrackTown USA, 2022c) were less accessible, leading to part of the narrative about the DNA of the city and its historic connection to the sport being lost.

All the track and field events were held in Hayward Field, except for road races—walking competitions and the marathons, which were held in the city and ended outside Autzen Stadium—the football stadium of the Oregon Ducks (WCH Oregon22, 2022). Through the road events, some other known places in Eugene were more visible or experienced, including the famous Pre Trail—named after Prefontaine. Furthermore, the brand of the UO, the brand of the university's athletic teams The Oregon Ducks, and the high-level facilities they use, were also visible. Hayward Field contains around 12,500 seats, and temporary stands were added for the championships, increasing the capacity to around 15,000 (Perlman, 2022). Even in its extended form, it was still significantly smaller than any other competition, especially in comparison to the stadiums in London, Beijing, and Moscow that could accommodate over 60,000 spectators. Despite the intimate and compact organization, Hayward Field was rarely in full capacity during the competitions. The overall ticket sales of the 15 sessions (10 evening sessions and 5 morning sessions) were around 146,000, with the organizers arguing several evening sessions being sold out (Manning, 2022a). Yet, these numbers pale in comparison to other championships, and with many empty seats in the stands visible through the 10 days of competitions, American and international athletes and sports administrators publicly wondered if the sport of track and field to grow beyond its diehard fans, Eugene is too small to remain the American capital of the sport (Greif, 2022).

Regional

The regional level pertains to the branding of the State of Oregon, and of Lane County, beyond the neighbor cities of Eugene and Springfield. Unlike previous competitions that were named after the hosting city, the 2022 World Athletics Championships were branded as Oregon22—after the state. Such branding, along with the format of most events surrounding the campus of the UO in Eugene, created a cognitive dissonance. The competitions were branded as a statewide effort with the governor allocating $40 million, with projections of visitors spending over $50 million on the event itself and having an economic impact of over $200 million (Eugene, n.d.). Beyond the name, the branding of the State of Oregon was manifested mostly through a campaign named "Extraordinary is Ordinary" with ads broadcasted during the competitions focusing on the state's natural beauty and resources such as Oregon rocks, Oregon water, and Oregon soil (Oregon, 2022). Through the ads, the scenery and culture of Oregon were presented in animated and nonanimated forms, including landscapes raging from snowy Hood Mountain, Crater Lake, the wild coast, forests, and more, along with a diverse culture of outdoor activities, international food influences, and wine tasting. Yet, beyond the commercials, these attractive locations were not easily accessible for international stakeholders who spent over a week in Eugene around the competitions and relied on transportation by the organizing committee. As several journalists mentioned, commuting in Eugene was not easy, and the organization overhyping the expected crowds and hotel prices increasing led to limited exposure of the county, state, or even parts of the hosting city that were not around the stadium. While Travel Oregon as an official partner had promotional activities around the stadium, the integration with the organization was limited in terms of experiencing the state. For example, instead of capitalizing on the structure of the competitions and offering national and international journalists statewide tours in the morning that had no competitions or little competitions, and city/county-wide tours in the breaks between the morning and evening sessions, these gatekeepers who could have further exposed the state remained around the stadium.

There were some initiatives in which the championship was directly connected to the overall branding of the state. The slogan of the competition was "Hello, World. Meet. Oregon," a play of words both on Oregon welcoming the world, and an international track and field meet happening in Oregon. Some promos leading to competitions emphasized not just the significance of Eugene to track and field, but a state-wide culture of running and jogging in nature.

Perhaps the most noticeable one was the choice of Legend the Bigfoot as the mascot of Oregon22, having an imaginary creature that lives in the woods capitalizes on the mystic of the state and the connection to its natural resources. More organically, crowds at the stadium were fascinated by nesting ospreys, who build their nest on a platform overlooking the stadium, giving visitors a chance to see at least a small part of the state's wildlife (Frandino & Tennery, 2022). The natural scenery of Oregon along with its historic connection to track and field were also promoted as part of advertisements leading to the competitions (World Athletics Championships Oregon22, 2020), and the Oregon22 Heritage Trail, in which 22 athletes who made significant impact on the sport were recognized in various locations in Oregon that were meaningful to their lives or careers. Some of the most known were two-time Olympic Champion Ashton Eaton commemorated in his hometown Bend, OR; his Canadian wife, Olympic bronze medalist and Oregon Ducks alumni, Brianne Thiesen-Eaton commemorated in Eugene, where she studied; and Portland-native Dick Fosbury who revolutionized high-jump winning an Olympic gold, commemorated in Medford, where he attended high school (Eugene, Cascades & Coast, n.d.-b).

Some of the media hotels or pre-competition training facilities were outside the Eugene/Springfield areas, and Travel Oregon offered some brochures that had tour information on them, but beyond that, visiting locations across the state or the county and experiencing Oregon's mystic nature mostly required individual logistic arrangements and efforts. Commuting is not easy in Oregon, public ground transportation is limited, and prior to the championships the organization and the city constantly warned about using personal cars to limit traffic around the stadium, which all limited the ability to experience other parts of Oregon. As the airport in Eugene did not accommodate international flights and served mostly connections from major cities on the West Coast, many national and international journalists flew to Portland and either used the organization's transport system or rented a car to drive to Eugene. As part of the drive, journalists also noticed the wineries, farms, and billboards for dispensaries including "the sign that proclaims Linn County the 'grass seed capital of the world'" (Bishop, 2022), as the use of cannabis is legal in Oregon. The image of Oregon was about natural beauty, being ecologically sustainable, socially progressive, and doing things differently (Curtis, 2001; Noorda & Berens, 2020; Parkman, 2010; Smith, 2008), some aspects of the organization of hosting a competition on a small campus, not allowing plastic bottles in the stadium, encouraging using public transportations and bicycles to commute, advertising the outdoors, promoting social diversity (WCH Oregon22, 2022), and the championships described as "unique" (Tennery, 2022). So, authentic messages about the State of Oregon were communicated to international audiences and stakeholders who attended the competitions or watched the broadcasting, but firsthand experiences of the mystic of Oregon was mostly limited to the stadium and its surroundings. Overall, from a tourism-destination image, Oregon22 did not fully capitalize on the scenery and landscape of the city or state by showing a more natural and rural side of America, than the big city lights and signs of New York and Los Angeles.

National

The national level pertains to national identity in the USA. Oregon22 were consistently promoted as the first World Athletics Championships happening on US soil, with athletes speaking about the significance of competing at home, sending messages of the USA welcoming the world, while also calling American audiences to witness the USA taking on the world knowing that athletic success of Team USA can lead to more domestic interest (WCH Oregon22, 2022; World Athletics Championships Oregon22, 2020). National media outlets explained larger audiences the significance of Eugene to American track and field, even referring to it as "The Mecca" (Futterman, 2022), thus adding authenticity of the branding of TrackTown USA. From an athletic perspective, Oregon22 was an overwhelming success for the hosts, as Team USA continued to dominate the sport winning the most gold medals and most overall medals; American men sweeping the podiums in the 100 m, 200 m, and shot pot competitions; American women upsetting the favorite Jamaicans in the 4 × 100 relay; and Sydney Mclaughlin breaking the world record in 400 m. Waves of nationalism were not evident just by the "USA, USA" chants (Wilson, 2022) and the American anthem, but also through F15s and Black Hawk helicopters flyovers (Oregon22, LLC, 2022)—militaristic rituals associated with American football traditions (Hopsicker, 2017).

Internal power struggles in America also manifested through the way Oregon22 was hosted. The organization paid tribute to athletes and different social leaders who fought for social change in America through the RISE Road to Progress (n.d.) project in which the athletics and social achievements of dozens of athletes such as Jesse Owens, Wilma Rudolph, and UO alumni mixed-race African American and Native American Otis Davis were celebrated. As the UO was built on Kalapuya Ilihi land, "the traditional indigenous homeland of the Kalapuya people" (UO Libraries, n.d.), acknowledging Native American athletes adds to the social and historic significance of Eugene and Oregon on a national level. The project also celebrated athletes from other sports such as Muhammad Ali, Bill Russell, Michelle Kwan, and Serena Williams, along with social leaders such as Dr. Martin Luther King Jr. and landmark American legislations such as Title IX. Gender plays a role in American public diplomacy (Dubinsky, 2021b) through social engagement, educational laws, and official initiatives by the US Department of State. With the USA marking 50 years to Title IX, while the American Supreme Court overturned the Federal rights for abortions, it was important for the organizations and for USA Track and Field to emphasize gender equity and equality, dedicating an evening for women's appreciation, celebrating the success of revolutionary female athletes in the USA and abroad, and of the most decorated track and field athlete Allyson Felix, as the Olympic legend competed for the last time on the world stage. That appreciation was also manifested through Felix's teammates, including by Team USA sprinter Noah Lyles who complimented her courage to criticize Nike amid the company's policies during her pregnancy. Furthermore, as part of the wave of social activism in the summer of 2020, international governing bodies relaxed their stands about protests. In Oregon22, prior to the women's nights, American female athletes and celebrities celebrated the protest made by African American lesbian athlete Raven Saunders during the Tokyo 2020 Olympic Games (Lyons, 2022). Perhaps the strongest manifestation of social change occurred through the warm welcome Mexico City 1968 Olympic Games gold medalist Tommie Smith and bronze medalist Dr. John Carlos received in Hayward Field prior to the 200 m race. Smith and Carlos were scrutinized and sanctioned after protesting racial injustice on the podium during the Games in Mexico. Despite becoming leaders of what Professor Harry Edwards refers to as the 3rd Wave of Black Athletes Activism, only in recent years American sports governing bodies have started to embrace the athletes and added them to the Hall of Fame. Acknowledging the significance of Smith and Carlos prior to the 200 m final in which three African American athletes swept the podium demonstrated the change America seeks to project. US Track and Field also endorsed Smith and Carlos to light the cauldron in the Los Angeles 2028 Olympic Games (Kilgore, 2022a).

Despite Oregon22 being the most watch World Athletics Championships broadcasted in America (Press Release, 2022), there was much internal disappointment with the size of the stadium and the lack of coverage outside the broadcasting network NBC and its different platforms (Alexander, 2022; Kilgore, 2022b). For example, highlights of the competitions were rarely shown on ESPN's SportsCenter Top 10 (Alexander, 2022). Noah Lyles, who won the gold medal in the 200 m race and was one of the most charismatic athletes in the competitions, blamed poor advertising, and argued that "the ball has been dropped a little bit," referring to lost opportunities. BBC commentator and former American Olympic champion Ben Johnson also tweeted about lack of marketing, pointing out empty seats in the stand. The disappointment resulted in athletes suggesting hosting future events in other cities. "We can't keep relying on Eugene to be our epicenter of track and field" (Kilgore, 2022b), Lyles said to the Washington Post. He added:

> There are other places we can go. When we went to New York for the Grand Prix [in early June], their interaction was just as strong as the interaction I had at Prefontaine. We don't have to have everything in Eugene. We can get

the same interaction in other places. We just to have to market and get people knowing we're going there. (Kilgore, 2022b)

Lyles was not the only one sharing criticism on Eugene being the face of American track and field. Fred Kerley, 100 m gold medalist, tweeted "We need to have world champ in Miami" (Fred Kerley, 2022). USA Track and Field announced they plan to have a separate circuit of competitions taking place around the USA leading to LA28, to market the sport across America (Greif, 2022). Thus, while Eugene received some national spotlight, the small-town hosting and the limited interest in track and field also emphasized the shortcomings of the branding of the city as "TrackTown USA."

International

The international level pertains both to the branding of Eugene, Oregon, and the USA internationally, and to other countries using the World Athletics Champions for nation branding and public diplomacy purposes. By hosting the annual Prefontaine Classic Diamond League meet, Eugene and Hayward field were already known in the track and field international community. The Oregon22 World Athletics Championships were the reaffirmation of the significance of Eugene to the sport of track and field hosting over 1700 athletes from 179 different countries and a way to expose the city to a much larger audience of sports fans (Press Release, 2022). The branding of Eugene as TrackTown USA and the significance of Hayward Field as "the country's track and field Mecca" (Whittington, 2022) also reflected through international coverage. The significance of the place, and the love and appreciation of local fans were acknowledged by international athletes in post-competition interviews (My CIS, 2022) such as Canadian Andre de Grasse who won the gold medal in the 4 × 100 relay, 400 m hurdles gold medalist Brazilian Alison dos Santos, and British Dina Asher Smith who won the bronze medal in the 200 m sprint, who all praised the atmosphere. The international branding of Eugene as a track and field hub was enhanced with 15 different athletes in Oregon 22 being former UO student-athletes, representing not just the USA, but also Australia, the Dominican Republic, Jamaica, and Italy (Neel, 2022). While Jenna Pardini helped the American women to win the gold medal in the 4 × 100 relay, Kemba Nelson and Jamaica finished second in that final winning a silver medal. Perhaps one of the biggest disappointments was the disqualification of local hero Devon Allen, of having a 0.001 second false start. Although not a UO alumni, Oregon-born Ryan Crouser won the shotput competition breaking the championship's record, not only leading an American-swept podium, but also reaffirming his dominance in the sports adding a gold medal in the 2022 World Athletics Championships to the Olympic gold medal he won in Tokyo 2020 and the world record he broke in Eugene, during the Olympic Trials (Hatler, 2022).

For the host, the USA, Oregon22 was an opportunity to show the world the American lifestyle. Despite the unique compact hosting and the connection to college lifestyle, the organization did not capitalize on the significance of the UO as the place where cult movie *Animal House* was filmed—a revolutionary comedy influencing dozens of other college teen comedies. On the other hand, glorifying *Animal House*, a movie that also includes sexual scenes and a culture of sexual violence on college campuses, might not have served the purpose of the way the organization used gender to promote American values. The emphasis on gender correlates with diplomatic initiatives that the US Department of State holds around Title IX and refutes negative coverage of the Supreme Court overturning Roe v. Wade and the Federal abortions rights, the systematic sexual assaults in American gymnastics, and misogynistic comments by former President Donald Trump (Dubinsky, 2021b). The overwhelming success of Team USA winning 13 gold medals and 33 overall medals (Press Release, 2022) reinforced the role of the collegiate American system in athletes' developments, and the role of Title IX as a sustainable competitive advantage for American women. One of the only references to *Animal House* was the song "Shout" which appeared in the movie and adopted by the UO, played while the Americans received the inaugural team trophy. Perhaps the biggest criticism though against the USA and the organizers was about visa issues, as athletes and delegation members from Great Britain, India, Jamaica, Libya, South Africa, Iran, and other countries did not get their visas on time or got it in delays, which hurt the preparation (Rowbottom, 2022). The international criticism of handling visas added to the overall criticism about American immigration policies, and concerns about future events held in the USA, including the Los Angeles 2028 Olympic Games (The Gleaner, 2022).

From a product-country-image perspective, there were also missed opportunities not capitalizing on Nike's significance not just to Oregon and Eugene, or to the sport of track and field, but also as an

American-recognized brand. This left the door open to other countries to capitalize on that. In fact, the country that did leverage export branding into further achievements was Japan, having both Seiko and ASICS leveraging their sponsorships through Oregon22 with the former holding an on-field press tour explaining about their advanced technologies, and the latter having a hospitality zone on campus, where international stakeholders could relax, refresh, and further learn about the products. In the pre-competition press conference, World Athletics President Seb Coe said that Tokyo was chosen as the host of the 2025 World Athletics Championships, giving more international recognition to Japan.

Oregon22 did give international athletes a platform to shine, for countries such as Jamaica, Ethiopia, or Kenya to brand themselves as experts in specific disciplines. In the concluding press conference of the championships Coe compared the contribution of legendary retired Jamaican sprinter Usain Bolt to track and field to Muhammad Ali's to boxing, not just in terms of level of competition but also as a personality (AIPS Media, 2022). While Bolt might be irreplaceable, the dominant legacy of Jamaican sprinters continued in Oregon22. Despite settling for silver in the 4×100 race, Jamaican female sprinters Shelly-Ann Frayser Pryce, Sherick Jackson, and Elaine Thompson-Herah swept the podium in the 100 m final, and Jackson and Frayser-Pryce won the gold and silver in the 200 m final, respectively, with the bronze won by British Dina Asher Smith whose parents are Jamaican. Jamaican women also won the silver medal in the 4×400 relay. Frayser-Pryce's singlet from the competition was added to the Museum of World Athletics (MOWA) exhibition at the university, which featured memorabilia of Bolt and other legendary track and field athletes from around the world (Johnson, 2022). Two dominant counties in Oregon22 were Ethiopia and Kenya, continuing the dominance of African countries in long runs. The legacy of African countries dominating distance running goes back to Abebe Bikila, who won Olympic gold medals in marathon races in Rome 1960 and Tokyo 1964. Yet, perhaps the most surprising African success was Nigerian Tobi Amusan who won the gold medal in the 100 m hurdles race and broke the world record. The contribution of African athletes also manifested through other countries, as naturalized Kenyan 3000 m steeplechase female runner Norah Jeruto won a gold medal for Kazakhstan, Kenyan-born runner Lonah Chamtai-Salpeter won a bronze medal for Israel in the women's marathon, and Somalia-born marathon runner Bashir Abdi won a bronze in the men's competition.

As in other significant sports events, international politics also manifested through the Oregon22 World Athletics Championships. After Ethiopian runner Gudaf Tsegay won the 5000 m run, a man run into the field, lifting her and fifth place finisher Letesenbet Gidey, both from the Tigray region in Ethiopia (Gault, 2022). The separatist region has been a center of violence in Ethiopia causing thousands of deaths (Borenstein, 2021). Following the win, protesters marched around the stadium calling for "Free Tigray" and "End Tigray genocide" (Gault, 2022). Yet, perhaps the most significant political interference was the exclusion of Russian athletes from the competitions. World Athletics has been calling for strict punishments on Russian athletes since the exposure of a systematic-run doping system prior to the Rio de Janeiro 2016 Olympic Games. Following different legal appeals, international sports federations allowed cleaned athletes to compete under different regulations such as the Russian federations, but after the Russian invasion on Ukraine different sports organizations adopted different policies ranging from allowing Russian athletes to compete under neutral flags to overall ban of Russian and Belarusian athletes. World Athletics took the latter approach in the Oregon22 World Athletics Championships (Greif, 2022c). Much like in other competitions around the world, Ukrainian athletes who competed in Oregon, and especially the two high-jumping medalists, received special appreciation from the fans. As high-jumper silver medalist Yaroslava Mahuchikh said before the competition "we protect our country on the track" (Greif, 2022c). Thus, despite the size of the hosting city, participating countries and international stakeholders still found ways to use Oregon22 for place branding and public diplomacy purposes.

Global

The global level pertains to the exposure of Eugene and Oregon to worldwide audiences and border-crossing trends and challenges. With the World Athletics Championships branded as the third most significant international sports event after the Olympic Games and the FIFA World Cup and the second largest sports event a single international sports federation holds after the FIFA World Cup, and with a projected television audience of a billion viewers, Oregon22 World Athletics Championships put a global spotlight on Eugene, OR. While there was some potential to global appeal through connecting brands known worldwide as *The Simpsons* or Nike, as mentioned through the chapter, these aspects were not significantly leveraged. With that said, the formation of the competition as sustainable, not allowing plastic bottles and offering water refill stations in the stadium and for accredited stakeholders, did fall within rising demand for more responsible hosting. Yet, despite branding emphasis on natural resources and attempts for green organizations, with competitions held in the morning or afternoon local time to accommodate East Coast primetime television broadcasting, the heat and weather became worrisome as the West Coast headed towards the dry and wildfires season. World Athletics President Coe even raised concerns about the significance of climate change and the need to adjust the organization's schedule to better protect athletes (BBC Sport, 2022). Global warming, climate change, the hot summer and heat challenges were not unique to Eugene, as they affected the competition schedule in Doha, Qatar, in 2019, and the Olympic Games in Tokyo held in 2021 as well. As Coe said, if the competitions were held in London the organization would be facing the same challenges. Another global challenge that reflected through the competition was of course COVID-19. As of the summer of 2022, the USA was the only country reporting over a million deaths from the pandemic. Despite internal arguments about personal freedom in America, the organization required every accredited stakeholder, including athletes and the media, to upload vaccination information and take a COVID-19 test prior to picking up the credentials or traveling to the USA, and once COVID-19 cases were detected during the competitions, accredited stakeholders were required to wear a mask when indoors. These measurements enabled the competition to relatively run smoothly, having only three athletes needing to withdraw from the championship due to the pandemic (Krauss, 2022).

Socially, the organization tried to be aligned with progressive views of race and gender, highlighting significant achievements of social leaders in the USA and worldwide through the MOWA museum, RISE Road to Progress (n.d.) project, the invitations of Smith and Carlos, and a specially dedicated women's night. With that said, there is still much controversy around gender classification in sports, especially amid transgender athletes who were allowed to compete in Tokyo 2020, and female athletes with high-level testosterone. In Oregon22, the controversy reflected through South African Caster Semenya, who was banned by World Athletics from competing in the 800 m race she excelled in due to high-level testosterone, and competed in the 5000 m heats where she did not even qualify for the finals (Ingle, 2022). During the competitions, Coe reaffirmed the position of World Athletics on gender classifications, staying "I'm really over having any more of these discussions with second-rate sociologists who sit there trying to tell me or the science community that there may be some issue. There is not. Testosterone is the key determinant in performance" (Ingle, 2022). Such decisions and remarks are made by international sports organizations and not by the local organizing committee or the hosting city, state, or country, yet nevertheless, they might not be aligned with the progressive branding of a place like Oregon.

For world athletics the World Athletics Championships are the highlight of the sport, and for USA Track and Field, Oregon22 was a steppingstone towards a much larger goal—the Los Angeles 2022 Olympic Games. The impression by both organizations is that from an athletic standpoint Oregon22 were successful championships and Team USA excelled significantly, but that Eugene, as a host, is just too small to meet the ambitions of the organizations. Oregon22 received high viewership ratings in America in comparison to previous track and field competitions (Press Release, 2022), but it was not a transformative event that brought the sport to every household. Even in a relatively not packed period of the year, without directly competing with the NFL, March Madness, or the playoff season in major America sports leagues, other popular sports events such as baseball had higher viewership (Alexander, 2022). For Eugene, hosting World Athletics might have been the pinnacle of the branding as TrackTown USA on a global level, but it also exposed the city to everything it cannot be. Coe thanked Eugene for hosting and admitted that there were not a lot of options to choose from when giving the USA the rights to host the competitions for the first time (Greif, 2022b). Coe shared the opinion voiced by some of the American athletes who suggested that to grow the sport larger cities and markets in America should hold significant track and field events (Fred Kerley, 2022; Kilgore, 2022b). According to Coe, with the USA being the number one track and field powerhouse, the country is "not punching its weight" (Greif, 2022b) in terms of growing the popularity of the sport. Coe did not rule out future World Athletics Championships happening in the USA again but emphasized that the competitions should be held in a global city, saying: "It won't be Eugene. I want to be back into L.A. or Miami or Chicago" (Greif, 2022b). Somewhat paradoxically, by establishing its status as a global track and field hub as the first American host of the most prestigious event of the sport, Eugene, OR, made international and American administrators reconsider if indeed the city should remain the track and field capital of America or should larger cities host future international and high-profile events to grow the sports in lager markets, thus, potentially jeopardizing Eugene's status as "TrackTown USA."

Conclusion

The Oregon22 World Athletics Championships were a double-edged sword for the branding of Eugene as TrackTown USA. On one hand, hosting the most important competition of the sport cemented the significance of the place in the history of track and field in America, especially as this was the first time the event took place on US soil. With that said, with the spotlight on a small university town and with growth expectations by both international and American stakeholders, Oregon22 also exposed much of Eugene's limitations. While from an athletic standpoint the organization delivered exciting competitions, there was much disappointment about missed opportunities to make Oregon22 a transformative event both to the sport of track and field and for the city of Eugene and the state of Oregon. Unrealistic expectations along with limited place-branding strategies, created glocal dissonance, and prevented Eugene to fully capitalize on the potential of the competition. While the sustainable and small-scaled organization was authentic to the branding of Eugene and Oregon as eco-friendly and socially progressive, there was little direct orchestrated engagement with Oregon's nature and outdoors beyond the university's campus, or with internationally global brands associated with the place, such as Nike, *The Simpsons*, or the movie *Animal House*. National and international stakeholders were exposed to Hayward Magic and further exposed the historic significance of Prefontaine, and Bowerman, thus enhancing the authenticity of Eugene as a track and field capital. Much like Lausanne Capitale Olympique, and other cities recognized with sports, a small remote town in the Pacific Northwest with a regional airport and no money exchange services continued to manage to separate itself through authentic branding. With that said, there was also a growing realization that for the USA to grow the sport to larger audiences, new markets need to be engaged, even if it means that the home of American track and field will change.

REFERENCES

AIPS Media. (2022, July 27). World Athletics president Coe speaks on possible World Championships format change, Budapest 2023 and more. *AIPS*. Retrieved from https://www.aipsmedia.com/aips/pages/articles/2022/32643.html

Alexander, J. (2022, July 25). Alexander: Track and field's world championships met by apathy. *The Orange County Register*. Retrieved from https://www.ocregister.com/2022/07/25/alexander-track-and-fields-world-championships-met-by-apathy/

Amiri, S. (2022). City diplomacy: An introduction to the forum. *The Hague Journal of Diplomacy*, 17(1), 91–95.

Around the O. (2022, July 28). New viewer record set for WCH Oregon22 at Hayward Field. *Around the O*. Retrieved from https://around.uoregon.edu/content/new-viewer-record-set-wch-oregon22-hayward-field

Australian Bureau of Statistics. (2021). *Torquay (Vic). 2021 Census All Persons Quickstats*. Retrieved from https://abs.gov.au/census/find-census-data/quickstats/2021/SAL22551

BBC Sport. (2022, July 22). World Athletics could move events because of global warming, says Lord Coe. *BBC*. Retrieved from https://www.bbc.com/sport/athletics/62272758

Berendt, J., & Uhrich, S. (2016). Enemies with benefits: The dual role of rivalry in shaping sports fans' identity. *European Sport Management Quarterly*, 16(5), 613–634. https://doi.org/10.1080/16184742.2016.1188842

Bishop, G. (2022, July 19). Synonymous with Track and field, Eugene is an obvious – Yet unlikely – First U.S. host of the World Championships. *SI*. Retrieved from https://www.si.com/olympics/2022/07/19/eugene-oregon-host-world-track-championships-hayward-field

Borenstein, H. (2021, March 10). Despite conflict and uncertainty, women runners from Ethiopia's Tigray region becoming a rising force. *World Athletics*. Retrieved from https://worldathletics.org/news/feature/women-runners-from-tigray

Caballero, D. (2022, July 25). World Athletics Championships bring economic boost to Eugene. *KGW8*. Retrieved from https://www.kgw.com/article/sports/track/world-championships-eugene-track-field-oregon-hayward-field/283-2c7016c6-5444-40a9-aaa3-e286a9f9905e?fbclid=IwAR1rESOR4ZKoAw2djQTPKStf0UVCm1X7FiWcgwlfszZDhve4AADzCdwyc_Q

Carlson, M. (1998). *Brand Oregon tool kit*. The Oregon Economic and Development Department.

Chalip, L. (2006). Towards social leverage of sport events. *Journal of Sport & Tourism*, 11(2), 109–127. https://doi.org/10.1080/14775080601155126

Curtis, J. (2001). Branding a state: The evolution of Brand Oregon. *Journal of Vacation Marketing*, 7(1), 75–81. https://doi.org/10.1177/135676670100700107

Dennehy, C. (2022, July 25). First World Championships in the US give reasons to be cheerful. *Independent*. Retrieved from https://www.independent.ie/sport/other-sports/athletics/first-world-championships-in-us-give-reasons-to-be-cheerful-41863945.html

Diamond League. (2020). *Prefontaine Classic*. Retrieved from https://eugene.diamondleague.com/home/

Dinnie, K. (2004). Place branding: Overview of an emerging literature. *Place Branding, 1*(1), 106–110. https://doi.org/10.1057/palgrave.pb.5990010

Dubinsky, Y. (2019). From soft power to sports diplomacy: A theoretical and conceptual discussion. *Place Branding and Public Diplomacy, 15*, 154–164. https://doi.org/10.1057/s41254-019-00116-8

Dubinsky, Y. (2021a). Branding a City as a sports town: A conceptual model based on 'Track Town USA'. *Journal of Global Sport Management.*, 1–17. https://doi.org/10.1080/24704067.2021.2001354

Dubinsky, Y. (2021b). Sports, Brand America and U.S. public diplomacy during the presidency of Donald Trump. *Place Branding & Public Diplomacy*. https://doi.org/10.1057/s41254-021-00230-6

Eugene. (n.d.). *Oregon22 FAQs*. https://www.eugene-or.gov/4957/Oregon22-FAQs

Eugene, Cascades & Coast. (n.d.-a). *Welcome to Eugene, Cascades & Coast*. https://www.eugenecascadescoast.org/

Eugene, Cascades & Coast. (n.d.-b). *The Oregon22 Heritage Trail*. https://www.eugenecascadescoast.org/running/history/heritage-trail/#

Frandino, M., & Tennery, A. (2022, July 22). Nesting ospreys delight crowds at World Championships. *Reuters*. Retrieved from https://www.reuters.com/lifestyle/nesting-ospreys-delight-crowds-world-championships-2022-07-22/

Fred Kerley. (@fkerley99). (2022, July 22). We need to have world champs in Miami. *Twitter*. https://twitter.com/fkerley99/status/1550581252947836928

Front Runners. (2022). *Goodbye, World. Love Oregon*. University of Oregon. https://championships.uoregon.edu/

Futterman, M. (2022, July 16). Why is the World's biggest track meet in a small college town in Oregon? *The New York Times*. Retrieved from https://www.nytimes.com/2022/07/16/sports/eugene-world-athletic-championships.html

Gault, J. (2022, July 23). Meet the guy who stormed the track after the women's 5,000 at the 2022 Worlds. *LetsRun.com*. Retrieved from https://www.letsrun.com/news/2022/07/meet-the-guy-who-stormed-the-track-after-the-womens-5000-at-the-2022-worlds/

Gillen, K. (2022, May 1). 'The Cali dream was a bit tarnished': How Australia's surf culture became the envy of the world. *The Sydney Morning Herald*. Retrieved from https://www.smh.com.au/lifestyle/life-and-relationships/

the-cali-dream-was-a-bit-tarnished-how-australia-s-surf-culture-became-the-envy-of-the-world-20220430-p5ahe6.html
Greif, A. (2022, July 24). Despite huge success at world championships track popularity lags in U.S. *Los Angeles Times*. Retrieved from https://www.latimes.com/sports/olympics/story/2022-07-24/world-track-and-field-championships-american-popularity-lags
Greif, A. (2022b, July 28). Inside the 'crazy' plan to boost track and field's popularity before the L.A. Olympics. *Los Angeles Times*. Retrieved from https://www.latimes.com/sports/olympics/story/2022-07-18/usa-track-and-field-world-championships-popularity-plan
Greif, A. (2022c, July 14). On U.S. soil, Ukraine's athletes bring message: 'We protect our country on the track'. *Los Angeles Times*. Retrieved from https://www.latimes.com/sports/story/2022-07-14/world-track-field-championships-ukraine-athletes-war-russia
Grewal, D., & Levy, M. (2021). *Marketing* (7th ed.). McGraw Hill Education.
Hale, J. (2022, July 23). Activists march against World Athletics Championships, Nike in the streets of Eugene. *The Oregonian*. Retrieved from https://www.oregonlive.com/oregon22/2022/07/activists-march-against-world-athletics-championships-nike-in-streets-of-eugene.html
Hatler, C. (2022, July 18). Ryan Crouser leads an American sweep in the men's shot put. *Runner's World*. Retrieved from https://www.runnersworld.com/news/a40635978/world-championships-shot-put-results/
Hayward Field. (n.d.). *Setting the pace*. University of Oregon. Retrieved from https://hayward.uoregon.edu/
Hayward Magic. (2021). Retrieved from https://haywardmagic.com/
Hopsicker, P. M. (2017). 'Superbowling': Using the super Bowl's yearly commentary to explore the evolution of a sporting spectacle in the American consciousness. *The International Journal of the History of Sport*, 34(1–2), 23–45. https://doi.org/10.1080/09523367.2017.1334644
Howard-Grenville, J., Metzger, L. M., & Meyer, D. A. (2013). Rekindling the flame: Process of identity resurrection. *Academy of Management Journal*, 56(1), 113–136. https://doi.org/10.5465/amj.2010.0778
Hunt, J. (2018). *University of Nike: How corporate cash bought American higher education*. Melville House.
I am Torquay. (n.d.). Surfing in Torquay. *Great Ocean Road Regional* Tourism. Retrieved from https://torquaylife.com.au/explore/surfing/
IAAF. (2015). *Eugene awarded 2021 IAAF World Championship*. World Athletics press release (April 16). Retrieved from https://www.worldathletics.org/news/press-release/eugene-awarded-2021-iaaf-world-championships
Ingle, S. (2019, October 11). Nike Oregon Project shut down after Alberto Salazar's four-year ban. *The Guardian*. Retrieved from https://www.theguard-

ian.com/sport/2019/oct/11/nike-oregon-project-shut-down-after-alberto-salazars-four-year-ban

Ingle, S. (2022, July 15). Small town, big dreams: USA banks on hosting worlds to boost athletics. *The Guardian*. Retrieved from https://www.theguardian.com/sport/2022/jul/15/usa-world-athletics-championships

Johnson, D. (2022, July 23). Frayser-Pryce donates Oregon22 100m singlet to MOWA. *World Athletics*. Retrieved from https://worldathletics.org/competitions/world-athletics-championships/world-athletics-championships-oregon-2022-7137279/news/news/shelly-ann-fraser-pryce-jamaica-oregon22-100m-mowa

Kahl, D. (2022, August 14). Does Eugene have sights worth seeing? *The Register Guard*. Retrieved from https://www.registerguard.com/story/opinion/columns/2022/08/14/does-eugene-have-sights-worth-seeing/65397484007/

Kavaratzis, M., & Ashworth, G. (2015). Hijacking culture: the disconnection between place culture and place brands. *The Town Planning Review*, 86(2), 155–176. https://doi.org/10.3828/tpr.2015.10

Kilgore, A. (2022a, July 23). U.S. track CEO endorses John Carlos and Tommie Smith to light 2028 cauldron. *The Washington Post*. Retrieved from https://www.washingtonpost.com/sports/olympics/2022/07/22/john-carlos-tommie-smith-2028-olympics-max-siegel/

Kilgore, A. (2022b, July 24). At world championships, U.S. dominance on track, U.S fan apathy off. *The Washington Post*. Retrieved from https://www.washingtonpost.com/sports/olympics/2022/07/24/world-track-field-championships-american-fans/

Krauss, L. (2022, July 27). A look at attendance and records during the World Athletics Championships in Eugene. *The Register-Guard*. Retrieved from https://www.registerguard.com/story/news/local/2022/07/27/track-field-world-championships-attendance-road-closures-records-results-restauarants/65382595007/

Krieger, J. (2021). *Power and politics in world athletics – A critical history*. Routledge.

Lausanne Olympic Capital. (2020). *Home of international sport*. Retrieved from http://www.olympiccapital.ch/en.

Lyons, A. (2022, July 18). World Athletics Championships Oregon22 – Day Four. *Getty Images*. Retrieved from https://www.gettyimages.co.uk/detail/news-photo/jackie-joyner-kersee-shannon-rowbury-michelle-wolf-and-news-photo/1409582520

Manning, J. (2022a, July 27). Eugene charms athletes, fans as unlikely World Athletics Championships host. *The Oregonian*. Retrieved from https://www.oregonlive.com/oregon22/2022/07/eugene-charms-athletes-fans-as-unlikely-world-athletics-championships-host.html

Manning, J. (2022b, June 13). Track world heads to Eugene for World Athletics Championships 2022. Is Oregon ready? *The Oregonian*. Retrieved from https://www.oregonlive.com/pacific-northwest-news/2022/03/eugenes-star-turn-hosting-track-world-championships-looms-is-oregon-ready.html

Martin, D. (2007). *Rebuilding brand America: What we must do to restore our reputation and safeguard the future of American business abroad*. Amacom.

Murray, S. (2018). *Sports diplomacy: Origins, theory and practice*. Routledge.

My CIS. (2022). Flash Interviews. *World Athletics*. Retrieved from https://cis.worldathletics.org/7137279/flash-interviews.

NBA.com Staff. (2022, November 10). 2022–23 Nike City Edition uniforms unveiled. *NBA.com*. Retrieved from https://www.nba.com/city-edition-jerseys/2022-23

Neel, Z. (2022, July 25). Oregon22 Recap: How all 15 Ducks did in the World Track and Field Championships. *USA Today Sports*. Retrieved from https://duckswire.usatoday.com/lists/oregon22-recap-how-all-15-ducks-did-in-the-world-track-and-field-championships/

Nike by Eugene Events. (2022). Nike Athlete Inspiration Huddle. *Nike*. https://www.nike.com/experiences/details/1656371560722

Noorda, R., & Berens, K. I. (2020). "Keep Portland Weird"? Carvinalesque elements in the branding of the Portland Book Festival. *Studies in Book Culture*, *11*(2), 1–42. https://doi.org/10.7202/1070268ar

Oregon. (2022). Extraordinary is ordinary. *YouTube*. Retrieved from https://www.youtube.com/playlist?list=PLd7Qf9ipRYq78EbBOQpOPNJ4hX5OxXvm8

Oregon22, LLC. (2022, July 12). Media advisory: Flyovers planned during the first nights of the World Athletics Championships Oregon22. *World Athletics*. Retrieved from https://worldathletics.org/competitions/world-athletics-championships/world-athletics-championships-oregon-2022-7137279/news/news/media-advisory-flyovers-planned-during-the-first-nights-of-the-world-athletics-championships-oregon22

Parkman, I. (2010). The reciprocal relationship between corporate and regional brands in the creative industries: The case of sustainable architecture in Portland, Oregon, USA. *Tourism, Culture, & Communication*, *10*(3), 201–216. https://doi.org/10.3727/109830410X12910355180900

Perlman, R. (2022, July 26). Lane one: Eugene World Championships were inspiring and brilliant, but leave more questions than answers. *The Sport Examiner*. Retrieved from https://www.thesportsexaminer.com/lane-one-eugene-world-championships-were-inspiring-and-brilliant-but-leave-more-questions-than-answers/

Press Release. (2022, July 25). A look back at the World Athletics Championships Oregon22. *World Athletics*. Retrieved from https://worldathletics.org/competitions/world-athletics-championships/oregon22/news/press-releases/a-look-back-at-the-world-athletics-championships-oregon22

Preuss, H. (2015). A framework for identifying the legacies of mega sport event. *Leisure Studies*, 32(6), 643–664. https://doi.org/10.1080/02614367.2014.994552

RISE Road to Progress. (n.d.) *RISE road to progress*. http://roadtoprogress.risetowin.org/category/Oregon22/

Rowbottom, M. (2022, July 15). Visa delays for Oregon22 affecting many athletes as Britain's Thompson, 41, misses World debut. *Inside the Games*. Retrieved from https://www.insidethegames.biz/articles/1125728/oregon22-visa-hold-ups-100-athletes

Smith, P. J. (2008). Branding Cascadia: Considering Cascadia's conflicting conceptualizations – Who gets to decide? *Canadian Political Science Review*, 2(2), 57–83.

Smith, G. (2022, July 20). Officials weigh in on Oregon22 crowds and business impact. *KEZI News*. Retrieved from https://www.kezi.com/news/officials-weigh-in-on-oregon22-crowds-and-business-impact/article_2c5c2e94-089a-11ed-8d7a-4f6cf7006c9f.html

Tennery, A. (2022, July 24). Athletics – 'Unique' Eugene hosted truly global World Championships. *WKZO*. Retrieved from https://wkzo.com/2022/07/24/athletics-unique-eugene-hosted-truly-global-world-championships/

The Gleaner. (2022, July 19). If America wants to host sports events… *The Gleaner*. Retrieved from https://jamaica-gleaner.com/article/commentary/20220718/editorial-if-america-wants-host-sports-events

Theen, A. (2022, July 25). Did the 'Hayward Magic' return to Eugene?: Beat check podcast. *The Oregonian*. Retrieved from https://www.oregonlive.com/podcasts/2022/07/did-the-hayward-magic-return-to-eugene-beat-check-podcast.html

TrackTown USA. (2022a). About. https://gotracktownusa.com/about-ttusa/

TrackTown USA. (2022b). 20:22. https://www.gotracktownusa.com/2022

TrackTown USA (@TrackTownUSA). (2022c, July 15). You're not going to want to miss this. Tomorrow, July 16, you can attend the Nike Athlete Inspirational Huddle with running legends: Joan Benoit Samuelson @Carl_Lewis @SanyaRichiRoss it starts at 2pm at Nike by Eugene. *Twitter*. Retrieved from https://twitter.com/TrackTownUSA/status/1548081995833520135

Travel Oregon. (2022). *Extraordinary is ordinary*. Retrieved from https://traveloregon.com/

Travel Portland. (2022). *This is Portland*. Retrieved from https://www.travelportland.com/

UO Libraries. (n.d.). *Honoring native people and lands*. University of Oregon. https://library.uoregon.edu/honoring-native-peoples-and-lands

WCH Oregon22. (2022). *Media Guide*. World Athletics Championships Oregon22. Retrieved from https://drive.google.com/file/d/1vpeJfCOsYu_CJ_UZTaWU4ig5f9Qoz_9y/view

Whittington, J. (2022, July 17). Ceh cultivates his craft on quest for discus success in Oregon. *World Athletics*. Retrieved from https://worldathletics.org/competitions/world-athletics-championships/world-athletics-championships-oregon-2022-7137279/news/feature/kristjan-ceh-farming-discus-slovenia-oregon

Wilson, S. (2022, July 16). USA, USA, USA: Kerley leads American sweep of men's 100m in Oregon. *World Athletics*. Retrieved from https://worldathletics.org/competitions/world-athletics-championships/world-athletics-championships-oregon-2022-7137279/news/report/wch-oregon22-report-men-100m

Woods, D. (2022, July 25). World meet at Lucas Oil Stadium? Maybe not, but Indy could regain place as a track town. *Indianapolis Star*. Retrieved from https://www.indystar.com/story/sports/2022/07/25/oregon22-resounding-success-for-usa-track-and-field-could-indianapolis-host-world-championships/65381498007/

Woods, R., & Butler, N. (2021). *Social issues in sport* (4th ed.). Champaign, IL: Human Kinetics.

World Athletics. (2022, July 14). World Athletics Championships Oregon 22 – Press Conference. *YouTube*. Retrieved from https://www.youtube.com/watch?v=5iIsXHnISys

World Athletics. (n.d.). Medal Table. *World Athletics*. Retrieved from https://www.worldathletics.org/Competitions/world-athletics-championships/world-athletics-championships-oregon-2022-7137279/medaltable

World Athletics Championships Oregon22. (2020, November 23). Heart and Home of Track & Field in the USA. *YouTube*. Retrieved from https://www.youtube.com/watch?v=hmJJZgVZO0U

CHAPTER 9

Sport-Tech Diplomacy

Introduction

The purpose of this chapter is to discuss the growing role of the sport-tech ecosystem in nation branding and public diplomacy, as captured by the term sport-tech diplomacy, through the case of Israel. In analyzing the case of Israel, this chapter[1] identifies four necessary processes that apply to the use of sport-tech for nation branding and public diplomacy: (a) an authentic narrative of innovation, (b) innovation in sports, (c) a diverse sport-tech ecosystem, (d) galvanizing state and non-state actors around sport-tech diplomacy.

In the bestseller book *Start-up Nation: The Story of Israel's Economic Miracle*" (Senor & Singer, 2009), authors Dan Senor and Saul Singer discuss the innovative DNA of the State of Israel and the Jewish people. In the context of business, innovation is defined as "the process by which ideas are transformed into new products and services that will help firms grow" (Grewal & Levy, 2021, p. 276). Senor and Singer describe the creation of the state of Israel, its survival in difficult political and weather conditions, and its thriving industry as an economic miracle. Israel's image

---

[1] The chapter is an adjusted and updated version of the article: Dubinsky, Y. (2022). Sport-Tech Diplomacy: Exploring the intersections between the sport-tech ecosystem, innovation, and diplomacy in Israel. Place Branding & Public Diplomacy, 18(2), 169–180. https://doi.org/10.1057/s41254-020-00191-2

© The Author(s), under exclusive license to Springer Nature Switzerland AG 2023
Y. Dubinsky, *Nation Branding and Sports Diplomacy*,
https://doi.org/10.1007/978-3-031-32550-2_9

has been often associated with an armed conflict (Avraham, 2009; Gilboa, 2006). Some countries have been using sports to try and improve the country's image through nation branding and public diplomacy (Anholt, 2010; Murray, 2018). Although sports and physical activities are rooted in Israel's history and in the image change of Jewish people and Zionism (Harif, 2011; Kaufman & Galily, 2009), the Israeli-Arab dispute often manifested through hosting and participating in local and international competitions, limiting some branding opportunities (Dart, 2016; Dubinsky & Dzikus, 2018).

Several scholars argue that to improve that image, Israel should find a bypassing message to the conflict, such as focusing on its advanced technological ecosystem (Avraham, 2009; Gilboa, 2006). In his PhD dissertation, "Israel's use of sports for nation branding and public diplomacy" (2018), Dubinsky suggests to create a bypassing message through focusing on sports technologies. This chapter explores the term sport-tech diplomacy, and through the case of Israel, tries to identify key intersections between sports-technologies, nation branding, and public diplomacy through authenticity of innovation, sports diplomacy, people-to-people diplomacy (Handelman, 2012) and corporate diplomacy (Ordeix-Rigo & Durate, 2009; White, 2015).

What Is Sport-Tech Diplomacy?

The use of innovation and technology by states, non-state actors, private companies, and citizens in the contexts of sports and diplomacy is referred to in this chapter as "sport-tech diplomacy." The role of technology and diplomacy has been discussed through digital diplomacy and the use of internet, social media, and other digital platforms for soft power purposes (Cull, 2011; Duncombe, 2018; Manor, 2019). Terms such as "digital diplomacy," "virtual diplomacy," net diplomacy, or "public diplomacy 2.0" often related to the digital platforms such as the internet, social media, mobile platforms, etc. (Manor, 2019). While there can be some intersections between "sport-tech diplomacy" and digital diplomacy, sport-tech diplomacy also focuses on the sport-tech landscape and how it is used in the context of diplomacy.

As sports-related technologies are ever developing, there are various taxonomies and definitions to what sports-tech includes (Colosseum, 2020a; Frevel et al., 2020; Ratten, 2020). Sports technologies can range from different artificial intelligence (AI) technologies used for broadcasting and media, esports, smart-stadiums, different health-related mobile applications and other forms of technologies that enhance the sports experience (Colosseum, 2020a). Frevel, Schnidt, Beirberbeck, Penkert, and Subirna (2020) suggest a matrix to categorize the different technologies based on teach angle, and user angle. They suggest a framework of three main categories, and several levels of subcategories, such as (a) activity and performance (including wearables and equipment, performance tracking and coaching, and preparation), (b) management and organization (including organizations and venues, and media and commercial), and (c) fans and content (including news and content, fan experience and social platforms, and fantasy sports and betting). The international sports innovation group Colosseum (2020a) divides the sport-tech nation map into six categories: (a) athlete development, (b) fan engagement, (c) smart stadium, (d) health and fitness, (e) gaming and esports, and (f) media and broadcasting. While there might be several definitions and taxonomies to how technologies impact sports, the term sports-tech diplomacy refers to the use of such technologies for public diplomacy, soft power, and country image purposes.

Sports diplomacy embodies the connection and interaction between public diplomacy, soft power, and sports (Dubinsky, 2019a, b; Murray 2018; Pigman, 2014). Most countries in the world engage in some sort of sports diplomacy, as there are over 200 delegations marching with a country's flag in the opening ceremony of the summer Olympic Games (Dubinsky, 2019b). The Olympic Games are especially a popular platform for countries to try and achieve foreign policy goals because of the number of participating countries, the magnitude of the event, and the global exposure through international media. For example, hosting countries of the Olympic Games use the opening ceremonies to showcase their history and culture. According to Arning (2013) "Opening ceremonies enable countries to smuggle in and project soft power through the guise of Olympic stewardship" (p. 539).

There are ample examples of using the Olympic Games for public diplomacy purposes, including mass boycotts, exclusion, participation, protests, governmental-led doping systems to increase athletes' performance, renovating cities to improve tourism, exposing the country's products, etc. (Boykoff, 2016; Dubinsky, 2019a, b; Murray 2018; Pigman, 2014). Perhaps the most known example of sports diplomacy is "Ping Pong Diplomacy," a friendly game between American and Chinese table-tennis teams, that led to establishing official relations between the United States and the People's Republic of China during the Cold War (Carter and Sugden, 2011), Yet, using sports for public diplomacy purposes might backfire if it is used only for a photo-op or as a gimmick (Murray, 2012). Totalitarian countries received criticism for trying to use sports as a tool to reposition their image, not to be associated with negative values and especially not with human rights violations (Boykoff, 2016; Murray, 2018). Such attempts to launder a country's image are referred to as "sports-washing" (CNN, 2020).

Both sports and technologies impact public diplomacy and a country's image. Through hosting events, participation, or through performance, democratic, autocratic, first-world countries, developing countries, third-world countries, big countries, and small countries all find value in using sports as a tool to try and achieve social, political, and economic goals (Dubinsky, 2019a, b). Examples of achieving economic goals can include improving tourism by hosting an event, renovating a city, introducing new technologies, or exposing products through sponsorships. Countries have been using the Olympic Games to expose new technologies in different ceremonies or through the organization (Arning, 2013; Dubinsky, 2019b), trying to enhance their international reputation. Examples include Nazi Germany exposing live television broadcasting in the Berlin 1936 Olympic Games, Japan using the Tokyo 1964 Olympic Games and South Korea using the Seoul 1988 Olympic Games to expose their technological advancements and reposition the reputation of the country as global or regional leaders, Barcelona using the 1992 Olympic Games in an innovative way to create a positive urban legacy and become a tourism attraction, London using green technology in the 2012 Olympic Games for sustainability purposes, and so on (Dubinsky, 2019a). In 2021 the International Olympic Committee (IOC) (2021) updated its strategic plan and published Agenda 2020+5, which included 15 recommendations about the future of the movement. In most of the recommendations the IOC addressed technological needs (International Olympic Committee, 2021), with recommendation 8 pertaining specifically to grow digital engagement with people, and recommendation 9 to encourage the development of virtual sports and further engage with video gaming communities. Thus, the growth of the sport-tech ecosystem is aligned with future strategic goals of international sports.

The stakeholders that impact on a country's use of sports for nation branding and public diplomacy vary from public institutions and individuals such as governments and municipalities through politicians, leaders, and officers; the sports community through associations, clubs and teams, players, coaches, and owners; the private sector through sponsors, investors, and industry leaders, nongovernmental organizations such as sport for development and peace organizations or international associations and federations; and of course private citizens and individuals, and other pressure groups (Dubinsky, 2018, 2019a, b; Murray, 2018). The COVID-19 pandemic has changed the world of sports, as sports events around the world (Drewes et al., 2020; Pedersen et al., 2021) were postponed or cancelled, including the Olympic Games in Tokyo. Thus, impacting countries' public diplomacy efforts. Furthermore, countries that did host local or international sports events needed to adapt to a new reality, using innovative ways to conduct and broadcast sports events (Pedersen et al., 2021).

There are authentic connections between sports, diplomacy, and technology, due to their global nature, crossing borders and cultures, and ability to reach masses (Kelly, 2021). Much like with sports diplomacy, where many stakeholders are involved, or public diplomacy that includes different definitions related to the state, people, or corporations, the sport-tech ecosystem is also so diverse that there is not one agreeable method to rank countries based on their sport-tech ecosystem. According to the Sports Tech VC Report 2022 (SportsTechX, 2022), the top 10 leading countries by funding in 2022 were the USA, Hong Kong, Germany, India, Israel, the UK, Canada, Denmark, Australia and Brazil. When analyzing the period between 2018 and 2022 (SportsTechX, 2022), the USA was ranked first, followed by India, China, Canada, Germany, the UK, France, Brazil, Hong Kong, and Israel. In 2020, the Asian Sprots-Tech report ranked India in the first place, followed by Israel, China, Japan, and Singapore (Roy, 2020) Asian market was an early adopter of esports, and China, Japan, South Korea, and Singapore all have a developed sport-tech ecosystem. The UK and other Western countries who have developed economies and invest in sports technologies (Frevel et al., 2020; Statista, 2020) and the American system that generates billions and is analytics oriented are fertile grounds for both domestic sports-technologies companies and markets foreign companies target (Colosseum, 2020a, b, c). Australia will host some of the largest international sports-events in the upcoming decade and has both the public and private industries orientated towards sports technologies, including through the Australian Sports Technology Network (ASTN) (Frevel et al., 2020). Gulf countries such as the United Arab Emirates and Saudi Arabia invest in sport-tech as part of their soft power initiatives to host international events. Thus, countries across the globe understand that combining innovation through sports has international value. In Africa, South Africa has a vibrant sport-tech ecosystem with dozens of sports-related start-ups (Tracxn, 2022). With the sport-tech ecosystem ever-growing, more countries are investing to further their goals, such as in Ethiopia, which is world-known for its long-distance running programs, keeping its consistency at the top due to both knowledge along with social factors (Smyth, 2022), or Serbia encouraging their own start-up initiatives (Colosseum Sports Tech Serbia, 2019). Dubinsky (2022) analyzed how Japan used sports-related technologies for nation branding and public diplomacy during the postponed Tokyo 2020 Olympic Games, coming up with five observations about the practice of sport-tech diplomacy: (1) sport-tech diplomacy has merits and limits, (2) sport-tech diplomacy does not solve moral dilemmas, (3) sport-tech diplomacy has cultural equity, (4) successful sport-tech diplomacy requires authenticity and credibility, and (5) sport-tech diplomacy is multifaceted and growing. As the world of sports is facing new challenges such as protests, counter-movements against public spending, a global recession, and implication of a global pandemic, sport-tech diplomacy will become an integral part in public diplomacy as countries, communities, and other stakeholders will seek new innovative and technology-based solution to use sports for soft power and public diplomacy purposes.

An Authentic Narrative of Innovation

As both Cull (2010) and Dubinsky (2022) mention, diplomacy requires authenticity and credibility. In the context of sport-tech diplomacy, this means that there needs to be a narrative that key stakeholders can authentically relate to. While the term "Start-Up Nation" might have been coined by Senor and Singer (2009), the innovative DNA of Israel and of the Jewish people did not start with their book. A history of learning goes back thousands of years, to the nickname "people of book." Through never-ending debates in segregated Yeshiva communities, to reform and secular philosophers, scientists, studying, learning, thinking, and challenging the status quo were part of Jewish culture. From Karl Marx, through Sigmund Freud, Albert Einstein, to Ruth Bader Ginsburg, Jewish people have been associated with revolutionary thought. Although Jewish people make up only 0.2% of the world's population (Hacket & McClendon, 2017), over 20% of Nobel Prize recipients are Jewish or part-Jewish (JINFO, 2020).

Beyond a culture of learning, other reasons for the constant need for innovation are threat from antisemitism and racism, which pushed Jews to excel in professions that have international value, such as commerce, medicine, and science, not just to assimilate in their communities, but also to add value to others in case they are forced to leave due to hate-crimes. Furthermore, "Tikun Olam" (Hassman, 2008), the idea of repairing and improving the world, is integrated in Jewish culture, and adopted by the State of Israel. Such innovative thought also translated to a DNA of problem-solving, including meeting the challenges of building a country in a dry and hostile region, defending it, and growing its industry (Senor & Singer, 2009).

According to Avraham (2009) and Gilboa (2006), Israel enjoyed a positive image in the first decades since the country's independence in 1948. The struggle of Jewish people who did not only survive the holocaust but managed to build an independent country in a hostile region was perceived in the Western world as "David against the Goliath of the Arab countries, which failed to destroy it" (Avraham, 2009, 3). Yet, as the Israeli-Arab conflict continued and especially after the 1967 Six-Day War, when it tripled its size including occupying Gaza Strip and the West Bank, international media portrayed Israel as the Goliath of the conflict, including comparing Israeli policies to Apartheid and even Nazi Germany (Gilboa, 2006).

Wars and armed conflict create animosity towards a country's image (Heslop et al., 2008; Shoham et al., 2006). When examining Israel's deteriorating image, several scholars (Avraham, 2009; Dubinsky, 2018; Gilboa, 2006) recommended to try and create a bypassing message that disassociates the country from the ongoing armed dispute, in a way that foreign audiences could relate to without being forced to choose a side in a polarizing conflict. In recent years the Israeli government has tried to use technology to create a narrative that portrays Israel beyond the conflict (Avraham, 2015; Mashiah & Avraham, 2019).

Both the Israeli tech industry and the Israeli government adopted the branding of the country as a technological powerhouse. The necessities of the dry land and the political situation forced Israel to find creative solutions to survive (Senor & Singer, 2009). The founding generation used innovative methods for establishing new Jewish settlements in British-Mandated Palestine such as "Wall and Tower"—a speedy method of settlements building. The Israeli melting pot and the fusion of ideas from East and West in the Zionist movement led to an innovative collaborative form of living known as the kibbutz. Thus, adaptation and fusing ideas and cultures were part of the DNA of Israel even before Israel's independence in 1948. Informality and a culture of trial and error also formed the Israeli "Chutzpah"—a concept capturing rudeness, directness, loudness, and lack of boundaries, but also a fearlessness to try and push limits.

In the early decades of the State of Israel, the military and agricultural innovation were the focus of Israeli innovation (Aharoni & Grinstein, 2017). Since the 1990s, the technological bloom gave Israel and especially the Tel Aviv metropolitan the nickname "Silicon Wadi" (Roper & Grimes, 2005) due to its thriving high-tech industry. This transition was parallel to the collapse of the Soviet Union, the decline of some of the socialist ideals that shaped Israel, including the kibbutz. On the other hand, the immigration of Jewish people from Russia in the early 1990s brought more knowledge to further develop Israeli technology in the decades to come. As of 2020, Israel has the "largest number of start-ups per capita in the world" (Israel Innovation Authority, 2020), with over 6500 start-ups and over 300 hubs (Startup-Nation Finder, 2020). According to Startup-Nation Central (2020), Israeli start-ups focus on six major fields: (a) agritech, (b) cybersecurity, (c) digital health, (d) industry 4.0, (e) fintech, and (f) watertech. With over 350 research and development (R&D) centers, multinational corporations also find Israel as a worthy place to have offices in (Israel Innovation Authority, 2020).

Aharoni and Grinstein (2017) discuss the repositioning of the image of Israel between the years 2007 and 2015. After decades of not having a clear public diplomacy strategy (Gilboa, 2006), in 2003 American market-researchers worked with the Israeli Ministry of Foreign Affairs to reposition brand Israel (Aharoni & Grinstein, 2017). They found that most people are not interested or do not have an opinion on the Israeli-Palestinian dispute and that "ordinary people do not find Israel relevant to their lives nor can they emotionally relate to the country" (Aharoni & Grinstein, 2017, p. 301). In the reposition strategy they recommended to focus on Israel's creative energy. The following Israeli governments and ministries adopted that idea. Mashiah and Avraham (2019) analyzed the rhetoric use of Israel's innovation and technological advancement in the official speeches by Israeli Prime Minister Benjamin Nethanyahu in the United Nations. The authors found "that the speeches undertook a glorification ideology of Israeli high-tech and framed Israeli innovation as a sensational phenomenon and a huge contributor to humanity" (Mashiah

& Avraham, 2019, 24). Thus, the rhetoric on innovation and technologies tries to shape the narrative of Israel beyond the conflict.

The Ministry of Economy and Industry emphasized Israel's entrepreneurial spirit (Ministry of Economy and Industry State of Israel, 2020), the Ministry of Foreign Affairs underlined the country's innovation (Israel Ministry of Foreign Affairs, 2020), and the Ministry of Tourism launched the campaign "Land of Creation" (Israel Land of Creation, 2020), focusing on the rich history of the Israel as a place sacred to the three main monotheistic religions, and as a place that encourages creativity and modernity. Yet, according to Crilley and Manor (2020), Israel is also taking an non-nation-branding approach focusing on city branding in the Ministry of Tourism campaign "Two Cities. One Break." They argue that "branding Israel as a 'start-up nation' is unlikely to help Israel obtain legitimacy on the world stage'" (Crilley & Manor, 2020, p. 7), and by focusing on the historic significance of Jerusalem and the secularism of Tel Aviv, the cities disassociate with "brand Israel" (p. 7). The municipality of city of Tel Aviv Yafo is dedicated to these ideas and strategies, branding the city as a *Non-Stop City*, a smart city, and a global city, competing with the most attractive cities in the world (Tel Aviv Yafo, 2020a). The municipality is investing in brand itself as "Tel Aviv Startup City" (Tel Aviv Yafo, 2020b) through a variety of strategies supporting local startups and entrepreneurs ranging from training, property tax reductions, affordable working space models, and other initiatives (Tel Aviv Yafo, 2020c). According to the municipality, Tel Aviv Yafo has "the highest amount of startups per capita in the world" (Tel Aviv Yafo, 2020b), including 4000 startups in greater Tel Aviv and over 100 foreign R&D centers. Thus, while it can also be seen as somewhat contradictory, the branding of Israel through innovation and technology happens both by the Israeli government as part of public diplomacy, and by ministries and authorities trying to disassociate from Israel's official foreign policies.

A History of Innovation in Sports

To enhance authenticity, the narrative about innovation should also relate to the sports context. Innovation and sports are rooted in Jewish and Israeli history through the early stages of the Zionist Movement in the late nineteenth and early twentieth centuries (Dubinsky & Dzikus, 2019; Harif, 2011; Kaufman & Galily, 2009). In the second Zionist Congress in 1898, Max Nordau coined the term "Muscular Judaism" (Harif, 2011).

The term refers to a need to change the image of the segregated Torah-learning European Jew to a proactive one who will build and defend the future Jewish homeland (Harif, 2011; Kaufman & Galily, 2009). The Maccabiah Movement connects Jewish communities with each other and to the State of Israel through the Maccabiah Games—The Jewish Olympics"—a quadrennial international multi-sports event for Jews taking place in Israel. (Dubinsky & Dzikus, 2019; Harif, 2011; Kaufman & Galily, 2009). To be a homeland for Jewish people and to increase the Jewish demographic in the country, there are certain Israeli laws such as The Law of Return and the Citizenship Law, that grant Israeli citizenship to every Jewish person who makes "Aliyah" and immigrates to Israel (Dubinsky, 2018). After Israel's independence, numerous athletes made "Aliyah" after competing in the Maccabiah Games. The World Maccabiah Movement also serves as a networking web between Jewish communities around the world, and in times of need the movement helps resolve diplomatic issues (Dubinsky, 2018).

The innovative DNA in Jewish culture and history did not skip Jewish sports. While Jewish people account for about 0.2% of the world population, Jewish athletes won over 2% of medals won in the summer Olympic Games (Jewish Virtual Library, 2020; Statista Research Department, 2016). The Golden Age of Jewish sports happened in the early twentieth century, where Jewish clubs and Jewish athletes reached significant athletic success in Europe and the USA. Some of the roots of modern football can be traced back to the Danube School (Daskal, 2009), a group of Jewish coaches from Austria, Hungary, and Romania, including such as Bela Guttmann, Hugo Meisl, Dori Kurschner, and Ernest Erbstein, who were not just football coaches, but football philosophers. Each of these coaches revolutionized the game of football not only by creating some of the best teams, but through innovative tactics while spreading the game through Europe and globally to Brazil and South America. For example, the coaching methods and attacking style of play that Erbstein's Grande Torino was playing set the foundations for some of the most iconic football teams, such as the 1958 World Cup-winning Brazilian national team, and the famous Dutch "Total Football" (Daskal, 2009). The rise of Nazi Germany, and the holocaust, ended the Jewish Golden Age, forced clubs to close, and sent many athletes to death camps (Bolchover, 2019). In the United States, while Jewish athletes gained unproportionate success in the early twentieth century, most of the contribution to sports came from dozens of Jewish coaches, managers, owners, and administrators (Daskal,

2011). From Red Auerbach, through Theo Epstein, and Robert Kraft, Jews have been shaping, growing, and innovating American sports. In Dubinsky's PhD dissertation "Israel's use of sports for nation branding and public diplomacy" (Dubinsky, 2018), participants from sports organizations and governmental ministries argue that the best way to use sports to raise interest of a country is through performance. Yet, with only one Olympic gold medal, nine medals in the Olympic Games and one participation in the FIFA World Cup over 50 years ago, Israel has yet to become an athletic powerhouse. The exception is the Maccabi Tel Aviv Basketball Club, becoming one of the most successful clubs outside the USA winning six European Championships and over 100 domestic and international trophies, becoming the most decorated sports club in the world (Maccabi, 2020a). Part of the success was due to innovative collaborations with American athletes, during the Cold War, contributing to the opening of the borders for athletes between the USA and Europe. Tal Brody, an American-Jew who was drafted for the NBA but decided to play for Maccabi Tel Aviv after participating in the Maccabiah Games, revolutionized Israeli basketball (Dubinsky, 2018). Brody was the team captain when the club won its first European Cup in 1977. After beating Soviet giants CSKA Moscow and reaching the Final Four, Brody coined the most famous saying in Israeli sports: "We are on the map and we're staying on the map, not just in sports but with everything" (Maccabi, 2020a), making a connection between the success of Maccabi Tel Aviv and of the thriving of the State of Israel.

Another example of innovation in Israeli sports comes through the Paralympic Movement (Brittain & Hutzler, 2009; Dubinsky, 2018). Israel contributed to the development of the Paralympic Games in its early days and was one of the early adopters of the idea to use sports for rehabilitation, partly through the connection with Jewish doctor Ludwig Guttmann, who founded the movement. Israel was a pioneer in establishing holistic centers for rehabilitation for war veterans and polio patients, including the use of athletic competitions (Dubinsky, 2018). As a result, Israeli athletes were successful in the first versions of the Paralympic Games, Tel Aviv hosted the Paralympic Games in 1968, and other countries adopted similar models (Brittain & Hutzler, 2009; Dubinsky, 2018). By being early adopters and by finding the solutions to challenges Israeli society faced, Israeli innovations contributed to the growth of the Paralympic movement and to the rehabilitation of people with disabilities through physical activity.

International politics often overshadowed Israel's participation in international sports, including boycotts, exclusions, demands from exclusions, demonstrations, hiding Israeli symbols, cancelled and postponed events, hosting outside of the country, and even a deadly terror attack during the 1972 Olympic Games in Munich, West Germany (Dubinsky & Dzikus, 2018; Galily, 2007; Ber et al., 2017). According to Dart (2016), Israel is trying to associate itself with Western Europe through sports, rather than with its Middle Eastern neighbors. As a result of the manifestation of the Israeli-Arab dispute through sports, Israel is losing ample branding opportunities (Dubinsky & Dzikus, 2018). When discussing the intersection of sports, diversity and innovation, perhaps the best example is the Peres Center for Peace and Innovation founded by Shimon Peres, the late prime minister and president of Israel and a Nobel Peace Prize Awardee (Peres Center for Peace & Innovation, 2020). The Center uses sports for educational purposes and peacebuilding activities between Israelis and Arabs. Such interaction between innovation, diversity promotion, and sports attracts partnerships with international organizations, and sports clubs, like the United Nations Office for Sport for Development and Peace, FIFA Foundation, and even FC Barcelona (Peres Center for Peace & Innovation, 2020).

A Diverse Sport-Tech Ecosystem

One element that sports diplomacy and the sport-tech ecosystem have in common is diversity. There is not one clear definition of either, and both have multiple stakeholders, ranging from countries and governments, nongovernmental institutions, citizens, and corporate entities (Dubinsky, 2022; Murray, 2018). According to international sports innovation group Colosseum (2020a, b), the Israeli sports-tech ecosystem consists of over 200 companies, focusing on both B2B and B2C target audiences. They divide the Sports Tech Nation Map (Colosseum, 2020c) into six main fields: fan engagement, media and broadcasting, health and fitness, athlete development, smart stadium, and gaming and esports. The ecosystem is rich and diverse, providing a vast variety of innovative solutions targeting a wide audience from individuals and amateurs to professionals and global corporations (Colosseum, 2020c).

The evolution of the gaming, fantasy sports, and esports industry did not skip the Israeli market, with over a dozen start-ups focusing on these industries (Colosseum, 2020a, c). In 2021, following collaborations with

Maccabi World Union, Israel hosted the 13th International Esports Federation (IESF) World Championship in the south Eilat (Pavitt, 2021). Several top Israeli sports teams, such as Maccabi Tel Aviv Football Club and Maccabi Tel Aviv Basketball Club, adopted esports as well (Halickman, 2017; Maccabi, 2020b). In 2020, Maccabi Tel Aviv Basketball Club signed a 5-year naming rights sponsorship agreement with the Israeli international mobile-gaming company Playtika (Maccabi, 2020c), strengthening the connection between one of the leading companies in the Israeli sport-tech industry and the most successful brand in Israeli sports.

Israel's international reputation in sports production goes well beyond the sport-tech system. Israeli Alex Gilady revolutionized Israeli television, became a senior vice-president in NBC Sports, and in 1994 was elected as a member of the International Olympic Committee (International Olympic Committee, 2020). Gilady received several Emmy Awards for television production of Olympic Games. In 2012 an Israeli team produced the prestigious basketball tournament in the 2012 Olympic Games in London and was nominated for the Olympic Golden Rings Award (Nevo, 2012). Ample international companies and corporations and global sports organizations use services of innovative Israeli media and broadcasting companies and start-ups. In 2016 Intel bought Israeli-based Replay Technologies for 175 million dollars (Tsipori, 2016). The Israeli company developed multidimensional imaging technology. Before the acquisition, Intel has been collaborating for several years with Replay Technologies, including using its service during the Super Bowl 50 and the NBA All Star Weekend.

Several Israeli companies specialize in AI, developing automated production of sports events. The Israeli company PlaySight offers "affordable & automated live streaming and multi-angle video recording production" (PlaySight, 2020a, b). Organizations that use their service vary from high school teams and local clubs, through some of the most successful NCAA division 1 programs, including Ohio State among others, to some of the most prestigious professional sports franchises and clubs, including the Boston Celtics from the NBA, Manchester City in the English Premier League, and others. While PlaySight have offices across America, their R&D Center remains in Israel, near Tel Aviv. Pixellot (2020a), is another Israeli company providing automated production without the need for human intervention, used in 34 countries, including by FC Barcelona, ESPN, SONY, and others. LiveU, an Israeli-founded company focusing on innovative and cost affective production and broadcasting, was sold to Francisco Partners for 200 million dollars (Haimovich, 2019). LiveU has over 3000 customers in over 130 countries (LiveU, 2020), including popular sports leagues such as the Spanish La Liga, and broadcasting networks including ESPN and FOX Sports. While not all Israeli sport-tech companies manage to partner with global organizations, these are just a few examples out of dozens of media and broadcasting oriented Israeli start-ups that through innovative technology reach households across the globe (Colosseum, 2020c).

In regards to fan engagement, Israeli companies also create a wide variety of solutions. Pico provides personal fan communicated platform, working with teams from the NBA, NHL, and even German soccer powerhouse Bayern Munich (Pico, 2020). There are also a number of sport-tech companies focusing on enhancing the experience when attending a game, including ticket brokers (Sports Events 365, 2020), seat delivery services for food and merchandise (Seatserve, 2020), and other services. Israeli-founded company Tokabot (Levin, 2018) helps clubs, federations, and media outlets to engage with fans during games through their online platform. Among the organizations using the platform are Bwin betting, the popular German newspaper Sport Bild, and several German football organizations including the German Football Association (Tokabot, 2020). One of Dubinsky's (2018) recommendations is to focus more on participation-sports tourism, such as cycling, running, and swimming. The Israeli sport-tech ecosystem also provides solutions for such strategy and for popular-sports enthusiasts. For example, Pic2Go is working with running events in North America, Latin America, Europe, and countries across the world including India, Indonesia, South Africa, and New Zealand, providing digital race-experience sharing such as recognizing barcodes on race bibs (Pic2Go, 2020). Whether these companies are based in Israel, founded in Israel, or founded by Israelis, they offer solutions applicable to global markets.

Galvanizing State and Non-State Actors Around Sport-Tech Diplomacy

Due to the diverse nature of the sport-tech ecosystem and the various intersections between sports and diplomacy, successful sport-tech diplomacy relies on different stakeholders authentically aligning behind a common message. Whether it starts with the government, or with the private industry or through citizens, the sport-tech ecosystem needs to reflect through the country's institutions. The high-tech bloom in the Israeli industry did not skip the Israeli sports-technology industry. As of 2020, there are over 200 sport-tech start-ups in Israel (Colosseum, 2020a). Hype Sports Innovations was formed by Israelis and created an international network of over 40,000 members (Hype Sports Innovations, 2020; Ravet, 2019), including virtual accelerating programs converting sport-tech to business models. As Israel is a small market, to reach international audiences, Israeli start-ups and sport-tech stakeholders often have offices outside of Israel as well, usually in strategic global cities, especially in the United States and Europe (Colosseum, 2020a; LiveU, 2020; Pixellot, 2020a). Most of the biggest sports leagues in the world work with Israeli sports technologies, including some of the biggest sports clubs like FC Barcelona (Pixellot, 2020b), NBA teams, such as the Golden State Warriors (Refael, 2019) and dozens more. Furthermore, some of Israeli start-ups outsource their technologies, partner with, or even sell to global companies such as Intel, Nike, Apple, and others (Colosseum, 2020a).

There is an understanding within Israeli governmental ministries and through the more developed sports organizations that there is much mutual potential of collaborations between the state, the associations, and the private sectors through sport technologies (Dubinsky, 2018). The more developed Israeli sports organizations and most of the top football clubs and basketball clubs who participate in international competitions regularly usually use Israeli sports technologies on a consistent basis. Furthermore, the National Olympic Committee of Israel formed a partnership with the Technion—Israeli Institute of Technology—to establish a collaborative research center to improve Israel's Olympic sports (National Olympic Committee of Israel, 2018).

However, there are also ample challenges. The Israeli sports industry ecosystem only partly adopted Israeli technologies. According to Nachlieli and Siminian (2019) Israeli start-up companies struggle to find Israeli sports organizations as receptive beta-sites. Potentially, there is mutual benefit of having both sports organizations and sport-tech companies to collaborate, as start-up companies will be able to perfect their products before launching to larger international markets, and sports organizations can obtain highly developed technology at a very low cost. However, there are several obstacles as some Israeli sports clubs do to not work with data that can be used by the data-driven technological companies, some coaches see technologies as a threat, and some sports organizations do not have the means or the know-how to use new technologies or do not see the benefit in using them (Nachlieli & Siminian, 2019). Furthermore, the Maccabiah Movement, which is perhaps the most significant example of collaboration between the State of Israel and Israeli sports, did not acknowledge enough use of Israeli sport-technologies through hosting the 2017 Maccabiah Games (Dubinsky & Dzikus, 2019). Trying to improve and position themselves as early adopters, the Maccabiah announced it will incorporate esports in the 21st Maccabiah Games as an exhibition event and help bring international esports championships to Israel (Maccabi World Union, n.d.; TGSPOT, 2019). During 2022 Israel integrated the branding of the country as a sport-tech hub through several hosted sports events, including a sport-tech exhibition during the 2022 Maccabiah Games (Maccabiah, n.d.), Maccabi World Union was involved with the Eilat 2021 Esports World Championships (Pavitt, 2021) and Haifa hosted a pre-season competition between AC Rome and Tottenham Hotspur branded as the I-Tech Cup (Eccleshare, 2022).

Governmental investment alone will not necessarily create an authentic message if the narrative is not adopted by the people and reflected through them. In recent decades, Middle Eastern countries from the Gulf, namely, Qatar and the United Arab Emirates, used sports for soft power purposes through hosting sports events and sponsoring some of the largest sports teams in the Western world (Thani & Heenan, 2017). The Israeli government admitted that international sports clubs have been reluctant to accept official sponsorships that promote Israel (Dorsey, 2016; Dubinsky, 2018). Yet, that was bypassed through people-to-people diplomacy, especially by Jewish-Canadian billionaire, Sylvan Adams' cycling-related initiatives. Adams' initiatives in Israeli cycling include hosting 3 days of the 2018 Giro d'Italia (Keyser, 2020), building a velodrome in Tel Aviv, and especially investing in the Israeli cycling team Israel Cycling Academy (Israel Cycling Academy, 2019), naming it "Israel Start-Up Nation" (Walla! Sports staff, 2019) and having it compete in the prestigious 2020 Tour de France (Sprio, 2020). By doing so, and through collaborations with Start-Up Nation Central (Sprio, 2020) using other Israeli innovations, and through endorsements by the Peres Center for Peace (Walla! Sports staff, 2019), the sponsorship of Israel as an innovative powerhouse is brought to audiences worldwide.

Several Israeli athletes and team-owners have been involved in the start-up industry. Former Olympic swimmer Gal Nevo (Swimming World Editorial Team, 2019) cofounded the tech company SenSwim, providing automatic data for swimming coaches during training. Omri Casspi, who played 10 seasons in the NBA, invested in nutritional technological start-up DayTwo, which provides dietary recommendations based on analysis of the DNA of gut microbiomes (Ravet, 2018). Several Israeli entrepreneurs who made their fortune through start-up companies, invested in or owned Israeli sports club. Ori Allon became a billionaire after being involved in several start-up companies, including developing and selling the algorithms to Google and Twitter (Oron, 2018). Allon became the major shareholder of his childhood favorite team, Hapoel Jerusalem Basketball Club, which under his ownership won the club its first two national championships. Alona Barkat, wife of Nir Barkat—chairman of CheckPoint Software Technology and former mayor of Jerusalem—demonstrated entrepreneurship when in 2007 she purchased Hapoel Beer-Sheva, a modest football club from the south of Israel then in the second division (Halickman, 2020; Montague, 2017). Barkat was the first female owner of an Israeli football team and under her ownership and leadership the club won three straight championships, and achieved some success in international competitions (Halickman, 2020). The impact of the club on the Israeli periphery was acknowledged by *The New York Times*' article "An Israeli Desert City Blooms as a Soccer Power" (Montague, 2017). The journalist from *The New York Times* also complimented the growing high-tech industry in the region, writing "In many ways, the city and its team have risen together. Tech companies have moved in. The university has expanded, bringing young people in growing numbers. The economy is quietly booming" (Montague, 2017).

The social impact of Israeli tech-entrepreneurs on Israeli sports was also recognized by CNN (Schwartz & Masters, 2019). Beitar Jerusalem, one of Israel's most successful football clubs, is often negatively mentioned in international media as "an Israeli club infamous for the racist behavior of some of its fans towards Muslims" (Schwartz & Masters, 2019). Much of the critic focuses on the right-wing fan base "La Familia" and the history of the club not signing Arab Muslim players. Moshe Hogeg, who founded several Israeli start-up companies and applications, purchased Beitar Jerusalem in 2018 and promised to fight racism through individual lawsuits (Schwartz & Masters, 2019). Such efforts correlate with the suggested micro-marketing strategies of branding Israel through its people, lifestyle, diverse culture, and technology (Aharoni & Grinstein, 2017). Thus, it is not just the government, but the people who see value through sport-tech diplomacy.

Perhaps the most essential stakeholders to create an authentic sport-tech ecosystem and authentic sport-tech diplomacy strategies are corporations and companies who see both the commercial and branding value. Israel's corporate sport-tech diplomacy does not necessary result from private companies trying to engage in Israel's official diplomatic efforts, but from growing out of the complex geopolitical situation in Israel, creating innovative solution applicable to global audiences. Start-ups improving sports performance sometimes developed from Israel's unique social structure, including the Israeli army. The start-up company IntelliGym (2020) offers a software developed by Applied Cognitive Engineering (ACE) as a cognitive training platform to improve decision-making and concentration. The technology was developed in Israel for training purposes in the Israeli Air Force (Ynet, 2004). The Israelis who founded IntelliGym served together in the Israeli Force and applied the technology to sports (Kabir, 2017). Organizations that use the software vary from youth clubs, to professional football teams in Germany, the Netherlands, and Austria, to Hockey Canada (IntelliGym, 2020). There are several examples of collaborations between Israeli sports innovations and the Israeli military, including the launching of the WinTech Program in 2020, a collaborative between Wingate Institute—Israel's Sports Institute, sports organizations, and the IDF Medical Corps (Wingate, 2020).

There are dozens of start-ups oriented towards health and fitness, providing well-being solutions, targeting popular sports, individual users, and professional sports teams (Colosseum, 2020c). These start-ups provide innovative solutions through fitness, dietary, healthy living, self-measurements, and other applications that can be used by different segments of the market. Just to name a few, Likeaglove created an innovative smart measuring grams technology (LikeAGlove, 2020); Sleeprate provides sleeping solutions, targeting enterprises and athletes (Sleeprate, 2020); and Physimax created a platform for musculoskeletal self-assessment (Physimax, 2020) and is used by West Point, top NCAA college programs, and even Utah Jazz from the NBA. Focusing on health and fitness does not rely on having high-level competitive sports teams and is not directly impacted by the Israeli-Arab dispute, and could be applied almost anywhere. Another aspect the sport-tech system addresses is the concept of "Tikun-Olam"—repairing the world—which is also part of the Jewish tradition and in the DNA of the State of Israel (Hassman, 2008). For example, the Israeli military are among the first responders in disaster-struck areas building field hospitals and providing care. By focusing on global problems such as health and obesity, the Israeli sport-tech ecosystem also contributes to that.

The Israeli start-up ecosystem also joined the fight against the COVID-19 pandemic (CoronaTech Israel, 2020). Through the first months of the pandemic, Israeli stakeholders suggested innovative solutions related to sports through automated recording of games that reduce the number of people in stadiums and arenas (Pixellot Ltd, 2020), suggesting new competition formats to allow a more sustainable way to organize sports events (Ingbar, 2020), offering solutions for how to stay fit during quarantine and lockdown (Siminian & Macdowell, 2020) or even just by organizing dozens of free virtual panels with industry leaders across the world, brainstorming and fusing ideas of how to approach an unprecedented challenge humanity faces (Colosseum, 2020a, b, c; Hype Sports Innovations, 2020). In the foreseeable future, countries who seek to continue to use sports for nation branding and foreign policy purposes will need to find new innovative solutions, including in the realm of technology, thus making sport-tech diplomacy a new tool for soft power and public diplomacy. In the case of Israel, facing never-ending challenges and trying to meet them with innovating solutions to survive and grow is not a bug, it is a feature.

Conclusion

The chapter discussed the uniqueness of sport-tech diplomacy through the case of Israel, identifying several processes that give the strategy authenticity. Through analyzing Israel's unique challenges, a narrative of constant need to adapt and find innovative solutions is one that galvanizes diverse stakeholders, each finding their own goals and points of interest. As Cull (2010) rightfully argues, successful public diplomacy needs to be based on credible policies. Thus, successful sport-tech diplomacy needs to reflect an existing or growing sport-tech ecosystem. Whether it is the state and official institutions, citizens, or corporations, they all see value in the sport-tech ecosystem, not just through self-affiliation but in the country being branded as a technological hub. The chapter does not argue that by focusing on sport-tech diplomacy Israel will solve its security or political issues, or that Israel is the number one sport-tech country in the world. However, Israel does manage to create a message that internally different stakeholders can support, and through that foster relations with other countries regardless of an ongoing armed dispute. With the ever-evolving nature of sports, investments in the sport-tech ecosystem are likely to grow with more countries identifying foreign-policy-related opportunities. Thus, sport-tech diplomacy might not stay as a niche bypassing message, but can play a more strategic and central role in countries' soft power adapting to social, political, and technological change.

References

Aharoni, I., & Grinstein, A. (2017). How to (re)position a country? A case study of the power of micro-marketing. *Place Branding and Public Diplomacy, 13*(4), 293–307. https://doi.org/10.1057/s41254-017-0055-9

Anholt, S. (2010). *Places: Identity, image and reputation*. Palgrave Macmillan.

Arning, C. (2013). Soft power, ideology and symbolic manipulation in Summer Olympic Games opening ceremonies: A semiotic analysis. *Social Semiotics, 23*, 523–544.

Avraham, E. (2009). Marketing and managing nation branding during prolonged crisis: The case of Israel. *Journal of Place Branding and Public Diplomacy, 5*, 202–212.

Avraham, E. (2015). Case E: Cultural diplomacy and entrepreneurship as a means for image restoration: The case of Israel. In F. M. Go, A. Lemmetyinen, & U. Hakala (Eds.), *Harnessing place branding through cultural entrepreneurship*. Palgrave Macmillan. https://doi.org/10.1057/9781137465160_10

Ber, R., Yarchi, M., & Galily, Y. (2017). The sporting arena as a public diplomacy battlefield: The Palestinian attempt to suspend Israel from FIFA. *The Journal of International Communication, 23*, 218–230.

Bolchover, D. (2019, May 2). How the Nazis destroyed a Golden Age of Jewish soccer. *Haaretz*. Retrieved from https://www.haaretz.com/jewish/.premium-how-the-nazis-destroyed-a-golden-age-for-jewish-soccer-1.5978782

Boykoff, J. (2016). *Power games: A political history of the Olympics*. Verso.

Brittain, I., & Hutzler, Y. (2009). A social-historical perspective on the development of sports for persons with physical disability in Israel. *Sport in Society, 12*(8), 1075–1088. https://doi.org/10.1080/17430430903076365

Carter, T., & Sugden, J. (2011). The USA and sporting diplomacy: Comparing and contrasting the cases of table tennis with China and baseball with Cuba in the 1970s. *International Relations, 26*(1), 101–121.

CNN. (2020, April 27). Sportswashing: What is it and who practice it? *CNN*. Retrieved from https://edition.cnn.com/videos/sports/2020/04/27/sportswashing-history-saudi-arabia-newcastle-united-russia-china-football-world-cup-spt-intl.cnn

Colosseum. (2020a). Sport Tech: New decade new era. *Colosseum*. Retrieved from https://www.colosseumsport.com/reports

Colosseum. (2020b). *International sports innovation group.* Retrieved from https://www.colosseumsport.com/events

Colosseum. (2020c). *Sport Tech Nation Map.* Retrieved from https://b7fc3c6e-058a-4522-ac6e-eb904fb57c4a.filesusr.com/ugd/6f3e28_48ba38b6833b4e98b2928efc8fdb70e7.pdf

Colosseum Sports Tech Serbia. (2019, October). *Sports Tech Serbia.* Retrieved from https://www.colosseum-serbia.rs/Sports%20Tech%20Serbia_Report.pdf

CoronaTech Israel. (2020). Resource Center for Israeli CoronaTech Innovation. *CoronaTech Israel.* Retrieved from https://www.coronatech.org.il/

Crilley, R., & Manor, I. (2020). Un-nation branding: The cities of Tel Aviv and Jerusalem in Israeli soft power. In S. Amiri & E. Sevin (Eds.), *City diplomacy* (pp. 137–160). Palgrave Macmillan.

Cull, N. J. (2010). Public diplomacy: Seven lessons for its future from its past. *Journal of Place Branding and Public Diplomacy, 6,* 11–17.

Cull, N. J. (2011). WikiLeaks, public diplomacy 2.0 and the state of digital public diplomacy. *Place Branding and Public Diplomacy, 7*(1), 1–8. https://doi.org/10.1057/pb.2011.2

Dart, J. (2016). "Brand Israel": Hasbara and Israeli sport. *Sport in Society, 19,* 1402–1418.

Daskal, O. (2009, October 8). Israel's national team should play "Jewish Football". *Calcalist.* Retrieved from https://www.calcalist.co.il/sport/articles/0,7340,L-3363432,00.html. [Hebrew].

Daskal, O. (2011, May 2). "People of the book" dominate sports business. *Calcalist.* Retrieved from https://www.calcalist.co.il/sport/articles/0,7340,L-3516347,00.html. [Hebrew].

Dorsey, J. (2016, October 16). Israel suspends Israeli-Palestinian encounters on the pitch. *Huffington Post.* Retrieved from https://www.huffpost.com/entry/israel-suspends-israeli-p_b_8319008

Drewes, M., Daumann, F., & Follert, F. (2020). Exploring the sports economic impact of COVID-19 on professional soccer. *Soccer & Society, 17*(2), 85–95. https://doi.org/10.1080/14660970.2020.1802256

Dubinsky, Y. (2018). *Israel's use of sports for nation branding and public diplomacy.* Unpublished doctoral dissertation, University of Tennessee, Knoxville.

Dubinsky, Y. (2019a). Analyzing the roles of country image, nation branding, and public diplomacy through the evolution of the modern Olympic movement. *Physical Culture and Sport. Studies and Research, 84*(1), 27–40. https://doi.org/10.2478/pcssr-2019-0024

Dubinsky, Y. (2019b). From soft power to sports diplomacy: A theoretical and conceptual discussion. *Place Branding and Public Diplomacy,* 1–9. https://doi.org/10.1057/s41254-019-00116-8

Dubinsky, Y. (2022). Sport-Tech diplomacy at the Tokyo 2020 Olympic Games. *CPD perspectives on public diplomacy.* USC Center for Public Diplomacy and

Figueroa Press. Retrieved from https://uscpublicdiplomacy.org/sites/default/files/Sport-Tech%20Diplomacy_11.21.22.pdf

Dubinsky, Y., & Dzikus, L. (2018). Israel's country image in the 2016 Olympic Games. *Place Branding and Public Diplomacy.* https://doi.org/10.1057/s41254-018-0105-y

Dubinsky, Y., & Dzikus, L. (2019). Israel's strategic and tactical use of the 2017 Maccabiah Games for nation branding and public diplomacy. *Journal of Applied Sport Management, 11*, 1–13. https://doi.org/10.18666/JASM-2019-V11-I1-9170

Duncombe, C. (2018). Twitter and the challenges of digital diplomacy. *SAIS Review of International Affairs, 38*(2), 91–100. https://doi.org/10.1353/sais.2018.0019

Eccleshare, C. (2022, July 28). Spurs in Israel: Why a pre-season trip to Haifa to face Roma has proven so controversial. *The Athletic.* Retrieved from https://theathletic.com/3456616/2022/07/29/tottenham-roma-friendly-israel/

Frevel, N., Schmidt, S. L., Beiderbeck, D., Penkert, B., & Subirana, B. (2020). Taxonomy of sportstech. In S. L. Schmidt (Ed.), *21st century sports* (pp. 15–37). Springer. https://doi.org/10.1007/978-3-030-50801-2

Galily, Y. (2007). Sport, politics and society in Israel: The first fifty-five years. *Israel Affairs, 13*, 515–528.

Gilboa, E. (2006). Public diplomacy: The missing component in Israel's foreign policy. *Israel Affairs, 12*, 715–747.

Grewal, D., & Levy, M. (2021). *Marketing* (7th ed.). McGraw Hill.

Hacket, C., & McClendon D. (2017, April 5). *Christians remain world's largest religious group, but they are declining in Europe.* Pew Research Center. Retrieved from https://www.pewresearch.org/fact-tank/2017/04/05/christians-remain-worlds-largest-religious-group-but-they-are-declining-in-europe/

Haimovich, H. (2019, May 28). Israeli company LiveU acquired for 200 million dollars. *Geektime.* Retrieved from https://www.geektime.co.il/liveu-aqcuire/. [Hebrew].

Halickman, J. (2017, November 7). A first in Israel: Maccabi signs the Eligula brothers as FIFA players. *Maccabi Tel Aviv.* Retrieved from https://www.maccabi-tlv.co.il/en/2017/11/first-israel-maccabi-signs-eligula-brothers-esport-players/

Halickman, J. (2020, March 29). Alona Barakat bails on Hapoel Beersheva. *The Jerusalem Post.* Retrieved from https://www.jpost.com/israel-news/sports/alona-barkat-bails-on-hapoel-beersheba-622851

Handelman, S. (2012). The minds of peace experiment: A laboratory for people-to-people diplomacy. *Israel Affairs, 18*(1), 1–11. https://doi.org/10.1080/13537121.2012.634278

Harif, H. (2011). *Zionism of muscles – The political functions of representative sport in Eretz Israel ad in the State of Israel, 1898–1960.* Yad Izhak Ben-Zvi.

Hassman, R. (2008). *The Israel brand nation marketing under constant conflict* (Policy paper). Tel Aviv University Press.
Heslop, L. A., Lu, I. R. R., & Cray, D. (2008). Modeling country image effects through an international crisis. *International Marketing Review, 25*, 354–378.
Hype Sports Innovations. (2020). *About us*. Retrieved from https://www.hypesportsinnovation.com/
Ingbar, I. (2020, March 10). The Corona cancels sports competitions? Then innovate. *Calcalist*. Retrieved from https://www.calcalist.co.il/sport/articles/0,7340,L-3800150,00.html. [Hebrew].
IntelliGym. (2020). *Improve your game intelligence*. https://www.intelligym.com/
International Olympic Committee. (2020). Mr Alex Gilady. *Olympic*. Retrieved from https://www.olympic.org/mr-alex-gilady
International Olympic Committee. (2021). *Agenda 2020+5: 15 Recommendations*. Retrieved from https://stillmed.olympics.com/media/Document%20Library/OlympicOrg/IOC/What-We-Do/Olympic-agenda/Olympic-Agenda-2020-5-15-recommendations.pdf
Israel Cycling Academy. (2019). *About us*. Retrieved from http://israelcycling-academy.com/who-are-we/
Israel Innovation Authority. (2020). *Innovation in Israel*. Retrieved from https://innovationisrael.org.il/en/contentpage/innovation-israel
Israel Land of Creation. (2020). *Welcome to tourist information Israel*. Ministry of Tourism. Retrieved from https://info.goisrael.com/en/
Israel Ministry of Foreign Affairs. (2020). *Innovative Israel*. Retrieved from https://mfa.gov.il/MFA/InnovativeIsrael/Pages/default.aspx
Jewish Virtual Library. (2020). *Jews in sports: Jewish Olympic Medealists (1896-present)*. Retrieved from https://www.jewishvirtuallibrary.org/jewish-olympic-medalists-1896-present
JINFO. (2020). *Jewish Nobel Prize winners*. Retrieved from http://www.jinfo.org/Nobel_Prizes.html
Kabir, O. (2017, October 30). Calcalist's digital and mobile Summit – The sports technology team. *Calcalist*. Retrieved from https://www.calcalist.co.il/conference/articles/0,7340,L-3723461,00.html
Kaufman, H., & Galily, Y. (2009). Sport, Zionist ideology and the State of Israel. *Sport in Society, 12*, 1013–1027. https://www.jpost.com/israel-news/sports/israeli-participation-in-uae-world-tour-affects-more-than-the-race-track-619081
Kelly, S. (2021). Sports tech diplomacy: The new Olympics. *Dr. Sarah Kelly*. Retrieved from https://www.drsarahkelly.com.au/sports-tech-diplomacy-the-new-olympics/
Keyser, Z. (2020, March 1). Israeli participation in UAE World Your affects more than the race track. *The Jerusalem Post*. Retrieved from https://www.jpost.com/israel-news/sports/israeli-participation-in-uae-world-tour-affects-more-than-the-race-track-619081

Levin, Y. (2018, June 21). Tokabot founders interview in sport5 channel. *YouTube*. Retrieved from https://www.youtube.com/watch?v=qWm5kKNsTlE

LikeAGlove. (2020). *LikeAGlove*. https://likeaglove.com/

LiveU. (2020). *Innovation in Broadcast Technology*. Retrieved from https://www.liveu.tv/

Maccabi. (2020a). The Club. *The Official site of Maccabi FOX Tel Aviv*. Retrieved from http://www.maccabi.co.il/data.asp?id=153&lang=en

Maccabi. (2020b). Introducing Maccabi gaming team. *The Official site of Maccabi FOX Tel Aviv* Retrieved from http://www.maccabi.co.il/news.asp?id=7644&lang=en

Maccabi. (2020c, August 12). *Our new name: Maccabi Playtika Tel Aviv*. Retrieved from http://maccabi.co.il/news.asp?id=7704&lang=en

Maccabi World Union. (n.d.). Esport World Championship. *Maccabi World Union*. Retrieved from https://www.maccabi.org/sport/esport-world-championship

Maccabiah. (n.d.). Sport-Tech Exhibition. *Maccabi World Union*. Retrieved from https://www.maccabiah.com/en/maccabiah-events/sport-tech-exhibition

Manor, I. (2019). *The digitalization of public diplomacy*. Palgrave Macmillan.

Mashiah, I., & Avraham, E. (2019). The role of technology and innovation messaging in the public diplomacy of Israel. *Journal of Global Politics and Current Diplomacy, 7*(2), 5–28.

Ministry of Economy and Industry State of Israel. (2020). *Invest in Israel*. Retrieved from https://investinisrael.gov.il/Pages/default.aspx

Montague, J. (2017, February 15). An Israeli desert city blooms as soccer power. *The New York Times*. Retrieved from https://www.nytimes.com/2017/02/15/sports/soccer/hapoel-beer-sheva-europa-league-besiktas.html

Murray, S. (2012). The two halves of sports-diplomacy. *Diplomacy & Statecraft, 23*, 576–592.

Murray, S. (2018). *Sports diplomacy: Origins, theory and practice*. Routledge.

Nachlieli, N., & Siminian, O. (2019, August 28). Gone with the click: Israeli sports does not adopt technologies. *Calcalist*. Retrieved from https://www.calcalist.co.il/sport/articles/0,7340,L-3769179,00.html. [Hebrew].

National Olympic Committee of Israel. (2018, December 26). The Technion and the National Olympic Committee in Israel are building a centre to improve the Olympic sports in Israel. *Olympis.il*. Retrieved from https://www.olympicsil.co.il/ימיקמ-לארשיב-יפמילוא-דעווהו-ןוינכטה/הירוגטק-אלל/. [Hebrew].

Nevo, M. (2012, August 15). An Israeli crew is nominated to an award for broadcasting from London. Sport 5. https://www.sport5.co.il/articles.aspx?FolderID=3683&docID=127667. [Hebrew].

Ordeix-Rigo, E., & Durate, J. (2009). From public diplomacy to corporate diplomacy: Increasing corporations' legitimacy and influence. *American Behavioral Scientist, 53*(4), 549–564. https://doi.org/10.1177/0002764209347630

Oron, N. (2018, September 2). This time I don't want to sell. *Forbes Israel*. Retrieved from https://forbes.co.il/e/this-time-i-dont-want-to-sell/

Pavitt, M. (2021, November 15). Eilat poised to hold IESF World Championship Finals. *Inside the Games*. Retrieved from https://www.insidethegames.biz/articles/1115485/eilat-iesf-world-championship-finals

Pedersen, P. M., Ruihley, B. J., & Li, B. (2021). *Sport and the pandemic*. Routledge.

Peres Center for Peace & Innovation. (2020). *Sports*. Retrieved from https://www.peres-center.org/en/the-organization/projects/sports/

Physimax. (2020). *AI-powered musculoskeletal self-assessment & optimization platform*. Retrieved from https://pmax.co/

Pic2Go. (2020). *How it works*. Retrieved from http://www1.pic2go.com/how-it-works

Pico. (2020). *We are Pico*. Retrieved from https://www.picogp.com/we-are-pico

Pigman, G. A. (2014). International sport and diplomacy's public dimension: Governments, sporting federations and the global audience. *Diplomacy & Statecraft, 25*, 94–114.

Pixellot. (2020a). *Leading the automatic production revolution*. Retrieved from https://www.pixellot.tv/

Pixellot. (2020b). *Pixellot video technology is already tested and used by sporting directors, analysts and coaches in all Barcelona venues*. Retrieved from https://www.pixellot.tv/press-releases/pixellot-signs-partnership-with-fc-barcelona-to-bring-together-ai-automated-coaching-solutions-to-football-clubs-and-academies-worldwide/

Pixellot Ltd. (2020, May 11). Covid-19. *YouTube*. Retrieved from https://www.youtube.com/watch?v=TvIdBLsTXXE

Playsight. (2020a). *Smart sports AI technologies fi any level and every sports*. Retrieved from https://www.playsight.com/

Playsight. (2020b). *SmartCourt Locator*. Retrieved from https://my.playsight.com/courts#/smartcourt-carousel

Ratten, V. (2020). Sport technology: A commentary. *Journal of High Technology Management Research, 31*(1). https://doi.org/10.1016/j.hitech.2020.100383

Ravet, H. (2018, June 5). Basketball player Omri Casspi invest in gut microbiome analysis startup DayTwo. *CTech*. Retrieved from https://www.calcalistech.com/ctech/articles/0,7340,L-3739552,00.html

Ravet, H. (2019, April 3). Former Reebok President joins Hype, an Israeli investment fund in sports technologies. *Calcalist*. Retrieved from https://www.calcalist.co.il/internet/articles/0,7340,L-3759734,00.html. [Hebrew].

Refael, S. (2019, November 4). Warriors without borders: What made the Warriors an historic team, before the fall. *Walla!*. Retrieved from https://sports.walla.co.il/item/3321539. [Hebrew].

Roper, S., & Grimes, S. (2005). Wireless Valley, silicon Wadi and digital Island – Helsinki, Tel Aviv and Dublin and the ICT global production network. *Geoforum*, *36*(3), 297–313. https://doi.org/10.1016/j.geoforum. 2004.07.003

Roy, R. (2020, April 19). India becomes Asia's No. 1 SportsTech nation. *TechnoSports*. Retrieved from https://technosports.co.in/2020/04/19/india-becomes-asias-no-1-sportstech-nation/

Schwartz, M., & Masters, J. (2019, December 5). Beitar Jerusalem: Soccer club owner ready to sue 'racist' fans. *CNN*. Retrieved from https://edition.cnn.com/2019/07/24/football/beitar-jerusalem-ali-mohamed-racism-soccer-spt-intl/index.html

Seatserve. (2020). *Seatserve*. https://seatserve.com/

Senor, D., & Singer, S. (2009). *Start-up nation: The story of Israel's economic miracle*. Twelve.

Shoham, A., Davidow, M., Klein, J. G., & Ruvio, A. (2006). Animosity on the home front: The Intifada in Israel and its impact on consumer behavior. *Journal of International Marketing*, *14*(3), 92–114.

Siminian, T., & Macdowell, D. (2020, April 7). 12 Israeli sport-tech solutions that will help keep fit even during the corona days. *Forbes*. Retrieved from https://forbes.co.il/12-תונורתפ-טרופס-קט-ישיארלאיי-ומשל-ורזעיש-/. [Hebrew].

Sleeprate. (2020). *Sleeprate*. https://www.sleeprate.com/

Smyth, D. (2022, December 5). Why are Ethiopian endurance rubbers so successful? *Runner's World*. Retrieved from https://www.runnersworld.com/uk/training/motivation/a42108849/ethiopian-running-success/

Sports Events 365. (2020). *Find it. Book it. Watch it.* https://www.sportsevents365.com/

SportsTechX. (2022). Global Sports Tech VC Report 2022. *SportsTechX*. Retrieved from https://sportstechx.com/gstvcr/

Sprio, J. (2020, August 26). Team Israel Start-Up Nation partners with Sonovia to develop innovative SonoMasks for Tour de France. *CTech*. Retrieved from https://www.calcalistech.com/ctech/articles/0,7340,L-3846584,00.html

Start-Up Nation Central. (2020). *Start-Up Nation Finder*. Retrieved from https://finder.startupnationcentral.org/

Start-Up Nation Finder. (2020). Moshe Hogeg. *Start-Up Nation Central*. Retrieved from https://finder.startupnationcentral.org/angel_page/moshe-hogeg

Statista. (2020). Distribution of sports technology companies in Europe in 2018, by country. *Statista*. Retrieved from https://www.statista.com/statistics/948501/sports-technology-startup-companies-distribution-europe-by-country/

Statista Research Department. (2016, August 22). All-time Summer Olympics medal table by country 1896–2016. *Statista*. Retrieved from https://www.statista.com/statistics/262864/all-time-summer-olympics-medals-table/

Swimming World editorial team. (2019, October 18). Gal Nevo introduces SenSwim: Swim data collecting tool for the future. *Swimming World*. Retrieved from https://www.swimmingworldmagazine.com/news/gal-nevo-introduces-senswim-swim-data-collecting-tool-of-the-future/

Tel Aviv Yafo. (2020a). *Tel Aviv Nonstop City – The brand story*. Retrieved from https://www.tel-aviv.gov.il/en/abouttheCity/Pages/TelAvivBrand.aspx

Tel Aviv Yafo. (2020b). *Tel Aviv Startup City*. Retrieved from https://www.tel-aviv.gov.il/en/WorkAndStudy/Pages/StartupCity.aspx

Tel Aviv Yafo. (2020c). *Supporting local startups*. Retrieved from https://www.tel-aviv.gov.il/en/WorkAndStudy/Pages/Supporting-Local-Startups.aspx

TGSPOT. (2019, December 13). Israel will host the world championship in electronic sports for the first time. *TGSPOT*. Retrieved from https://www.tgspot.co.il/first-esport-tournament-in-israel/

Thani, S., & Heenan, T. (2017). The ball may be round but football is becoming increasingly Arabic: Oil money and the rise of the new football order. *Soccer & Society, 18*, 1012–1026. https://doi.org/10.1080/14660970.2015.1133416

Tokabot. (2020). *The number 1 contextual engagement platform for live events*. Retrieved from https://tokabot.com/

Tracxn. (2022, November 23). *Sports tech startups in South Africa*. Retrieved from https://tracxn.com/explore/Sports-Tech-Startups-in-South-Africa

Tsipori, T. (2016, March 9). Intel buys Israeli co Replay Technologies for $175m. *Globes*. Retrieved from https://en.globes.co.il/en/article-intel-acquires-israeli-co-replay-technologies-for-175m-1001108929

Walla! Sports staff. (2019, December 11). The cycling team "Israel Start-Up Nation" was presented: "An exciting chapter in history". *Walla!*. Retrieved from https://sports.walla.co.il/item/3328520. [Hebrew].

White, C. J. (2015). Exploring the role of private-sector corporations in public diplomacy. *Public Relations Inquiry, 4*, 305–321.

Wingate Institute. (2020, February 26). A Win Tech course for sports innovation was launched. *Wingate*. Retrieved from https://www.wingate.org.il/Index.asp?ArticleID=7006&CategoryID=100. [Hebrew].

Ynet. (2004, November 10). American basketballers train with an Israeli software. *Ynet Sport*. Retrieved from https://www.ynet.co.il/articles/0,7340,L-3000074,00.html. [Hebrew].

CHAPTER 10

Sports, Country Image, and the Global Order in an Ever-Changing World

Introduction

In 2015 the United Nations established the Sustainable Development Goals (SDGs), as "a shared blueprint for peace and prosperity for people and the planet, now and into the future" (United Nations, n.d.). The goals pertain to 17 areas and topics: 1. no poverty; 2. zero hunger; 3. good health and well-being; 4. quality education; 5. gender equality; 6. clean water and sanitation; 7. affordable and clean energy; 8. decent work and economic growth; 9. industry, innovation, and infrastructure; 10. reduced inequalities; 11. sustainable cities and communities; 12. responsible consumption and production; 13. climate action; 14. life below water; 15. life on land; 16. peace, justice, and string institutions; and 17. partnerships for the goals. Simon Anholt, author of several books on place branding and who leads The Good Country Index that measures the contribution of each country to the world, and Professor Nicholas Cull, one of the leading voices in public diplomacy from the University of Southern California Anneberg School of Communications, have been recording a podcast during 2021 and 2022 named "People, Places, Power" as part of a collaboration with USC Center for Public Diplomacy (CPD, n.d.). One of the repeating themes through the dozens of recorded podcasts, which also reflects in Anholt's Good Country Index (Anholt, 2020; The Good Country Index, n.d.), and Cull's publications on public diplomacy, is that

© The Author(s), under exclusive license to Springer Nature Switzerland AG 2023
Y. Dubinsky, *Nation Branding and Sports Diplomacy*,
https://doi.org/10.1007/978-3-031-32550-2_10

the image of the country eventually reflects good policies (Cull, 2008, 2010). So, if countries want to have a good reputation, they need to have positive contribution. The Good Country Index (2022) ranks countries based on their contribution to the world on science and technology, culture, international peace and security, planet and climate, prosperity and equality, and health and wellness. The top five ranked countries in the 1.5 version of the index that was mostly based on data from 2020 (The Good Country Index, 2022) are: Sweden, Denmark, Germany, Netherlands, and Finland, with Canada (6) being the only non-European country in the top 10, and Australia (18) and New Zealand (19) the only other non-European ones in the top 20. Part of the message that New Zealand prime minister Jacinda Ardern tried to send in her speech prior to the drawing of the Australia & New Zealand 2023 FIFA Women's World Cup was that New Zealand did not just want to use the event to show it is a progressive country and one of the best countries in the world, but also as one of the best countries *for* the world (nzherald.co.nz, 2022).

The years 2020, 2021, and 2022 required every country to adapt to a new reality. As the pandemic became and endemic, the world found ways to live along the virus and resume some of the stopped, canceled, and postponed activities—including sports. Yet, that does not mean that normalcy will look exactly like 2019 or that countries should aspire to go back to 2019, rather than move forward. As mentioned through the book, 2020, 2021, and 2022, did not just result in health crises, but also in financial, social, and political turmoil and exposed already existing vulnerabilities including their manifestations through sports. Civic resistance rising against governments and sports governing bodies over corruption, abuse, gentrification, racism and discrimination, public spending, greenwashing, and even protesting the need for mega sports events, all challenge the ways countries can and will use sports for nation branding and public diplomacy. Beyond that, the hegemony of the global north is being challenged through developing economies such as China and Russia and through the global south as seen through mega events held in Beijing and Qatar. In 2021, the IOC updated Agenda 2020 to Agenda 2020+5 (International Olympic Committee, 2021), making 15 recommendations on five fields that will shape the future of the Olympic Movement: solidarity, digitalization, sustainable development, credibility, and economic and financial resilience. This chapter argues that the following five areas will shape how countries will use sports for nation branding and public diplomacy: a. sustainability and the environment, b. social justice, c. economic vulnerabilities, d. geopolitics, and e. technology and innovation.

Sustainability and the Environment

One of the biggest global challenges the world is facing is climate change. Extreme heat waves, uncontrolled wildfires, hurricanes, typhoons, tornados, tsunamis, and floods became more frequent and cause death and destruction worldwide (NCEI, 2022; WMO, 2022). This challenge is global, impacting life on the planet. Western Europe and the USA are no more immune from deadly fires than remote rainforests in the Amazon or the Australian outback, and in the years 2020 to 2022, climate change became a disruptor in the sports events calendar (Orr et al., 2022). Despite scientists and ecologists warning about unsustainable industrialism and pollution causing greenhouse effect that leads to extreme weather, increasing temperatures, rising sea levels, melting icebergs (WMO, 2022), the fight against climate change and for protecting the planet became a political one. This polarization was manifested in the USA as Donald Trump withdrew from The Paris Agreement on climate change when he was elected (Dubinsky, 2021a), and Joe Biden rejoined it after his inauguration. Such inconsistent policies, by the world number one powerhouse, add to the instability of the global system. According to The Good Country Index (2022), the leading countries in the world in the fight against climate change and to preserve the planet are northern and Western European countries, other members of the European Union, Canada, Australia, and small countries such as Malta, who find a place branding niche to contribute to global efforts despite their small size. The fight against climate change and for a more sustainable planet embody many diplomatic opportunities, including regional, international, and global collaborations. Yet it also results in divisions and uncertainty especially as two of the world's largest economies, the USA and China, are part of the problem, ranked 81 and 50, respectively (The Good Country Index, 2022). The political turmoil associated with climate change also challenges hegemonic use of the topic for public diplomacy. Climate-change diplomacy in the USA also manifests through a rise in city-diplomacy, with cities disassociating from the reluctance of Trump's White House and try to brand themselves as green and sustainable (Dinnie & Sevin, 2020). The fight against climate change and reduction of carbon emission, means forcing changes to create a more sustainable lifestyle, putting limitations on industrial fishing, urban planning with improved public transportation, making cities and places more accessible, etc. Thus, the fight against climate change is not unrelated to other global challenges such as poverty, inequalities, or even racism and with cities developing their own place branding agendas, countries do not necessarily act as unified actors when facing such a challenge.

The nation branding attempts by governments of emerging global economies come at the expense of much needed public support for education and health care, which only widens social gaps, and the greenwashing policies leave permanent damage on the environment. Climate change has of course immense implications on sports, with unexpected weather conditions forcing sports organizations to be able to adapt and plan for unpredictable conditions. For example, league matches cancelled and postponed due to hurricanes and unhealthy air following wildfires, changing schedules in the Olympic Games because of a potential typhoon or moving the marathon to a different city because of the heat, or using artificial snow in the Winter Olympic Games, poor air quality during the Australian Open following the bushfires, heatwaves in Europe during the Tour de France, etc. (Dubinsky, 2022b; Orr et al., 2022). The Winter Olympic Games are weather challenges with less countries, regions, and cities, having appropriate climate to host the competitions (Orr et al., 2022).

Unsustainable hosting of mega sports events is part of the problem. There is no shortage of examples for how unnecessary public spending for place branding and country image goals led to catastrophic outcomes. The people of Quebec finished paying the debt of the 1976 Montreal Olympic Games only in 2006, and the Olympic Stadiums, first known as "The Big O" due to its shape, became known as "The Big Owe." Despite the Olympic Movement entering what Dubinsky (2022b) refers to as "The Legacy-Oriented Era," the first decades of the twenty-first century led to skyrocketing costs, abandoned stadiums and facilities, and greenwashing becoming a practice organizing committees, governments, and international institutions use when damaging the environment while claiming to have sustainable policies by taking minor or unsignificant measures. Brazil (2014 FIFA World Cup, Rio de Janeiro 2016 Olympic Games), India (Delhi 2010 Commonwealth Games), China (Beijing 2008 Olympic Games), Russia (Sochi 2014 Winter Olympic Games, 2018 FIFA World Cup), and South Africa (FIFA World Cup 2010), the five major emerging economies known as the BRICS countries, all hosted mega-sports events in the first two decades of twenty-first century leading to environmental damage and international criticism.

The years 2020, 2021, and 2022 do not show a better trajectory, as while international sports organizations claim to take sustainable measures, the postponed UEFA Euro 2020 required delegations and fans to fly thousands of miles between stadiums, Tokyo 2020 was held against the will of Japanese people who did not have access to the Games they financed, Beijing was divided with fences for the 2022 Winter Olympic Games, and the Qatar 2022 FIFA World Cup costs hundreds of billions of dollars and was held in stadiums that cost the lives of unknown amount of immigrant workers who built them. The aftermath of the Tokyo 2020 might have not led to a spread of a new variation of COVID-19, but did result in chaos, including indictments over corruption, protests on future events, and extreme violence with the assassination of former Japanese prime minister Shinzo Abe, who was one of the strongest advocates for the Games and their postponement. Looking forwards, 2022 ended with the next most prestigious mega sports events awarded to Western democracies in developed countries with Paris hosting the Olympic Games in 2024, Los Angeles in 2028, Brisbane in 2032, Milano-Cortina the Winter Olympic Games in 2026, and the USA hosting the 2026 FIFA World Cup along with Canada and Mexico, and Australia and New Zealand hosting the 2023 FIFA Women's World Cup. All these bids and organizations emphasize green policies and the significance of positive sustainable legacy using existing facilities and being diverse and community oriented.

It would be simplistic and superficial to associate greenwashing only with developing or authoritarian countries. The fossil fuel industry sponsors over a dozen leagues in Australia (Sherry et al., 2022), the 2026 FIFA World Cup will require fans to fly regularly between stadiums and cross three different countries and time zones, and despite the International Olympic Committee (IOC) amending its bidding regulations, local communities continue to protest against hosting the Olympic Games leading to both Vancouver and Barcelona withdrawing from the bid for the 2030 Winter Olympic Games. As mentioned, climate change affects other social issues such as environmental justice and social justice, including through sports. For example, the rise in sea level impacts urbanization, community displacement, and gentrification (Sivels, 2023), which means that areas prone to extreme weather need weather-resilient stadiums that not only enable hosting sports events but can also serve as emergency shelters. Postlethwaite, Jenkin, and Sherry (2022) conducted a comprehensive integrative review of over 200 research articles connected to sports diplomacy. They (Postlethwaite et al., 2022) conclude that sports diplomacy is multidisciplinary, that most research has been historical, and future research is needed on the sport industry contribution to the UN Sustainable Development Goals. Tourism is a source for greenhouse gas emission and a key contributor to climate change (Kennelly, 2023), and countries use sports as a nation branding tool for tourism destination image (TDI) purposes. The rise of community resistance against greenwashing in mega-events and the concerns raised by younger generations about the future of the planet, have nation branding implications in the ways countries will use sports as part of their climate-change diplomacy as they seek to project a positive international image.

Social Justice

The fifth wave of black athletes' activism was sparked by social protests in the USA in the summer of 2020 (Williams, 2022). The fourth wave of black athletes' activism was influenced by Black Lives Matter (BLM) and characterized by influential athletes such as LeBron James and Colin Kaepernick using their social and economic power to protest against police brutality and racial injustice who galvanized other American athletes and sports organizations to take a stand, or a knee. The fifth wave took protests for social justice a few steps further, galvanizing athletes from different sports, and linking between racial injustice in America to other social struggles in the USA and worldwide. The protests against systematic racism also manifested with professional and college athletes demanding the removal of confederation symbols, leading to NASCAR banning the use of the confederation flag in races or even Mississippi replacing the confederate flag with a magnolia flower in its state flag. While Black Lives Matter led to protest against racial injustice worldwide, including kneeling before European soccer games, the Americans were the ones behind in terms of reconciling with the crimes of settler colonialism against indigenous and aboriginal communities. Other former British colonies were oriented towards the cultural heritage of aboriginal communities when planning the 2023 FIFA Women's World Cup in Australia and New Zealand or a Canadian bid for Vancouver 2030 Winter Olympic Games (which eventually collapsed due to lack of public financial support). Both Australia and New Zealand emphasize the aboriginal name of the lands on which competitions will take place and both had trailblazing female leaders as the faces of the competition. New Zealand prime minister Jacinda Ardern repeatedly mentioned the significance of first nations and indigenous culture in the country, and the iconic flipping goal celebration of Australian football star Sam Kerr, a mixed-raced LGBTQ athlete, who idolized Cathy Freeman (Kerr & Harris, 2021), the torch lighter of the Sydney 2000

Olympic Games who celebrated her gold medal with both the Australian and Aboriginal Flags, was projected on the Sydney Opera House, one of Australia's most iconic tourism destination venues.

In the USA it took a wave of social justice to push sponsors to pressure sports teams to correct long-overdue racial practices. As the fifth wave of athletes activism forced the USA to revisit its racial history, it also had implications on other social causes including the traumas of Native Americans due to settler colonialism, leading to statues of settlers who colonized native lands removed from college campuses and American sports teams such as the Washington Redskins and the Cleveland Indians to change their names to the Commanders and Guardians, respectively. Yet, despite some changes made, settler colonialism of indigenous First Nations continues to exist through building stadiums on native land, and dehumanize indigenous communities in racist cartoonish ways through mascots and symbols in professional teams such as Blackhawks, Chiefs, and Braves (Ali-Joseph et al., 2023). Thus, at least in North America, and especially in the USA, the success of social struggles to lead to change are very much tied to marketing implications.

From a public diplomacy perspective, the rise of athletes activism came from people-to-people diplomacy, with citizens leading the charge, rather than traditional public diplomacy. In fact, the civic resistance came as protest to populist leadership in America by Donald Trump's White House, and spread globally according to local situations in other countries. Athletes supporting BLM in America influenced football players such as Marcus Rashford and Raheem Sterling to lead social protests against racism in the UK, which also evolved into one of the best British Olympians in history Mo Farah, to speak about being trafficked from Somalia as a child, raising awareness to further systemic racism, human trafficking, and exploitation of Africa. There is nothing new about the connection between human trafficking, sports, and entertainment, going back to the use of slaves fighting for their lives as gladiators in the Ancient Roman Colosseum, or children from Bangladesh, Pakistan, and Sudan as child jockeys in deadly camel races in the Arabian Gulf up to even the first years of the twenty-first century, which is of course not unrelated to the casual exploitation of migrant workers from Africa and South Asia who built the stadiums Qatar used in the 2022 FIFA World Cup. American athletes supporting BLM and protesting a history of systemic racism going back to segmentation and slavery inspire international athletes to shed light on human trafficking and other forms of modern slavery.

The strive for better social justice transcends race. For example, if looking at gender and American soccer icon Megan Rapinoe who received the Medal of Freedom from President Joe Biden in 2022, she received an official apology from US Soccer during the summer of 2020 after told not to kneel when being one of the first white athletes to support Colin Kaepernick in 2016. Rapinoe was in the front of the US Women's National Team (USWNT) fight for equal pay , legal dispute, and negotiations with US Soccer that led not just to a compromise and improvement of the USWNT conditions but to unprecedented equal revenue distribution of FIFA's prize money. That struggle came in an international environment where other soccer federations such as Norway and Netherlands were already distributing equal money between the men's and women's national teams, and helped growing the voices of female soccer players not just for better payments but for better working environment and against toxic masculinity by coaches and administrators. The #MeToo Movement, which led to gymnasts to speak out against the systematic abuse in American gymnastics, continues to lead to more female athletes speaking out against their oppressors in other sports and other countries. These fights for gender equality do not stay or end on the athletic field, as seen with athletes across the globe supporting the brave protests of Iranian women taking off their hijabs as protests against Iran's modesty police and moreover against the control of the authoritarian Iranian regimes on women's bodies and minds.

There is of course backlash to athletes activism, not just from conservative ends of the political spheres or from populist leadership calling to ban the use of critical race theory from the education system, but from athletes themselves. As mentioned, the strife for social justice crosses borders, genders, and nationalities. And with that also comes the expectation to support further social and political causes. BLM, for example, associated itself also with the Palestinian struggle, a cause that was supported by leading international Muslim soccer players such as Senegalese Sadio Mane, Egyptian Mohamed Salah, and Frenchman Paul Pogba. While the waves of activism led the IOC to relax Rule 50 and enable contained forms of protest prior to the beginning of competitions in Tokyo 2020, the majority of the athletes who were asked about potential changes did not want to allow complete freedom of on-field protests during the Olympic Games fearing an escalation in further politization of the Olympic Movement. Yet, the IOC and other sports federations did take measures against Russia, which again brought criticism about sports organizations prioritizing some political causes over others. The interconnectivity between social causes also led athletes to criticize each other for picking causes according to their marketing agendas rather than social justice, as demonstrated from Turkish-American NBA player Enes Kanter Freedom who called out the hypocrisy of American athletes and sponsors taking a stand on racial injustice in the USA but keeping silent amid human rights violations in China not to jeopardize their market growth. The Qatar 2022 FIFA World Cup was especially dividing regarding social justice, blocking attempts to show support for the LGBTQ community, yet allowing and even enhancing support of Palestine. When facing international scrutiny about human rights violations, the Qataris blamed Western media with hypocrisy, orientalism, and even Islamophobia, emphasizing cultural differences between the Global North and the Global South, giving different interpretations to social justice.

From a product-country-image (PCI) perspective, two of the most known sports brands associated with their country-of-origin are Nike with the USA (Martin, 2007) and Adidas with Germany (Akdeniz Ar & Kara, 2012). While both companies capitalized on the waves of activism, supporting social causes with Nike endorsing Colin Kaepernick and Adidas issuing a Pride Collection (Adidas, n.d.), both are also highly scrutinized for hypocritical policies when corporate marketing goals conflict with social justice. Nike, which endorsed the lack of activism in the 1990s and switched its social stands over the years according to commercial interest and played a role in forcing the change of the Redskins name, was more hesitant to take social stands in the Chinese markets they wanted to capitalize on. German footwear giants Adidas dropped the support of rapper Kanye West following his antisemitic remarks despite his profitable clothing line, yet continued to capitalize on its affiliation with the national football team of Germany and sponsor the Qatar 2022 FIFA World Cup despite the deadly outcomes of the tournament and the host's discriminative policies against the LGBTQ community. No country or federation wants to find itself as framed of being in the wrong side of history, yet the global nature of athletes-activism, along with the interconnectivity between communities and issues, also mean that through traditional public diplomacy, people-to-people diplomacy, and corporate-diplomacy, the strive for social justice is inconsistent, both galvanizing and polarizing, ever-evolving, and full of internal contradictions. Whatever the evolution of athletes' activism will look like, social justice will not remain within the context of one community or place, and every stakeholder in the nation branding process will be impacted and pushed to pick a side or form a country image strategy.

Economic Vulnerabilities

The economic turmoil caused in the years 2020, 2021, and 2022 both exposed the vulnerabilities and problems of the existing sports ecosystem and displayed its significance as countries compromised on their normative dimensions (Dubinsky, 2022a, b) to find ways to keep this $2.3 trillion industry (Best & Howard, 2022) going. The European Super League (ESL) fiasco in the spring of 2021 displayed the unsustainable state of the current structure of European football. Foreign ownerships, geopolitical pressures, and unsustainable policies, led 12 top clubs to withdraw from the prestigious UEFA Champions League and create their own tournament, before most of them withdrew due to public pressure and resistance from their local communities. Yet, despite the failed attempt, the economic problems remain. Gaps between clubs within leagues are widening, and the FIFA Fair Play attempt to regulate transfers and budgets has not proven to create a more sustainable system. With wealthy foreign ownerships, at times associated with their governments, transfer fees are skyrocketing. And as not all countries generate the same economic revenues, a cross-continental salary cap as used in the American leagues, is not applicable. UEFA keeps revising its competition system to try and adjust to the contradicting pressures of small countries and markets seeking involvement in prestigious competitions, along with clubs that became international franchises pressuring to capitalize on a global market. Global ambitions of foreign ownerships from the Arabian Gulf, East Asia, and North America along with the unsustainable system, push the top clubs and leagues to find new sources of revenues, such as outsourcing super-cup games to other countries, or exploring new formats of a Super League type of competition. Foreign investments do not only challenge the structure of football, as seen with the LIV Golf tour, which is supported by Saudi Arabia's Public Investment Fund, and challenges the Professional Golf Tours (PGA) as the hegemonic governing body of the sport.

As mentioned, all these issues that will shape the future are intertwined, especially through financial power struggles and the economy. The fight for social justice in America also challenges the political economy of the

American collegiate system. In 2021 already a significant change was made, with the National Collegiate Athletics Associations (NCAA) and athletic conferences and universities allowing student-athletes who are still considered amateurs to receive compensation based on their name, image, and likeness. This change did not happen due to the goodwill of the organizing institutions, but after long pressure on politicians to change state legislations that will bend the NCAA's hand. This already challenges the existing system and power dynamics between schools, athletes, and sponsors. Yet, student athletes are still not paid for their labor, and with African American athletes overrepresented in the billion-dollar industries of collegiate American football and men's basketball, there are also growing demands and legal appeals to abolish amateurism regulations or at least find a revenue-distributing channel so athletes could benefit a portion from the money they generate per sport. Should student-athletes be allowed to unionize and reach revenue-sharing agreements similar to the NBA and the NFL based on their sports, men's football players will earn over $200,000 and men's basketball players over $300,000 per year (Beer, 2020; Witty, 2021). This is one of the most contested issues in the sociopolitical economy in American sports, as not paying student-athletes in revenue-generating sports exploits the labor of African Americans, but paying them their market value widens the gender disparities even within the education system. As seen with the fights for social justice, power struggles in the USA have global implications that impact public diplomacy and nation branding as well. The NIL regulations, and any future changes to the amateur status of student-athletes will have trickle-down effects on non-revenue-generating sports, on women's sports and Title IX, on international student-athletes who are not allowed to earn money due to visa regulations and the diplomatic roles of the American collegiate system, on coaches' salaries, on athletes development towards the Olympic Games, and overall on the normative image of Brand America.

The protest against gigantism and public spending associated with mega-events will lead to new forms of hosting, including through joint collaborations between regions, countries, and maybe even continents, which inevitably have diplomatic implications. The 2023 Women's World Cup hosted in Australia and New Zealand; the 2026 FIFA World Cup in the USA, Mexico, and Canada; and the surfing competitions of the Paris 2024 Olympic Games planned to be held in Tahiti are a few immediate manifestations of such approaches. Despite the IOC's attempted reforms in Agenda 2020 and Agenda 2020+5, pressure groups such as NOlympics and growing public resistance challenge the bidding process as cities are reluctant to bid or withdraw from bids due to lack of domestic support. So mega-events are changing to accommodate financial pressures, but they are still growing with FIFA approving expanding the 2023 Women's World Cup to 32 participants and the 2026 World Cup to 48. Such expansions have financial logistic effects on host cities, but also diplomatic implications on participating federations as more countries are represented in global events watched by over a billion viewers. The developing women's game is a contested field for nation branding and public diplomacy power struggles. The advantage of countries who invest in women's football—many of them liberal democracies—along with growing popularity and exposure of the game globally, create a situation of uncompetitive matches and sheds lights on disparities and inequalities that reflect on national priorities of developing countries including criticizing their normative and functional dimensions of their images. Thus, from nation branding and public diplomacy perspectives, the growing popularity of sports as reflected through the growth of exposure and media rights revenues incentivizes countries to be part of the process, despite the economic challenges that can lead to domestic or international criticism.

Geopolitics

Definitions of public diplomacy vary between geopolitical and international relations scholars, with some focusing on communication with foreign public as part of foreign policy, and others also look at more actors such as citizens in people-to-people diplomacy, companies in corporate-diplomacy, or different forms of cultural diplomacy such as gastro-diplomacy or even sports diplomacy (Dubinsky, 2019a). Thus, the definition itself of sports diplomacy is also contested, whether it is directly related to governmental attempts to use sports for soft power purposes or about the interactions between actors with diplomatic potential such as leagues, clubs, associations, international governance structures, sponsors, investment firms, and governments (Rofe, 2016). Even under the umbrella of sports the word diplomacy is used to describe relations such as ping-pong diplomacy, stadium diplomacy, sport-tech diplomacy, etc. (Dubinsky, 2021b, 2022c; Rofe, 2016). Such terminological variations and nuances indicate that there is not one accepted coherent definition of sports diplomacy, or on the significance counties see in sports for foreign policy and country image. China, Qatar, and Saudi Arabia all have strategic 2030 plans on how the countries will look in the future, and they all include sports as part of their vision. Part of the manifestation of nation branding is through jersey-diplomacy, through advertisements of countries such as Curacao or Rwanda on the sleeves of Ajax Amsterdam and FC Arsenal (Visit Rwanda, n.d.), airlines officially sponsoring top sports teams through the name of the country (Chadwick, 2022), Saudi-owned team Newcastle United issuing a third jersey in the colors of the Arab country, Mexico issuing official kits for the 2022 FIFA World Cup with imagery acknowledging Aztec and African culture, Algeria and Morocco disputing about jersey designs and cultural appropriation (News Agencies, 2022), or Denmark and its sponsor Hummel using a toned down jersey to protest the deaths of migrant workers in Qatar.

Power balances in the international system are shifting. Populist leaders such as Donald Trump, Boris Johnson, and Jair Bolsonaro, who incited chaos during the pandemic in the USA, the UK, the European Union, and in South America, have been replaced or resigned, yet the legitimacy of populist, nationalist, and even fascist politicians and parties continues to gain momentum in democratic countries, including Italy, France, and Israel. Fake news and conspiracy theories have been undermining public trust in institutions, and the history of corruption in sports organizations add to the sense of anarchy. Science deniers, now branded as free-thinkers, lead to new conspiracy theories and further waves of hate, as seen through basketball star Kyrie Irving sharing an antisemitic film, and support of Kanye West's antisemitic comments projected outside an American college football game in Florida, contributing to a toxic and chaotic climate in America that even escalated into political violence targeting Speaker of the House Congresswoman Nancy Pelosi 2 weeks prior Congress elections in America. While it is irresponsible to assume the decline of the USA as the world's most influential superpower, China and Russia have successfully challenged the west, exposing limitations and vulnerabilities of the democratic system and liberal ideologies. The term sportswashing embodies these shifting powers, as the attempts of autocratic countries to use sports as a soft power tool are criticized for not meeting Western standards. Yet, there is much criticism on that approach, including accusation of hypocrisy that the Global North has also used sports for non-liberal purposes (Boykoff, 2022), to establish itself as the hegemon, and is now reluctant to share power (Hussain & Cunningham, 2022).

The Western approach towards Qatar and the 2022 FIFA World Cup, focusing on corruption accusations, death of migrant workers, and anti-LGBTQ policies (Hussain & Cunningham, 2022), has been met with criticism over lack of understanding of orientalism and even Islamophobia. China, Russia, and the Arabian Gulf have proven themselves to be influential economic players in the global markets, and attract support despite human rights violations. They also expose double standards and internal contradictions within Western perception, forcing the Global North to ask itself if being liberal also means sharing power with non-liberal countries. As of the end of 2020, being gay is forbidden by law in 69 countries (BBC News, 2021). If Qatar is being delegitimized for having anti-LGBTQ regulations, should all these dozens of countries be subjected to the same standard, including sprinting power-house Jamaica, long-run powerhouse Kenya, the future host of the 2026 Youth Olympic Games Senegal, and dozens of others in Asia, the Americas, and Oceania?

The Middle East is going through changes as well. Beyond the growing influence of GCC countries in international sports, the Abraham Accords open diplomatic collaborations between Arab countries and Israel, which also manifest through athletic competitions between countries and athletes from Saudi Arabia competing against Israelis (Dubinsky, 2022b). Israel could see some diplomatic achievements with the official commemorations of the 11 Munich 1972 victims and there were even speculations about hosting an Olympic event in the country as part of a creative Berlin 2036 bid, but as long as a peace process with the Palestinians is stagnant, the framing of Israel in international sports continues to be in the context of an armed dispute.

The world of sports endures how authoritarian countries use sports, and in some cases international organizations even prefer to work with nondemocratic countries with less pressures to answer to (Boykoff, 2022). Yet, when systemic violations of regulations can no longer be compensated with financial benefit and when political aspirations turn into sheer violence, the world of sports is also forced to react. Banning Russia and Belarus from international sports competitions came only after the unprovoked military invasion to Ukraine. Vladimir Putin has violated the Olympic Truce multiple times before the winter of 2022, including during the Beijing 2008 Olympic Games when invading Georgia and when hosting the Sochi 2014 Paralympic Games invading the Crimea Peninsula in Ukraine. On both occasions the IOC and most major international sports organizations have not sanctioned Russia. The invasion of Ukraine came after a series of violations, including systemic doping and cover-up and even potential child abuse, that tested the patience and challenged the credibility of international sports institutions. Ronald Reagan's Star Wars-inspired framing of the Soviet Union as "the evil empire" during the Cold War has been replaced by Biden's warning of "a nuclear Armageddon." It is in the eyes of the beholder to interpret if the ban was an attempt by international sports institutions to add pressure on the Russians to end the violence and prevent an escalation towards another Cold War or even a World War, or it was a "lifetime achievement award" for the ongoing repeating violations. There are precedents of the IOC excluding Germany following World War I and II, but there are also different policies different sports organizations are taking towards allowing Russian athletes to compete. Either way, in 2022 a line in the sand has been drawn, leading to pressure groups demanding further bans and exclusions based on other countries' involvement in warfare. Examples include calls for banning Iran from the Qatar 2022 FIFA World Cup following the country's military ties with Russia, comparing between the glorification of the bravery of Ukrainian and the Palestinian struggles, or criticism about ignoring victims of armed conflict in the Global South.

Despite all the geopolitical challenges in sports, every country sees value in participation, so the power struggles are less likely to manifest through mass boycotts such as during the Cold War, but in attempts to be better positioned within the system. Yet the balance of power is shifting, especially new countries and regions trying to strip the Global North from a perception of entitlement on international sports and more broadly a front seat in the world order. Political scientist Amitav Acharya (2018) argues that the global order is changing, and although the military superiority of the USA is not contested, Western dominance is transitioning into a pluralistic multiplex world without a hegemonic construction. The role of militarism in American society is integrated though national competitions and especially in American football (Zirin, 2022). That has not changed during the pandemic (Dubinsky, 2022a), and was even amplified when hosting the Oregon22 World Athletics Championships, and the USA will continue to host major international sports event in the upcoming decade. However, according to Acharya (2018), China's economic growth can threaten the American dominance, and the world certainly does not come to the USA for leadership on global issues. China was the only country to have economic growth during the first year of the pandemic and separated itself from the rest of the BRICS countries. Despite Western criticism, hosting the Beijing 2022 Winter Olympic Games established the Chinese as Olympic royalty with its capital becoming the only city to host both summer and winter Olympics. Yet, the zero-COVID policy led China to postpone, cancel, or have future sports events moved to other countries, which limits President Xi Jinping's ambitious plan to become the world's largest sport economy by 2030. GCC countries entered that vacuum, and especially Qatar who used to the 2022 FIFA World Cup not just to display its own country but to position itself as the face of the global south, and try to capitalize on the championship's legacy with the 2023 AFC Asian Cup that was moved from China and the 2030 Asian Games. The framing of the Global South as sportswashers, or focusing on over 120 deaths in a stadium disaster in Indonesia (Reuters, 2022), or protests on genocide in Ethiopia during the Athletics World Championships, does not just negatively portray other countries, but reaffirms the functional, normative, cultural, and sympathetic dimensions of the country images of those in power.

Francis Fukuyama's (1992) post–Cold War argument in The End of History about Western liberalism prevailing and Samuel Huntington's (1996) global analysis as a clash of civilizations have been received with much criticism from orientalist scholars (Said, 1994, 2003). One of the most critical scholars was Edward Said, who used the terms orientalism (2003) and cultural imperialism (1994) to argue that the west established its privileges through unprecedented colonization and imperialism since the nineteenth century over the Global South and superficially classifies and misunderstands other countries and especially Muslim and Arab ones. From a geopolitical perspective, the Global South is fighting to challenge Western hegemony by any means available. The corruption in the world of sports is not new; did not start with Russia, Qatar, or China in the twenty-first century; and Germany, the USA, Australia, France, England, and Switzerland have a long and controversial history of shaping modern sports to play to their advantage (Boykoff, 2016, 2022). In this context, whataboutism became a useful tool for disrupters, whether from progressive liberal movements and by authoritarian regimes to highlight power imbalances and double standards. Yet, by justifying and excusing unethical conduct and policies and even terrorism or human rights violations, can have catastrophic geopolitical implications, perpetuating rising fascist forces, conspiracies, and ideologies in an age of disinformation.

Technology and Innovation

The ever-growing technological advancements continuously change the sports business ecosystem and have nation branding and public diplomacy implications. As communication with foreign publics is in the essence of public diplomacy (Cull, 2008), from Johannes Guttenberg's printing invention in the fifteenth century to social media in the twenty-first century, technological innovations reshaped social communications (Bjola et al., 2019), and, through that, public diplomacy. There are countless examples for how technological communication advancements changed geopolitics in the twenty-first century, from Qatar using Al Jazeera for soft power purposes to undermine regimes with state-owned media during the Arab Spring, the role of social media in framing every escalation in the Israeli-Arab dispute, Russia's use of social media platforms to spread disinformation and influence elections in America, Twitter banning the account of former American President Donald Trump, etc.

Media rights fuel the sports business ecosystem. Thus, every technological development, such as shifts to streaming services using a second mobile screen for social media, fantasy apps, or betting, embody further business opportunities and more options to connect between stakeholders. The pandemic forced countries, people, and organizations to adapt to new realities, including grounding people to consume content from home, or forcing organizations to find innovative solutions to meet safety guidelines such as social distancing or reduced capacities. The growing and diverse sport-tech ecosystem provided different solutions to meet demands, such as digital platforms for content consumption, artificial intelligence in broadcasting that required smaller production staff, health applications, esports and gaming options, and others.

As professional sports teams seek to maximize their performance and marketing potential, they become more science-oriented relying on analytics of big data for future decision-making processes. This means leagues and clubs need more statisticians who might have not been top athletes but have advanced degrees in data analysis, leading to a more diversified job market in terms of gender, ethnicities, and backgrounds. The health, financial, economic, political, and social crises all add to the already existing lack of trust of centralized governance. It is with the mindset of this geopolitical turmoil that blockchain technology, the metaverse as an alternative social sphere, and cryptocurrency as a new decentralized marketplace grew rapidly and globally fostering irregulated trades of non-fungible tokens (NFT). The world of sports quickly embraced the new digital platforms with athletes such as LeBron James endorsing Crypto, which also received the naming rights of the home arena of the Los Angeles Lakers and Los Angeles Clippers, and other cryptocurrency companies paying millions of dollars for creative ads during the Super Bowl, and leagues and organizations extending their products with NFTs. Thus, sports and technology have similarities as both are essentially global, ever-changing, not restricted to one country, and embody people-to-people, corporate, and traditional public diplomacy opportunities.

With Gen Z being digital natives, growing up with mobile phones and available internet, consumption patterns have shifted as well towards content that is immediately available and individually tailored. One of the main shifts in sports consumption in the past 10–15 years was the move towards over-the-top (OTP) consumption, including through streaming services such as Netflix, Hulu, Amazon Prime, etc. Their success led broadcasting networks to develop their own OTP platforms, top professional sports organizations either create ones of their own such as online subscription for NBA League Pass, NFL Red Zone; collaborate with existing ones such as the UEFA Champions League broadcasted in the USA through Paramount+; and add online available movies through the Olympic Channel or sports documentaries for binge streaming. The growing available content provides organizations from more countries to share their stories. The series *Ted Lasso* that evolved from a promotional sketch for the English Premier League comically depicts the differences between soccer and American football, and became one of the most popular shows through Apple TV+ as it both displays cultural differences between the USA and England and focuses on common challenges such as mental health. From place branding lenses, documentaries following clubs or even high school sports for periods of times, often also project the images of their communities, cities, or small towns. The documentary series *The Last Dance* on Michael Jordan and the Chicago Bulls that came out right after the outbreak of the pandemic and the documentary movie *The Redeem Team* both frame the image of the USA through basketball, and are available on Netflix. Thus, as OTP consumption grows, so will nation branding opportunities.

One of the fastest growing markets is esports especially with Gen Z. The industry passed over $1 billion (Murray et al., 2020) and is continuing to grow worldwide from online gaming and competitions filling out arenas. Esports popularity bloomed in Asian countries such as China, Korea,

Japan, Indonesia, and the Philippines, leading American and European markets to join and adopt it. The potential of this growing global phenomena was not lost on sports governing bodies, who want to capitalize on the youth of the world and on new markets. Big professional sports leagues use esports to penetrate Asian markets, which also has public diplomacy implications being reluctant to criticize China amid human rights violations as they see their growth is financially invested in the country. The IOC focused on gaming as part of its Agenda 2020+5 strategic plan, recommending to "encourage the development of virtual sports and further engage with video gaming communities" (International Olympic Committee, 2021, p. 21). Murray, Birt, and Blackmore (2020) describe the network of intersections between governing bodies, governments, and other stakeholders as esports-diplomacy. Japan used gamming as part of a cultural diplomacy tool through referencing the Nintendo game Super Mario in promoting the Tokyo 2020 Olympic Games, and playing themes from SEGA games during the parade of nations in the opening ceremony. Saudi Arabia targets esports as part of its soft power initiatives, which is already classified as sportswashing in Western media. Whether the Olympic Movement or other governing bodies will officially embrace esports as a medal event in their programs or not, its popularity among younger generations, economic growth, and international outreach will continue to foster not just people-to-people diplomacy or corporate-diplomacy, but also have geopolitical manifestations.

By becoming a leading country in the sport-tech ecosystem, countries engaged in sport-tech diplomacy (Dubinsky, 2022c) try to enhance their functional dimension, aesthetic dimension, and sympathetic dimension through fostering international collaborations. According to Dubinsky (2022c), through traditional public diplomacy, people-to-people diplomacy, corporate-diplomacy, and even philanthropy-diplomacy, the state of Israel and Israeli stakeholders enhance the image of the country as a start-up nation, despite not all of them having political affiliations with the government. Digitalization can also provide international collaboration opportunities regarding global problems, such as climate change becoming a disruptor in sports (Orr et al., 2022), by tackling ecologic challenges through weather and disaster monitoring, air quality monitoring, digital facility management technologies, or digital applications for personal use (Orr & Ross, 2022). Of course, there can also be backlash about normative dimensions of countries using sport-tech diplomacy, including accusations of Israeli sportswashing attempts, criticizing Japan and China for violating personal freedom when using monitoring technologies as part of health protocols when hosting the Tokyo 2020 and Beijing 2022 Winter Olympic Games, or Qatar for funding free trips to attend the 2022 FIFA World Cup in exchange for noncritical coverage on social media. As the sport-tech ecosystem keeps growing and diversifying, so will the ways to use it for nation branding and public diplomacy.

Conclusion

The years 2020, 2021, and 2022 brought unprecedented challenges to every country in the world. On one hand, the cancellations and postponements of leagues, competitions, and championships showed that sports is not in the highest priorities of countries and international institutions, seeing public health as more important. The suspension of Russian and Belarusian athletes as a sanction for attacking Ukraine also prioritized hard power in international relations even if it means that innocent athletes will not be allowed to compete in international competitions due to their nationalities. With that said, from the spread of the virus to global reach of activism, sports was both a cause and an outcome of all the social, political, and economic challenges and struggles the world went through. The book discussed the conceptual and theoretical connections between nation branding, public diplomacy, and country image, and identified emerging trends, such as sportswashing and sport-tech diplomacy. Beyond theory, it also focused on place branding tactics on local, regional, national, international, and global levels through the case of the Oregon22 World Athletics Championships hosted in "TrackTown USA." Through discussing historical developments through the evolution of the FIFA World Cup or reflecting on 50 years to Title IX in America, global implications, the new era of the Olympic Movement, or globalization in European football, the book demonstrated how social power struggles emerge through sports into international geopolitics. The book ends with a reflection on the changing global order, identifying five areas in which the intersections between sports, nation branding, and public diplomacy will continue to grow in the future. While the book argues that traditional practices for using sports for nation branding and public diplomacy are challenged and changing, it also emphasized that despite all the turmoil, the significance of sports as a soft power tool has not declined, suggesting that as long as people walk on this planet, they will also be playing, running, and jumping, finding ways to compete between themselves, and their countries and communities will use that to try and improve their images to achieve social, political, and economic goals. And that is not going to change.

REFERENCES

Acharya, A. (2018). *Global order: Agency and change in world politics*. Cambridge University Press.

Adidas. (n.d.). *Pride collection*. Retrieved from https://www.adidas.com/us/pride

Akdeniz Ar, A., & Kara, A. (2012). Country of production biases on consumer perceptions of global brands: Evidence from an emerging market. *Journal of Global Marketing*, 25(3), 161–179. https://doi.org/10.1080/08911762.2012.740155

Ali-Joseph, A., Leonard, K., & Welch, N. M. (2023). Indigenous environmental justice in U.S and Canada. In Kellison, T. (Ed.). *Sport stadiums and environmental justice* (pp. 32–454). New York, NY: Routledge.

Anholt, S. (2020). *The good country equation*. Berrett-Koehler Publishers Inc.

BBC News. (2021, May 12). Homosexuality: The countries where it is illegal to be gay. *BBC*. Retrieved from https://www.bbc.com/news/world-43822234

Beer, T. (2020, September 1). NCAA athletes could make $2 million a year if paid equitably, study suggests. *Forbes*. Retrieved from https://www.forbes.com/sites/tommybeer/2020/09/01/ncaa-athletes-could-make-2-million-a-year-if-paid-equitably-study-suggests/?sh=5c7da3dd5499

Best, R., & Howard, D. (2022). *The global sports industry*. Independently Published.

Bjola, C., Cassidy, J., & Manor, I. (2019). Public diplomacy in the digital age. *The Hague Journal of Diplomacy*, 14(1–2), 83–101.

Boykoff, J. (2016). *Power games: A political history of the Olympics*. Verso.

Boykoff, J. (2022). Toward a theory of sportswashing: Mega-events, soft power, and political conflict. *Sociology of Sport Journal*, 1–10. https://doi.org/10.1123/ssj.2022-0095

Chadwick, S. (2022). From utilitarianism and neoclassical sport management to a new geopolitical economy of sport. *European Sport Management Quarterly*, 1–20. https://doi.org/10.1080/16184742.2022.2032251

CPD. (n.d.). *People places power*. USC Center on Public Diplomacy. Retrieved from https://uscpublicdiplomacy.org/tags/people-places-power

Cull, N. J. (2008). Public diplomacy: Taxonomies and histories. *Annals of the American Academy of Political Science*, 616(1), 31–54.

Cull, N. J. (2010). Public diplomacy: Seven lessons for its future from its past. *Journal of Place Branding and Public Diplomacy*, 6, 11–17.

Dinnie, K., & Sevin, E. (2020). The changing nature of nation branding: Implications for public diplomacy. In N. Snow & N. J. Cull (Eds.), *Routledge handbook of public diplomacy* (pp. 137–144). Routledge.

Dubinsky, Y. (2019a). From soft power to sports diplomacy: A theoretical and conceptual discussion. *Place Branding and Public Diplomacy, 15*, 154–164. https://doi.org/10.1057/s41254-019-00116-8

Dubinsky, Y. (2021a). Sports, Brand America and U.S. public diplomacy during the presidency of Donald Trump. *Place Branding & Public Diplomacy*. https://doi.org/10.1057/s41254-021-00230-6

Dubinsky, I. (2021b). China's stadium diplomacy in Africa. *Journal of Global Sport Management*, 1–18. https://doi.org/10.1080/24704067.2021.1885101

Dubinsky, Y. (2022a). Country image, cultural diplomacy, and sports during the COVID19 pandemic: Brand America and Super Bowl LV. *Place Branding & Public Diplomacy*, 1–17. https://doi.org/10.1057/s41254-021-00257-9

Dubinsky, Y. (2022b). The Olympic Games, nation branding, and public diplomacy in a post-pandemic world: Reflections on Tokyo 2020 and beyond. *Place Branding & Public Diplomacy*, 1–12. https://doi.org/10.1057/s41254-021-00255-x

Dubinsky, Y. (2022c). Sport-Tech Diplomacy: Exploring the intersections between the sport-tech ecosystem, innovation, and diplomacy in Israel. *Place Branding & Public Diplomacy, 18*(2), 169–180. https://doi.org/10.1057/s41254-020-00191-2

Fukuyama, F. (1992). *The end of history and the last man*. The Free Press.

Huntington, S. P. (1996). *The clash of civilizations and the remaking of world order*. Simon & Schuster.

Hussain, U., & Cunningham, G. B. (2022). The Muslim community and sport scholarship: A scoping review to advance sport management research. *European Sport Management Quarterly*, 1–23. https://doi.org/10.1080/16184742.2022.213443

International Olympic Committee. (2021). Olympic agenda 2020+5: 15 recommendations. *International Olympic Committee*. Retrieved from https://stillmedab.olympic.org/media/Document%20Library/OlympicOrg/IOC/What-We-Do/Olympic-agenda/Olympic-Agenda-2020-5-15-recommendations.pdf.

Kennelly, M. (2023). COVID-19 and sport tourism. In S. Frawley & N. Schulenkorf (Eds.), *Routledge handbook of sports and COVID19* (pp. 161–172). Routledge.

Kerr, S., & Harris. (2021). *Sam Kerr: Kicking goals: The flip out*. Simon & Schuster.

Martin, D. (2007). *Rebuilding brand America: What we must do to restore our reputation and safeguard the future of American business abroad*. Amacom.

Murray, S., Birt, J., & Blakemore, S. (2020). eSports diplomacy: towards a sustainable 'gold rush'. *Sport in Society*, 1–19. https://doi.org/10.1080/17430437.2020.1826437

NCEI. (2022). *U.S. billion-dollar weather and climate disasters*. NOAA National Centers for Environmental Information. Retrieved from https://www.ncei. noaa.gov/access/billions/

News Agencies. (2022, October 1). Morocco demands Adidas withdraw Algeria's football Jersey. *Al Jazeera*. Retrieved from https://www.aljazeera.com/ sports/2022/10/1/morocco-demands-adidas-withdraw-algeria-football-jersey

Nzherald.co.nz. (2022). Draw for the FIFA Women's World Cup|nzherald.co.nz. *YouTube*. Retrieved from https://www.youtube.com/watch?v=vjg1P8Q9XVY

Orr, M., & Ross, J. W. (2022). Chapter 26 Digital technology and sport ecology. In M. L. Naraine, T. Haydukk III, & J. Doyle (Eds.), *The Routledge handbook of digital sport management* (pp. 346–354). Routledge.

Orr, M., Murfree, J., & Stargel, L. (2022). (Re)scheduling as a climate mitigation and adaptation strategy. *Managing Sport and Leisure*, 1–6. https://doi.org/1 0.1080/23750472.2022.2159501

Postlethwaite, V., Jenkin, C., & Sherry, E. (2022). Sport diplomacy: An integrative review. *Sport Management Review*, 1–22. https://doi.org/10.108 0/14413523.2022.2071054

Reuters. (2022, October 2). Timeline: Major football stadium disasters over the last 40 years. *Al Jazeera*. Retrieved from https://www.aljazeera.com/ sports/2022/10/2/timeline-major-stadium-disasters-over-the-last-40-years

Rofe, S. J. (2016). Sport and diplomacy: A global diplomacy framework. *Diplomacy & Statecraft*, *27*(2), 212–230. https://doi.org/10.1080/09592296.2016. 1169785

Said, E. W. (1994). *Culture and imperialism*. Vintage Books.

Said, E. W. (2003). *Orientalism*. Penguin Classics.

Sherry, E., McCullough, B. P., & Bramley, O. (2022, October 26). Out of bounds: How much does greenwashing cost fossil-fuel sponsors of Australian sport? *The Conversation*. Retrieved from https://theconversation.com/out-of-boundshow-much-does-greenwashing-cost-fossil-fuel-sponsors-of-australiansport-192720?utm_source=twitter&utm_medium=bylinetwitterbutton

Sivels, L. (2023). Old and new stadium development in Miami. In T. Kellison (Ed.), *Sport stadiums and environmental justice* (pp. 118–129). Routledge.

The Good Country Index. (2022). *Results – Version 1.5*. Retrieved from https:// index.goodcountry.org/

The Good Country Index. (n.d.). *About The Good Country Index*. Retrieved from https://www.goodcountry.org/index/about-the-index/

United Nations. (n.d.). *Transforming our world: The 2030 Agenda for Sustainable Development*. Retrieved from https://sdgs.un.org/2030agenda

Visit Rwanda. (n.d). *About the partnership*. https://www.visitrwanda.com/ arsenal/

Williams, L. A. (2022). The heritage strikes back: Athlete activism, black lives matter, and the iconic fifth wave of activism in the (W)NBA bubble. *Cultural Studies ↔ Critical Methodologies, 22*(3), 266–275. https://doi.org/10.1177/15327086211049

Witty, A. (2021. College athletics spending and the movement towards revenue sharing. *ADU*. Retrieved from https://athleticdirectoru.com/articles/student-athlete-revenue-sharing/

WMO. (2022). *Provisional state of the global climate 2022*. World Meteorological Organization. Retrieved from https://www.ncei.noaa.gov/access/billions/

Zirin, D. (2022). Behind the shield. *Media Education Foundation*. Retrieved from https://go.mediaed.org/behind-the-shield

Index[1]

A
Abdoul-Jabbar, Kareem, 12, 171
Abe, Shinzo, 5, 80, 91, 255
Aboriginal, 10, 83, 256
Abraham Accords, 4, 11, 175, 264
Abramovich, Roman, 132, 135, 144, 148, 166, 169
Abu Dhabi, 40, 132, 134, 137, 145, 172
AC Milan, 129, 130, 132, 133, 136, 141, 142, 146, 172
Activism, 1, 11–13, 17, 20, 40, 66, 78, 84–86, 148, 165, 171, 174, 207, 256–260, 270
Adams, Sylvain, 177
Adidas, 133, 259
Afghanistan, 4, 76, 166, 171
Africa, 3, 4, 8, 9, 11, 27, 39, 42, 54, 58–60, 62, 83, 134, 143, 146, 160, 162, 176, 181, 228, 257
Agenda 2020, 5, 82, 91–93, 95, 226, 252, 261, 269
Agenda 2020+5, 91, 92, 95, 226, 252, 261, 269
Agnelli, Andrea, 141
Ajax Amsterdam, xiii, 135, 147, 263
Alexander the Great, 37, 157
Algeria, 61, 88, 263
Ali, Muhammad, 27, 171, 206, 210
Al Jazeera, 65, 143, 172, 174, 267
Allen, Devon, 209
Amateurism, 6, 19, 76, 80, 116, 118, 157, 158, 160, 165, 180, 234, 261
Amnesty, 159, 171, 173, 177
Amusan, Tobi, 210
Ancient Greece, 1, 25, 37, 41, 42, 157
Ancient Rome, 37, 257
Animal House, 197, 209, 214
Antetokounmpo, Giannis, 11
Antisemitism, 160, 177, 259, 263
Apartheid, 25, 30, 37, 160, 177, 229
Arabian Gulf, 11, 18, 19, 40, 43, 86, 134, 144, 158, 260, 264

---

[1] Note: Page numbers followed by 'n' refer to notes.

Arab Spring, 171, 172, 174, 267
Ardern, Jacinda, 10, 252, 256
Argentina, 8, 14, 54, 55, 58–60, 149, 160, 178
Armstrong, Lance, 81, 179
Arsenal FC, 129, 132–134, 136, 138, 145, 172, 176, 263
Asher Smith, Dina, 208, 210
Asia, 6, 8, 10, 11, 27, 54, 62, 145, 257, 260, 264
Asian Games, 8, 164, 266
ASICS, 202, 210
Atletico Madrid, 129, 130, 132, 133, 136, 140, 141, 176
Australia, 10, 14, 27, 36, 37, 40, 67, 83, 94, 172, 194, 208, 227, 252, 253, 255, 256, 261, 266
Australian Open, 10, 254
Austria, 55, 57, 232, 240
Azerbaijan, 133, 140, 176

B

Bach, Thomas, 75, 82, 84
Bader Ginsburg, Ruth, 228
Bahrain, 4, 171–173
Bangladesh, 257
Barshim, Mustaz Essa, 88
Basketball Africa League (BAL), 11
Battle of the Sexes, 108
Bayern Munich, 133, 142, 236
Beckham, David, 143
Beitar Jerusalem, 239
Belarus, 89, 169, 211, 264, 270
Berlusconi, Silvio, 136, 141, 142
Bermuda, 88
Berry, Gwen, 85, 111
Biden, Joe, 4, 105, 113, 121, 253, 258
Bikila, Abebe, 83, 210
Biles, Simone, 14, 85, 107
Bird, Sue, 109, 121

Black Lives Matter, 4, 11–13, 85, 89, 109, 111, 148, 256–258
Black Power Salute, 38, 76
Blatter, Sepp, 61, 64
Bolsonaro, Jair, 3, 14, 263
Bolt, Usain, 83, 210
Bosman Rule, 59
Bowerman, Bill, 194, 198, 201
Boycotts, 13, 18, 30, 38, 41–44, 55, 58, 88, 92, 145, 158, 163, 164, 166, 168, 225, 234, 265
Brand America, 17, 35, 102–106, 118, 120, 195, 261
Brazil, 3, 8, 14, 54, 56, 61–64, 182, 227, 232, 254
Brexit, 3, 4, 18, 148
BRICS, 254, 266
British Empire, 37, 180
Brody, Tal, v, 233
Brundage, Avery, 84, 160
Bryant, Kobe, 14
Bundesliga, 143
Burkina Faso, 88
Bush, George W., 113

C

Californization, 40
Cameroon, 8, 59
Canada, 9, 39, 43, 66, 81, 85, 182, 196, 227, 240, 252, 253, 255, 261
Capitalism, 7, 13, 40, 59, 60, 92, 102, 112, 118, 146, 158, 166, 170, 195
Caribbeans, 60, 87
Carlos, John, 12, 84, 198, 207
Caslavska, Vera, 165
Catalonia, 63, 132
Catchings, Tamika, 113
Ceaușescu, Nicolae, 160
Chamtai-Salpeter, Lonah, 210

Chastain, Brandy, 110
Chelsea FC, 129, 132, 133, 135, 136, 138, 144, 166, 169, 172
Chile, 54
China, 4, 6, 8–10, 18, 30, 33, 35, 36, 41–43, 62, 80, 82, 86, 87, 131, 132, 134, 146, 158, 161–165, 169, 172, 174–176, 182, 183, 197, 225, 227, 252–254, 259, 262–266, 268, 269
Christmas Truce, 30
City diplomacy, 29, 195, 253
Civil Rights Movement, 12, 113, 171, 198
Clash of civilizations, 158, 170, 266
Climate, 5, 10, 20, 39, 68, 93, 103, 118, 142, 212, 251–256, 263, 269
Climate change, 5, 10, 20, 39, 67, 68, 93, 118, 212, 253–256, 269
Coe, Sebastian, 199–202, 210, 212, 213
Cold War, 4, 12, 26–29, 38, 54, 58–60, 64, 76, 80, 83, 87, 102, 103, 112, 158, 160, 162, 165, 179, 197, 225, 233, 265
Colonialism, 1, 19, 37–40, 58, 161, 256, 257, 266
Comaneci, Nadia, 83, 160
Commonwealth Games, 10, 37, 136, 180, 183, 254
Communism, 30, 59, 160, 162, 165, 166, 170
Corporate diplomacy, 29, 93, 104, 113, 119, 134, 145, 224, 259, 262, 269
Corruption, 11, 43, 44, 54, 57, 62–66, 77, 81, 88, 93, 107, 141, 144, 147, 149, 167, 173, 178, 181, 252, 255, 263, 266
Country image, 21, 27, 32
Country-of-origin, 32, 105, 118, 133, 259
COVID-19, 1–3, 5, 7–13, 15, 16, 18, 20, 65, 67, 77, 79, 80, 162–165, 199, 212, 227, 255
Crimea Peninsula, 43, 167, 264
Critical race theory, 40
Crouser, Ryan, 209
Cruyff, Johan, 140
Cuba, 39
Cultural diplomacy, 15, 26, 29, 35, 36, 44, 90, 91, 112, 168, 262, 269
Cultural Olympiad, 90

D
Davis, Otis, 206
De Coubertin, Pierre, 39
De Grasse, Andre, 208
Denmark, 227, 252, 263
Diamond League, 194, 199, 208
Digitalization, 91, 95, 252, 269
Disney, 164
  Disneyfication, 40
Division I, 105, 106, 115–117
Djokovic, Novak, 10, 14
Dominican Republic, 208
Doping, 42–44, 81, 87, 107, 158, 165, 167, 168, 179, 211, 225, 264
Dos Santos, Alison, 208
Dubai, 172

E
Eaton, Ashton, 204
Edwards, Harry, 12, 84, 171, 207
Einstein, Albert, 228
Ekecheiria, 26, 30, 41
El Salvador, 58
Embiid, Joel, 11

England, xiii, 5, 8, 9, 13, 14, 18, 54, 55, 57, 58, 129, 131, 132, 135, 137–139, 141, 146, 172, 180, 183, 266, 268
Equal pay, 110, 258
Erdogan, Tayyip, 178
ESPN, 6, 114, 142, 207, 235
Ethiopia, 4, 39, 87, 210, 211, 228, 266
Etihad, 172
Eurocentrism, 171
European Super League (ESL), 18, 67, 68, 129–149, 260
European Union (EU), 3, 4, 37, 59, 142, 144, 147, 148, 169, 178, 181, 253, 263
Eusebio, 57

F

The FA, 137–139, 180
Falkland Islands, 131
Falklands War, 58
Farah, Mo, 257
Fascism, 43, 54, 55, 57, 136, 141, 143, 263, 266
FC Barcelona, 63, 129, 132, 134, 136, 139, 140, 148, 172, 234, 235, 237
Felix, Allyson, 87, 107, 113, 121, 198
FIFA, 10, 11, 14, 16, 19, 27, 39, 43, 51–68, 51n1, 75n1, 86, 106, 107, 110, 111, 131, 134, 136, 140, 141, 143, 144, 146–149, 159, 160, 167, 173, 175, 181–183, 193, 211, 233, 234, 252, 254–261, 263, 265, 266, 270
FIFA Fair Play, 130, 130n2, 143–145, 260
FIFA Women's World Cup, 10, 106, 107, 110, 252, 255, 256

FIFA World Cup, 10, 11, 14, 16, 19, 27, 39, 43, 51–68, 51n1, 75n1, 86, 131, 134, 136, 140, 141, 143, 144, 146, 147, 149, 159, 160, 167, 173, 175, 181–183, 193, 211, 233, 254, 255, 257, 259, 261, 263, 265, 266, 270
Fiji, 38
First nations, 10, 256, 257
Floyd, George, 13, 84
Fly Emirates, 133, 172
Fosbury, Dick, 198, 204
France, 3, 18, 51, 54, 55, 59–62, 83, 94, 131, 137, 142–144, 149, 157, 171, 172, 176, 178–180, 182, 227, 238, 254, 263, 266
Franco, Francisco, 139, 160
Frayser Pryce, Shelly-Ann, 210
Freeman, Cathy, 83, 256
Freud, Sigmund, 228

G

Garra Charrua, 54, 56, 131
Gastro diplomacy, 262
Gaza Strip, 177, 229
Gazprom, 15, 167, 169
Gender equality, 4, 10, 13, 60, 109, 111, 113–115, 119–121, 198, 251, 258
Genocide, 11, 13, 160, 164, 176, 211, 266
Gen Z, 91, 268
Germany, 3, 5, 10, 12, 18, 29, 38, 42–44, 54, 57, 59, 61–64, 76, 83, 87, 131, 137, 141–144, 160, 164, 170, 177, 181, 183, 226, 227, 229, 232, 234, 240, 252, 259, 265, 266
Gilady, Alex, 235
Giro d'Italia, 176, 177, 238
Glazer, Joel and Avram, 132, 135, 145

INDEX 279

Globalization, 16, 19, 37–40, 59, 104, 118–120, 137, 195, 270
Global North, 259, 263–265
Global South, 4, 171, 259, 265, 266
Glocalization, 18, 19, 139, 140, 195, 200, 214
Good Country Index, 103, 251, 253
Great Britain, 36–38, 137, 157, 171, 209
Greece, vi, xiii, 36, 37, 89
Greenwashing, 11, 42, 66, 92, 93, 159, 182, 252, 254–256
Griner, Brittney, 110, 114
Gu, Eileen, 164
Gulf Cooperation Council (GCC), 170–176, 178, 182, 183, 264, 266
Gulf War, v, 171
Guttmann, Bela, 232
Guttmann, Ludwig, 233

H
Hamm, Mia, 110
Hammon, Becky, 111
Hard power, 33, 34, 82, 102, 103, 146, 159, 167, 171, 175, 270
Hassan, Sifan, 88
Havelange, João, 61
Hayward Field, 194, 198, 199, 202, 207, 208
Hayward, Bill, 198
Hegemony, 40, 158, 252, 266
Henry, John, 132, 145
Hitler, Adolf, 43, 44, 143, 160
Honduras, 58
Hong Kong, 3, 163, 227
Hooliganism, 137
Human rights, 9, 10, 13, 18, 19, 43, 52, 65, 80, 89, 134, 144, 158, 159, 161–165, 167, 169, 173–176, 178, 182, 183, 226, 259, 264, 266, 269
Human trafficking, 173, 257
Hungary, 43, 57, 165, 232

I
Ibrahimovich, Zlatan, 143
Imboden, Race, 85
Imperialism, 171, 266
India, 3, 38, 62, 172, 209, 227, 236, 254
Indonesia, 142, 177
Infantino, Gianni, 174
Inter Milan, 129, 130, 132, 134, 136, 141, 142, 146, 177
International Olympic Academy, v, vii, xiii
International Olympic Committee (IOC), 5, 13, 21, 25, 38, 39, 41, 43, 52, 75, 77–86, 88–95, 111, 119, 160, 163, 164, 168–170, 177, 180, 182, 194, 226, 235, 252, 255, 258, 261, 264, 265, 269
IOC Rule 50, 84, 258
Iran, 4, 60, 88, 145, 171, 172, 175, 178, 209, 258, 265
Iraq, v, 4, 103, 112, 171
Irving, Kyrie, 14, 263
Islam, 12, 158, 170, 171, 174, 239
Islamophobia, 65, 172–174, 259, 264
Israel, v, xiii, 3, 4, 16, 20, 33, 58, 132, 175, 177, 182, 210, 223, 223n1, 224, 227–241, 263, 264, 269
Italy, 3, 5, 9, 14, 18, 29, 43, 54–56, 59, 60, 88, 129, 131, 132, 136, 137, 141–142, 159, 172, 177, 182, 208, 263

J

Jamaica, 39, 107, 208–210, 264
James, LeBron, 13, 256, 268
Japan, 3, 4, 6, 9, 10, 13, 17, 39, 40, 54, 61, 62, 64, 75n1, 78–80, 87, 90, 91, 93, 94, 108, 172, 182, 210, 226, 227, 269
Jinping, Xi, 146, 162, 164, 266
Jogo Bonito, 14, 54, 56, 63, 131
Johnson, Boris, 3, 130, 138, 263
Jones, Marion, 81
Jordan, Michael, 12, 199, 268
Juventus, 60, 129, 130, 132, 134, 136, 141, 142, 146, 148, 149

K

Kaepernick, Colin, 13, 84, 110, 256, 258, 259
Kafala, 65, 66, 173, 174
Kanter Freedom, Enes, 178, 259
Kazakhstan, 82, 163, 176, 210
Kenya, 11, 39, 87, 210, 264
Kerley, Fred, 208, 213
Kerr, Sam, 256
Khashoggi, Jamal, 175
King, Billie Jean, 108, 109, 111, 121
King Charles III, 180
Knight, Phil, 194, 198, 199, 201
Kroenke, Stan, 145
Kuwait, 171, 172
Kwan, Michelle, 113, 206

L

Lausanne Capitale Olympique, 194, 214
Ledecky, Katie, 87, 107, 113
LGBTQ, 65, 86, 110, 159, 167, 173, 174, 256, 259, 263
Liberalism, 60, 66, 158, 170, 178, 266

Libya, 171, 209
Ligue 1, 143
Liverpool, xiii, 129, 132, 134–136, 138, 145, 148
Lloyd, Carli, 110
Los Angeles 2028, 77, 80, 180, 207
Luther King Jr., Martin, 12, 108, 206
Lyles, Noah, 206, 207

M

Maccabiah Games, 33, 177, 232, 233, 238
Maccabi Tel Aviv, 42, 233, 235
Mafia, 64, 141, 179
Major League Soccer (MLS), 177, 196
Malcom X, 12
Malta, 253
Manchester City FC, 129, 132, 134, 136, 138, 145, 147, 172, 235
Manchester United, 129, 132, 134, 136, 138, 145, 148
Mandela, Nelson, 25, 37, 62
Mane, Sadio, 258
Maori, 34
Maradona, Diego Armando, 14, 58
March Madness, 109, 213
Marx, Karl, 228
Marxism, 40, 170
Mbappé, Kylian, 149
McKeon, Emma, 88
Mclaughlin, Sydney, 206
Mental health, 5, 11, 14, 85, 86, 111, 268
Merkel, Angela, 5, 181
Messi, Lionel, 140, 148
MeToo Movement, 85, 148, 258
Mexico, 12, 38, 54, 66, 67, 76, 84, 165, 171, 198, 207, 255, 261, 263
Middle East, 3, 4, 10, 19, 66, 145, 264

INDEX   281

Migrant workers, 54, 65, 66, 173, 257, 263
Militarism, 265
Milla, Roger, 59
Miller, Cheryl, 109
MLB, 111
Mollaei, Saeid, 88
Mongolia, 88
Moore, Maya, 109
Morgan, Alex, 110, 113
Morocco, 4, 66, 174, 263
Mozambique, 57
Munich 1972, 38, 62, 76, 89
Munich Massacre, 10, 76, 170, 177
Muscular Judaism, 177, 231
Mussolini, Benito, 43, 54, 55, 141, 159

N

Name, Image and Likeness (NIL), 110, 117, 120, 261
Nassar, Larry, 81, 85, 114, 180
National Collegiate Athletic Association (NCAA), 101, 105–110, 115, 116, 199, 200, 235, 240, 261
National identity, 27, 33–34, 63
Nationalism, 3, 32, 33, 43, 55, 60, 137, 139, 158, 181, 206
National Women's Soccer League (NWSL), 196
Nation branding, v, vii, xiii, 2, 5, 9, 15–18, 20, 21, 26, 26n1, 27, 30–33, 36, 37, 40, 42, 44, 51–53, 61, 62, 66, 67, 75, 75n1, 76, 80, 86, 90, 94, 95, 101–105, 107, 111, 114, 118, 120, 131, 133, 136, 140, 143, 144, 146, 157–159, 162, 165, 168, 174, 208, 223, 224, 226, 228, 231, 233, 241, 252, 254, 256, 260–263, 267, 268, 270
Nation building, 33, 65, 149, 173
Native Americans, 13, 206, 257
Naturalization, 87, 161, 164, 210
Nazism, 10, 12, 38, 42–44, 57, 62, 76, 83, 143, 160, 164, 181, 183, 226, 229, 232
NBA, 6, 9, 11, 12, 14, 111, 117, 165, 176, 178, 195, 196, 233, 235–237, 239, 240, 259, 261, 268
Nethanyahu, Benjamin, 230
Netherlands, xiii, 57, 63, 240, 252, 258
Newcastle United, 11, 149, 175, 263
New Zealand, 3, 10, 34, 38, 67, 79, 85, 160, 236, 252, 255, 256, 261
Neymar, 148
NFL, 13, 111, 117, 198, 213, 261, 268
NHL, 9, 236
Nigeria, 59
Nike, 19, 81, 105, 119, 179, 194, 198, 199, 202, 207, 209, 211, 214, 237, 259
Nixon, Richard, 30, 101
Nobel Prize, 228
NOlympics, 39, 94, 261
North America, 3, 7, 8, 51n1, 80, 129n1, 134, 145, 157, 161, 162, 236, 257, 260
North Korea, 4, 81, 86
Norway, 39, 107, 258
Nuclear disaster, 79
Nye, Joseph, 134

O

Obama, Barack, 108, 113
Occupation, 4, 131, 177
Oceania, 8, 38, 145, 264

Oligarchs, 15, 135, 144, 166, 169
Olympia, vi, 26, 30, 75, 157, 194
The Olympic Charter, 91
Olympic Games, v, xiii, 1, 5, 6, 8–13, 16, 18, 19, 25, 27, 33, 36, 38, 39, 42, 43, 52, 62, 75–90, 75n1, 92–94, 102, 103, 106, 109, 111, 113, 118, 136, 137, 143, 146, 157, 159, 160, 162–171, 175, 178, 179, 181–183, 193, 197, 201, 207, 209, 211, 213, 225–228, 232–235, 254–256, 258, 261, 264, 266, 269, 270
   Athens 1896, 76
   Athens 2004, 36
   Atlanta 1996, 36, 107, 109
   Barcelona 1992, 36, 226
   Beijing 2008, 36, 162, 163, 167, 254, 264
   Berlin 1936, 10, 12, 38, 76, 160, 164, 165, 169, 181
   Brisbane 2032, 77, 80, 83, 94, 182, 255
   London 1908, 76
   London 2012, 33, 36, 106, 107
   Los Angeles 1984, 36, 76, 80, 109, 166, 201
   Los Angeles 2028, 80, 208, 209, 255
   Mexico City 1968, 12, 38, 76, 84, 165, 171, 198, 207
   Montreal 1976, 76, 92, 160
   Moscow 1980, 36, 76, 166
   Munich 1972, 10, 264
   Paris 1900, 76
   Paris 2024, 75, 80, 95, 255, 261
   Rio de Janeiro 2016, 6, 91, 106, 182, 211, 254
   Seoul 1988, 36
   St. Louis 1904, 76
   Stockholm 1912, 198
   Sydney 2000, 36, 83, 256
   Tokyo 2020, 5, 6, 8–10, 13, 16, 17, 75–95, 75n1, 102, 106, 108, 111, 118, 168, 182, 207, 209, 212, 228, 255, 258, 269, 270
The Olympic Partners, 80
Olympic Trials, 194, 198, 199, 209
Olympic Truce, 30, 89, 169, 183, 264
Olympism, 41, 42, 91
Oman, 4, 171, 172
Orientalism, 65, 171, 173, 174, 259, 264, 266
Orwell, George, 10, 25, 80, 163
Osaka, Naomi, 14, 85, 111
Owens, Jesse, 12, 83, 206

P
Pakistan, 35, 38, 257
Palestine, 4, 10, 11, 42, 66, 89, 170, 171, 174, 177, 229, 230, 258, 259, 265
Pan-American Games, 85, 111
Paralympic Games, 43, 78, 89, 167, 169, 170, 183, 233, 264
The Paris Agreement, 253
Paris Saint Germain, 133, 134, 142–144, 147–149, 172
Parker, Candance, 109
Parlow Cone, Cindy, 110
Pele, 14
Pelosi, Nancy, 263
People-to-people diplomacy, 29, 83, 86, 113, 134, 224, 238, 257, 259, 262, 269
Peres, Shimon, 234
Perez, Florentino, 140
Philippines, 27, 88, 269
Ping Pong Diplomacy, 30, 41, 103, 197, 225
Place branding, 19, 27, 31, 32, 118, 133, 136, 193, 194, 201, 211, 251, 253–254, 268, 270

Pogba, Paul, 258
Populism, 3, 7, 20, 40, 86, 257, 258, 263
Portugal, 8, 57, 147
Pound, Richard, 169
Prefontaine, Steve, 194, 198, 199, 201
Premier League, 11, 130, 132, 134, 137–140, 148, 166, 175, 176, 235, 268
Prince, Sedona, 109
Product-country-image, 2, 32, 62, 67, 105, 133, 172, 209, 259
Public diplomacy, v, vii, xiii, 2, 5, 10, 15–18, 20, 26–30, 26n1, 32, 34–44, 53, 55, 58, 62, 67, 75, 75n1, 76, 79, 80, 86, 89, 90, 94, 95, 102–104, 107, 112, 114, 118, 119, 134, 135, 139, 144, 157–159, 162, 177, 197, 206, 208, 211, 223–227, 230, 231, 233, 241, 251–253, 257, 259, 261, 262, 267–270
Putin, Vladimir, 4, 15, 19, 43, 52, 64, 65, 144, 164, 166–170, 183, 264

Q
Qatar, 10, 16, 19, 27, 33, 51, 54, 64–66, 75n1, 86, 88, 134, 140, 143, 144, 149, 161, 171–175, 183, 200, 212, 238, 252, 255, 257, 259, 262, 263, 265–267, 270
Qatar Airways, 172
Queen Elizabeth II, 3, 180

R
Racism, 12–14, 58, 84, 85, 103, 116, 159, 160, 180, 198, 229, 252, 253, 256, 257
Raisman, Aly, 107

Rapinoe, Megan, 13, 84, 110, 258
Rashford, Marcus, 257
Reagan, Ronald, 4, 162, 265
Real Madrid, 63, 129, 130, 132, 133, 135, 136, 139–141, 146, 149, 172
Referendum, 82, 83
Refugee Olympic Team, 89
Resistance, 12, 13, 17, 18, 39, 40, 77, 80, 82, 86, 94, 109, 135, 143, 170, 182, 252, 256, 257, 260, 262
Robinson, Jackie, 12
Roe v. Wade, 115, 121, 209
Rogge, Jacque, 82
Ronaldo, Cristiano, 11, 141, 149, 175
Rudolph, Wilma, 206
Rugby World Cup, 11, 37–38
Rumble in the Jungle, 27
Russell, Bill, 12, 206
Russia, 4, 8, 9, 15, 18, 43, 51, 54, 61, 63, 64, 67, 86, 87, 89, 110, 114, 131, 132, 137, 144, 158, 161, 165–170, 174–176, 182, 183, 230, 252, 254, 258, 263, 264, 266, 267
Rwanda, 11, 176, 263

S
Salah, Mohamed, 258
Salazar, Alberto, 81, 179
Samoa, 38
San Marino, 88
Saudi Arabia, 10–11, 35, 66, 88, 140, 145, 149, 171, 172, 175, 182, 227, 260, 262, 264, 269
Saunders, Raven, 85, 207
Semenya, Caster, 212
Senegal, 8, 11, 264
September 11, 6, 104, 112, 170, 172
Serbia, 228

Sexual abuse, 14, 81, 82, 115
Sheikhs, 145, 176
Shuai, Peng, 163
The Simpsons, 197, 211, 214
Singapore, 3, 227
Six-Day War, 177, 229
Smart power, 102, 112, 146, 159, 165, 167, 176
Smith, Tommie, 12, 84, 198, 207
Social identity theory, 27–28, 33, 135
Socialism, 135
Social justice, 9, 13, 39, 89, 94, 109–111, 119, 161, 252, 255–261
Soft power, 2, 3, 15, 16, 19, 20, 26, 26n1, 27, 34–37, 40, 42–44, 52, 58, 64, 67, 91, 102, 107, 112, 120, 134, 143, 144, 149, 159, 167, 172, 173, 175, 176, 181–183, 224, 225, 227, 228, 238, 241, 242, 262, 263, 267, 269, 270
Solo, Hope, 110
Somalia, 210, 257
South Africa, 3, 11, 25, 30, 37, 54, 61, 62, 64, 160, 209, 228, 236, 254
South America, 8, 9, 11, 35, 56, 63, 232, 263
South Korea, 3, 36, 54, 61, 62, 226, 227
Soviet Union, v, 4, 12, 28, 30, 36, 40, 43, 64, 76, 87, 102, 157, 158, 162, 165, 166, 168, 170, 176, 179, 230, 265
Spain, 3, 9, 18, 36, 54, 59, 63, 129, 131, 132, 137, 139–141, 160, 182
Spanish La Liga, 132, 138, 236
Sports diplomacy, 1–21, 25–44, 26n1, 83, 87, 101–121, 165, 224, 225, 227, 234, 255, 262

Sports for development and peace, 41
Sportswashing, 11, 16, 18, 19, 43, 52, 55, 64, 65, 67, 68, 88, 144, 158–161, 164, 165, 168, 170, 173–179, 181–183, 226, 263, 269, 270
Sport-tech, 20, 42, 91, 104, 119, 223–228, 223n1, 234–242, 262, 267, 269, 270
Sport-tech diplomacy, 20, 42, 91, 104, 119, 223, 224, 228, 236, 239–242, 262, 269, 270
Stadium diplomacy, 42, 162, 262
Staley, Dawn, 111
Start-up nation, 223
Sterling, Raheem, 257
Sudan, 4, 88, 257
Summit, Pat, 109
Super Bowl, 5, 27, 52, 103, 165, 183, 197, 235, 268
Switzerland, 27, 54, 179, 266
Syria, 4

T
Tahiti, 261
Taiwan, 3, 162, 163
Tamberi, Gianmarco, 88
Taurasi, Diana, 109
Terrorism, 6, 10, 62, 65, 76, 104, 112, 160, 170, 174, 183, 234
Thailand, 137
Thiesen-Eaton, Brianne, 204
Thompson-Herah, Elaine, 210
Thorpe, Jim, 198
Thrilla in Manila, 27
Thuram, Lilian, 60
Tibet, 162, 163
Tigray, 4, 211
Title IX, 17, 39, 60, 87, 101–121, 198, 206, 209, 261, 270
Tokyo 1964, 78, 210

Tonga, 38
Tottenham Hotspur, 129, 132, 135, 136, 138, 147, 178, 238
Tour de France, 173
Tourism destination image, 2, 31, 136, 172, 256
Track Town USA, 19, 27, 193–214, 270
Transgender, 14, 85, 101, 212
Trump, Donald, 3–5, 7, 13, 14, 102, 103, 110, 115, 209, 253, 257, 263, 267
Tsunami, 79
Turkey, 178
Turkmenistan, 88

U
UEFA, 5, 8, 9, 65, 130, 130n2, 140, 143, 144, 147, 148, 160, 166, 168, 169, 178, 260, 268
UEFA Champions League (UCL), 8, 9, 65, 130, 140, 166, 167, 169, 178, 260, 268
Uganda, 87
Ukraine, 4, 8, 10, 15, 19, 43, 65, 89, 148, 167, 169, 170, 183, 211, 264, 270
United Arab Emirates (UAE), 11, 133, 140, 144, 145, 171–173, 227, 238
United Kingdom, 3, 227, 257, 263
United Nations, 14, 41, 92, 182, 230, 234, 251
United Nations Sustainable Development Goals, 92, 251, 255
United States, xiii, 2–5, 7, 9, 12, 17–19, 30, 36–38, 43, 52, 54, 59, 60, 66, 67, 77, 79–85, 87, 89, 94, 101–107, 109–116, 118–120, 131, 132, 137, 146, 157, 158, 160, 162, 163, 165, 166, 168, 172, 179, 182, 183, 193–200, 202, 205, 206, 208, 209, 212–214, 225, 227, 232, 233, 237, 253, 255–257, 259, 261, 263, 265, 266, 268
United States Olympic and Paralympic Committee (USOPC), 77, 81–85, 115
Universalism, 158
Universiade Games, 162, 164, 167, 178
University of Oregon, vii, xiii, 19, 109, 194, 197, 198, 200–203, 206, 208, 209
Uruguay, 54, 56, 131, 172, 178
U.S. Women's National Soccer Team (USWNT), 60, 81, 103, 105–107, 110, 111, 113, 121, 258
Uyghurs, 164

V
Valieva, Kamila, 168
Viera, Patrick, 60
Vietnam War, 12, 171
Vuelta a Espana, 176

W
Wambach, Abby, 110
West Bank, 177, 229
West, Kanye, 259, 263
Whataboutism, 65, 174, 179, 182, 266
White House, 110, 116, 253, 257
William, Prince of Wales, 138, 180
Williams, Serena, 105, 121, 199, 206
Williams, Venus, 111
Wimbledon, 8, 27, 169

Winter Olympic Games, 6, 8–10, 13, 19, 52, 75n1, 80–82, 136, 163–165, 168, 181, 254, 255
   Beijing 2022, 6, 8–10, 13, 18, 19, 75n1, 80, 81, 86, 89, 163, 164, 168–170, 266, 270
   Milano-Cortina 2026, 255
   PyeongChang 2018, 168
   Salt Lake City 2002, 81, 180
   Sochi 2014, 43, 52, 167, 168, 254, 264
WNBA, 6, 7, 13, 109, 113, 114
Woods, Tiger, 199
World Anti-Doping Agency (WADA), 168
World Athletics Championships, 8, 11, 19, 167, 169, 170, 193–214, 265, 270
World's Fair, 76, 172
World War I, 29, 30, 34, 38, 53, 76, 170, 171, 265
World War II, 12, 34, 38, 43, 54, 56, 57, 76, 79, 89, 137, 157, 160, 162, 165, 170, 181, 265

Y

Youth Olympic Games (YOG), 78, 163, 164

Z

Zedong, Mao, 30, 162
Zidane, Zinedine, 60, 61
Zionism, 33, 177, 224, 229, 231

Printed in the United States
by Baker & Taylor Publisher Services